DATA BREACH AND ENCRYPTION HANDBOOK

Lucy Thomson, Editor

ABA SECTION OF
SCIENCE & TECHNOLOGY LAW

AMERICAN BAR ASSOCIATION
Defending Liberty
Pursuing Justice

Cover design by ABA Publishing.

The materials contained herein represent the opinions and views of the authors and/or the editors, and should not be construed to be the views or opinions of the law firms or companies with whom such persons are in partnership with, associated with, or employed by, nor of the American Bar Association or the Section of Science & Technology Law, unless adopted pursuant to the bylaws of the Association.

Nothing contained in this book is to be considered as the rendering of legal advice, either generally or in connection with any specific issue or case; nor do these materials purport to explain or interpret any specific bond or policy, or any provisions thereof, issued by any particular franchise company, or to render franchise or other professional advice. Readers are responsible for obtaining advice from their own lawyers or other professionals. This book and any forms and agreements herein are intended for educational and informational purposes only.

Printed in the United States of America.

15 14 13 12 11   5 4 3 2

Library of Congress Cataloging-in-Publication Data

Data breach and encryption handbook / Lucy L. Thomson, editor.
    p. cm.
    Includes index.
    ISBN 978-1-60442-989-3
    1. Data protection—Law and legislation—United States. 2. Computer networks—Law and legislation—United States—Criminal provisions. 3. Privacy, Right of—United States. 4. Records—Access control—United States. 5. Computer security—Law and legislation—United States. 6. Data encryption (Computer science)—Law and legislation—United States. 7. Computer crimes—United States. 8. Identity theft—United States. 9. Computer security—Standards. I. Thomson, Lucy L. II. Title.

    KF1263.C65D37 2011
    342.7308'58—dc22

                                                                                          2011001891

Discounts are available for books ordered in bulk. Special consideration is given to state bars, CLE programs, and other bar-related organizations. Inquire at Book Publishing, ABA Publishing, American Bar Association, 321 North Clark Street, Chicago, Illinois 60654-7598.

www.ShopABA.org

Contents

CHAPTER **2**

Despite the Alarming Trends, Data Breaches Are Preventable

CHAPTER **3**

The Aftermath of Data Breaches: Potential Liability and Damages

CHAPTER **4**

The Underground World of Online Identity Theft: An Overview

PART IV Technology

CHAPTER 10
Encryption: The Basics

CHAPTER **11**

Encryption Best Practices   **191**

Preface

Data breaches are a manifestation of the crisis in information security that currently threatens governments and business around the world. These cybersecurity risks pose some of the most serious economic and national security challenges of the 21st century.[1] Data breaches are increasing at an alarming rate, leading to identity theft and fraud and devastating financial losses and disruption for millions of individuals. Organized crime groups and sophisticated international hackers are suspected of being responsible for some of the major breaches, which threaten the integrity of the critical infrastructure of the United States and its allies.[2] Other data breaches—many of which occurred at major retailers, financial institutions, payment card processors, universities, healthcare providers, law firms, and government agencies—were caused by exceedingly lax security that reveals a cavalier disregard for protecting important client and customer records.

This *Data Breach and Encryption Handbook* is designed to be a comprehensive reference, bringing together information that attorneys, business owners, technology professionals, and policymakers in business and government must have to understand data breach laws and to address the problem of data breaches. It is the result of a year-long effort by a group of legal and technology experts affiliated with the American Bar Association Section of Science & Technology Law.[3] Focusing on prevention of data breaches, the book addresses the problem of escalating data breaches and its legal ramifications. Prevention is a complex and challenging problem that encompasses law and technology—as well as the many individuals and institutions engaged in the collection, storage, processing, and sharing of sensitive information.

With the objective of developing solutions to address the problem of data breaches, this book focuses in great depth on the law and its implications, encryption technology, recognized methods of resolving a breach, and many related aspects of information security. To better illustrate the complex challenges of data breaches, chapters 3 and 5 examine a number of the major data breach incidents from a variety of legal and technology perspectives; instructive graphics help pinpoint the methodologies hackers used to cause each of these breaches. Unlike a treatise on information security or encryption, this book is designed

---

1. The White House, Cyberspace Policy Review: Assuring a Trusted and Resilient Information and Communications Infrastructure, at iii and 1, *available at* http://www.whitehouse.gov/assets/documents/Cyberspace_Policy_Review_final.pdf; Ctr. for Strategic and Int'l Studies, Securing Cyberspace for the 44th Presidency (Dec. 2008), *available at* http://csis.org/files/media/csis/pubs/081208_securingcyberspace_44.pdf.

2. U.S. Dep't of Homeland Sec., 2009 National Infrastructure Protection Plan, *available at* http://www.dhs.gov/files/programs/editorial_0827.shtm. The critical infrastructure of the United States includes agriculture and food, banking and finance, communications, defense industrial base, energy, information technology, national monuments and icons, transportation systems, and water. *See* United States v. Gonzalez No. 09-cr-626 (D.N.J. 2009).

3. The American Bar Association (ABA) Section of Science & Technology Law (SciTech) is widely recognized as the premier global authority on science and technology law.

to enable attorneys and technology professionals alike to understand the root causes of the security failures while also gaining fluency in the complexities of the problem of data breaches so that the practitioner will ask the right questions to address the issues raised by data breaches and how to prevent them.

Chapters 10–15 demystify encryption by first identifying it as a basic scientific concept that has existed for thousands of years. Leading encryption experts then explain what encryption really is, what encryption keys are, and how the pieces of the encryption puzzle fit together. For many people, the concept of encryption is cloaked in intrigue and mystery with notions of wars, spies, and code breaking.[4] Some people focus on the complexity of encryption algorithms and encryption keys and dismiss this topic as one they cannot begin to master. In fact, with the knowledge of how modern encryption works, it becomes relatively easy to understand how to think about good and bad practices for using encryption. For attorneys and security professionals with a more complete understanding of information security, chapter 12 discusses how encryption can be circumvented or undermined by poor security practices and chapter 14 provides an inside look into the future of encryption with an essay by the developer of the self-encrypting hard drive. Chapter 15 provides a practical assessment of some of the basic encryption technology.

Chapter 4 provides a fascinating inside look at the criminal underground and reveals the thriving global market of websites known as "carding forums"—places where criminals sell stolen personal and financial information. The latest information on the crisis in information security should serve as a wake-up call for everyone with responsibility for safeguarding sensitive personal records. The past five years have seen a huge increase in the number of data breaches reported publicly. A recent breach requiring not only technical prowess but also unparalleled global cooperation among criminals provides a dramatic illustration of the escalating international threat. A group of hackers operating from Russia, Estonia, and Moldova masterminded the breach of RBS WorldPay in Atlanta, Georgia, exploiting technology vulnerabilities and executing an extraordinarily well-coordinated global scheme to steal 1.5 million prepaid payroll account cards and then use a small number of them to obtain $9.5 million from ATMs in 280 cities in eight countries around the world. The serious threats and risks to data security that exist and are well known to potential attackers are highlighted in chapters 1 and 5; they are increasing dramatically as hackers launch attacks from abroad and the proliferation of mobile devices enables transactions from often insecure platforms.

In order to comply with all the state data breach laws and HITECH—the federal data breach notification law for health records—attorneys, executives, and regulators will find the discussion of the data breach notification laws in chapters 6, 7, and 8 an essential resource that surveys the legal landscape, highlights the differences between the laws, and makes sense of the encryption technologies that underlie the legal requirements. For companies conducting business in multiple states, chapters 6 and 7 can help them develop strategies for overcoming the complexities and redundancies of competing state

---

4. *See,* e.g., SINGH, SIMON, THE CODE BOOK: THE SECRET HISTORY OF CODES AND CODE BREAKING. KAHN, DAVID, THE CODEBREAKERS: THE COMPREHENSIVE HISTORY OF SECRET COMMUNICATIONS FROM ANCIENT TIMES TO THE INTERNET. WRIXON, FRED B., CODES, CIPHERS, SECRETS AND CRYPTIC COMMUNICATION (Black Dog & Leventhal Publishers, 2005).

laws. The HITECH regulations issued by the U.S. Department of Health and Human Services and the Federal Trade Commission (FTC) are complex, nuanced, and conflicting; the in-depth analysis provided in chapter 8 not only sets forth the regulatory requirements, it also highlights the new and difficult areas that must be addressed to ensure compliance. Companies doing business internationally must comply with the country laws governing cross-border data flows and data breach notification. The international guide in chapter 9 is an invaluable starting point for this analysis.

Preparation is the key to preventing data breaches by putting in place comprehensive information security controls that are appropriate and effective; the latest thinking about prioritized approaches is discussed in chapter 16.[5] Likewise, the need to be prepared to respond to a data breach is essential. Company officials and their counsel must have at their fingertips the data breach notification requirements of all the states where the company is doing business and where their customers live, and a plan for making a quick response. Chapter 17 provides an essential guide to the necessary steps to comply with the data breach notification laws if a breach does occur.

Ignore the problem of data breaches at your peril. Lawsuits have been filed in almost every case involving a major data breach. The recently enacted HITECH Act increased the penalties for actions leading to a data breach involving health care providers. The aftermath of data breaches has been devastating to the companies subject to a breach, including huge settlements given to consumers and banks, investigations and fines by federal and state agencies, the imposition of onerous auditing requirements, costly breach notification procedures, business disruption, intensely negative publicity, and, in some cases, bankruptcy. Litigation stemming from the most serious data breaches is analyzed in chapter 3—highlighting the causes of action that have been successful, and those that failed in this new and developing area of the law. Insurance protection for security breaches is often overlooked. Businesses that may face liability or loss from a security breach should assess the extent of their exposure, as explained in chapter 19, and purchase appropriate insurance.

The state data breach laws and HITECH embrace encryption as a means of protecting sensitive personal records—if personal records are encrypted and a data breach occurs, individuals do not need to be notified. This "safe harbor" approach sounds straightforward, but how can it be reconciled with the need to notify individuals who entrusted their personal information to an organization when the data is compromised so they may take action to protect themselves from the serious consequences of identity theft and financial losses? A close look behind the scenes of some of the largest and most serious data breaches reveals a serious flaw in relying on encryption alone. In a number of these massive data breaches in which millions of personal records were compromised, personal records were "encrypted." Chapter 5 presents an anatomy of these data breaches and illustrates how the theft of "data in the clear" occurred. Missing was the end-to-end encryption required to protect credit and debit card data as it flowed through the payment card authorization process. Comprehensive information security controls are required.

---

5. *See* Thomas Shaw, Information Security and Privacy—A Practical Guide for Global Executives, Lawyers and Technologists, ABA (2011) (a comprehensive guide to information security and privacy law by the ABA Section of Science & Technology Law).

Amid the intense focus on the minutia of data breach notification procedures, no one should forget the fact that encryption is only one important building block of an information security system. A wide range of practical solutions to avoid data breaches has been developed, such as data leak prevention, identified as one of the "hottest technologies" and discussed in chapter 18. Security best practices now emphasize the need to prioritize security controls and solutions to address the greatest risks, and to automate the implementation and tracking of the controls where possible to enable continuous security monitoring. Chapter 16 on information security provides an overview of the latest thinking to address cybercrime and the proliferation of data breaches.

The *Data Breach and Encryption Handbook* will have accomplished one of its goals if it generates discussion and debate about the best approaches to preventing data breaches. This includes an assessment of whether the state data breach notification laws and HITECH address the real problem—maintaining the security of sensitive personal information—or simply focus on the aftermath of a broken system. The goal of legislation (state, federal, and international) should be to prevent data breaches rather than to enact complex and costly requirements that provide little assistance to individuals after their information has been compromised through breaches that result from failed security. Many questions arise as others are answered: Do the state and federal data breach laws facilitate the development of appropriate solutions to prevent data breaches? Does encryption prevent data breaches? Is it enough to encrypt the sensitive data on mobile devices? As m-commerce expands, enabling a variety of business transactions to take place on mobile devices such as cell phones and PDAs, how must information security be configured and applied to protect the security of these mobile transactions, including mobile banking?

A concluding thought is that data breaches should not be permitted, condoned, or accepted as inevitable under any circumstances. Organizations and individuals who collect, use, store, or share personally identifiable information should be held responsible for protecting it. This includes the requirement for having appropriate information security. Fundamentally, information security requires discipline and precision—a system of managerial, operational, and technical controls that is designed based on a risk assessment, tailored to the data and information in the particular organization or information system, and, implemented appropriately, carefully maintained, and regularly monitored. Hackers are well-positioned to exploit weaknesses and vulnerabilities, so anything less will be inadequate and ineffective.

Acknowledgments

This book is the result of a year-long effort by a group of legal and technology experts affiliated with the American Bar Association (ABA) Section of Science & Technology Law (SciTech) to address the problem of escalating data breaches and its legal ramifications. The extraordinary lawyers, scientists, and technology professionals in SciTech are a source of continuing inspiration. In the words of past SciTech Chair and former Oracle General Counsel Ray Ocampo, the members of this section are "diverse, cool, and highly intelligent."

Many thanks go to the team who made this book possible—past SciTech Section Chairs Tom Smedinghoff and Ruth Hill Bro, current Chair Steve Wu, past Section Council member Kim Kiefer Peretti, members of the SciTech Information Security and e-Discovery and Digital Evidence (EDDE) committees, Hoyt Kesterson, Eric Hibbard, Bob Thibadeau, Serge Jorgensen, Ben Tomhave, Jennifer Kurtz, Renee Abbott, and the other colleagues who contributed their considerable expertise to this project: Arthur Peabody, Lorie Masters, and Tom Hahler. Dennis Monroe provided invaluable assistance, insight, and expertise, creating the graphics that illustrate the massive data breaches and data breaches trends.

The ABA thanks the curators of the Open Security Foundation (OSF) for their assistance, and in particular Jay Dyson, for preparing a chart on data breach trends. OSF, which runs the DataLossDB (http://datalossdb.org/), is a research project aimed at documenting known and reported data loss incidents worldwide. We also commend the Identity Theft Resource Center (http://www.idtheftcenter.org) for their excellent work collecting and analyzing critical information about data breaches and providing assistance to victims of data breaches. This information is an important part of the book.

The guiding light for this project was Sarah Orwig, Executive Editor of ABA Publishing, who offered extraordinary support and advice from the day the project was conceived to the day it was completed. Shawn Kaminski, SciTech Executive Director, was, as usual, extremely helpful, providing encouragement and assistance. The chairs of the SciTech Book Publishing Committee contributed invaluable guidance throughout the project: past Chair Eric Drogin, who is now SciTech Chair-Elect, and Steve Brower, current Book Publishing Chair.

This book represents the wisdom of cutting-edge thinkers in the area of information security. As the initial comprehensive work to address the growing epidemic of data breaches, each contributor brought a unique perspective, not merely to diagnosing the problems, but to prescribing a cure. Indeed, we are fortunate to have individuals who are not only leaders in this field, but many who are the "original thinkers" of bringing encryption and data management practices together to prevent what all recognize as unacceptable breaches of personal information—breaches that invade privacy and expose both individuals and businesses to economic damage and potentially irreparable harm.

By examining the problem of data breaches from a variety of different legal, technology, and policy perspectives, we have endeavored to provide insight and ideas that will inspire those who collect, use, store, and share sensitive personal information to take aggressive steps to safeguard it.

About the Editor

LUCY L. THOMSON, J.D., M.S., CIPP/G, focuses her practice at the intersection of law and technology. As a Senior Principal Engineer, Information Security, and Privacy Advocate at CSC, a global technology company, she has addressed a wide range of legal, technical, and policy issues in major IT and information-sharing programs. She works on teams building modernized information systems for very large organizations, and has developed strategies to safeguard sensitive information at the nation's ports, as well as for the government's key financial systems.

Appointed Consumer Privacy Ombudsman in 10 federal bankruptcy cases, Ms. Thomson has overseen the disposition of 125 million electronic consumer records and developed privacy and information security standards that were adopted by the courts.

Ms. Thomson is Vice Chair of the ABA Section of Science & Technology Law, is a member of its Section Council, and serves in the ABA House of Delegates. She founded and co-chairs the e-Discovery and Digital Evidence (EDDE) Committee. Ms. Thomson was the editor of the Symposium on Homeland Security in *Jurimetrics: The Journal of Law Science and Technology* (2007) and is the author of *Critical Issues in Identity Management—Challenges for Homeland Security* and *Cybercrime Across Borders*. She organized and moderated a panel on the state and federal data breach laws at the RSA Conference 2010.

A career U.S. Department of Justice attorney, Ms. Thomson served in senior positions in the Criminal and Civil Rights Divisions. In the Fraud Section of the Criminal Division, she litigated complex white-collar crime cases and pioneered the use of electronic evidence at trial. As head of the FBI Laboratory Task Force, she directed a review of scientific laboratory evidence in thousands of the government's most high-profile criminal cases.

She holds an M.S. degree from Rensselaer Polytechnic Institute and a J.D. degree from the Georgetown University Law Center. An avid sailor, Ms. Thomson is a National Women's Intercollegiate Sailing Champion.

In addition to editing the book, Ms. Thomson wrote chapter 1, "Cybercrime and Escalating Risks"; chapter 2, "Despite the Alarming Trends, Data Breaches Are Preventable"; chapter 5, "Anatomy of the Major Data Breaches—Encrypted Records—Failed Security"; chapter 7, "State Data Breach Laws and the Duty to Provide Information Security"; and chapter 16, "Security Best Practices—The Watchword Is Prioritize!"; and co-wrote chapter 8, "HITECH—The First Federal Data Breach Notification Law."

Contact: (703) 798-1001, lucythomson1@mindspring.com

About the Authors

RENEE A. ABBOTT is a recent graduate of The Catholic University Columbus School of Law in Washington, D.C. Her primary practice areas are technology, criminal law, and litigation. Prior to law school, Ms. Abbott spent 10 years working at ConAgra Foods in the areas of logistics, demand planning, and sales and marketing. Her last five years at ConAgra were spent working in the area of information technology. She has experience as a project manager for several multimillion-dollar software development projects. She was appointed to the leadership committee for the enterprise-wide SAP implementation. She gathered substantial experience with full lifecycle software development. She spent a year as an intern in the U.S. Department of Agriculture Office of the Chief Information Officer where she crafted agency policy on e-mail retention and protection of personally identifiable information.

Ms. Abbott is a member of the ABA Section of Science & Technology Law and its e-Discovery and Digital Evidence (EDDE) and Cyberlaw committees. She is a barrister member of The Catholic University of America Thurgood Marshall Inn of Court. As an active alumni, she volunteers as a judge and coach for Moot Court and Alternative Dispute Resolution student teams.

Contact: (408) 391-7285, rraabbott@aol.com

RUTH HILL BRO advises businesses on privacy and information management strategy and global compliance. She is a Past Chair of the ABA Section of Science & Technology Law and has served as a Council Member since 2002. She also founded and currently chairs the Section's Committee for the Advancement of Science and Technology Law and Education and the Membership and Diversity Committee. She founded and chaired the ABA E-Privacy Law Committee from 2000-2005. In 2009, she was appointed to the ABA's Standing Committee on Technology and Information Systems.

Ms. Bro has been featured as a speaker on privacy, information management, data security, e-workplace, and e-business issues by corporations (in-house training), industry groups, universities, and bar and trade associations over 100 times in the past decade. She has also published over 85 works on these topics, including the 2004 ABA book, *The E-Business Legal Arsenal: Practitioner Agreements and Checklists*. She is a member of the Advisory Board of BNA's *Privacy & Security Law Report*, the Editorial Board of *Internet Law & Strategy*, and the U.S. Panel of Experts of *DataGuidance*. She has been recognized as a leader in her field by numerous organizations, including Chambers USA, the Legal 500 US, Lawdragon 500 (New Stars, New Worlds), and Ethisphere Institute's first annual list of *Attorneys Who Matter* (2009). She won *New York Law Journal's* 2006 Annual Fiction Contest for her short story, "Privilege."

Ms. Bro received her B.A. degree from Northwestern University and her J.D. degree from the University of Chicago Law School.

Contact: (312) 861-7985, ruth.bro@comcast.net

THOMAS L. HAHLER is an information security expert at a global technology company that provides consulting systems and technical services to homeland security, defense, and intelligence clients. Mr. Hahler currently serves as a Certifying Agent at U.S. Customs and Border Protection where he oversees the certification and accreditation of the IT modernization program.

Having worked with computer networked systems for over 25 years, Mr. Hahler has experience with the full range of communications through implementation of a network access language. In addition, he has over 15 years of experience in all phases of security management from planning through implementation of security features. His extensive software development background includes emphasis on protocols and structured design. He is working on issues related to the implementation of encryption solutions to safeguard sensitive government and private sector information.

Contact: (703) 343-0874, hahler@his.com

ERIC A. HIBBARD is the Chief Technology Officer Security and Privacy for Hitachi Data Systems where he is responsible for storage security strategy, identifying and defining new storage security architectures, and designing new storage networking infrastructures. Mr. Hibbard is a senior security professional with 30-plus years' experience in information and communications technology, working for government, academia, and industry.

Mr. Hibbard is active in formal storage and security standardization as well as organizations involved with data security and protection. He serves as the International Representative for INCITS/CS1 Cyber Security, Vice Chair of the e-Discovery and Digital Evidence (EDDE) Committee of the ABA Section of Science & Technology Law, Vice Chair of the IEEE Information Assurance Standards Committee, Vice Chair of IEEE P1619 Security in Storage Work Group, and Chair of the Storage Networking Industry Association Security Technical Working Group. He is also involved with INCITS/T11, Information Systems Audit and Control Association (ISACA), ISSA, Trusted Computing Group, IEEE-USA Critical Infrastructure Protection Committee, IETF, W3C, and the Distributed Management Task Force.

Mr. Hibbard currently holds the International Information Systems Security Certification Consortium CISSP certification as well as the ISSAP, ISSMP, and ISSEP concentration certifications. He also holds the ISACA CISA and the SNIA SCSE certifications. His educational background includes a B.S. in Computer Science and a credential in Data Communications.

Contact: (408) 970-7979, eric.hibbard@hds.com

SERGE JORGENSEN is the Chief Technology Officer for the Sylint Group and provides technical input in the areas of information security, system design, and incident response. He has received various patents in engineering and math-related fields while developing secure, low-bandwidth data transmission techniques and methodologies. Mr. Jorgensen works closely with the FBI and industry in addressing information security needs to safeguard critical infrastructure processes and components. In this work, he is responsible for developing and implementing secure communication protocols, traffic analysis techniques, and malware identification and remediation efforts. Mr. Jorgensen is an active member of the ABA e-Discovery and Digital Evidence (EDDE) Committee, and works nationally and internationally to mitigate the effects of malicious attacks against corporate and government enterprises.

Contact: (941) 951-6015, sjorgensen@usinfosec.com

JENNIFER ANN KURTZ is a Denver-based consultant with 16 years of experience in building and managing resilient and sustainable technology systems and processes for companies, state agencies, and communities. She worked with Echelon One in California and was director of strategic relations and communications at Purdue University's Center for Education and Research in Information Assurance and Security. She also served a two-year appointment as director of eCommerce for the State of Indiana, where she led the state broadband study and eGov Task Force committees, authored the Governor's Technology Roundtable report, and initiated the Indiana Industries of the Future program. Other government sector experience includes work at the National Security Council, the U.S. Department of State, and the White House.

Ms. Kurtz's private sector experience includes senior IT management at Delco Remy International and security and technology analysis for a division of DynCorp in Fairfax, Virginia, where she co-authored the 10-year telecommunications strategy plan for the U.S. Department of the Treasury.

Ms. Kurtz earned her B.A. in International Studies from American University, and an M.B.A. from Anderson University. She taught as adjunct faculty member in telecommunications management at Ball State University and is on the Industrial Advisory Board of Purdue's College of Technology. She was recognized as Indiana's "Hi Tech Woman of the Year" in 2003 and has published articles and book chapters on information security, eGovernment, and telecommunications topics.

Contact: (317) 372-2658, kurtz_jennifer@hotmail.com or jennifer.ann.kurtz@gmail.com

LORELIE S. MASTERS is a partner at Jenner & Block LLP in Washington, D.C., and has more than 25 years of experience representing policyholders in disputes over coverage in product liability, technology and e-commerce issues, and directors' and officers', property, and business interruption insurance. Ms. Masters served as trial counsel in obtaining a jury verdict for policyholder Hoechst Celanese Corporation in what the *National Law Journal* called one of the "most significant jury verdicts of 1997." She prevailed in representing policyholders in London arbitrations under the Bermuda Form and in other litigations, arbitrations, mediations, and settlements, recovering millions of dollars for her clients.

She is coauthor of two treatises, *Insurance Coverage Litigation* (Aspen Law & Business 2000 & Supp. 2008), and *Liability Insurance in International Arbitration: The Bermuda Form* (Hart 2004). She is a past Chair of the Insurance Coverage Litigation Committee of the ABA Section of Litigation. Ms. Masters is a member of the ABA Commission on Women in the Profession and a past President of the Women's Bar Association of the District of Columbia. She is recognized in Chambers and has been named a Best Lawyer and Super Lawyer in insurance coverage from 2007 to the present.

Contact: (202) 639-6076, lmasters@jenner.com

DENNIS R. MONROE is a senior technology consultant with more than 30 years of business application project management, design, and integration experience. He specializes in data architecture, real-time high volume data management, and enterprise architecture.

Mr. Monroe is responsible for a nationwide government production environment supporting the U.S. Customs and Border Protection Modernization program, including the trade industry and participating government agencies. His commercial experience has been with national and international corporate business systems, including the payment card industry. As assistant to the Regulatory Director of Maryland Bank of North America, he was responsible for project management, development, and technical delivery of semiannual MasterCard and Visa regulatory upgrades to all credit card processing systems at the Dallas, Texas, national service center.

Contact: (469) 556-1256, drmonroe@aol.com

ARTHUR E. PEABODY, JR. is Lead Medicare Counsel for the BlueCross BlueShield Association. He litigates complex multimillion-dollar Medicare reimbursement cases brought by hospitals, nursing homes, and rehabilitation facilities. He coordinated a demonstration project to evaluate arbitration as a means to resolve disputes over Medicare coverage of home health care benefits.

As an Assistant U.S. Attorney for the Eastern District of Virginia (the "rocket docket"), Mr. Peabody litigated civil cases representing federal agencies as both plaintiff and defendant, including health care fraud actions alleging mis-billing, kickbacks, and regulatory noncompliance. He spearheaded an initiative to improve conditions in Virginia's worst nursing homes by creative use of the False Claims Act. For the past 10 years, he has served as a volunteer mediator for the U.S. District Court for the District of Columbia.

For many years Mr. Peabody served as Chief of the Special Litigation Section of the Civil Rights Division at the U.S. Department of Justice. He managed all aspects of the investigation and litigation of novel federal court actions brought to vindicate the constitutional and federal statutory rights of juveniles and elderly and disabled persons. Many of these cases formed the basis for statutes, regulations, and the development of Supreme Court precedents. He has appeared in 34 different federal courts across the nation.

Mr. Peabody is serving his second term as an elected member of the Alexandria City School Board. He earned his J.D. degree from Cornell.

Contact: (202) 798-1002, arthurpeabody@mindspring.com

KIMBERLY KIEFER PERETTI, J.D., LL.M., CISSP, was a senior litigator in the Computer Crime & Intellectual Property Section (CCIPS), Department of Justice (DOJ), Washington, D.C., and recently joined PricewaterhouseCoopers' Forensic Technology Services practice to address the prevention, response and remediation of data breaches, cyber intrusions, economic espionage, Intellectual Property theft, and privacy. In 2009, *SC Magazine* recognized Ms. Peretti as a top "industry pioneer" in the information security industry. At CCIPS she led several benchmark investigations and prosecutions, including the prosecution of the infamous TJX hacker Albert Gonzalez who is currently serving 20 years in prison for his role in the largest hacking and identity theft case ever prosecuted by the Department of Justice. She is a frequent keynote speaker and lecturer on the topic of data breaches, cyber investigations and cyber crime.

Ms. Peretti's law review article entitled "Data Breaches: What the Underground World of Carding Reveals," resulted in a hearing before the U.S. House of Representatives Homeland Security Committee to consider vulnerabilities in the payment card industry. Ms. Peretti is a Certified Information Systems Security Professional (CISSP) and holds an LL.M. (Masters of Law) from the University of Munich, Germany, and a J.D. from Georgetown University Law Center (magna cum laude).

Contact: (703) 918-1500, kimberly.k.peretti@us.pwc.com

THOMAS J. SMEDINGHOFF is a partner at the law firm of Wildman Harrold in Chicago, where his practice focuses on new legal issues relating to the developing field of information law and electronic business activities. He is recognized internationally for his leadership in addressing emerging legal issues regarding electronic transactions, information security, and authentication from both a transactional and public policy perspective. He has been retained to structure and implement e-commerce and information security legal infrastructures for a variety of government agencies and businesses including banks, insurance companies, investment companies, and certification authorities. He has also been actively involved in developing legislation and policy in the area of electronic business at the state, national, and international levels.

Mr. Smedinghoff serves as a member of the U.S. Delegation to the United Nations Commission on International Trade Law (UNCITRAL), where he participates in the Working Group on Electronic Commerce and helped to negotiate the 2005 United Nations Convention on the Use of Electronic Communications in International Contracts. He is also chair of the International Policy Committee of the ABA Section of Science & Technology Law. Previously, he was chair of the ABA Section of Science & Technology Law (1999–2000) and the ABA Electronic Commerce Division (1995–2003).

Mr. Smedinghoff is the author of *Information Security Law: The Emerging Standard for Corporate Compliance* (IT Governance Publ'g, 2008), and the editor and primary author of *Online Law: The Legal Guide to Doing Business on the Internet* (Addison Wesley, 1996).

Contact: (312) 201-2021, Smedinghoff@wildman.com

ROBERT THIBADEAU, Ph.D., is a Senior Vice President at Wave Systems, which delivers software for managing hardware-secured data on laptops and desktops in enterprise environments. In 25 years at Carnegie Mellon University, he was one of the seven founding directors of the Robotics Institute and later, after experiencing malicious data breaches in the mid-1990s, taught and performed research in security and privacy. He retired with an Adjunct Professorship in 2007, but continues teaching a graduate course in computer security and the Trusted Infrastructure Workshops sponsored by the National Science Foundation (http://www.cylab.cmu.edu/tiw/).

Beginning in 1998, he authored the Phoenix Secure Core, the European Java reference code for W3 P3P privacy, and a new generation of disk drives, optical drives, and solid state drives for laptops, desktops, and enterprise. He is recently retired as Chief Technologist at Seagate Technology, where he architected encrypting disk drive technology, which through his roles representing Seagate in the Trusted Computing Group, Storage Workgroup, and Board of Directors, is now shipping in standardized forms from Seagate, Samsung, Toshiba, Fujitsu, Hitachi Global Storage Technologies, IBM, and LSI. Wave Systems is the largest volume supplier of software that supports the encrypting disk drives, with over 60 million clients in the field. At Wave Systems, Dr. Thibadeau founded the Security and Privacy Consultancy to bring security and privacy to organizations and enterprises seeking to employ the finest and most transparent control over Internet, insider, and device theft threats.

Contact: (412) 370-1245, rht@cs.cmu.edu or rthibadeau@wavesys.com

BENJAMIN L. TOMHAVE is a Senior Security Analyst with Gemini Security Solutions in Chantilly, VA, specializing in solutions architecture, security planning, security program development and management, and other strategic security solutions. He holds a Master of Science degree in Engineering Management with an Information Security Management concentration from The George Washington University, and is a Certified Information Systems Security Professional (CISSP). He is a member of ISSA, OWASP, the American Bar Association Information Security and Electronic Discovery and Digital Evidence Committees, and the IEEE Computer Society.

Mr. Tomhave worked previously in a variety of security roles for companies including BT Professional Services, AOL, Wells Fargo, ICSA Labs, and Ernst & Young. He is a published author and an experienced public speaker.

Contact: (703)282-8600, tomhave@secureconsulting.net

STEPHEN S. WU is a partner in the Silicon Valley law firm Cooke Kobrick & Wu LLP. He advises clients concerning data security and privacy, electronic commerce, e-discovery, electronic records retention, and digital evidence. His practice also includes technology transactions, intellectual property litigation, and commercial litigation. Before forming CKW, Mr. Wu was VeriSign, Inc.'s second in-house attorney where he was in charge of the company's worldwide policies and practices governing its digital certification secure e-commerce services. Prior to joining VeriSign, Mr. Wu practiced with Jones Day Reavis & Pogue and Kirkpatrick & Lockhart LLP in the areas of computer law, intellectual property, general litigation, and technology transactions. He clerked with a U.S. District Judge in Columbus, Ohio. Mr. Wu was cochair of the ABA Information Security Committee from 2001 to 2004. He is currently Chair of the ABA Section of Science & Technology Law.

Mr. Wu is a frequent speaker on secure electronic commerce and information security topics, as well as e-discovery, digital evidence, and electronic records retention. He has written or cowritten five books on information security, including *Guide to HIPAA Security and the Law* (ABA 2007); *Information Security: A Legal, Business, and Technical Handbook* (ABA 2004); *Risk Management for Consumer Internet Payments* (NACHA 2002); and *Digital Signatures* (RSA Press 2002). Mr. Wu received his B.A., summa cum laude, from the University of Pittsburgh in 1985, and his law degree, cum laude, from Harvard Law School in 1988.

Contact: (650) 917-8045, swu@ckwlaw.com

PART I

Crisis in Information Security

CHAPTER 1

Cybercrime and Escalating Risks

Lucy L. Thomson

Cybersecurity risks pose some of the most serious economic and national security challenges of the 21st century.[1] The global impact is unmistakable. A recent cyberspace report by the Center for Strategic and International Studies (CSIS) declared that cybersecurity is a strategic issue "on par with weapons of mass destruction and global jihad." CSIS concluded that the damage from cyberattack is real, and "a growing array of state and nonstate actors are compromising, stealing, changing, or destroying information and could cause critical disruptions to U.S. systems."[2]

The problem of data breaches and the search for solutions must be considered in the context of global cyberthreats. Behind the data breach statistics is a complex picture of heightened threats to data security from sophisticated criminals who are targeting the most valuable corporate and government assets and information and exploiting vulnerabilities in the critical infrastructure. The picture is further complicated by the proliferation of mobile devices and wireless technology that enable mobile commerce (m-commerce) and a continually expanding array of applications that present many vulnerable points in the flow of sensitive data in computer networks. The final piece of the data breach picture is the lack of security resulting in unencrypted data on computers, laptops, and other mobile devices that are lost or unaccounted for. Electronic records are not the only issue—examples of lax security include volumes of paper documents as well. Many data breaches occur when documents containing personal information are discarded where they can be retrieved by strangers.

Because of the notification requirements in the state data breach laws, the past five years have seen a huge increase in the number of data breaches reported publicly. Data

---

1. Ctr. for Strategic and Int'l Studies, Securing Cyberspace for the 44ᵗʰ Presidency. Wash., D.C. (Dec. 2008), at 15, *available at* http://csis.org/files/media/csis/pubs/081208_securingcyberspace_44.pdf. National Seurity Council, The Comprehensive National Cybersecurity Initiative, *available at* http://www.whitehouse.gov/sites/default/files/cybersecurity.pdf. *See generally Symposium on Homeland Security,* in Jurimetrics: J.L. Sci. & Tech. (2007); Lucy Thomson, *Critical Issues in Identity Management,* 47 Jurimetrics 257–356 (2007).

2. The White House, Cyberspace Policy Review: Assuring a Trusted and Resilient Information and Communications Infrastructure, at iii, *available at* http://www.whitehouse.gov/assets/documents/Cyberspace_Policy_Review_final.pdf; CSIS Comm'n on Cybersecurity for the 44th Presidency, Threats Posed by the Internet, *available at* http://csis.org/files/media/csis/pubs/081028_threats_working_group.pdf.

breaches in the United States rose almost 50 percent in a single year, from 425 data breach incidents reported in 2007 to 656 breach incidents in 2008.[3] In the first three quarters of 2010, 561 data breaches were reported, up from 498 data breaches reported in 2009.[4]

This chapter focuses on the nature of the threats, both national and international, and their impact on individuals and organizations, and particularly on threats that are the result of technology advances. As information systems become both more extensive and more complex, the risks to personal information grow. In the absence of adequate security measures, the stakes are high for governments and business entities, as well as individuals.

EXPANDING GLOBAL CYBERSECURITY THREATS

The number of cyberattacks against the U.S. government is rising sharply, and many of the attacks are believed to be coming from Chinese state and state-sponsored entities. During 2008, for example, there were more than 50,000 cyberattacks against the U.S. Department of Defense.[5] Many other types of malware have been unleashed by sophisticated hackers against corporate and government networks around the globe.

Advanced Persistent Threats

Advanced persistent threats (APTs) are among the most serious type of cyberattacks because their focus is espionage. Originating in the Asian Pacific countries, these threats employ undetectable zero-day exploits and social engineering techniques against company employees to breach networks. They are rarely detected by antivirus and intrusion detection programs. Through the intrusions, hackers grab a foothold into a company's network, sometimes for years, even after the company has discovered them and taken corrective measures.[6] Mandiant, a firm that has directed APT investigations, describes APT attacks as an "orchestrated deployment of sophisticated and perpetual attacks that have systematically compromised computer networks in the public and private sector for years. The APT hides in plain sight and avoids detection by making outbound connections using common network ports and services, providing remote access to critical infrastructure controls and sensitive information."[7]

IM DDOS Botnet

The emergence of the IM DDOS botnet illustrates the increasingly brazen and unrestrained efforts by criminals to promote global cybercrime. Launched in March 2010, the IM DDOS botnet is a commercial service for delivering Distributed Denial of

---

3. Identity Theft Res. Ctr., 2008 ITRC Breach Report, *available at* http://www.idtheftcenter.org.

4. Identity Theft Res. Ctr, 2010 Data Breach Stats (Oct. 26, 2010) and 2009 Data Breach Stats (March 24, 2010), *available at* http://www.idtheftcenter.org.

5. 2009 REPORT TO CONGRESS OF THE U.S.-CHINA ECONOMIC AND SECURITY REVIEW COMM'N, 111th Cong., First Session (Nov. 2009), *available at* http://www.uscc.gov/annual_report/2009/annual_report_full_09.pdf.

6. Kevin Mandia, *M-Trends*, MANDIANT, Jan. 27, 2010, *available at* http://www.mandiant.com/products/services/m-trends; Kelly Jackson Higgins, *Anatomy of A Targeted, Persistent Attack*, DARK READING, Jan. 27, 2010, *available at* http://www.darkreading.com/database_security/security/attacks/showArticle.jhtml?articleID=222600139.

7. *Id.*

Service (DDoS) attacks against any desired target.[8] Operated by a criminal organization in China, it is a publicly available service that allows anyone for lease to establish an online account, input the domain(s) they wish to attack, and pay for the service.[9]

Damballa, the organization that documented the existence of this botnet, explains how it works: "A Denial of Service (DoS) attack is a technique used to overwhelm a website/domain in an effort to reduce its responsiveness, or completely eliminate its ability to respond to new communication attempts. DoS attacks have been used to 'take down' political sites, abuse sites, commercial business websites and even military command centers as part of a coordinated targeted campaign. A Distributed Denial of Service (DDoS) attack utilizes multiple PCs or servers to initiate a coordinated attack against a targeted system."[10]

The criminals establish the botnet by installing malicious software (malware) on victim machines (hosts). The botnets are used to rally and command unwitting victim machines into participating in the attacks. The infected hosts are instructed to launch a coordinated DDoS against the victim of choice. The more assets involved in the attack, the larger the flood of requests and data that can be targeted at the victim.

The proliferation of the IM DDOS botnet is but one illustration of the daunting global challenge facing business owners to maintain the security of their computer networks, and thus to protect their critical information assets from theft and fraud. From the standpoint of a business concerned about potential liability, an organization with an infected computer that is used to launch an external attack may be identified as a "facilitator" of the attack, and may be responsible for failing to adequately secure its own networks.[11]

Zeus Trojan

In October 2010 the FBI arrested 20 persons charged with bank fraud in an international cyber crime network. An attack attributed to the "Zeus Trojan" malware allegedly allowed hackers to access victims' bank accounts from thousands of miles away, compromising dozens of individual and business accounts in the U.S. and transferring more than $3 million under false identities.[12] According to the FBI, the thefts were perpetrated

---

8. Damballa, a security firm that specializes in tracking botnets and their criminal operations, announced its discovery of the new IM DDOS botnet in September 2010. *The IMDDOS Botnet: Discovery and Analysis,* Damballa Threat Research, *available at* http://www.damballa.com/downloads/r_pubs/Damballa_Report_imDDOS.pdf.

9. Damballa Threat Research, *id,* page 2. Two individuals in the U.S. who created a botnet and launched DDoS attacks on web hosting providers to demonstrates its potential to a customer, pleaded guilty to criminal charges of damaging a computer. *See* United States v. Smith, (N.D. Texas 2010), *available at* http://www.justice.gov/usao/txn/PressRel10/smith_edwards_hacking_ple_pr.html (June 10, 2010).

10. *Id. See* US-CERT, National Cyber Alert System, Cyber Security Tip ST04-015, National Cyber Alert System, Understanding Denial of Service Attacks, *available at* http://www.us-cert.gov/cas/tips/ST04-015.html.

11. Damballa, *The IMDDOS Botnet, supra* note 8, page 15.

12. Federal Bureau of Investigation, Cyber Banking Fraud: Global Partnerships Lead to Major Arrests (October 1, 2010), *available at* http://www.fbi.gov/news/stories/2010/october/cyber-banking-fraud/cyber-banking-fraud/?searchterm=trojan%20zeus. A trojan horse provides a "back door" into a computer system. The hacker may hide malicious or harmful code inside another program, video or game. Once a trojan is installed, a hacker can have access to all the files on a hard drive, a system's e-mail, or even create messages that pop up on the screen. Trojans are often used to enable even more serious attacks.

by hackers from Russia and Eastern Europe who used the Zeus banking trojan to break into computers at small businesses and small municipalities and steal online banking credentials that they transferred to a remote server. The Zeus Trojan was distributed as an attachment or link in spam e-mail to users who downloaded it onto their computers. The hackers then used the banking credentials to access bank accounts of these businesses and municipalities, withdraw money in amounts just under $10,000, and transfer it to fraudulent bank accounts opened using fictitious names and fake passports. Ten (10) percent of the proceeds were kept by the "mules" who opened the fraudulent bank accounts and the rest was wired to the masterminds of the scheme in Eastern Europe.[13]

The Zeus Trojan is spread by the Zbotnet. According to Damballa, it has infected 3.6 million computers in the United States, or one percent of all the computers in the country. Its Eastern European developers provide a support network, it is easy to use, and ad-ons have been created to defeat efforts by banks to thwart the criminals.[14] A Zeus toolkit is available that lets users tailor the botnet to break the security of specific banks, and to evade anti-virus detection.[15]

Kneber Botnet

An intrusion affecting 75,000 computer systems at nearly 2,500 companies was discovered in January 2010.[16] Named the Kneber botnet,[17] it targeted proprietary corporate data, e-mails, credit card transaction data, and login credentials at companies in the health and technology industries, educational institutions, energy firms, financial companies, and Internet service providers in 196 countries, including the United States, Saudi Arabia, Egypt, Turkey, and Mexico, according to officials at NetWitness, the security firm that discovered it.[18] The Kneber botnet is believed to be run by a criminal group based in Eastern Europe that uses very sophisticated command and control methods to infiltrate targeted company computers and networks and harvest login credentials and passwords, which it uses to hack into other systems. A report by NetWitness reveals details about the nature of this threat:

> Deeper investigation revealed an extensive compromise of commercial and government systems that included 68,000 corporate login credentials, access to email systems, online

---

13. Federal Bureau of Investigation New York, Department of Justice Press Release, Manhattan U.S. Attorney Charges 37 Defendants Involved in Global Bank Fraud Scheme Who Used "Zeus Trojan" and Other Malware to Steal Millions of Dollars from U.S. Bank Accounts, Defendants Allegedly Compromised Dozens of Accounts and Transferred More Than $3 Million in Stolen Funds to Hundreds of Accounts Opened Under False Identities (Sept. 30, 2010), *available at* http://newyork.fbi.gov/dojpressrel/pressrel10/nyfo93010.htm.

14. Damballa, *The IMDDOS Botnet, supra* note 8, at 7–8.

15. Kelly Jackson Higgins, *Anitvirus Rarely Catches Zbot Zeus Trojan*, DARK READING (Sept. 16, 2009), available at http://darkreading.com/xxx; Tim Greene, *Despite recent busts, ZeuS Trojan will be around awhile; ZeuS malware is resilient, distributed, effective*, NETWORK WORLD (October 2, 2010), *available at* http://www.networkworld.com/cgi-bin/mailto/x.cgi?pagestosend=/news/2010/100210-zeusXXX.

16. Press Release, NetWitness, NetWitness Discovers Massive ZeuS Compromise: "Kneber Botnet" Targets Corporate Networks and Credentials (Feb. 18, 2010), *available at* http://www.netwitness.com/resources/pressreleases/feb182010.aspx.

17. A botnet (for robot NETwork) consists of compromised computers that are used to create and send communications (spam or viruses that flood a network with messages such as a denial of service attack) to other computers on the Internet. The computer receives commands from the person(s) in control of the botnet.

18. Ellen Nakashima, *Large Worldwide Cyber Attack Is Uncovered*, WASH. POST, Jan. 18, 2010, at A1.

banking sites, Facebook, Yahoo, Hotmail and other social networking credentials, 2,000 SSL certificate files, and dossier-level data sets on individuals including complete dumps of entire identities from victim machines. . . .

Conventional malware protection and signature based intrusion detection systems are by definition inadequate for addressing Kneber or most other advanced threats. Organizations which focus on compliance as the objective of their information security programs and have not kept pace with the rapid advances of the threat environment will not see this Trojan until the damage already has occurred. Systems compromised by this botnet provide the attackers not only user credentials and confidential information, but remote access inside the compromised networks.[19]

Hackers responsible for several of the recent massive data breaches showed increasing sophistication, targeting organizations that process and store vast amounts of valuable personal information, as well as major businesses and government agencies that make up the critical infrastructure of the nation.

Aurora Botnet and the Google Attack

In January 2010 Google announced that it had been the victim of a targeted attack and identified over 34 additional organizations that had also been breached. The attack is believed to have originated in China and to have used botnets to access victim networks and steal confidential business systems and information.[20] This breach is particularly dangerous for the companies involved because the hackers used social engineering and phishing attacks to trick company officials into opening e-mail attachments or linking to a malicious website and downloading malware. According to news reports, the hackers stole from Google "source code for a password system that controls access to almost all of the company's web services."[21]

DATA BREACH RISKS

The risks to individuals of identity theft, fraud, and violations of privacy are becoming more serious as large amounts of information of greater sensitivity become accessible in electronic form to people and organizations that may not have an appropriate and adequate level of security protection. The effect of a data breach and identity theft on the victims can be devastating, and in some cases, irreparable.[22] Law firms collect and store large amounts of critical, highly valuable corporate records. In November 2009 the FBI issued a warning that hackers are targeting U.S. law firms to steal confidential information. Criminals are using spear phishing or targeted socially engineered e-mail designed

---

19. NetWitness, *supra* note 16.

20. DAMBALLA, THE COMMAND STRUCTURE OF THE AURORA BOTNET, March 2, 2010, *available at* http://www.damballa.com/downloads/r_pubs/Aurora_Botnet_Command_Structure.pdf; Robert McMillan, *McAfee: "Amateur" Malware Not Used in Google Attacks*, IDG NEWS SERV., Mar. 31, 2010, *available at* http://www.networkworld.com/news/2010/033110-mcafee-amateur-malware-not-used.html.

21. Ellen Nakashima, *Google Hackers Duped Company Personnel to Penetrate Networks*, WASH. POST, Apr. 21, 2010, at A-15.

22. Press Release, Identity Theft Res. Ctr., Identity Theft: The Aftermath 2008 (June 30, 2009), *available at* http://www.idtheftcenter.org/artman2/publish/m_press/Identity_Theft_The_Aftermath_2008.shtml. See Federal Trade Commission, Guide for Assisting Identity Theft Victims (Oct. 28, 2010), *available at* http://www.idtheft.gov/probono.

to compromise a network by bypassing technological network defenses.[23] Appearing to originate from a trusted source, the messages are designed to entice users to click on an attachment or link, which launches a self-executing file and, through a variety of malicious processes, attempts to download another file. Once in the network, a hacker can install a trojan computer program that will allow him to send sensitive files to a remote server, often in another country. The hacker can also create a "back door" that will allow hackers to get back into the network at a later time. Network defense against these attacks is difficult as the e-mail subject lines are spoofed, or crafted to uniquely engage recipients with content appropriate to their specific business interests. Risks to the confidentiality of personal information are present in a variety of environments. These range from the most simple—such as when printouts containing Social Security numbers and other personal information are thrown in the trash for others to retrieve—to the technologically complex—such as a community bank that uses an encryption algorithm for its customer debit card PIN codes that could be broken, creating the weakest link in a security system, or when sensitive health records are exposed through a peer-to-peer file-sharing system installed on the same computer where the health records were stored.

AGGREGATED ELECTRONIC INFORMATION AT RISK[24]

Credit Card, Driver's License, Bank Account, and Social Security Numbers

Retail establishments, payment card processors, educational institutions, credit bureaus, financial institutions, data brokers, healthcare providers, and other organizations collect—in person and online—and store massive amounts of personally identifiable information about individuals without having appropriate information security controls in place to protect this sensitive information.

The more personal information that is aggregated and stored electronically, the greater the risk to the individual. These institutions routinely violate one of the principal tenets of fair information practice—to collect and store the minimum amount of data required to meet their business requirements.[25] Many organizations have not developed and implemented data retention and destruction policies to ensure that sensitive personal information will be deleted promptly when it is no longer required. Examples abound of organizations that have suffered massive data breaches and put customers at risk of identity theft because they retained far too much personal information—retail establishments that needed credit card numbers only for three months to complete pur-

---

23. FBI, Spear Phishing E-mails Target U.S. Law Firms and Public Relations Firms, *available at* http://www.fbi.gov/scams-safety/e-scams/archived_escams.

24. Sensitive information refers to information that requires some degree of heightened protection from unauthorized access, use, disclosure, disruption, modification, or destruction because of the nature of the information, e.g., personally identifiable information and proprietary commercial information. It includes privileged information.

25. This is a core principle of the Payment Card Industry Data Security Standard (PCI DSS) Milestones for Prioritizing Compliance Efforts. *See* PCI SEC. STANDARDS COUNCIL, THE PRIORITIZED APPROACH TO PURSUE PCI DSS COMPLIANCE (Feb 2009) *available at* https://www.pcisecuritystandards.org/index.shtml ("Remove sensitive authentication data and limit data retention. This milestone targets a key area of risk for entities that have been compromised. Remember—if sensitive authentication data and other cardholder data are not stored, the effects of a compromise will be greatly reduced. If you don't need it, don't store it.").

chases but collected and saved them for "research purposes," copied the information onto backup tapes, or otherwise saved the information in local databases.

Medical Records

As the government target to create an electronic health record for every American by 2014 approaches, the most personal records of all Americans will be collected, copied, stored, and shared by multiple parties around the globe. The records may be accessed for years to come by a wide range of medical and nonmedical personnel including physicians, office assistants, technicians, vendors, and government and university officials—not only to provide medical care to individual patients, but for "research" by government agencies and universities.

Obviously, the privacy risks to patients increase as the number of people who have access to their medical records grows. At present, it is not only the obvious institutions and individuals—doctors, hospitals, and pharmacies—that have access to patient medical records. Under various government Prescription Drug Monitoring Programs (PDMP), state officials have access to prescription records and monitor the use of certain controlled substances and other medications. In addition, they maintain individually identifiable records of persons diagnosed with specified diseases such as cancer.[26] Some technology companies collect and store patient pharmacy records, ostensibly on behalf of insurance companies. Some have gone beyond merely serving as a processor of electronic pharmacy records to amassing databases of individual records and assigning "risk scores" that assess the medications prescribed, even though these companies have no information about the medical diagnoses of the patients or the reasons the medications were prescribed.

Technology companies that have created online personal electronic health records (EHR) systems are creating huge databases of the most sensitive patient records. Google has undertaken a pilot project with the Cleveland Clinic to create a system of electronic patient health records called Google Health. Kaiser Permanente, the nation's largest HMO, is conducting a pilot project to link its health records system to Microsoft's consumer health storage platform, HealthVault. Revolution Health, founded by AOL cofounder Steve Case, is a "consumer-centric health company" that allows consumers to make "informed choices and offers more convenience and control over their individual healthcare decisions."[27] These electronic health records management systems exchange data among diverse public and private constituents, and will enable local, regional, and national health networks. They will provide the flexibility to integrate applications such as lab systems, practice management systems, EHR, analytics tools, and other capabilities. While advocates of EHR cite numerous benefits to patients—including better quality of patient case, improved outcomes, lower costs, and increased efficiencies for the healthcare community—the challenge of securing systems such as these are major because security is only as good as the weakest link, and these interconnected systems

---

26. National Conference of State Legislatures, Prescription Drug Monitoring Programs, *available at* http://www.ncse.org/default.aspx?tabid=12726.

27. About Revolution Health, *available at* http://www.revolutionhealth/about/index.

present a variety of weak links that provide vulnerable points that hackers may be able to penetrate.[28]

Tax and Financial Records

Confidential financial records—tax records submitted to the IRS—may now be at risk. Consider this: to apply for a mortgage, loan applicants are required to submit a detailed application with demographic and financial information, a credit report with bank and investment account numbers, credit card numbers, employment verification, and tax returns for the past two or three years. Virtually all the personal information that a hacker would need to completely assume a person's "identity" is contained in these documents. While each of these items individually is sensitive, in this context, the information is gathered together and stored in one electronic file, thus greatly increasing the risk that if the aggregated information is stolen, identity theft will be successful. Pursuant to a 2009 Fannie Mae policy, mortgage lenders have been directed to obtain transcripts of tax returns for all mortgage loan applicants for multiple years, regardless of the applicants' sources of income.[29] Tax returns submitted to the IRS are safeguarded with sophisticated security controls and criminal law prohibits IRS employees from browsing through tax returns.[30] However, with electronic tax records available to multiple mortgage lenders and investors, individuals may not be informed of who will have access to their records and how they will be safeguarded. State and federal laws contain data retention requirements for mortgage-related documents, such as nondiscrimination provisions that are at odds with the privacy "collection limitation" principle, putting this information at risk for many years.

Likewise, data brokers are amassing huge amounts of personal information about individuals without their consent, and in most cases, without their knowledge. The consequences for individuals if this information is revealed or otherwise misused are irreparable. Compromise of these records could lead to denial of employment or insurance, theft from financial accounts, identity theft, and prying by family members, neighbors, and acquaintances.

Law Firm Records

Law firms collect and store large amounts of highly sensitive business and personal information and communications about clients and their legal and business activities,

---

28. Lucas Mearian, *As health data goes digital, security risks grow—Encryption alone won't be enough to protect online patient data*, COMPUTERWORLD, March 22, 2010, *available at* http://www.computerworld.com/s/article/print/9173198/As_health_data_goes_digital_security_risks_grow?taxonomyName=Security&taxonomyId=17.

29. In this era of electronic records, individuals applying for mortgages who sign an IRS Form 4506-T authorize loan officers or mortgage investors to obtain electronic copies of their tax returns from the IRS. Fannie Mae Selling Guide, Announcement 09-02 (Feb. 6, 2009), *available at* https://www.efanniemae.com/sf/guides/ssg/annltrs/pdf/2009/0902.pdf ("The borrower must complete and sign Form 4506 *Request for Copy of Tax Return* or 4506-T *Request for Transcript of Tax Return* granting the lender permission to request copies of federal income tax returns directly from the IRS. The lender must obtain the IRS copies of the returns or the transcript and validate the accuracy of the tax returns provided by the borrower prior to the loan closing.").

30. Even at the IRS, the Government Accountability Office (GAO) found that newly identified and unresolved information security control weaknesses in key financial and tax processing systems continue to jeopardize the confidentiality, integrity, and availability of financial and sensitive taxpayer information. GAO Info. Sec., IRS Needs to Continue to Address Significant Weaknesses, GAO 10-355 (Mar. 2010).

and highly valuable corporate records—do their computer networks have robust security controls that cannot be breached?[31] In November 2009 the FBI issued a warning that hackers are targeting U.S. law firms to steal confidential information. Criminals are using spear phishing or targeted socially engineered e-mail designed to compromise a network by bypassing technological network defenses.[32] Appearing to originate from a trusted source, the messages are designed to entice users to click on an attachment or link, which launches a self-executing file and, through a variety of malicious processes, attempts to download another file. Once in the network, a hacker can install a Trojan computer program that will allow him to send sensitive files to a remote server, often in another country. The hacker can also create a "back door" that will allow hackers to get back into the network at a later time. Network defense against these attacks is difficult as the e-mail subject lines are spoofed, or crafted to uniquely engage recipients with content appropriate to their specific business interests. Is the highly sensitive personal information about clients, opposing parties, and third parties obtained through electronic discovery secured and deleted appropriately?

Mortgages and Consumer Loans

An extraordinary risk of identity theft could be posed if a Securities and Exchange Commission (SEC) proposed rule that would require the public release of individual information for all mortgage and consumer loans being sold through an asset-backed security is adopted.[33] Conceived of as a way to improve transparency for investors, the proposed rule would require the disclosure of "loan-level information" about characteristics of the property securing the loan, and the individuals who received mortgages and other consumer loans, including credit information about the borrower, cash out, credit scores, length of employment, income, monthly debt, liquid assets/cash reserves, and other details regarding individual borrowers. In comments filed with the SEC, a coalition of privacy organizations asserted that the proposal is a "direct and substantial threat to the privacy of every individual who obtains a mortgage. If adopted, the proposal would be an unprecedented release of individual-level financial data and would greatly increase borrowers' risk for identity theft and other problems related to the public release of detailed financial information."[34]

Using publicly available information about property sales, data brokers could easily identify individual borrowers and combine the personal financial data the SEC proposes be released with demographic information, retail transaction records, and credit information. Similarly, criminals, such as those from other countries who have been responsible for some of the major data breaches, could precisely target individuals and use this previously private financial information to assume their identity. The President's Identity Theft Task Force recommended reducing the amount of sensitive

---

31. Karen Sloan, *Firms Slow to Awaken to Cybersecurity Threat*, Nat'l L.J., Mar. 9, 2010, *available at* http://www.law.com/jsp/lawtechnologynews/PubArticleLTN.jsp?id=1202445899467&Firms_Slow_to_Awaken_to_Cybersecurity_Threat.

32. FBI, Spear Phishing E-mails Target U.S. Law Firms and Public Relations Firms, *available at* http://www.fbi.gov/scams-safety/e-scams/archived_escams.

33. 75 Federal Register 23328 (May 3, 2010), available at http://edocket.access.gpo.gov/2010/pdf/2010-8282.pdf.

34. World Privacy Forum, *available at* http://www.worldprivacyforum.org/pdf/WPFcommentsSEC_02August2010fs.pdf.

financial information circulating about consumers. The consumer groups argued that the proposed SEC rule directly contravenes the Task Force recommendations by greatly increasing the amount of sensitive financial information about individual borrowers that would be made publicly available.[35]

Mergers and Acquisitions

"Corporate restructuring puts every organization in a state of heightened IT risk."[36] Mergers, acquisitions and organizational changes present serious security challenges. These require the integration of disparate business processes, business cultures, and information technology. "Any material weaknesses or deficiencies at the acquired company may impact the acquirer." As the movement and integration of information systems take place in merged companies, sensitive personal information may be at risk. Of the total breaches in 2010, the Verizon team reported that 9 percent of the breaches involved organizations that had recently been involved in a merger or acquisition. Another 9 percent had been restructured in some way.[37]

Cloud Computing

Cloud computing is an information technology infrastructure that is transforming the way information services are delivered to companies and individuals. However, it introduces IT security and privacy risks related to outsourcing the administration and physical control of sensitive data to a third party vendor, and maintenance of the data on shared computing platforms, risks that will need to be carefully evaluated and addressed.[38]

The cloud computing business model emphasizes increased flexibility and lower cost to organizations when the major components of computing—hardware, software, storage, networking, data, and information—are available on-demand and paid for through a subscription, variable costs, usage, or pay-per-use arrangement.[39] It is designed to maximize the use and flexibility of computing resources—multiple operating systems can run simultaneously on the same hardware—and increase organizational efficiency because it can optimize computer workloads and adjust the number of servers in use to match demand, thereby conserving energy and information technology resources.

35. Comments of the World Privacy Forum, the Center for Digital Democracy, Consumer Action, the Center for Financial Privacy and Human Rights, Privacy Rights Clearinghouse, and Privacy Activism to the Securities and Exchange Commission Regarding SEC Notice of Proposed Rulemaking on Asset-Backed Securities, File Number S7-08-10 (August 2, 2010), *available at* http://www.worldprivacyforum.org/pdf/WPFcommentsSEC_02August2010fs .pdf.

36. Jackie Gilbert, *Navigate Your Company Through an M&A Transition,* SC MAGAZINE (May 12, 2009), *available at* http://www.scmagazineus.com/navigate-your-company-through-an-ma-transition/article/136554/.

37. 2010 Verizon Report, *Ibid.* at 11.

38. The FTC hosted a series of public roundtable discussions to explore the privacy challenges posed by 21st century technology and business practices that collect and use consumer data, including cloud computing; *available at* http://www.ftc.gov/bcp/workshops/privacyroundtables/index.shtml.

39. NIST defines cloud computing as: "a model for enabling convenient, on-demand network access to a shared pool of configurable computing resources (e.g., networks, servers, storage, applications, and services) that can be rapidly provisioned and released with minimal management effort or service provider interaction." NIST Special Publication 800-125, *Guide to Security for Full Virtualization Technologies,* (July 21, 2010), *available at* http://csrc .nist.gov/publications/PubsDrafts.html.

The technology consists of a shared pool of computing resources that are available as a (1) private cloud (enterprise owned or leased), (2) community cloud (shared infrastructure for a specific community), (3) public cloud (services to the public), or (4) hybrid cloud (composed of two or more clouds).

Cloud computing provides the data owner diminished control over the information. Data may be fragmented and dispersed, making it difficult to account for it; it can be exposed to foreign governments; it may become a target for hackers; and data ownership issues may arise between the entity that provides the data and the cloud vendor.

Data breaches involving Google cloud computing services illustrate the risks of having data maintained remotely on a server in the cloud. In one breach, individuals' private documents stored on Google Docs were shared with other users without their permission in March 2010.[40] Google sent letters to some users stating that certain identified documents may have been shared without their knowledge with persons with whom they had previously shared documents, but whom the users had not authorized to receive the identified documents.

In another breach by an insider, a Google engineer/programmer, who was subsequently fired, reportedly searched a Google database to access the accounts of teenagers he was interested in.[41] The employee reportedly abused his privileges to access confidential user information. The risk of this type of breach is evident in a cloud or other outsourcing arrangement in which an organization relies on third-party service providers to process or analyze their confidential information, payment transactions, etc.

NEW TECHNOLOGIES, NEW RISKS

Mobile Devices

The proliferation of mobile devices such as laptops, thumb drives, cellular telephones, and personal digital assistants (PDAs) are creating two kinds of risks: (1) they are repositories for the collection and storage of large amounts of important personal information, and (2) these devices enable the sharing of that personal information, or they enable m-commerce such as mobile banking. Security experts predict that hacking of mobile devices and m-commerce transactions will be among the most serious criminal activity of 2010.[42]

---

40. The privacy group Electronic Privacy Information Center (EPIC) has asked the FTC to investigate Google for privacy breaches related to Google Docs and other Google services—and to ban Google from offering any cloud services, including Gmail, Google Docs, and others until the company can prove it is capable of safeguarding people's privacy. The complaint alleges that Google's inadequate security is an unfair and deceptive business practice. *Available at* http://epic.org/privacy/ftc/google/epic_complaint.pdf.

41. Audrey Watters, Google's Internal Security Breach Raises Questions About Trust and the Cloud (September 16, 2010), *available at* http://www.readwriteweb.com/cloud/2010/09/googles-internal-security-brea.php.

42. Kevin Prince, *Top 10 Information Security Threats of 2010,* NETWORK SECURITY EDGE, January 29, 2010, *available at* http://www.networksecurityedge.com/content/top-10-information-security-threats-2010; Blake Wiedman, Mobile Security Threats and Prevention, Governmentsecurity.org, October 3, 2009, *available at* http://www.governmentsecurity.org/articles/mobile-security-threats.html; Sophos, Security Threat Report: 2010, at 25, *available at* http://sophos.com/sophos/docs/eng/papers/sophos-security-threat-report-jan-2010-wpna.pdf; Leo King, *Facebook poses mobile working 'security threat,'* NETWORK WORLD, June 14, 2010, *available at* http://www.networkworld.com/news/2010/061410-facebook-poses-mobile-networking-security.html.

Mobile Marketing

A retail marketing initiative that is certain to expose large amounts of sensitive personal information to possible compromise is the use of mobile coupons by entities such as department stores, grocery stores, and fast food outlets. For those who have enrolled in the program, companies send digital coupons to customers' cell phones; they are redeemed in stores when scanned by a cashier.[43] While individuals opt-in to take advantage of the discounts, these programs also provide retailers the opportunity to build profiles on their customers. When scanned, digital information from special bar codes on the coupons is captured, including the individual's cell phone number, carrier's name, date and time the coupon was obtained, viewed and redeemed, and the store where it was used; in some cases the Internet search terms used to obtain the coupon may be captured as well.

The scanner may place a "cookie" on the phone to track user's Internet use. As the technology develops, the process of scanning the phone may also enable the company to obtain other information stored there—consider that smart phones may contain identifying information, address book, contact list, calendar, multiple e-mail accounts, voice mail, GPS locations, and sensitive data stored on the memory card. When an enterprise has identified its customers individually through a phone number, identifying information on the phone, participation in a retail buying program, or the credit card number used in the transaction, it can "enhance" the information it has collected by purchasing from a data broker a wide variety of demographic, commercial, and public information. Contrary to the privacy principle that organizations limit the amount of information collected and maintained on individuals, mobile marketing can expand exponentially the volume of sensitive information stored and used, making these retail databases prime targets for hackers engaged in identity theft and fraud.[44]

Peer-to-Peer File Sharing

The Kneber botnet hackers penetrated file-sharing sites looking for sensitive corporate documents. Personal information, including sensitive data about customers and/or employees, and health and financial records, may be at risk on many computers and computer systems when peer-to-peer (P2P) file-sharing programs are installed. P2P technology may be used to make online telephone calls (e.g., Skype), play games, and, through P2P file-sharing software, to share music, video, and documents. It is not unusual, however, for users to download corrupt P2P programs or to misconfigure the software and unintentionally allow all of the files on their computer to be shared to the

---

43. Ariana Eunjung Cha, *Mobile Coupons Help Retailers Track Customers*, WASHINGTON POST, June 27, 2010 at G01.

44. Concerned about privacy risks and the potential for identity theft, the FTC has addressed the issue of tracking consumers' online sctivities (web searches, pages visited, content viewed) in the report Self-Regulatory Principles for Online Behavioral Advertising, February 2009, *available at* http://www.ftc.gov/os/2009/P08540behavadreport .pdf. Expanding on the definition of PII, the report states that the privacy protections should cover any data that "reasonably can be associated with a particular consumer or computer or other device." The report articulates four principles, including the need for companies to provide reasonable security for any data they collect for behavioral advertising and to retain data only as long as it is needed to fulfill a legitimate business or law enforcement need.

community.[45] This technology creates a significant risk of a breach when it is installed on the same computer as the personal information—when the P2P file-sharing software is not configured properly, sensitive records not intended for sharing may be accessible to anyone on the P2P network.

Two individuals were indicted in San Diego and charged with using account login information and passwords inadvertently exposed to the peer-to-peer file-sharing network. The defendants are alleged to have accessed the bank accounts of the victims, transferred funds to prepaid credit cards that the hackers obtained in their own names, and used the cards to purchase goods and obtain cash.[46]

FAILED SECURITY

The State of Information Security in the 21st Century?

The highly publicized data breaches of Heartland, Hannaford, RBS WorldPay, TJX, DSW, CardSystems, and others discussed throughout this book should serve as a wake-up call to organizations around the globe that adequate information security is required to protect personal records. Consider this: a hacker breached the financial records of 192,000 consumers maintained by D.A. Davidson, an investment firm that provides financial services to clients nationwide and obtained highly confidential consumer financial information.[47] The Financial Industry Regulatory Authority (FINRA), which fined the firm $375,000, found that prior to January 2008, the firm did not employ adequate safeguards to protect the security and confidentiality of customer records and information stored in a database housed on a computer Web server with a constant open Internet connection. The unprotected information included customer account numbers, Social Security numbers, names, addresses, dates of birth, and other confidential data. Furthermore, the firm's procedures for protecting that information were deficient in that the database was not encrypted and the firm never activated a password, thereby leaving the default blank password in place. The firm had failed to implement basic safeguards to protect that data—even though it had been advised before this incident to implement an intrusion detection system.[48]

---

45. The FTC has notified almost 100 organizations that personal information, including sensitive data about customers and/or employees, has been shared from the organizations' computer networks and is available on P2P file-sharing networks to any users of those networks, who could use it to commit identity theft or fraud. News Release, Fed. Trade Comm'n, Widespread Data Breaches Uncovered by FTC Probe: FTC Warns of Improper Release of Sensitive Consumer Data on P2P File-Sharing Networks (Feb. 22, 2010), *available at* http://www.ftc.gov/opa/2010/02/p2palert.shtm.

46. *See* News Release, Office of the U.S. Att'y, S. Dist. Cal., *available at* http://www.cybercrime.gov/girandolaIndict.pdf (announcing indictment of Jeffrey Steven Girandola and Kajohn Phommavong on 16 counts of conspiracy, computer fraud, access device fraud, and aggravated identity theft).

47. Three members of an international criminal group were extradited from Eastern Europe, and pleaded guilty in federal court in Montana to charges of criminal conspiracy, extortion and fraud in this case. *See* U.S. Department of Justice, District of Montana, News Release (June 10, 2010), *available at* http://www.justice.gov/usao/mt/pressreleases/20100610162515.html.

48. FINRA News Release, Financial Industry Regulatory Authority, FINRA Fines D.A. Davidson & Co. $375,000 for Failure to Protect Confidential Customer Information (April 12, 2010), *available at* http://www.finra.org/Newsroom/NewsReleases/2010/P121262.

FINRA mandated changes in Davidson's information security practices,[49] including:

- Sensitive data must be encrypted
- Vendor passwords should be changed from default settings
- Network logs should be actively managed and reviewed sufficiently to identify network intrusions
- Firewalls and application services should be configured to minimize direct connections to the public internet (including databases)
- An active detection solution should be employed, such as Network Intrusion Detection.

No one knows how pervasive this problem of a total lack of security is throughout the nation's businesses. Failed security has resulted in massive data breaches that lead to the loss or compromise of millions of personally identifiable individual records.[50] Individuals and organizations have cause for serious concern. Sophisticated underground enterprises have created a thriving market for stolen personal information that is used for unauthorized financial transactions and widespread identity theft.[51] Data breaches are so pervasive because they are not only the result of hacker attacks, but they are also caused by sloppy security practices, resulting in the loss of laptops and other mobile devices containing unencrypted personal information.

Serious threats and risks to sensitive data and information exist and are well-known to potential attackers. These threats cannot be ignored any longer. Individuals and organizations that collect sensitive personal information have the highest duty and responsibility to protect and safeguard those records. The hundreds of data breach incidents indicate that some collectors have not merely failed to protect the information but have failed to provide reasonable security protections. Information security must be addressed in a disciplined and professional manner in any information system that collects, stores, or shares sensitive data and information. Lawyers will play a critical role in ensuring that the organizations they represent safeguard the sensitive data entrusted to them.

---

49. *Id.*
50. *See* chapter 5, Encrypted Records—Failed Security.
51. *See* chapter 4, The Underground World of Online Identity Theft: An Overview.

CHAPTER 2

Despite the Alarming Trends, Data Breaches Are Preventable

Lucy L. Thomson

It is critical for business executives and their counsel, and technology professionals, to know and understand the causes of data breaches in order to protect one of the most valuable and vulnerable assets of the business—its information. This is not only good business practice, it will avoid the high costs associated with responding to data breaches, potential liability, negative press, embarrassment, and ultimately loss of customers and business. In almost all cases, the data breaches that occurred could have been prevented by proper planning and the correct design and implementation of appropriate security solutions.[1]

Maintaining consumer trust and confidence is essential to the business, as the impact of data breaches can be devastating. Individuals whose identity has been stolen face an uphill battle to address the myriad of problems that follow, including closing accounts, canceling fraudulent debts, changing identification numbers, removing incorrect information, and restoring credit.

ALARMING TRENDS

The past five years have seen a dramatic increase in the number of data breaches reported publicly.[2] Data breaches in the United States rose almost 50 percent in 2008.[3] Data breaches in 2010 are up—more breaches have been reported in the first three

---

1. The high costs of responding to data breaches have been well documented. As the notification requirements in the data breach laws become more complex, and the liability imposed by courts and administrative agencies for data breaches increases significantly, these costs are likely to rise dramatically. See chapters 6, 7, and 8 for a detailed discussion of the requirement for an assessment of harm and the conduct of risk assessments in some of the state data breach laws.

2. The American Bar Association thanks the curators of the Open Security Foundation (OSF) for providing the graphic in Figure 2.3 of this chapter. OSF, which runs the DataLossDB, is a research project aimed at documenting known and reported data loss incidents worldwide. For more information, see http://datalossdb.org.

3. IDENTITY THEFT RES. CTR., 2009 ITRC BREACH REPORT (Jan. 6, 2010), *available at* http://www.idtheftcenter.org.

TABLE 2.1
Records Compromised in the Largest Data Breaches

Company	Date	Records Breached
Heartland	January 2009	30,000,000
RBS WorldPay	December 2008	1,500,000
Hannaford	February 2008	4,200,000
TJX	January 2007	45,600,000
TOTAL		81,300,000

Source: Compiled from information maintained by the Open Security Foundation (OSF) DataLossDB and the Identity Theft Resource Center (ITRC).

quarters of 2010 than were reported in 2009.[4] According to Identity Theft Resource Center (ITRC) reports, in 2009 only six of 498 organizations that reported breaches had either encryption or other strong security feature protecting the exposed data.[5] Equally small numbers were reported for 2008, when the ITRC declared, "It is obvious that the bulk of breached data was unprotected by either encryption or even passwords."[6]

The largest data breaches ever were reported in 2007, 2008, and 2009. These massive data breaches, involving Heartland, RBS WorldPay, Hannaford, and TJX, compromised the personal records of 81,300,000 individuals, exposing them to potential identity theft and fraud.[7] The numbers are staggering (see Table 2.1).

According to the data breach statistics compiled by the ITRC, the 498 data breaches reported in 2009 exposed 222,477,043 individual records.[8] The year 2009 was distinguished by the massive size of several breaches rather than the total number of reported breaches, which were fewer in 2009 than in 2008, but more than the number of breaches in 2007. In 2008, 656 data breach incidents were reported, in which 35,691,255 records were exposed. These numbers are up from 425 breaches reported in 2007 and 483 breaches in 2006. Figure 2.1 shows comparative data on the number of data breach incidents for the years 2001 through 2009.

DATA BREACH INCIDENTS BY INDUSTRY

Significant numbers of data breaches have occurred in five industry sectors: business, government/military, education, health/medical, and banking/credit/financial. Of the five industry sectors, the largest number of data breach *incidents*—more than

---

4. Identity Theft Res. Ctr, 2010 Data Breach Stats (Oct. 26, 2010), *available at* http://www.idtheftcenter.org.
5. Identity Theft Res. Ctr., Breaches 2009, Data Breaches: The Insanity Continues, (Jan. 8, 2010), *available at* http://www.idtheftcenter.org/artman2/publish/lib_survey/Breaches_2009.shtml.
6. Identity Theft Res. Ctr., Security Breaches 2008 (Mar. 26, 2009), *available at* http://www.idtheftcenter.org/artman2/publish/lib_survey/Breaches_2008.shtml.
7. Chapter 5 provides an in-depth analysis of the causes of each of these data breaches.
8. The Open Security Foundation Data Loss database reports slightly lower numbers: total incidents: 480; total records affected: 220,596,330. OPEN SEC. FOUND., DATA LOSS DATABASE—2009 YEARLY REPORT, *available at* http://datalossdb.org/yearly_reports/dataloss-2009.pdf.

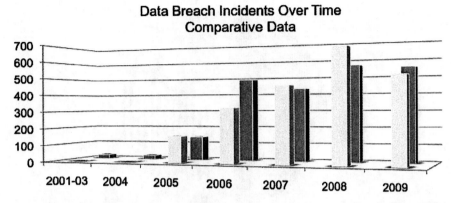

FIGURE 2.1
Incidents Over Time

Source: Compiled from information maintained by the Open Security Foundation (OSF) DataLossDB and the Identity Theft Resource Center (ITRC).

40 percent—occurred in the business sector. There has been a steady upward trend of breaches occurring in retail businesses and payment card processors. Government agencies at the federal, state, and local levels and the military experienced the next largest incidence of data breaches—18 percent—followed by educational institutions, where 15 percent of the data breaches occurred. Healthcare organizations and financial institutions suffered 13 and 11 percent of the breaches respectively.[9] Table 2.2 presents the

TABLE 2.2
Percent of Breaches by Industry Sector

Industry	2009	2008	2007	2006
Business	41.2	36.6	29.3	20.9
Government/Military	18.1	16.8	24.5	30.5
Educational	15.7	20.0	24.7	24.9
Health/Medical	13.7	14.8	14.5	14.0
Banking/Credit/Financial	11.4	11.9	7.0	9.7

Source: Compiled from information maintained by the Identity Theft Resource Center.

9. Based on the data breaches investigated by the Verizon risk team and the United States Secret Service (USSS), the 2010 Verizon Breach Report provides a somewhat different perspective on the nature of data breaches. It reports the percent of data breaches by industry groups in the Verizon-USSS caseload as follows: Financial Services—33%; Hospitality—23%; Retail—15%; Manufacturing—6%; Tech Services—5%; Business Services—4%; Government—4%; Media—4%; Healthcare—3%; Other—4%.

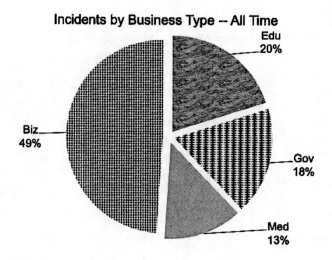

FIGURE 2.2
Incidents by Business Type

Source: Compiled from information maintained by the Open Security Foundation (OSF) DataLossDB.

percentages for the years 2006 through 2009. Figure 2.2 illustrates the distribution of data breaches by industry sector over the past decade.

Number of Records Breached by Industry

Comparing the number of *records breached* for each industry presents a more dramatic picture than focusing solely on the number of data breach incidents. These figures are contained in Table 2.3.

The largest number of records breached in 2009 occurred in the business sector, where a record 132,402,177 consumer records were exposed. Thus, nearly 60 percent of the records breached occurred in retail companies and payment card processors. Similarly, in 2007, breaches in the business sector accounted for 80 percent of the total records breached that year. Overall, the massive breaches of Hannaford, Heartland, and TJX reported in 2009 and 2007 contributed to the size of these numbers.

Government agencies and the military accounted for more than 35 percent of the records breached in 2009 and 2006. The government percentage was so large in 2009 because of the major breach of the U.S. military involving 76 million records. In 2008, the financial sector accounted for 52 percent of the records breached—because of RBS WorldPay, the second largest ATM processor in the United States.

Millions of Medical Records Breached

Healthcare breaches have increased from 13 percent in 2009 to 26.4 percent in 2010. 148 of the 561 U.S. companies and organizations that endured a significant data breach in the first three quarters of 2010 were healthcare providers.[10] Healthcare organizations

---

10. *Id.*

TABLE 2.3
Records Breached by Industry Sector

Industry	2009	2008	2007	2006
	Percent/Number			
Business	59.3	16.5	82.6	23.2
	132,402,177	5,886,950	105,544,377	4,433,350
Government/ Military	35.6	8.3	6.4	38.5
	79,470,963	2,954,373	8,156,682	7,362,790
Educational	0.4	2.3	0.9	11.5
	803,667	806,142	1,184,575	2,198,830
Health/ Medical	4.7	20.5	3.1	14.3
	10,461,818	7,311,833	3,997,133	2,741,101
Banking/ Credit/ Financial	0.0	52.5	6.9	12.5
	8,364	18,731,947	8,834,476	2,401,773
Total Number of Records Breached	223,146,989	35,691,245	127,717,243	19,137,844

accounted for half of the top 10 largest breaches reported for 2009. Data breaches are occurring at healthcare organizations at a much higher rate than in any other industry, a trend that reflects both the vast amount of personal data housed at hospitals and medical centers and the comparatively lax security employed by these organizations.[11] Overall, there were 68 breaches involving health care institutions in which 11,311,818 records were compromised. The breach of millions of personal medical records is not just limited to 2009: 7,311,833 records were breached in 2008, 3,997,133 records were breached in 2007 and 2,741,101 records were breached in 2006.

Medical identity theft is a particularly devastating event for individuals whose medical records have been stolen.[12] In light of the government initiatives to create electronic health records, these breaches illustrate starkly the challenges ahead for policymakers and healthcare providers. These breaches underscore the need for renewed vigilance to address the problem of data breaches among healthcare providers.

---

11. Identity Theft Res. Ctr, 2010 Data Breach Stats, *supra* note 4.
12. WORLD PRIVACY FORUM, MEDICAL IDENTITY THEFT: THE INFORMATION CRIME THAT CAN KILL YOU, at 26, (Spring 2006), *available at* http://worldprivacyforum.org/pdf/wpf_at 26,_medidtheft2006.pdf.

CAUSES OF DATA BREACHES

Assessing the causes of the data breaches is critically important to developing solutions to prevent them from occurring. The types of breaches that have occurred over the past decade are illustrated in Figure 2.3. In order to prevent data breaches, it is essential to analyze and understand the root causes of the security failures and to develop a specific plan to address each of them. Analysis of the types of breaches that have occurred is very illuminating—for the conclusion that most of these breaches did not have to happen.

Approximately one third of data breaches were caused by hackers. Nearly 60 to 80 percent of the personal records breached in the years 2009 and 2007, respectively, were stolen from retail establishments and payment card processors by hackers who exploited serious weaknesses in their computer networks.

There are a number of causes of data breaches in the business sector. Hackers have targeted retailers and payment card processors because of the high value for identity theft of the consumer information collected and maintained by these entities. At the same time, business executives have failed to address the multitude of vulnerabilities in their networks, making them prime targets for hackers to exploit. Another aspect of lax security that lead to large breaches is the theft or loss of laptops, computers, hard drives, backup tapes, PDAs, and other portable media containing unencrypted personal information.

Finally, many organizations collect too much sensitive data and save it much longer than is necessary to accomplish their business purposes. They must have data retention and destruction plans in place and delete (sanitize) sensitive data on a regular basis. All of these factors must be addressed in order to prevent data breaches.

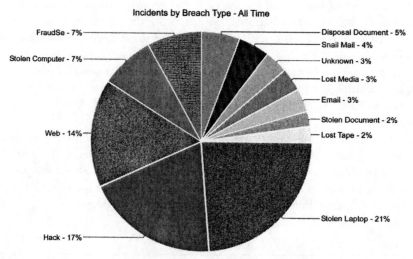

FIGURE 2.3
Types of Incidents

Source: Open Security Foundation (OSF) DataLoss DB.

Lost and Stolen Computers, Laptops, and Portable Devices

More than one third of data breaches resulted from the theft or loss of laptops, computers, hard drives, backup tapes, PDAs, or other portable media containing unencrypted personal information. During 2009 and the beginning of 2010, an astounding 7 million of the most sensitive medical records and personal information about students were stolen or "disappeared." Nearly 2 million medical, financial, and social services records of individuals were breached on stolen or lost laptops. More than 8 million personal, financial, and medical records were stolen or lost in just three incidents during 2007, 2008, and 2009 while they were being transported on tapes or CDs to offsite storage facilities. None of this personal information was encrypted.

The ITRC has analyzed the problem this way: "This is 100% avoidable, either through use of encryption, or other safety measures. Laptops, portable storage devices and briefcases full of files, outside of the workplace, are still 'breaches waiting to happen.' With tiered permissions, truncation, redaction and other recording tools, PII [personally identifiable information] should be left where it belongs—behind encrypted walls at the workplace."[13]

The breaches described in Table 2.4 illustrate the sheer magnitude of the exposure of personal records and the potential damage to millions of individuals. In light of the available security measures and their widespread acceptance within the information security community, there is no excuse for organizations that collect and store PII to fail to fulfill their duty to protect this personal information.

These types of breaches can be prevented easily both by encrypting the data on the devices and by enforcing procedures that do not permit individuals to transport sensitive data unencrypted on moveable media or without proper authorization, keeping careful track of the devices, and having the highest standards and requirements for couriers to move backup tapes and CDs to offsite storage facilities or from one location to another.

Improper Disposal of Paper Documents

Equally egregious are incidents involving paper records that were not shredded and were placed in the trash for others to find. Paper breaches accounted for nearly 26 percent of known breaches (an increase of 46 percent over 2008). Five percent of the breaches were caused by the improper disposal of paper and electronic records in the trash. This behavior should never be permitted to happen.

A Nevada mortgage broker was fined $35,000 by the FTC for discarding 40 boxes of sensitive consumer financial records in a publicly accessible dumpster. The records included tax returns, mortgage applications, bank statements, photocopies of credit cards and drivers' licenses, and at least 230 credit reports. The FTC charged Gregory Navone with failing to take reasonable measures to protect credit report information from unauthorized access during its disposal in violation of the Fair Credit Reporting Act and the FTC Disposal Rule.[14]

---

13. Identity Theft Res. Ctr., Breaches 2009, *supra* note 5.

14. FTC v. Gregory Navone, FTC File No. 072 3067 (D. Nevada), *available at* http://www.ftc.gov/os/caselist/07 23067/100120navonestip.pdf. *See* FTC Fair and Accurate Credit Transaction Act of 2003 (FACTA) Disposal Role, *available at* http://www.ftc.gov/opa/2005/06/disposal.shtm.

TABLE 2.4
Data Breaches That Should Never Have Happened

Lost and Stolen Laptops

Blue Cross Blue Shield Highmark—850,000 Records Breached—August 2009

A laptop was stolen from an employee of the BC/BS national office. It contained information on about 50,000 doctors, or 90 percent of the physicians nationwide. The employee violated company policy and downloaded an unencrypted version of the database onto a personal laptop.

Naval Hospital Pensacola—38,000 Records Breached—August 2009

A laptop containing 38,000 pharmacy services customers' Social Security numbers and dates of birth were lost.

Vavrinek, Trine, Day and Co.—Customers of 50 Banks—April 2009

Six laptop computers were stolen from an auditing firm in California. They contained bank files including customer account name, number, and balance as of August 2008.

Oklahoma Department of Human Services—1,000,000 Records Breached— April 2009

A computer containing names, Social Security numbers, and dates of birth of people who received state assistance was stolen from a worker's car.

Lost External Hard Drives and Tapes

Educational Credit Management Corporation (ECMC)—3,300,000 Records Breached—March 2010

Computer backup discs containing student names, addresses, dates of birth, and Social Security numbers were stolen in a burglary of the ECMC offices. This breach affects 5 percent of all students with federal loans in the United States and represents 8.9 million loans. ECMC, a nonprofit located in St. Paul, Minnesota, is a guarantor of federal student loans. The breach announcement is posted online at http://www.ecmc.org/details/Announcement.html.

Health Net—1,500,000 Records Breached—May 2009

A portable external hard drive containing seven years of personal and medical information on about 1.5 million Health Net customers (including Social Security numbers and medical records) "disappeared" and is still missing from the insurer's Northeast headquarters in Shelton, Connecticut.

Blue Cross Blue Shield Tennessee—2 Million Records Breached—October 2009

Sixty-eight hard drives were missing from the BC/BS Tennessee office. It is suspected that they contained medical files and personal information.

Tapes Stolen in Transit to Offsite Storage Facilities

Peninsula Orthopaedic Associates—100,000 Records Breached—March 2009

Tapes containing patient personal information (including Social Security numbers and employer and health insurance plan information) were stolen while in transit to an off-site storage facility.

Georgia Department of Community Health—2,900,000 Records Breached— April 2007

A CD was lost containing names, Social Security numbers, and addresses of people on Medicaid and Peach Care. A computer services company lost the CD while it was being transported by a private carrier.

Bank of New York Mellon Corporation—4,500,000 Records Breached— February 2008

A box of unencrypted tapes with personal and financial information (including names, Social Security numbers, and dates of birth) was lost by third-party vendor Archive America during transport to an off-site facility.

A related type of breach resulted from not properly sanitizing electronic media. Improper destruction of hard drives and other media is the source of many breaches. Destruction of electronic records should be overseen by information technology professionals; these types of breaches should never occur.

Accidental Exposure

Through careless handling, personal information is often exposed in postal mailings. It is also posted on websites where it is exposed to individuals who are not intended to access it. Peer-to-peer (P2P) file-sharing technology creates a significant risk of a breach when it is installed on the same computer as the personal information—when the P2P file-sharing software is not configured properly, sensitive records not intended for sharing may be accessible to anyone on the P2P network.[15]

Insider Threats

Malicious insiders pose a serious threat to the security of sensitive information and their activities accounted for another third of the breaches. Individuals who abused administrative privileges lead to a significant number of breaches, and security failures such as not suspending system access for terminated employees caused many breaches. Data breaches by malicious insiders must be addressed as carefully as hacker attacks, since individuals who abuse their system access and privileges can cause the compromise and loss of millions of sensitive records. Insider breaches often involve system and network administrators, but may also be committed by other types of employees.[16] During 2007, 2008, and 2009, 214 data breaches caused by insiders were reported. Three of the most egregious insider breaches, including WikiLeaks, are described in Table 2.5. Twenty-four percent were perpetrated by employees who had some type of job change—fired, resigned, newly hired, or changed roles within the organization.[17]

Defending an organization's perimeter from external attack does not protect against valuable information seeping out because of insider malfeasance, whether that behavior is characterized as malicious, mischievous, or ignorant/accidental.[18] Carnegie Mellon University recommends a list of 16 best practices[19] to minimize the risk of insider threat.

---

15. The FTC has notified almost 100 organizations that personal information, including sensitive data about customers and/or employees, has been shared from the organizations' computer networks and is available on P2P file-sharing networks to any users of those networks, who could use it to commit identity theft or fraud. News Release, Fed. Trade Comm'n, Widespread Data Breaches Uncovered by FTC Probe: FTC Warns of Improper Release of Sensitive Consumer Data on P2P File-Sharing Networks (Feb. 22, 2010), *available at* http://www.ftc.gov/opa/2010/02/p2palert.shtm.

16. 2010 Verizon Report, *supra* note 9 at 34.

17. 2010 Verizon Report, *supra* note 9 at 29.

18. *CSO*, 2006 eCrime Watch Survey (Sept. 6, 2006), *available at* http://www.cert.org/archive/pdf/ecrimesurvey06.pdf. The survey was conducted by *CSO* magazine in cooperation with the U.S. Secret Service, Carnegie Mellon University Software Engineering Institute's CERT Coordination Center, and Microsoft Corp.

19. DAWN CAPPELLI, ANDREW MOORE, TIMOTHY J. SHIMEALL & RANDALL TRZECIAK, COMMON SENSE GUIDE TO PREVENTION AND DETECTION OF INSIDER THREATS (July 2006), *available at* http://www.cert.org/insider_threat/.

TABLE 2.5
Insider Data Breaches

> *WikiLeaks—approximately half a million confidential government documents and messages—July and November 2010*
> The publication by WikiLeaks of confidential American diplomatic cables and messages about the Iraq and Afghanistan wars revealed the largest insider data breach ever.[20] Members of Congress characterized the breach as "espionage" and a "breach of national security" and called on the Pentagon to identify the high-ranking individuals responsible. A junior military man is suspected of leaking the information to WikiLeaks.
>
> *Bank of New York Mellon—Identity Theft of 2,000 Employees— October 2009*
> A computer technician who worked in the bank's IT department stole the identities of 2,000 bank employees and opened bank and brokerage accounts. He then used them to steal more than $1.1 million from charities, nonprofit groups, and other entities. The individual was convicted and pleaded guilty to a "massive identity theft scam."[21]
>
> *Certegy Check Services—8.4 Million Records Breached—July 2007*
> Certegy, which provides check authorization services to retailers, maintained financial information (credit card numbers, bank accounts, and other personal information) on millions of individuals, including those who had not written a check for more than a decade. A senior database administrator (DBA) compromised customer records by selling the information to a data broker. The Certegy DBA, who was responsible for defining and enforcing data access rights in the computer network, abused his position of trust at the company. The data was then sold to various marketing firms.[22]
>
> A settlement with the Florida Attorney General's Office requires Certegy to maintain a comprehensive "Information Security Program" that assesses internal and external risks to consumers' personal information, implements safeguards to protect that information, and regularly monitors and tests the effectiveness of those safeguards. Certegy will also adhere to payment card industry data security standards.
>
> The widespread effect of this data breach was more harmful to consumers than would have been expected. Strategia Marketing, LLC purchased and used the stolen data to engage in "negative option" telemarketing to sell buyer discount programs, travel clubs, and other products to unwitting consumers using techniques that were found by the FTC to constitute unfair and deceptive business practices and that violated the telemarketing sales rule.[23]

20. Mark Landler and J. David Goodman, Clinton Says U.S. Diplomacy Will Survive 'Attack,' New York Times, November 29, 2010, available at http://www.nytimes.com/2010/22/30/w0rld/30reax.html?_r=1; WikiLeaks, New York Times, December 16, 2010, *available at* http://topics.nytimes.com/top/reference/timestopics/organizations/w/wikileaks/index.html; The Defense Department's Response, New York Times, October 22, 1010, *available at* http://www.nytimes.com/2010/10/23/world/middleeast/23response.html.

21. New York County District Attorney's Office, District Attorney Vance Announces Guilty Plea in Massive Identity Theft Scam, Computer Technician Stole Personal Information of 2,000 Bank of New York Employees Orchestrated More Than $1.1 Million in Thefts from Charities and Nonprofits (July 1, 2010), *available at* http://www.manhattanda.org/whatsnew/press/2010-07-01.shtml.

22. Certegy was fined $975,000 by the Florida Attorney General. *See* http://www.myfloridalegal.com/newsrel.nsf/pv/889FA9C2A2A31AA88525770700578C1B; Ellen Messmer, *Fidelity: Ex-Worker Stole 2.3 Million Customer Records*, PC WORLD (July 4, 2007), *available at* http://www.pcworld.com/article/134154/fidelity_exworker_stole_23_million_customer_records.html.

23. Suntasia Marketing Defendants Pay More Than $16 Million to Settle FTC Charges; Massive Telemarketing Scheme Affected Nearly One Million Consumers Nationwide (January 13, 2009), *available at* http://www.ftc.gov/opa/2009/01/suntasia.shtm; http://www.ftc.gov/os/caselist/0623162/090113suntasiaftnorder.pdf.

Hacker Attacks

An assessment of data breach trends over the past several years reveals that hacking accounts for about one-third of the hundreds of breaches of computer networks or websites. Web applications rank first in the number of breaches and the amount of data compromised. In 2010, web applications accounted for 54 percent of the breaches and 92 percent of the total records breached.[24] Organizations that collect, process, or store large amounts of personally identifiable information, particularly credit card numbers and related information of high value to criminals, have become targets of overseas organized crime.[25]

Payment cards are prized by criminals because they are an easy form of data to convert to cash. Personal information and bank account data were the second and third most compromised data types. Like payment cards, both are useful to criminals for committing fraud. Bank account data is also important due to the many cases of insider misuse at financial institutions.[26]

Several of the largest and most recent data breaches resulted from hackers infiltrating information systems at vulnerable points—where sensitive personal records were unsecured—even though those same records were encrypted when stored in company networks. The RBS WorldPay breach illustrates the increasing aggressiveness of global hackers. As the FBI observed, "in just one day, an American credit card processor was hacked in perhaps the most sophisticated and organized computer fraud attack ever conducted."[27]

Chapter 5 profiles eight of the major data breaches and provides insight into the need for organizations to exercise extreme care and develop appropriate security solutions to protect sensitive records in large systems.

WHAT INFORMATION HAS BEEN COMPROMISED IN DATA BREACHES?

In 35 percent of the data breaches, names, addresses, and Social Security numbers were among the data included. Huge numbers of credit and debit cards, and financial and medical records were exposed in the major breaches as well.

Twenty-eight percent of breaches in 2009 (compared with 12 percent in 2008) were the result of social tactics that involved deception, manipulation, intimidation, etc. to exploit users. The targets of these attacks are usually regular employees and customers.[28] Verizon-USSS cases reveal that the social tactics used for breaches include solicitation/ bribery (someone outside the organization conspired with an insider to engage in illegal behavior, the insider often placed there by an organized criminal group); phishing (fraudulent e-mails soliciting personal information); pretexting (invented scenario to deceive target); spoofing/forgery (fake website, documents, etc.); extortion (blackmail, threat of violence); hoax/scam; elicitation (subtle extraction of information through conversation); and spam (unsolicited messaging).[29]

---

24. 2010 Verizon Report, *supra* note 9 at 30.

25. Chapter 1 discusses cybercrime and the escalating risks to businesses and individuals.

26. 2010 Verizon Report, *supra* note 9 at 41.

27. News Release, U.S. Dep't of Justice, Alleged International Hacking Ring Caught in $9 Million Fraud (Nov. 10. 2009), *available at* http://www.justice.gov/opa/pr/2009/November/09-crm-1212.html.

28. *Id.* at 31–32.

29. *Id.* at 31.

In addition to the well-publicized types of PII, many other important and sensitive pieces of data have been breached (see Table 2.6). Consider the impact that exposure of these records can have on the individuals whose information is stolen.

DATA BREACHES CAN AND MUST BE PREVENTED

Organizations that collect, use, store, and share sensitive personal data must accept responsibility for protecting the information and ensuring that it is not compromised by hackers or malicious insiders or inadvertently accessed, lost, or stolen. The WikiLeaks breach and others illustrate starkly the critical questions executives of all government and private sector organizations must address—how should the organization's most valuable information be classified and what level of protection is required; who may have access to each type of information and should it be compartmentalized (particularly in information-sharing arrangements); what mechanisms will be used to enforce the access controls; and how will potential breaches be detected and prevented?[30]

The intense focus on response after a data breach has occurred is very costly to organizations, and does little to remediate the losses of the individuals whose personal information has exposed them to identity theft or fraud. Business owners, data custodians, and their attorneys in the private sector and in government around the globe must redouble their efforts to understand the risks of collecting, storing, and sharing sensitive and personal information, the many ways data can be breached, and the tools available to protect the data. They must develop the expertise to avoid these breaches, and to address them in a meaningful way if and when they occur. This includes an appreciation of the fact that there is no one solution that is appropriate for every organization. Information security must be tailored based on the type(s) of data to be protected, the potential threats and risks to the data, and the nature of the information systems of the organization, including the hardware, software, applications, and interconnections. As well, business owners must understand that appropriate implementation and periodic auditing are as important as the initial security controls that are put in place.

Most of the reported data breaches are a result of lax security and the failure to create or enforce appropriate security policies, rules, and procedures. Lost laptops and mobile devices containing vast amounts of unencrypted sensitive and personal information, lost backup tapes and computers, lost devices by delivery services, and posting of sensitive information on websites are all examples of the lack of reasonable security measures that have led to major breaches.

Appropriate information security controls, including encryption, must be implemented and enforced in a rigorous and disciplined manner so that a *data breach never occurs*. Following are a number of steps that should be considered when developing an information security solution that involves encryption.[31]

---

30. Viola Gienger, WikiLeaks Secrecy Breach May Prompt U.S. to Reverse Post-9/11 Data Sharing, Bloomberg, Dec. 1, 2010, *available at* http://www.bloomberg.com.

31. For an insightful (and entertaining) view of what an organization should do to protect itself from the sophisticated, persistent, and well-funded hackers, see Ryan Naraine and Dancho Danchev, *Advanced Persistent Threats: Should Your Panties Be in a Bunch, and How Do You Un-Bunch Them?*, ZDNet, Mar. 11, 2010, http://blogs.zdnet .com/security/?p=5691&page=5&tag=col1;post-5691.

TABLE 2.6
Types of Personal Information Compromised in Data Breaches

Birth dates	Names
Phone numbers	Addresses
Demographic information	Social Security Numbers (SSN)
Family size	SSN of children
User name and computer passwords	Federal tax information
Photocopies of driver's licenses	Tax returns—taxes owed
Employer information	Tax IDs
Occupation	Detailed medical history
Passport numbers	Hospital medical records
Visa applications	Patient medical records of a physician
Photographs	Pension-related information
Salary information	Insurance information
Payroll information	Medicare benefit premium information
Lists of assets	Donations to university
Telephone bills	Veterans' records—VA physicians and patients
Bank account numbers	
Credit and debit card numbers	Workers' compensation information
Commercial loan information	City voting records
College Board standardized test scores	GED recipients and sensitive info
College student grades	SSA disability applications
University student records	Phone numbers of family members
Info on prospective students	Work history
Biographical info on university alumni	State purchasing card numbers
	Patent and intellectual property
	Federal legal cases

ACTION PLAN TO PREVENT DATA BREACHES—ENCRYPTION CONSIDERATIONS[32]

1. Conduct a risk assessment—security controls must address all risks in the risk assessment.
2. Develop a comprehensive information security plan specifically designed to prevent data breaches.

---

32. Lucy Thomson, Thomas J. Smedinghoff, Eric A. Hibbard & Robert Thibadeau, *Untangling the Web of the State and Federal Data Breach Laws*, RSA Conference, 2010 (March 2010).

3. Develop a data retention and destruction plan so personal data is not at risk—sanitize regularly.
4. When information is encrypted, notification is not required; but all data must be protected (e.g., see chapter 5, which describes how TJX and Heartland encrypted records stored in databases but transmitted them unencrypted "in the clear" where they stolen).
5. Match the encryption solution to the risk.
   Strength of security ECB (simplest of the encryption modes) versus XTS (more specialized encryption mode).
   Approach of encryption solution (self-encrypting disks versus file-level encryption).
   Pedigree/certification of encryption for particular users (Common Criteria, FIPS 140).
6. Use data classification (even rudimentary) to help guard against overprotection (cafeteria menu) or underprotection.
7. Bear in mind that compliance-driven encryption necessitates proof-of-encryption capabilities.
8. Inadequate/inappropriate key management can result in data breaches and/or loss of data.
9. Analyze audit logs on a regular basis; look at increase or decrease in log size and length of lines within logs for evidence of a possible data breach.[33]

Finally, remember that while encryption will assist in avoiding certain types of data breach incidents, it is not a panacea. For instance, a common threat approach consists of a criminal or organized crime entity enlisting an "insider" to assist in extracting sensitive information. An insider with valid access credentials will not find encryption to be an obstacle in any way. As a result, encryption is one of many valuable tools for information protection, not the entire solution.

---

33. The Verizon team reported that it has seen log entries increase by 500 percent following a breach. They have seen them completely disappear for months after the attacker turned off logging. They have noticed SQL injection and other attacks leave much longer lines within logs than standard activity. 2010 Verizon Report, *supra* note 9 at 50.

CHAPTER 3

The Aftermath of Data Breaches: Potential Liability and Damages

Arthur E. Peabody, Jr. and Renee A. Abbott

INTRODUCTION

Massive data breaches have had a devastating impact on both businesses and consumers alike.

- Lawsuits have been brought by business entities, consumers, and banks. Consumers have brought actions alleging an array of state and common-law violations; banks have likewise brought actions, including class actions seeking to recover the costs of fraud and other damages.
- Investigations have been initiated by federal agencies, including the U.S. Department of Justice, Federal Trade Commission (FTC), Secret Service, and state Attorneys General. Settlement agreements impose strict information security measures on businesses that have subjected consumers to breaches and require information security audits for decades.
- Non-governmental regulators have acted to fine companies falling within the scope of their regulatory authority substantial sums for failing to protect confidential customer information.
- Consumers have been subjected to identity theft and fraud. Social Security and credit card numbers have been stolen. Consumers have been required to obtain new credit cards, driver's licenses, and personal ID numbers; lose credit in "rewards programs"; and close and open new accounts.
- Some businesses have been so damaged that they could not remain viable and have declared bankruptcy. Settlements have cost businesses millions of dollars; some view the highest expense as attorneys' fees.
- Businesses have been fined by credit card companies such as Visa and MasterCard for failing to comply with their contracts requiring "reasonable security" by the implementation of security standards promulgated by the

Payment Card Industry Data Security Standards (PCI DSS) Council. Other companies have been terminated as credit card processors.

- Businesses have been required to notify millions of customers of the breaches; upgrade the security of their information systems; and obtain fraud alerts from credit bureaus for customers, thereby incurring the costs of credit reports for consumers.
- Federal law now requires "risk assessments" of breaches of health care data; other laws impose new and additional costs on businesses to ensure the security of data and notification of breaches to customers.

Data breaches almost always result in lawsuits. This chapter identifies the serious impact of data breaches and the approaches both consumers and banks have taken in the courts to recover their damages.

- Most of the lawsuits brought to recover damages resulting from data breaches have been based on state law claims; the law is still emerging in this area. Many contract and tort claims have been dismissed based on the contours of state law.
- Plaintiffs need to draft their complaints carefully. A small or bankrupt business's only viable asset following a massive data breach may be its insurance policies; contract claims are not covered under many policies.
- Likewise, due to significant potential liability, businesses need to review their insurance policies to determine if they have adequate coverage for massive data breaches, scrutinize their information security policies, ensure compliance with information security standards, and be prepared to conduct a professionally based risk assessment should any breach occur.[1]
- Federal laws are effective in achieving systemic relief but do not result in the recovery of damages for individuals; the FTC has been successful in requiring business to adopt professional security practices and to require periodic audits to ensure appropriate security measures are in place.
- Criminal cases have been brought to prosecute hackers under federal criminal laws.

Recent civil cases decided in the federal courts have identified a major problem for consumers whose PII has been breached by the failure of a corporation or bank to have an information system that is secure. Courts continue to rule against plaintiffs bringing actions primarily based on state law and common law principles; finding that a breach alone is insufficient to prove liability and damages; a plaintiff must demonstrate some real harm or financial loss to have a viable claim.

A recent ruling by the 9th Circuit Court of Appeals is the latest in a series of cases where individuals whose personal information was exposed, subjecting them to potential identify theft and other fraud from a data breach, have been unable to successfully pursue claims due to the lack of actual harm suffered by those individuals whose data was breached. In *Ruiz v. Gap,*[2] the plaintiff had submitted personal information as part

---

1. For more on the insurance aspects of this issue, see chapter 19, Insurance Protection for Security Breaches.
2. 622 F. Supp. 2d 908 (N.D. Cal. 2009).

of an online employment application. Two laptops belonging to a contractor for Gap were stolen. The laptops contained data on some 750,000 Gap job applicants, including the plaintiff. He filed suit alleging negligence, breach of contract, and other California state regulations. His claim was dismissed by the United States District Court for the Northern District of California on the ground that the plaintiff had failed to prove any loss or actual injury as a result of the breach of his personal information.[3] A mere breach or exposure to potential harm is inadequate; real losses or damages are required. The 9th Circuit affirmed.[4]

A federal judge in Pennsylvania dismissed a class action lawsuit arising out of a data breach involving Aetna. The court found that the plaintiffs lacked standing to sue due to the failure to allege an "injury in fact."[5] The court opined that the plaintiff's alleged injury in the form of alleged increased risk of identity theft was too speculative to afford the plaintiff standing to sue.[6] On July 12, 2010, a federal district court in New York granted summary judgment dismissing consumer class action claims against the Bank of New York allegedly arising from the loss of unencrypted back-up tapes.[7] The court held, *inter alia*, that an alleged increased risk of identity theft constituted neither sufficient injury to confer standing to sue nor, in the alternative, a legally compensable injury under the causes of action asserted in the complaint. The plaintiffs had alleged negligence, breach of contract, breach of fiduciary duty, and violations of state consumer protection statutes.

Likewise in August 2009, a federal court in Washington dismissed two class actions lawsuits for the failure to state a claim. The complaints were filed following the theft of a laptop containing names, Social Security numbers, and addresses of approximately 97,000 Starbucks employees. One plaintiff alleged misuse of his information, *i.e.*, a bank account was opened in his name without his consent. The bank had closed the account before any unauthorized charges had been made; no connection between the loss of the information and the opening of the account was established. In this circumstance, the court dismissed the complaint.[8]

These rulings are consistent with what appears to be a growing trend in data breach litigation to require some showing of actual harm or injury resulting from the breach. Yet lawsuits continue to be filed—both by consumers and state law enforcement officials alike[9] as serious breaches continue to occur.[10]

---

3. *Id.*

4. 2010 WL 2170993 (9th Cir.).

5. Allison v. Aetna, C.A. No. 09-2560 (E.D. Pa. March 9, 2010).

6. See discussion of motions to dismiss, M. Kozubek, *Plaintiffs Data Breach Suits Fail Where They Can't Prove Damages*, INSIDE COUNSEL, *available at* www.insidecounsel.com.

7. Hammond v. Bank of New York Mellon, 2010 WL 2643307.

8. Kozubek, *supra* note 6.

9. See, *e.g.*, A. Gonsalves, February 1, 2010, *Health Net Sued over Data Breach*, INFORMATION WEEK, *available at* www.informationweek.com/shared/printableArticleSrc.jhtml.

10. *See, e.g.*, P. Basken, March 26, 2010, *Personal Data on 3.3 Million Student-Loan Borrowers Is Reported Stolen*, CHRONICLE OF HIGHER EDUCATION, *available at* www.chronicle.com/article/Personal-Data-on-33-Million/64870; D. Kravets, February 11, 2010, Facebook Denies "All Wrongdoing" in Beacon Data Breach, *available at* www.wired .com/threatlevel/2010/02/facebook-denies-all-wrongdoing-in-beacon-data-breach; J. Vijayan, June 4, 2010, *Insurer Says It's Not Liable for University of Utah's $3.3M Data Breach*, NETWORKWORLD, *available at* www.networkworld .com/cgi-bin/mailto/x.cgi?pageto send=/news/2010/060510-insure.

Irrespective of the outcome of litigation, corporations, banks, hospitals, and other business entities are learning that breaches of personal information are expensive. For example, the University of Utah Hospitals and Clinics has incurred upwards of $3.4 million in costs following the theft of approximately 1.5 million patient billing records on computer tapes. Although the University sent notices to affected patients, numerous lawsuits resulted. In June 2010, a Colorado insurance company filed a lawsuit in federal court against the corporation, Perpetual Storage, responsible for the storage of the University's patient data.[11] On April 10, 2010, Certegy, a financial services company, settled a class action lawsuit arising out of a massive data breach that exposed personal information from 5.9 million consumer files. Under the settlement, the company will ensure that safeguards are in place to protect consumer data; consumers are able to request credit monitoring at the company's expense.[12]

Non-governmental regulators have stepped into the fray. On April 12, 2010, the Financial Industry Regulatory Authority (FINRA) announced that it had fined D.A. Davidson of Great Falls, Montana, $375,000 for failing to protect confidential customer data that was hacked by an international crime group.[13] The agency found that the company stored information in a database on a computer web server with a constantly open Internet connection. The database was not encrypted and the firm had never activated a password, thereby leaving a blank password in place. As such, the information was completely unprotected. Earlier, the company had ignored the advice of independent auditor to act to protect their database.

Although courts have yet to open the floodgates to successful consumer class action litigation, plaintiffs continue to pursue such claims in court as entities subjected to breaches suffer significant damages to their business reputations and the costs of notification, credit monitoring, credit card replacement, and a host of other associated costs.

LIABILITY AND DAMAGES RESULTING FROM MAJOR DATA BREACHES

TJX

TJX is an off-price retailer selling apparel and home fashions in over 2,500 stores worldwide. It suffered a massive data breach affecting 45.6 million credit and debit card numbers in 2007. The breach also compromised the personal information of approximately 455,000 consumers who had made unreceipted merchandise returns. This personal information included personal ID numbers, including some Social Security numbers.

As a result of the data breach, issuing banks claimed tens of millions of dollars in fraudulent charges on some of the breached accounts. One bank alleged fraud losses involving Visa cards ranging from $68 million to $83 million spread across 13 countries.

---

11. *See*, K. Truong, *Insurer Denies Reimbursement to University of Utah in Data Breach*, The Chronicle, *available at* www.Chronicle.com/blogPost/Insurer-Denies-Reimbursement.

12. Attorney General Reaches Settlement Agreement with Certegy Check Services over Data Breach," news release *available at* www.myfloridalegal.com/newsrel.nsf/pv/889FA9C2A2A31AA88525770700578C1B.

13. F. McMorris, *D.A. Davidson to Pay FINRA Fine*, Financial Planning, April 12, 2010, *available at* www.financial-planning.com/news/finra-da-davidson-2666466-1.html.

Issuing banks have cancelled and reissued millions of credit and debit cards—costs that the banks sought to recover as damages in various lawsuits.

Consumers holding these cards were unable to use them to access their credit and bank accounts until they received replacement cards. Further, some consumers have obtained or will have to obtain new personal ID numbers, such as new driver's licenses.[14]

In June 2009, TJX reported that it would pay nearly $10 million to settle lawsuits brought by the attorneys general of 41 states.[15] In this agreement, the company agreed to implement measures to enhance its security of credit card data.[16] By June 2010, TJX had to set aside $178 million cash reserves to settle lawsuits.[17]

In September 2009, commentators reported that TJX could be expected to pay out up to $200 million in lawsuits settlements.[18] One analyst predicted that the figure could reach $1 billion over the next several years.[19] The company set aside $180 million for settlements of claims resulting from the massive breach.[20]

Consumers filed a class-action lawsuit in the U.S. District Court for the District of Massachusetts, alleging negligence for failing to maintain adequate security of consumer credit and debit card data and not disclosing the breach for at least one month.[21]

Banks, required to reissue millions of credit and debit cards, also filed a class action.[22] Plaintiff banks claimed that TJX failed to adequately safeguard its computer system and, as a result, unauthorized individuals gained access to customers' personal and financial information and stole this information to commit fraud and identity theft. More specifically, the complaint alleged breach of contract, negligence, negligent misrepresentation, and a violation of Chapter 93A of Massachusetts General Laws (deceptive practices). Defendants moved to dismiss.

The court dismissed the plaintiff banks' contract claim on the ground that they were not lawfully third-party beneficiaries of agreements between TJX and MasterCard and Visa because those contracts explicitly barred third-party status on other parties, that is, the contracts barred any application of terms beyond the specific parties to the contract. Likewise, the court dismissed the negligence claim on the ground that the losses incurred by the plaintiff banks were economic losses not recognized by Massachusetts negligence law. The negligent misrepresentation and Chapter 93A claims survived. These claims were based on the alleged failure of TJX to advise the banks that a majority of its retailers did not comply with data security standards.

---

14. TJX Companies, FTC No. 072-3055, Agreement Containing Consent Order, Analysis of Proposed Consent Order to Aid Public Comment at 2, www.ftc.gov/os/caselist/0723055/080327/analysis.pdf.

15. *Id.*

16. *Id.*

17. *See,* S. Hammond, Liability for data breaches goes beyond customer lawsuits, *available at* www.docucrunch.com/liability-for-data-breaches-goes-beyond-customer-lawsuits.

18. Jaikumar Vijayan, *TJX Agrees to Settle Another Breach Lawsuit for $525,000,* COMPUTERWORLD, Sept. 3, 2009, *available at* http://www.computerworld.com/s/article/9137491/TJX.

19. *Id.*

20. *Id.*

21. TJX Faces Class Action Lawsuit in Data Breach, www.krowenlaw.com/tjx3.htm.

22. This action represents the consolidation of at least five federal court actions brought against TJX by banks and citizens in Massachusetts, Alabama, and Puerto Rico. *See In re* TJX Cos., Inc., Customer Data Breach Litig., 493 F. Supp. 2d 1382 (Judicial Panel on Multi-District Litigation 2007); *In re* TJX Cos. Retail Sec. Breach Litig., 524 F. Supp. 2d 83 (D. Mass. 2007).

However, the federal district judge declined to certify the class, finding that many banks were in too many different situations to permit class certification.[23] More specifically, the court found that concerns regarding the adequacy of class representation and the great number of individual questions on fundamental issues of the banks' claims made class certification inappropriate.[24] It is noteworthy that the court observed that many of the banks purported to be represented in the class action "did not wish to pursue an action" and that the interests between different banks were in "fundamental conflict."[25] Further, each individual bank would have to show that it had relied on TJX's negligent misrepresentations and suffered financial loss.

The court held that liability could not be made on a class basis.[26] The court observed that some banks considered only one factor—keeping up with the competition—in making a decision to issue credit cards. Another bank conceded that a merchant's failure to comply with data security standards would not cause the bank to decline to issue credit cards.[27] Yet another bank, according to the court, indicated that its beliefs about the adequacy of TJX's security activities did not influence the security measures the bank implemented.[28]

In addition, the court observed that the banks would have difficulty proving that TJX's negligent security practices resulted in all the fraud, identity theft, and other damages they alleged. For example, the banks would have the burden to prove that the identity theft and other damages had not occurred when an individual consumer lost his or her wallet and the credit card(s) contained in the wallet, an incident the court labeled as "unrelated fraud."[29] As a result the case was remanded to state court "should the plaintiffs elect to press their suit there."[30] Many banks pursued individual actions—but not without attempting to amend their complaint to bring new claims to the district court.[31] In turn, the court addressed these additional claims.

On December 18, 2007, the district court dismissed the plaintiffs' conversion claim filed in a proposed amended complaint—the banks claimed that they had a "protectable property interest" in cardholder data and information that had been breached. The court promptly disposed of this claim, finding the cardholder data and information to be "intangible property" not falling within the scope of coverage of traditional conversion claims because "it would be impossible to access TJX's computer system and simply print out reports replete with the information that is the subject of the plaintiffs' claims."[32]

All parties appealed to the First Circuit.[33] The circuit affirmed the district court's decision that the banks had a claim for negligent misrepresentation, finding that the "claim

23. *In re* TJX Cos. Retail Sec. Breach Litig., 246 F.R.D. 389 (D. Mass. 2007).
24. *Id.* at 400.
25. *Id.* at 394–95.
26. *Id.*
27. *Id.* at 396.
28. *Id.*
29. *Id.* at 392, 398.
30. *Id.* at 401.
31. *In re* TJX Cos. Retail Sec. Breach Litig., 527 F. Supp. 2d 209 (D. Mass. 2007).
32. *Id.* at 213.
33. *In re* TJX Cos. Retail Sec. Breach Litig., 564 F.3d 489 (1st Cir. 2009).

survives, but on life support."[34] The court cast doubt on the viability of a claim that "by accepting credit cards and processing payment authorizations, defendants impliedly represented that they would comply with MasterCard and Visa regulations."[35] The court questioned whether "merely doing credit card transactions with issuing banks is a representation to third parties that all defendants will comply with the detailed security specifications of Visa and MasterCard."[36] The court was more charitable in sustaining the Chapter 93A state deceptive trade practices claim.[37] The court cited FTC standards and some state precedents that convinced the court that TJX's conduct might be viewed as "inexcusable and protracted reckless conduct, aggravated by failure to give prompt notice when lapses were discovered."[38] The court affirmed the district court's holding on all other issues, including the negligence claim, even reversing the district court's transfer of the case to state court.[39]

In the context of individual bank claims, as recently as September 2009, TJX agreed to pay four banks $525,000 for damages resulting from the 2007 breach.[40] Banks appear to have been more successful in settling claims than in pursuing protracted litigation.

Finally, banks and credit unions that issued more than 95 percent of the cards and consumers affected by the TJX breach reached a settlement and a recovery of up to $40.9 million.[41] In addition to the bank settlements, TJX agreed to compensate consumers for any time they lost "as a result of the intrusion" at a rate of $10 per hour. Consumer compensation was limited to $60 per person; $30 vouchers were sent to consumers for purchases at TJX stores.

Similar claims—for breach of contract, negligence, and equitable indemnification—were brought by Sovereign Bank against Fifth Third Bank (a member of the Visa network) as a result of a breach of credit and debit card data.[42] Electronic data on some credit cards had been copied and used fraudulently to obtain goods and services after cardholders had used their cards at BJ's Wholesale Club.[43] The Third Circuit affirmed the district court's dismissal of the bank's negligence claim on the same ground as the district court in Massachusetts—state law precludes negligence actions for purely economic damages; some element of "property damage" must be alleged.[44] Likewise, the Third Circuit found no basis for an indemnification claim. However, unlike the federal court in Massachusetts, the Third Circuit was unwilling to affirm the dismissal of the contract claim. While the court used the same analysis as the Massachusetts court—was Sovereign Bank a third-party beneficiary of the contract between Visa and its member

34. *Id.* at 495.
35. *Id.* at 494.
36. *Id.*
37. *Id.* at 495.
38. *Id.* at 496.
39. *Id.* at 501.
40. J. Vijayan, *supra* note 10.
41. The consumer and bank class actions were consolidated into one case. The federal district court in Massachusetts was assigned responsibility for all TJX breach litigation. *In re* TJX Cos. Consumer Data Breach Litig., 493 F. Supp. 1382 (Judicial Panel on Multidistrict Litigation 2007). *See In re* TJX Cos. Retail Sec. Breach Litig., 584 F. Supp. 2d 395 (D. Mass. 2008).
42. Sovereign Bank v. BJ's Wholesale Club, 533 F.3d 162 (3d Cir. 2008).
43. *Id.* at 166.
44. *Id.*

banks issuing credit cards?—the court found that there was a genuine issue of material fact as to whether Sovereign was an intended beneficiary.[45]

TJX's massive breach did not evade scrutiny by federal officials. The FTC filed a complaint against TJX alleging that 2,500 TJX stores worldwide failed to use reasonable and appropriate security measures to prevent unauthorized access to personal information on its networks.[46] Specifically, the agency charged that TJX

- Created an unnecessary risk to personal information by storing it on, and transmitting it between and within, its various computer networks in clear (that is, unencrypted) text;
- Did not use readily available security measures to limit wireless access to its networks, thereby allowing an intruder to connect wirelessly to its networks without authorization;
- Did not require network administrators and others to use strong passwords or to use different passwords to access different programs, computers, and networks;
- Failed to use readily available security measures, such as firewalls, to limit access among its computers and the Internet; and
- Failed to employ sufficient measures to detect and prevent unauthorized access to computer networks or to conduct security investigations, such as patching or updating antivirus software.

The FTC settlement with TJX requires the company to establish and maintain a comprehensive security program designed to protect the security, confidentiality, and integrity of personal information about consumers. It also requires administrative, technical, and physical safeguards and for TJX to retain independent, third-party security auditors to assess the security programs twice a year for the next 20 years. The FTC specified the procedures to be implemented. TJX must designate an employee to coordinate the information security program; identify internal and external risks to the security and confidentiality of personal information; design and implement safeguards to control the risks identified in risk assessments; and develop reasonable steps to select and oversee service providers that handle personal information.[47]

Heartland Payment Systems

Following a massive breach, Heartland Payment Systems was subjected to multiple lawsuits. In December 2007, a group of hackers was indicted for criminal fraud for launching a "Structured Query Language" (SQL) attack on Heartland's computer network. Over the course of 2008, the hackers managed to steal 130 million credit and debit card numbers.[48]

---

45. *Id.* at 173. The Third Circuit's opinion outlines in detail the nature of the contractual relationships between Visa and its member banks, including a helpful description of how a credit card transaction is processed and how the various contracts between Visa, its member banks, and merchants regulate their relationships. *See* Sovereign Bank v. BJ's Wholesale Club, 533 F.3d 162, 164–66 (3d Cir. 2008).

46. *In re* TJX Cos., Inc., FTC File No. 072-3055, *available at* http://www.ftc.gov/os/caselist/0723055/index.shtm.

47. *Id.*

48. *In re* Heartland Payment Sys. Sec. Litig., 2009 WL 4798148.

Heartland provides bank card payment processing services to merchants in the United States. The company facilitates the exchange of information and funds between merchants that accept credit and debit card payments and the cardholder's financial institutions. Heartland maintained millions of credit and debit card numbers on its computer network.[49]

Initially launched against the corporation's payroll manager application, the damage was not confined to this part of the network. The attack resulted in hidden, malicious software being placed on Heartland's network. This "malware" infected the credit card payment system that stored consumer credit and debit card data.[50]

Heartland did not discover the breach until January 2009. Following disclosure of the breach and subsequent disclosures about the potential impact of such a massive breach, Heartland's stock fell from more than $15 per share to $5.34 by February 24, 2009. If measured by the highest price of its stock in 2008, Heartland's stock declined in value by about 80 percent.[51]

At least 20 lawsuits have been filed against the credit card payment processing company by consumers and 10 on behalf of financial institutions, and an additional four cases initiated on security fraud theories.[52] In light of the large number of suits brought in federal court, a Multidistrict Litigation Panel consolidated the actions and transferred them to the U.S. District Court for the Southern District of Texas, the venue of Heartland's computer operations.[53]

The complaints in this litigation alleged breach of implied contract, negligence, negligent misrepresentation, common law negligence, and violation of state consumer protection statutes. Banks referenced damages arising from the costs of reissuing new credit and debit cards, mailing costs, and salaries paid to the employees issuing new cards. Consumers alleged identify theft and fraud.

By May 2010, Heartland had resolved many lawsuits that were brought against the company. Most recently, Heartland announced a settlement with MasterCard for $ 41.4 million. Commentators following the many lawsuits report that this settlement brings the total Heartland has committed to pay out to consumers, banks, and credit card companies to around $140 million.

On January 10, 2010, Heartland Payment Systems announced a settlement agreement under which issuers of Visa-branded credit and debit cards will have an opportunity to obtain a recovery from Heartland with respect to losses they may have incurred from the 2008 criminal breach of Heartland's payment system environment.[54] Heartland agreed to pay up to $60 million to fund the settlement program.

---

49. *Id.*

50. *Id.*

51. *Id.*

52. Tom Field, *Heartland Data Breach: Legal Update from Attorney Richard Coffman*, BANK INFO. SEC., June 25, 2009, http://www.bankinfosecurity.com/articles.php?art_id=1574.

53. The litigation consists of 19 federal court actions pending in eight states. The order transferring the 19 cases to Texas references five additional lawsuits pending in five states characterized as "potential tag-along actions. *In re* Heartland Payment Sys. Customer Data Sec. Beach Litig., 626 F. Supp. 2d 1336 (U.S. Jud. Pan. Mult. Lit. 2009). Individuals have filed cases on their own behalf—with mixed results. *See, e.g.*, Hinton v. Heartland Payment Sys., 2009 WL 704139 (D.N.J.).

54. *See* Press Release, Visa, Heartland Payment Systems Agrees on Settlement to Provide Visa Issuers up to $60M for Data Security Breach Claims (Jan. 8, 2010), http://www.corporate.visa.com/media-center/press-releases/press974.jsp.

The Visa/Heartland settlement agreement is contingent upon acceptance by financial institutions representing 80 percent of the eligible issuers' U.S. accounts that Visa considered to have been placed at risk of compromise during the Heartland data breach. Heartland will fund up to $59.2 million of the amounts to be made available to Visa and its issuers under the settlement program. Additionally, Visa will credit the full amount of intrusion-related fines it previously imposed and collected from Heartland's sponsoring bank acquirers toward the $60 million maximum funding of the program. It appears that the settlement amount represents a significant recovery to Visa issuers for losses they may have suffered from the Heartland data security breach. By February 4, 2010, most affected financial institutions had accepted the terms of the settlement.[55]

Visa will notify eligible issuers with details about the program and how to participate; eligible issuers will be required to opt-in to participate.

RBS WorldPay

In December 2008, the Atlanta-based U.S. payment processing arm of the Royal Bank of Scotland Group, RBS WorldPay, reported that a hacker had gotten into the electronic payment processing services provider's computerized recordkeeping system and digitally unearthed the financial account information of 1.5 million cardholders. For 1.1 million among them, Social Security numbers were also exposed. RBS immediately promised customers that they will not be held financially responsible for any resulting fraud; the company is also offering 12 months' complimentary credit monitoring.[56]

This breach involved electronic payroll cards. These prepaid cards, which Internetnews .com describes as "reloadable stored value cards companies use to pay their employees' wages," were among the types of account information targeted. Thieves also obtained account numbers associated with "open-loop" gift cards, prepaid cards endorsed by credit card companies like Visa and MasterCard.

A number of lawsuits by consumers seeking to recover damages incurred as a result of this massive breach were transferred to Georgia by the U.S. Panel of Multidistrict Litigation.[57] RBS WorldPay's parent company, the Royal Bank of Scotland (RBS), received an $8.9 million fine from the UK financial services regulator, The Financial Services Authority, for negligent IT governance.[58]

Hannaford Bros.

In February 2008 Hannaford, an East Coast supermarket chain, suffered a major breach exposing 4.2 million credit cards exposed to theft and subsequent fraud.[59] Nearly two dozen cases arising out of the Hannaford data breach were consolidated into a single

---

55. www.corporate.visa.com/media-center/pressreleases/press998.jsp.

56. SC Magazine, December 29, 2008, *available at* www.scmagazines.com/15-million-individuals-affected-in -rbs-worldpay-breach/article/123386.

57. 626 F. Supp. 2d. 1322 (2009).

58. L. McGlasson, *RBS WorldPay Extradition*, BankInfoSecurity, August, 2010, *available at* www.bankinfosecurity .com/articles.php?art_id=2830.

59. Jerry Harkavy, *Malware Cited in Supermarket Data Breach*, USA TODAY, March 28, 2008, www.usatoday .com/tech/news/computersecurity/2008-03-08-malware-supermarket_N.htm.

class-action lawsuit.[60] The gravamen of the lawsuit alleged that the company failed to maintain adequate security measures to safeguard its customers' data. More specifically, claims were asserted alleging breach of implied contract, breach of implied warranty, breach of duty of a confidential relationship, failure to advise customers of the theft of data, strict liability, negligence, and violation of Maine's Unfair Trade Practices Act (UTPA).[61] Alleged facts constituting these claims were recited in the complaint as follows:

- Customers' debit cards and credit cards were exposed to and subjected to unauthorized charges.
- Their bank accounts were overdrawn and credit limits exceeded.
- They were deprived of the use of their cards and access to their funds.
- They lost accumulated miles and points toward bonus awards and were unable to earn points during the interval their cards were inactivated.
- Those customers who requested that their cards be cancelled were required to pay fees to issuing banks for replacement cards.
- Those customers who had registered their cards with online sellers were required to cancel and change their registered numbers.
- Their preauthorized charge relationships were disrupted.
- Customers expended time, energy, and expense to address and resolve these financial disruptions and mitigate the consequences.
- They suffered emotional distress.
- Their credit card information became at increased risk of theft and unauthorized use.
- Some customers purchased identity theft insurance and credit monitoring services to protect themselves against the possible consequences.[62]

The court examined all the issues under Maine state law. As the court stated, "The answer [to all the claims] depends solely on state law, and state law is still undeveloped."[63] Unlike the law of some other states, Maine law recognizes that a contract may have "unarticulated implied terms."[64] As such, the court found that "in a grocery transaction where a customer uses a debit or credit card, a jury could find that there is an implied contractual term that Hannaford will use reasonable care in its custody of consumers' card data."[65] The court found no implied breach of warranty because the court reasoned that the term "good[s]" in the applicable statute does not include the payment mechanism.[66]

The court dismissed the "confidential relationship" claim, finding that essential elements to make out this claim were lacking, and further finding that lack of such a confidentiality claim precluded any claim for a breach of duty to advise customers of the

---

60. *In re* Hannaford Bros. Co. Customer Data Sec. Breach Litig., 613 F. Supp. 2d 108 (D. Me. 2009). The court declined to accept a case brought by Floridians in Florida because the suit alleged only violations of Florida state law. This action was remanded to the Florida state courts.

61. *Id.*

62. *Id.* at 116.

63. *Id.* at 115.

64. *Id.* at 118.

65. *Id.* at 119.

66. *Id.* at 120.

theft of their data. "The plaintiffs present no Maine cases to show that Maine common law recognizes this claim—breach of a duty to advise customers of the theft of their data once it occurred—as a stand-alone claim."[67] Finding that Maine's common law strict liability doctrine applies only to "extra hazardous activities," the court dismissed the strict liability claim.[68]

The court sustained the negligence claim, finding that Maine law had not adopted the broad doctrine that "purely economic damages" would never be the subject of a tort claim,[69] as well as the UTPA claim (deceptive practices), relying on a circuit decision endorsing the FTC definitions of unfair and deceptive practices. Finally, the court found that any plaintiff must have suffered a "cognizable injury," meaning that "consumers who did not have a fraudulent charge actually posted to their account cannot recover;" only customers with fraudulent charges they have been required to pay may assert a claim.[70]

In brief, the federal court applied a strict reading of Maine law to all claims; as to those few claims the court sustained, an "injury in fact" standard was applied. Customers whose payment data have been stolen can recover against a merchant only if the merchant's negligence caused a direct loss to the customer's account.[71]

In further opinions and orders, the court identified three categories of plaintiffs: (1) those who had never experienced a fraudulent charge; (2) the sole plaintiff who still had outstanding fraudulent charges; and (3) those who had fraudulent charges that had been reversed.[72] Citing numerous data breach cases from other jurisdictions, the court determined that the first category of plaintiffs experienced only a risk of injury and, therefore, had no recoverable damages.[73] For the plaintiff in the second category, the court found that the fraudulent charges on her account were a cognizable injury.[74] Finally, the court found for those plaintiffs who had already been compensated, their claims failed because any losses were "too speculative."[75] After the court's ruling, the remaining one plaintiff was reimbursed, effectively ending the litigation.[76]

In the final "act" in the drama, the plaintiffs moved for reconsideration, arguing that the time and effort each expended to avoid or remediate harm from fraudulent charges was a cognizable loss.[77] The federal court certified the issue to the Maine Supreme Judicial Court that ruled in a June 16, 2010 opinion that Maine tort law did not recognize

---

67. *Id.* at 124.
68. *Id.* at 126.
69. *Id.* at 128.
70. *Id.* at 131. The court carefully analyzed the factual claims of those who were at risk of being subjected to fraudulent charges and those who had them posted yet reversed. The court found these potential damages to be "too remote, not reasonably foreseeable, and/or speculative," to state a claim. *Id.* at 134. The court also dismissed claims for emotional distress and alleged losses resulting from a "rewards program," or points accumulated through the use of various credit cards. *See id.* at 134–35.
71. *Id.* at 135.
72. *In re* Hanford Bros. Co., 613 F. Supp.2d 108, 131–35 (D. Me. 2009).
73. *Id.*
74. *Id.* at 133.
75. *Id.* at 134.
76. 660 F. Supp. 2d 94, 97 (D. Me. 2009).
77. *Id* at. 101.

lost time as an actionable injury, opining that the law did not compensate individuals for the "typical annoyances and inconveniences of life."[78]

Discount Shoe Warehouse (DSW)

Columbus, Ohio-based Discount Shoe Warehouse, DSW Inc., operates approximately 190 stores in 32 states. The company generates over $100 billion in revenue annually. In 2004 and 2005, DSW collected and maintained credit card, debit card, and checking account numbers and other confidential personal financial information of approximately 1.5 million customers.[79]

During March 2005, unauthorized persons obtained access to the information of approximately 96,000 customers.[80] Customers whose personal financial information was breached were exposed to increased risk of identity theft and fraud; in addition, out-of-pocket expenses were incurred in connection with closing their accounts, ordering new checks, and obtaining credit reports and monitoring of their accounts.[81] According to Securities and Exchange Commission (SEC) filings, as of July 2005, DSW exposure for losses related to the breach ranged from $6.5 million to $9.5 million.[82]

Individual customers filed a number of ill-fated class-action lawsuits. In *Key v. DSW, Inc.*,[83] the plaintiff filed a putative class action alleging negligence, breach of contract, conversion, and breach of fiduciary duty. The district court dismissed the action finding that the plaintiff had not suffered any injury in fact and that, as a result, lacked standing to sue. The court found that the complaint had "bifurcated" claims. Although it was alleged that a number of class members had been injured, the complaint only alleged that the named plaintiffs had been "subjected to a substantial increase in their risk of identity theft and other financial crimes."[84] The court relied on decisions by other federal courts finding in the identity theft context that, as a general rule, an alleged increase in risk of future injury is not an actual or imminent injury required to allege legally cognizable injury and standing. As such, the court ruled that the class action could not proceed; defendant DSW's motion to dismiss the action was granted.[85]

In *Richardson v. DSW*,[86] a federal diversity case removed from state court, plaintiffs in this class action raised claims based on "implied contract and bailment theories" and violations of the Illinois Fraud Act (deceptive practices).[87] The court declined to dismiss the implied contract theory but dismissed the other claims. The court found that there was no basis to allege a bailment because there was no agreement by DSW to return credit card information to consumers; the requirement of returning property being a

---

78. *In re* Hannaford Bros. Co. Customer Data Breach Litigation, 4 A.3d 492, 497 (2010).
79. News Release, Fed. Trade Comm'n, DSW Inc. Settles FTC Charges (Dec. 1, 2005), *available at* http://www.ftc.gov/opa/2005/12/dsw.shtm.
80. *Id.*
81. *Id.*
82. DSW, Inc., Annual Report 2005, SEC Form 10K, www.sec.gov/Archives/edgar/data/1319974/000095015208002818/130952a110vk.htm#106.
83. 454 F. Supp. 2d 684 (S.D. Ohio 2006).
84. *Id.* at 686.
85. *Id.* at 691.
86. 2005 WL 2978755 (N.D. Ill.),
87. *Id.*

key element of the common law cause of action labeled "bailment."[88] In dismissing the state law claim, the court found there was no intent by DSW to cause the security breach that resulted in the misappropriation of the plaintiffs' credit card information, a requirement the court viewed as critical to the vitality of the claim.[89] The court sustained the implied contract claim, stating that "DSW and its non-cash customers have a contractual relationship—namely, by accepting credit cards as a basis for payment, the corporation agreed to take reasonable measures to keep the information secure."[90]

To strengthen their case, the plaintiffs subsequently filed a motion to amend their complaint.[91] The court reinstated the state law claim alleging deceptive practices on the ground that DSW failed to meet its contractual obligations with credit card companies to properly handle and maintain credit card information.[92] The court observed that DSW failed to implement proper security practices in order to reduce costs, that is, to save money.[93] Finally, the court observed that it was reasonably foreseeable that hacking of insecure information would occur.[94]

The FTC filed a complaint against DSW that was settled in December 2005. The settlement required DSW to establish and maintain a comprehensive security program that included administrative, technical, and physical safeguards. In addition, DSW must be audited every two years for the next 20 years by a qualified, independent, third-party audit professional.[95] The State of Ohio filed a similar action.[96]

CardSystems Solutions

Prior to bankruptcy, CardSystems processed more than $15 billion in credit card and online transactions each year for Visa, American Express, MasterCard, and Discover on behalf of more than 105,000 small to medium businesses. It also processed online transactions and electronic benefit transfer transactions—cards used by the government to distribute social welfare benefits such as food stamps and unemployment payments. It suffered a data breach of 40 million accounts affecting various credit card brands. Information on MasterCard accounts was taken from CardSystems' database, potentially affecting one out of every seven credit cards issued in the United States.[97]

Plaintiff customers brought a putative class action in a California state court setting forth state law claims that CardSystems negligently maintained consumer credit data. This action was removed to federal court and, subsequent to CardSystems' bankruptcy, plaintiffs sought to transfer the action to the District of Arizona so the action could be consolidated with CardSystems' bankruptcy proceedings. Finding that the plaintiffs had

---

88. *Id.*
89. *Id.*
90. *Id.*
91. *Richardson v. DSW*, 2006 WL 163167.
92. *Id.*
93. *Id.*
94. *Id.*
95. *Id.*
96. *See Ohio Sues DSW over Customer Data Theft*, CONSUMERAFFAIRS.COM, June 7, 2005, http://consumeraffairs .com/news04/2005/ohio_dsw.html.
97. *Credit Card Data Processing: How Secure Is It?: Hearing Before the U.S. House of Representatives*, 109th Cong. (July 21, 2005) (statement of John M. Perry, President and CEO, CardSystems Solutions), *available* at http://financial -services.house.gov/media/pdf/072105jmp.pdf.

alleged only California state law claims, the court remanded the proceeding to a California state court.[98]

Other litigation sought to define the liability of various other parties to the credit card transactions exposed in the massive breach of consumer information.

In *Cumis Insurance Society v. Merrick Bank Corp.*,[99] a federal court examined the liability of CardSystems, the processor of the transactions and the holder of the credit card information; Merrick Bank, the guarantor of CardSystems' compliance with industry rules, which assumed responsibility for CardSystems' noncompliance and thereby agreed to indemnify third parties for losses by fraud; and Savvis, the entity retained to certify CardSystems' compliance with industry standards. Industry standards required that information systems be secure; and more specifically, that magnetic-stripe data not be retained.[100] Cumis is an insurer that provides insurance to credit unions. As a result of the breach, Cumis paid millions of dollars in payments to its credit union insureds for credit and debit card fraud losses suffered by its individual members.[101]

The court applied Arizona state law. The court found that Cumis had claims against both Merrick and Savvis for restitutionary disgorgement (funds paid by Cumis to Merrick for credit and debit card transactions); negligence (Arizona does not endorse the economic loss rule limiting tort claims to claims for personal injury and property loss); and breach of contract (Cumis was a third-party beneficiary of the promises made by Merrick and Savvis to ensure the security of the data).[102]

Merrick Bank thereafter sued Savvis in an effort to place all liability for the breach on the company hired to certify that CardSystems was in compliance with industry data security standards.[103] The court transferred the case to the District of Arizona, the venue of the CardSystems' litigation, for disposition. On January 11, 2010, the district court found that the bank had a cause of action against Savvis, the company retained to report on CardSystems' compliance with security standards.[104]

As a result of CardSystems' bankruptcy, issues of liability are a part of the maze of bankruptcy proceedings.[105]

Data Breaches Continue

A data breach at Internet domain administrator and host Network Solutions compromised personal and financial data for more than 573,000 credit and debit cardholders in June 2009. Network Solutions was PCI compliant at the time of the breach, *i.e.*, it was certified as in compliance with standards issued by the Payment Card Industry Council, standards, discussed below, that are designed to protect against breaches.

The breach was the result of hackers planting rogue code on the company's Web servers used to host mostly small online stores, intercepting financial transactions between

---

98. Parke v. CardSystems Solutions, 2006 WL 2917604 (N.D. Cal. 2006).
99. 2008 WL 4277877 (D. Ariz. 2008).
100. *Id.*
101. *Id.*
102. *Id.*
103. Merrick Bank v. Savvis, Inc., 2008 WL 5146545 (E.D. Mo. 2008).
104. 2010 WL 148201.
105. *See In re* CardSystems Solutions, Inc., Debtor, 2007 WL 4166184 (D. Ariz. 2007); 2007 WL 4287834 (D. Ariz.); 2008 WL 4964011 (D. Ariz.); 414 B.R. 572 (D. Ariz. 2008); 2009 WL 2983211 (D. Ariz.).

the sites and their customers. Compromised data was captured between March and June 2009, when the breach was discovered.

Network Solutions provides service to more than 10,000 merchant websites. The ecommerce customers are mainly small businesses, commonly characterized as "Mom and Pop" type retailers across the country.[106]

ROLE OF SECURITY STANDARDS

In light of the many actions brought on grounds of negligence, security standards have received renewed focus. Beginning in 2006, the Payment Card Industry Security Standards Council has issued Data Security Standards (PCI DSS) that are incorporated by the major credit card processing companies in contracts as a means of insuring that retailers properly safeguard cardholder accounts and other personal information.[107] The PCI Council was formed by American Express, Discover Financial Services, JCB (Japan Credit Bureau) International, MasterCard Worldwide, and Visa Inc.

Overall, these standards require businesses with computerized information systems to:

- Build and maintain a secure network
- Protect credit card data
- Maintain a vulnerability management system
- Implement strong access control measures
- Regularly monitor and test networks
- Maintain an information security policy

There are two sets of standards: Payment Application Data Security Standard (PA-DSS), which applies to software applications, and PCI DSS, which applies to merchants that accept payment cards. Compliance requirements vary by business transaction volume.

The PCI Security Standards Council serves as an advisory group and manages the underlying PCI security standards. Each payment card brand is responsible for its own compliance programs and has set different deadlines for compliance for software providers and merchants. Visa's final security deadline was July 1, 2010—if that deadline is not met, merchants risk losing their ability to use credit cards. The goal of the credit card processing companies is to ensure that all their merchants use only PA-DSS compliant applications and PCI DSS policies and procedures.

Beginning in January 2010, the State of Nevada mandated PCI DSS compliance for businesses accepting credit cards.[108] In doing so, Nevada became the first state to transform these standards into state law. Commentators have suggested that a domino effect may result as states seek to find ways to protect consumers and businesses from the damage caused by massive data breaches.

---

106. L. McGlasson, Network Solutions Data Breach: 573,000 Cardholders at Risk, *available at* www.bankinfosecurity.com/articles.php?art_id=1660.

107. *See* Gretchen McCoy, *How Should You Ensure PCI DSS Compliance?*, SC MAGAZINE, Mar. 9, 2009, http://www.scmagazineus.com/how-should-you-ensure-pci-dss-compliance/article/128484/.

108. NEV. REV. STAT. §§ 603A.010 *et seq.*

These standards may serve to provide a basis for a court to determine what constitutes "reasonable security" in the context of a negligence claim or allegations of federal regulatory violations. Although the reported decisions have not, to date, explored the parameters of these standards, courts are likely to do so in the future. Risk managers should understand whether a merchant has been negligent by failing to employ "reasonable security measures" by looking to compliance with PCI DSS standards.[109]

CRIMINAL PROSECUTIONS

The U.S. Department of Justice has prosecuted hackers under applicable criminal law. For example, hacker Albert Gonzalez, accused of masterminding the massive data thefts at TJX and several other retailers, pleaded guilty in September 2009 to criminal charges related to computer hacking and credit card fraud. Gonzalez was a member of a group of hackers that stole millions of credit and debit card numbers from TJX and other retailers. He pleaded guilty to 19 counts of conspiracy, computer fraud, wire fraud, access device fraud, and aggravated identity theft.[110] Gonzalez was also indicted in New Jersey and charged with conspiracy and computer fraud for allegedly hacking into Heartland Payment Systems, Hannaford Bros., ATMs stationed in 7-Eleven stores, and two unnamed national retailers. In March 2010, Gonzales was sentenced to serve two consecutive 20-year prison sentences for his role in the TJX and Heartland attacks. A co-conspirator was sentenced to 5 years in April 2010.[111]

In November 2009, eight men from Estonia, Russia, and Moldova were indicted in the Northern District of Georgia for allegedly hacking into the Atlanta-based bank card processing company RBS WorldPay and stealing $9.5 million in cash from ATM machines around the world in a span of hours.[112]

CONCLUSION

Credit card processing companies have been subjected to financial ruin and paid out millions of dollars in damages as a result of massive data breaches. Surviving companies have settled most claims as a means of ending negative publicity and preserving the remnants of their business reputations. As a result, all businesses involved in handing personal information should reexamine the security of their information systems, adhere to professional standards, and act proactively to minimize or eliminate the risk of data breaches. The potential liability resulting from breaches of consumer and other personally identifiable information should cause all businesses to review the terms of

---

109. Kevin P. Kalinich, *ID Theft Liability Standard Emerging for Merchants*, RISK & INS. (Nov. 1, 2009), *available at* http://www.riskandinsurance.com/story.jsp?storyId=279882143.

110. *See, e.g., Hacker Gonzalez Pleads Guilty to 20 Charges*, OFFICE OF INADEQUATE SEC., Sept. 11, 2009, http://www.databreaches.net/?p=7087.

111. A. Moscaritolo, *Hacker Gonzalez Receives 20 Years in Prison*, SC MAGAZINE, March 20, 2010, *available at* www.scmagazineus.com/hacker-albert-gonzalez-receives-20-years-in-prison/article/166571.

112. United States v. Pleshchuk et al., Criminal Indictment, 1:09-CR-491 (N.D. Ga.) November 10, 2009, *available at* www.scribd.com/doc/22377006/RBS-WorldPay-Indictment.

their business liability insurance policies to ensure that the myriad claims that may be brought against them as a result of a breach are covered by the policies they hold.[113]

Consumers and banks have tried various approaches, as individuals, as institutions, and in class actions, to recover damages potentially or actually incurred as a result of data breaches. State law causes of action have brought only modest results as many common law theories have been found by courts to lack vitality either because the specific legal doctrine does not apply on its own terms or the facts of the case do not fit the theory. For example, breach of contract causes of action have been sustained based on some state laws, but not on others. In other cases, the courts have been reluctant to sustain claims absent injury in fact—or the posting of a fraudulent claim on their stolen credit card for which they were required to pay. The lesson here is that there may be some viable state law causes of action in the context of a breach. The viability of the specific state claim will depend on the contours of state law.

On the other hand, the FTC has successfully invoked federal law to impose measures to ensure that personal data is protected and to require audits of the offending institutions for decades to come to ensure compliance. Yet the credit card industry itself has the responsibility for ensuring that entities comply with professional standards, including PCI DSS standards, and acting to prevent breaches in the future. As for the hackers themselves, the Department of Justice has brought effective prosecutions to hold such persons accountable under federal criminal laws.

---

113. Readers interested in the insurance aspects of these issues should see chapter 19, Insurance Protection for Security Breaches.

CHAPTER 4

The Underground World of Online Identity Theft: An Overview[1]

Kimberly Kiefer Peretti

Individuals have been at risk of having their personal information stolen and used to commit identity-related crimes long before the emergence of the Internet. What the Information Age has changed, however, is the method by which identity thieves can access and exploit the personal information of others. One method in particular leaves hundreds of thousands, and in some cases tens of millions, of individuals at risk for identity theft: large-scale data breaches by skilled hackers. In this method, criminals remotely access the computer systems of government agencies, universities, merchants, financial institutions, credit card companies, and data processors, and steal large volumes of personal information on individuals. Often, these large-scale data breaches involve the compromise of personal financial information, such as credit or debit card account information. Three of the larger, more highly publicized data breaches in recent years, involving DSW, Inc.,[2] CardSystems Solutions, Inc.,[3] and TJX

---

1. This chapter was originally published in Volume 25 of the *Santa Clara Computer and High Technology Law Journal* (http://www.chtlj.org) in an article entitled "Data Breaches: What the Underground World of 'Carding' Reveals."

2. DSW, Inc., FTC File No. 053-3096 (Mar. 14, 2006). The Federal Trade Commission (FTC) alleged that DSW stored personal information from the magnetic stripes of credit and debit cards on its computer networks, and failed to take reasonable security measures to protect this sensitive customer data. *Id.* DSW responded by issuing press releases that transaction information involving 1.4 million credit cards was stolen from DSW customers who shopped at certain stores between November 2004 and February 2005. Press Release, DSW, DSW Releases Findings from Fraud Investigation into Credit Card and Other Purchase Information Theft (Apr. 18, 2005), *available at* http://www.retailventuresinc.com/PressReleases/2005/ccAprilUpdate.pdf.

3. CardSystems Solutions, Inc., FTC File No. 052-3148 (Feb. 23, 2006), *available at* http://www.ftc.gov/os/caseli st/0523148/0523148CardSystemscomplaint.pdf. CardSystems is a payment card processor that provides merchants with authorization services for approving credit and debit card purchases. The FTC alleged that CardSystems stored magnetic stripe data on its computer systems and failed to take reasonable security measures to protect this data. *Id.* The complaint specifically alleged that, in September 2004, hackers exploited a vulnerability in CardSystems' security system and stole the magnetic stripe data for tens of millions of credit and debit cards. *Id.* at 2.

Companies, Inc.,[4] have compromised millions of credit and debit card account numbers. In these cases, hackers targeted the credit and debit card account information held by merchants or third-party data processors as the result of credit and debit card retail transactions.

Large-scale data breaches would be of no more concern than small-scale identity thefts if criminals were unable to quickly and widely distribute the stolen information for subsequent fraudulent use (assuming, of course, that the breach would be quickly detected). Such wide-scale global distribution of stolen information has been made possible for criminals with the advent of criminal websites, known as "carding forums," dedicated to the sale of stolen personal and financial information. These websites allow criminals to quickly sell the fruits of their ill-gotten gains to thousands of eager fraudsters worldwide, thereby creating a black market for stolen personal information.

The process by which large volumes of data are stolen, resold, and ultimately used by criminals to commit fraud is revealed in an underground world known as "carding." In its narrow sense, the term "carding" refers to the unauthorized use of credit and debit card account information to fraudulently purchase goods and services. The term has evolved in recent years, however, to include an assortment of activities surrounding the theft and fraudulent use of credit and debit card account numbers including computer hacking, phishing, cashing-out stolen account numbers, reshipping schemes, and Internet auction fraud. Individuals engaged in criminal carding activities are referred to as "carders."

Carders are often members of one or more carding forums that facilitate the sale of, among other contraband, stolen credit and debit card numbers, compromised identities, and false identifications. Carding forums often share a common pattern of organization, which may include a small group of "administrators" who serve as a governing council, "moderators" who oversee and administer one or more subject-matter-specific forums on the website, "reviewers" who examine and/or test the criminal products and services, and "vendors" who advertise and sell the criminal products and services after the product or service had received a favorable written review from a reviewer.

To engage in carding on these websites, members advertise their products and services by posting messages to various informational and discussion forums. To conceal their activity, carders have adopted a vernacular when advertising their products and services in various posts on the carding websites.

One of the products frequently for sale is the "dump," which generally refers to information electronically copied from the magnetic stripe on the back of credit and debit cards. In the credit card industry, this information is referred to as "full-track data," referencing the two tracks of data (Track 1 and Track 2) on the magnetic stripe.[5] Track

4. On January 17, 2007, TJX, the parent company of T.J. Maxx, Marshalls, HomeGoods, and other retail stores, reported an unauthorized intrusion into its computer systems, potentially exposing credit and debit card account information on customers. News Release, TJX Cos., Inc., The TJX Companies, Inc. Victimized by Computer Systems Intrusion (Jan. 17, 2007), https://www.home-savings.com/files/tjxalert.pdf. TJX initially identified 45.7 million credit and debit cards that had been compromised. Amended Consol. Class Action Complaint at 3, *In re* TJX Cos. Retail Sec. Breach Litig., No. 1:07-cv-10162-WGY (D. Mass. Jan. 9, 2008).

5. VISA INC., VISA FRAUD INVESTIGATIONS AND INCIDENT MANAGEMENT PROCEDURES: WHAT TO DO IF COMPROMISED 16 (2007), *available at* http://usa.visa.com/download/merchants/cisp_what_to_do_if_compromised .pdf?it=r|/merchants/risk_management/cisp_if_compromised.html.

1 is alphanumeric and contains the customer's name and account number.[6] Track 2 is numeric and contains the account number, expiration date, the secure code (also known as the card verification value, or CVV), and discretionary institution data.[7] Dumps typically contain at least Track 2 data, but often contain both Tracks 1 and 2. Carders also refer to BINs (bank identification numbers) and PINs (personal identification numbers) in the course of selling dumps. Each bank that issues credit cards is issued a unique BIN. The first six digits of any valid credit card number is this unique BIN of the bank that issued the card number.[8] Carders are interested in BINs because they allow them to identify and target more vulnerable financial institutions, and spread thefts across a wide range of institutions. Often, carders will advertise "BIN lists" for sale. The term "PIN," used in the credit card industry as a means of cardholder identification,[9] is also a carding term of art indicating a credit card or debit card for which the personal identification number has also been obtained, allowing for direct cash withdrawals. Often, carders will advertise "dumps with PINs" for sale.

In more recent years, carders have introduced a new product known as "full-infos" that contain more personally identifiable information on individuals than dumps. "Full Info" or "Fulls" is a carding term that refers to a package of data about a victim, including, for example address, phone number, Social Security number, credit or debit account numbers and PINs, credit history report, mother's maiden name, and other personal identifying information.

In addition to providing a forum for the online trading of stolen account information, carding forums also provide a forum for trading in a variety of counterfeit identification documents. Examples of the types of counterfeit documents for sale on the carding forums include counterfeit passports, driver's licenses, Social Security cards, credit cards, debit cards, birth certificates, college student identification cards, health insurance cards, bills, diplomas, or anything that can be used as an identity document. Carders often refer to these fraudulent identification documents simply as "IDs" or "novs." The term "nov" (short for novelty) was originally adopted by carders in an attempt to appear to be engaged in the legitimate activity of producing documents for novelty purposes.

There are several methods by which carders obtain the stolen financial account information to resell on the carding forums. Most often, carders purchase the information in bulk from hackers, who steal it from entities that hold large amounts of financial account information, including credit card service providers and data processors, financial institutions, merchants, restaurants, and government agencies. Federal carding-related prosecutions have revealed that hackers use sophisticated techniques, such as wardriving (driving with a laptop computer and high-powered antenna to locate, and potentially exploit, vulnerable wireless computer systems),[10] installation of "sniffers" (malicious code that allows for the capture of data in real-time as it transverses

---

6. *Id.* at 17.
7. *Id.*
8. *Id.* at 15.
9. *Id.* at 17.
10. *See, e.g.,* Indictment at 2, United States v. Salcedo, No. 5:03-cr-00053-LHT-1 (W.D.N.C. 2006); Indictment at 3, United States v. Gonzalez, No. 1:08-cr-10223-PBS-1 (D. Mass. 2008).

computer networks),[11] and SQL injections (Internet-based attacks that exploit vulner-abilities in database-driven websites),[12] to access computer systems remotely and steal financial information. The compromise of computer systems by these methods allows hackers to obtain large quantities of financial account information, often on millions of potential victims.

A second method by which carders obtain the financial account information on large numbers of individuals is phishing. Indeed, the carding forums often provide assistance to carders on phishing in the form of "how to" tutorials and selling prebuilt kits that allow carders to set up fraudulent websites within minutes. Carders with hacking skills also engage in phishing that targets vulnerable computers of individual cardholders. This occurs, for example, by infecting the computers with data-mining viruses or other types of malicious code.

Once the stolen information is obtained, vendors advertise their product or service by posting a message on the carding forum. The vendor then arranges for the particular sale with the purchaser through instant messaging or private e-mail. The carder pur-chasing the stolen information, in turn, typically uses the information to engage in one of four types of credit or debit card fraud, referred to in the criminal underworld as "carding online," "in-store carding," "cashing," and/or "gift card vending."

"Carding online" simply refers to using stolen credit card information to make pur-chases of goods and services online from merchants, whereas "in-store carding" refers to the process of presenting a counterfeit credit card that had been encoded with sto-len account information to a cashier at a physical retail store location. Because in-store carding requires the carder to physically visit the store, it is more risky for the carder than carding online. In-store carding also requires a higher level of technical sophisti-cation than carding online because the carder must create a counterfeit credit card. In order to make a counterfeit card, a criminal must possess several pieces of equipment, including, for example, laminators, embossers, encoders, scanners, and printers, each of which is easily available for purchase on the Internet.

A third form of carding is known in the criminal world as "cashing." Broadly speak-ing, the term cashing refers to the act of obtaining money, rather than retail goods and services, with the unauthorized use of stolen financial information. One particular method of cashing, known as "PIN cashing," requires the carder to obtain dumps with PINs (i.e., credit or debit card account or bank account information with personal iden-tification numbers), encode the dump onto the back of a piece of plastic, and use the counterfeit card with the corresponding PIN at an ATM to obtain cash.

Finally, some carders engage in a practice known as "gift card vending," which involves purchasing gift cards from retail merchants at their physical stores using coun-terfeit credit cards and reselling such cards for a percentage of their actual value. Such gift cards can be resold in several ways, including on a carding website or in face-to-face transactions to unwitting purchasers.

---

11. *See, e.g.*, Indictment at 3–4, United States v. Yastremskiy, No. 2:08-cr-00160-SJF-1 (E.D.N.Y. 2008); Indict-ment at 3, United States v. Gonzalez, No. 1:08-cr-10223-PBS-1 (D. Mass. 2008).

12. *See, e.g.*, Indictment at 5, United States v. Gonzalez, No. 1:08-cr-10223-PBS-1 (D. Mass. 2008).

During the past several years, federal law enforcement agencies have been actively engaged in investigating the carding community. These investigations have resulted in several benchmark prosecutions. In 2004, several top-tier members of a criminal carding organization were charged with conspiracy based on their activities and membership in the online organization.[13] In 2007, a major supplier of tens of thousands of credit card accounts to carding forums was indicted for wire fraud and identity fraud.[14] Finally, in 2008, the Justice Department announced the largest hacking and identity theft case ever prosecuted, in which an international hacking ring allegedly stole over 40 million credit and debit card numbers.[15] These investigations and prosecutions have shed light on the global nature of carding organizations. In particular, criminals worldwide belong to, and actively participate in, these carding organizations. In addition, specific criminal carding activity, such as PIN cashing discussed above, often involves, and in some cases requires, the active participation of carders from more than one country. Finally, these investigations have also revealed that stolen information can be immediately and widely distributed across the globe.

As companies increasingly rely on computer systems and the Internet in the Information Age, it has become increasingly clear that criminals have the tools to access and exploit for financial gain large volumes of personal information. As a result, prosecuting and punishing criminals continues to be an essential element in addressing the large-scale data breach problem.

---

13. Indictment at 2, United States v. Mantovani, No. 2:04-cr-00786-WJM-1 (D.N.J. 2006).

14. Indictment at 2–3, United States v. Butler, No. 2:07-cr-00332-MBC-1 (W.D. Pa. Sept. 17, 2007).

15. Press Release, U.S. Dep't of Justice, Retail Hacking Ring Charged for Stealing and Distributing Credit and Debit Card Numbers from Major U.S. Retailers (Aug. 5, 2008), http://www.cybercrime.gov/gonzalezIndict.pdf. In March 2010, the ringleader of the organization, Albert Gonzalez, was sentenced to 20 years imprisonment. Press Release, U.S. Dep't of Justice, Leader of Hacking Ring Sentenced for Massive Identity Thefts from Payment Processor and U.S. Retail Networks (Mar. 26, 2010), http://www.justice.gov/opa/pr/2010/March/10-crm-329.html.

PART II

Anatomy of the Major Data Breaches

CHAPTER 5

Encrypted Records— Failed Security

Lucy L. Thomson[1]

It is widely assumed that if sensitive records are "encrypted," they will be safe.[2] However, information security is only as good as the weakest link. Data breaches have occurred even where sensitive records were "encrypted" at some point in the information lifecycle. As a result, millions of consumer records have been stolen and individuals have been exposed to risks of identity theft and fraud.[3] This chapter takes you behind the statistics and into the security of companies that suffered major data breaches. A close look at the root causes of security failures in the major breaches reveals that even if implemented, encryption does not always protect sensitive records—other critical security controls must also be in place.

The important protection provided by encryption, however, should not be minimized. When computers, laptops, backup tapes, thumb drives, cell phones, PDAs, and other devices are lost or stolen, encryption is a critical factor in protecting personal records from unauthorized access. Going forward, in addition to encrypting records, individuals and organizations must also devise strategies to ensure that these devices are not lost, stolen, or otherwise compromised so that no breach occurs. Encryption can also protect data and information from compromise by external hackers or malicious insiders if it is used appropriately and implemented in conjunction with other security controls.[4]

---

1. Dennis Monroe, an expert in enterprise architecture, created all the graphics for this chapter and provided invaluable assistance.

2. This is the premise underlying a number of the state data breach notification laws, and the new federal breach law for health records (Health Information Technology for Economic and Clinical Health Act, HITECH), which require notification of consumers in the event of a data breach of "unencrypted" records. Chapters 6, 7, and 8 describe in detail the various schema and definitions of encryption in these laws.

3. Chapter 4 provides an inside look into the underground where criminals market stolen personal information.

4. Chapter 2 reviews the data breach trends and the incidence of hacking and insider breaches that are important to assess in preventing future breaches.

No one should assume that merely encrypting sensitive records is adequate without a careful review of the potential risks to the data and information throughout the system.[5] Encryption is one important tool in a much broader information security program. The risk assessment must identify the sensitive data and information an organization collects, uses, stores, and shares, and determine where those records may be vulnerable.[6]

An assessment of data breach trends over the past several years reveals that hacking accounts for about one third of the thousands of data breaches. Organizations that collect, process, or store large amounts of personally identifiable information, particularly credit card numbers and related information of high value to criminals, have become targets of overseas organized crime.[7] Several of the largest data breaches resulted from hackers infiltrating information systems at vulnerable points—where sensitive personal records were unsecured—even though those same records were encrypted in company networks.

This chapter focuses on several of the largest data breaches ever reported, including Heartland, Hannaford, RBS WorldPay, TJX, and DSW. The case studies show that even when personal records are encrypted at some point, failed security can lead to massive data breaches in a number of ways: sensitive data transmitted "in the clear"—that is, unencrypted—either within or outside a corporate network may be intercepted and stolen; personal identification number (PIN) codes encrypted with outdated encryption algorithms can be stolen and "reverse engineered;" encrypted access to a Web site does not provide protection for records subsequently stored there unencrypted; encryption keys that are not protected may be used to compromise encrypted records; weak encryption with a serious design flaw may be breached easily; wireless systems provide opportunities for hackers to breach a network; and overall information security controls that are inadequate may lead to a breach.

Massive data breaches have caused many businesses to suffer significant financial losses and reputation damage and have put consumers at risk for fraud and even bankruptcy—with resulting criminal indictments and civil damage actions.[8]

Criminal cases bring us into direct contact with the schemes that produced many of the largest and most publicized data breaches. The indictment of the RBS World-Pay hackers and the prosecution of Albert Gonzalez for the breaches of Heartland,

---

5. See NAT'L INST. OF STANDARDS & TECH., RISKS MANAGEMENT GUIDE FOR INFORMATION TECHNOLOGY SYSTEMS, Special Pub. 800-30 (July 2002), available at http://csrc.nist.gov/publications/nistpubs/800-30/sp800-30.pdf.

6. Appropriate information security controls and procedures (technical, operational, and managerial) include user identification and authentication, user provisioning and identity management, authorization and access control, audit and logging, encryption, boundary protection, system monitoring, security incident handling, secure data storage, personnel security, and physical and environment protection. Chapter 16 provides an overview of the issues related to developing and implementing an appropriate information security program.

7. The global cyberattacks that pose some of the most serious economic, national security, and privacy challenges of the 21st century are discussed in chapter 1.

8. For example, TJX stated in its SEC Form 10-K filing: "From the time of the discovery of the Computer Intrusion late in fiscal 2007, through the end of fiscal 2010, we cumulatively expensed $171.5 million (pre-tax) with respect to the Computer Intrusion. As of January 30, 2010, our reserve balance was $23.5 million, which reflects our current estimate of remaining probable losses with respect to the Computer Intrusion, including litigation, proceedings and other claims, as well as legal, monitoring, reporting and other costs." The TJX Cos., Inc., SEC Form 10-K (FY ended Jan. 30, 2010), available at http://www.faqs.org/sec-filings/100330/TJX-COMPANIES-INC-DE-_10-K/#ixzz0ln03WBlp.

Hannaford, TJX, and DSW provide illuminating insights into the massive data breaches occurring in major American businesses. This insider look at a number of the largest data breaches is based on facts found by federal courts in civil litigation, breach statistics gathered by professional organizations, corporate filings with the Securities and Exchange Commission (SEC), and settlements with federal agencies, including the Federal Trade Commission (FTC).

The goal of this chapter is to identify the weaknesses in the information systems that permitted these breaches to occur—notwithstanding the security measures, including encryption, that many of the companies had implemented. Although encryption of sensitive data may play a critical role in an overall information security program, it does not provide the entire answer.

How a Hacker Attack Unfolds

A hacker attack on a computer network is generally conducted systematically following several logical steps. The process begins by conducting reconnaissance of the organization to create a profile of its information technology environment and security posture and continuing with penetration and, if successful, ultimately gaining control over the network.[9]

- *Footprinting—Reconnaissance—Target Selection.* Hackers gather target information about the organization's Internet, remote access, intranet, and extranet presence.[10] To facilitate the use of social engineering, hackers identify and target system administrators and individuals with privileged access to the network.
- *Enumeration.* There are a variety of tools available on the Internet to identify potential networks and to determine the network typology and potential paths into the network. Hackers scan the network to determine which services are running or listening, identify open ports, and detect the operating system.
- *Penetration—Exploitation.* Hackers identify valid user accounts or poorly protected resources shares, guess weak passwords, eavesdrop on password exchanges, engage in social engineering, and establish a user account. They establish a direct connection to the system, install backdoors, exploit server application vulnerabilities, and may conduct denial-of-service attacks.[11]
- *Privilege Escalation.* Once attackers have obtained a user account, they try to obtain an administrator account with elevated privileges or "root" access.

---

9. Stuart McClure, Joel Scambray & George Kurtz, Hacking Exposed: Network Security Secrets and Solutions (5th ed., 2005).

10. According to the Indictment of Albert Gonzalez, the hackers found their targets on a list of Fortune 500 companies and then did reconnaissance to determine the payment-processing systems the companies used. They then uncovered vulnerabilities in the systems that they could exploit.

11. The Gonzalez Indictment revealed that hackers broke into the Heartland and Hannaford networks using a SQL injection attack. Once on the networks, the hackers installed back doors to provide them with continued access. They tested their malware against 20 different antivirus programs to make sure they would not be detected, and also programmed the malware to erase evidence from the hacked networks to avoid forensic detection.

- *Consolidating Power.* Hackers install additional tools to spread their influence; these include malware, network eavesdropping tools, sniffers, and rootkits.[12] In recent breaches, hackers have gained command and control over the entire network infrastructure.[13] The hackers locate track 2 data (information found on the magnetic stripes of credit and debit cards, including cardholder account data and encrypted PINs), as well as internal accounts and proprietary files.[14] They then use malware to transmit the stolen data to a hacking platform outside the company.
- *Covering Tracks—Concealing the Attacks.* Finally, the hackers disable auditing, change the file history, clear the event log, and hide files.

Federal prosecutions have revealed that hackers used sophisticated techniques, such as wardriving (driving with a laptop computer and high-powered antenna to locate vulnerable wireless computer systems),[15] installation of sniffers,[16] and SQL injections (Structured Query Language; Internet-based attacks that exploit vulnerabilities in database-driven Web sites),[17] to access computer systems remotely and steal financial and other sensitive information.

The Basics of Payment Card Processing

Of the eight case studies in this chapter, six involve credit and debit card transactions and processing. A brief overview of the payment card authorization process is necessary to understand the security failures that lead to the breaches.[18] Authoritative sources explain that

> Authorization is the process by which card issuers either approve, refer (i.e., contact the card processor for further instructions), or deny requests to accept transactions. Approval is based on a validation of the account number and expiration date to verify

---

12. Malware (for "malicious software") is a program or file that is harmful to a computer user. It includes computer viruses, worms, Trojan horses, and also spyware, programming that gathers information about a computer user without the user's permission. Sniffers are malicious codes that allow for the capture of data in real-time as it transverses computer networks. A rootkit is a software or hardware device designed to gain administrator-level control over a computer system without being detected. A rootkit is used to perform malicious operations on a target host computing system without the knowledge of the administrators or users of that system.

13. DAMBALLA, THE COMMAND STRUCTURE OF THE AURORA BOTNET (March 2010), *available at* http://www.damballa.com/downloads/r_pubs/Aurora_Botnet_Command_Structure.pdf.

14. Indictment at 2, United States v. Gonzalez, No. 1:08-cr-10223-PBS-1 (D. Mass. 2008).

15. *See, e.g.,* Indictment at 2, United States v. Salcedo, No. 5:03-cr-00053-LHT-1 (W.D.N.C. 2006); Indictment at 3, United States v. Gonzalez, No. 1:08-cr-10223-PBS-1 (D. Mass. 2008).

16. *See, e.g.,* Indictment at 3–4, United States v. Yastremskiy, No. 2:08-cr-00160-SJF-1 (E.D.N.Y. 2008); Indictment at 3, United States v. Gonzalez, No. 1:08-cr-10223-PBS-1 (D. Mass. 2008).

17. *See, e.g.,* Indictment at 5, United States v. Gonzalez, No. 1:08-cr-10223-PBS-1 (D. Mass. 2008).

18. This chapter reflects information provided on the New York State Department of Taxation and Finance Web site, http://www.tax.state.ny.us/evta/guidelines_credt_authorization.htm, and the court's opinion in *Sovereign Bank v. BJ's Wholesale Club*, 533 F.3d 162 at 164–66 (3d Cir. 2008). The Third Circuit's opinion outlines the nature of the contractual relationships between VISA and its member banks, including a helpful description of how a credit card transaction is processed and how the various contracts between VISA, its member banks, and merchants regulate their relationships.

that a cardholder's account is open, and that the transaction will not place the account above any credit limit. Since most authorization requests are approved, the term "authorization transaction" refers to an approved authorization request.

Authorization requests to Visa, MasterCard, American Express and Discover are transmitted to the card processor (e.g., Heartland and CardSystems), which routes the request to the appropriate card issuer. Authorization requests are routed directly to American Express and Discover.

Authorization performed on-line is completed in seconds.[19] Each transaction is authorized separately as it occurs, and the authorization status is returned immediately after the transaction is submitted for approval. If an on-line authorization is declined, the cardholder will immediately be made aware that their transaction was not completed with the card used for payment. A denial means the transaction was simply declined. A referral may occur if a cardholder is over their credit limit, has not paid their balance due in a timely fashion, or has used the card frequently in short period of time.[20]

The graphics throughout this chapter illustrate the various points in the payment card authorization process where the breaches occurred. While the authorization process is similar in each case, the points where hackers exploited vulnerabilities and the security failures took place are different. Two of the cases involve e-commerce Web sites where records were "encrypted" but serious security failures resulted in data breaches. Sensitive data and information must be protected with appropriate security controls, including encryption, every step of the way in the information lifecycle. The use of end-to-end security is imperative.

HEARTLAND: TRANSMISSION OF SENSITIVE DATA IN THE CLEAR

Heartland Payment Systems, based in Princeton, New Jersey, is the sixth largest processor of credit and debit card transactions in the United States.[21] It facilitates the exchange of information and funds between merchants and cardholders' financial institutions. Heartland provides electronic bank card payment processing services to 250,000 businesses.[22] Forty percent of the transactions come from small to midsize restaurants across the country. The company handles more than 100 million card transactions per month; this amounts to more than 4 billion card transactions annually.

---

19. New York State Department of Taxation and Finance Web site, http://www.tax.state.ny.us/evta/guidelines_credit_authorization.htm. An alternative to online authorization is batch authorization, in which large numbers of transactions are submitted for authorization at a scheduled time, usually at the end of the day. This method is used for transactions that will not be completed immediately, such as mail order approvals.

20. *Id.*

21. http://www.heartlandpaymentsystems.com.

22. Heartland Payment Sys., Heartland Q4 2008 Earnings Call Transcript, *available at* http://seekingalpha.com/article/122440-heartland-payment-systems-q4-2008-earnings-call-transcript?page=2; *see* Press Release, Heartland Payment Sys., http://www.2008breach.com.

What Sensitive Information Was Stolen?

Hackers broke into the Heartland network in 2007 and stole payment card transaction data, including the digital information encoded onto the magnetic stripe built into the backs of credit and debit cards with card numbers, expiration dates, and names.[23]

Heartland executives claimed that cardholder Social Security numbers, unencrypted PINs, addresses, or phone numbers were not compromised, and that only consumer data, not confidential merchant business data, were affected. However, a thief could use this information to clone stolen debit card data to make a fake card and swipe the card as a credit card, as was done in the RBS WorldPay and TJX breaches.

Anatomy of the Breach

Hackers broke into the Heartland network using a SQL injection attack. They planted malware capable of sniffing payment card data as it moved across the company's network. According to Robert Baldwin, Heartland's president and chief financial officer, "As the transaction is being processed, it has to be in *unencrypted form* to get the authorization request from Heartland to the card brands."[24]

Albert Gonzalez and two other hackers were indicted for criminal acts resulting from executing a SQL injection attack on the Heartland corporate computer network that resulted in malware being placed on its payment processing system.[25]

Figure 5.1 depicts the flow of a payment card authorization transaction and illustrates the vulnerable points that lead to the Heartland breach.

1. Card information at a business or restaurant is captured from the magnetic stripe of a credit or debit card by swiping the card through a point-of-sale terminal, or by entering the card and payment information into the payment device. Information from the card (e.g., card type, account number, expiration date) is combined with information about the transaction (e.g., dollar amount), to create the authorization request.[26]

2. The payment processor's system recognizes the authorization request as being for a Visa, MasterCard, American Express, or Discover card. In the case of Visa or MasterCard, the request was transmitted unencrypted to the appropriate association, which, in turn, routed the request to the member bank that issued the card.[27] The payment processor transmits the authorization request directly to American Express or Discover, respectively.

23. Heartland Payments Sys., SEC Form 10-K (FY ending Dec. 31, 2008), *available at* http://www.sec.gov/Archives/edgar/data/1144354/000119312509055621/d10k.htm; *also see* How Stuff Works, How Does a Magnetic Stripe on the Back of a Credit Card Work?, http://www.money.howstuffworks.com/personal-finance/debt-management/magnetic-stripe-credit-card1.htm.

24. L. McGlasson, Heartland Payment Systems, Forcht Bank Discover Data Breaches, Bank Info Security, January 21, 2009, http://bankinfosecurity.com/articles.php?art_id=1168; also see Baldwin Carr statements, January 29, 2009, quoted at http://www.storefrontbacktalk.com/securityfraud/heartland-breach-hit-at-its-unencrypted-point.

25. United States v. Gonzalez, No. 09-cr-626 (D.N.J. 2009).

26. The payment device connects to the payment processor's system and transmits the authorization request via one of five communications methods: dial-up, leased line, host-to-host, ISDN, or wireless.

27. Baldwin and Carr statements, *supra* note 24.

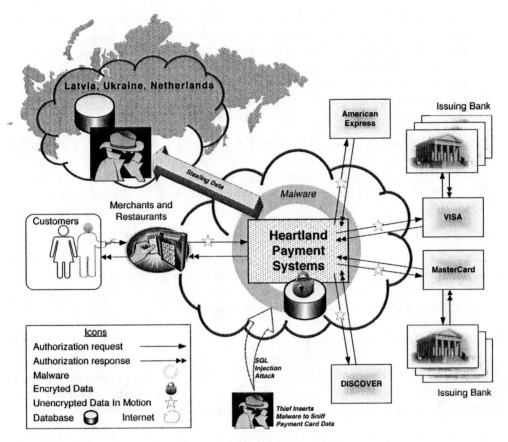

FIGURE 5.1
Breach of the Heartland Payment Card Authorization Process

3. *Breach Part 1:* Using a SQL injection attack, hackers broke into the Heartland network. Once on the network, the hackers installed back doors to provide them with continued access. They tested their malware against 20 different antivirus programs to make sure they would not be detected.[28]
4. The initial breach into Heartland was confined to the company's corporate network, which was separate from its card-processing network. By May 2008 the hackers had jumped to the processing network. Heartland discovered the hackers on its network only in January 2009 after being told by credit card companies that it might have been breached.[29]
5. The malware that infected Heartland's systems could read and collect unencrypted data-in-motion. Data, including card transactions sent over Heartland's internal processing platform, were sent unencrypted. After consumers

---

28. *Supra* note 25.
29 *Id.*

swiped their cards, sniffer software captured the card data as Heartland transmitted it for authorization by major payment companies and banks.[30]

6. *Breach Part 2:* The intruders used sophisticated hacker tools to take data out of Heartland's system. They broke the data into batches suitable for wholesale distribution over the Internet and transmitted it to remote locations in encrypted data streams. The hackers also programmed the malware to erase evidence from the hacked networks to avoid forensic detection.

Even though Heartland encrypted some of its data, its information security "failed" at multiple points. There were opportunities for personal data to be intercepted when they were unencrypted on the company network and when the authorization requests were transmitted in the clear to the card brands and member banks that issued the cards.

HANNAFORD: SECURITY FAILURES AT CRITICAL JUNCTURES

Established in 1883 on the Portland, Maine, waterfront, Hannaford is an East Coast supermarket chain that operates 167 stores in Maine, Massachusetts, New Hampshire, New York, and Vermont. It is now owned by the Belgium-based Delhaize Group, a global company and one of the world's largest food retailers.

What Sensitive Information Was Stolen?

In February 2008 Hannaford Brothers suffered a major breach that exposed 4.2 million credit card accounts to unauthorized access.[31] Hackers intercepted card data stored on the magnetic stripe of payment cards.[32] That information included card numbers and expiration dates but not customer names. The attack has resulted in 700 known cases of fraud.[33]

Anatomy of the Breach

Using a SQL injection attack, hackers infiltrated the Hannaford computer network in November 2007. The data breach disclosed in March 2008 involved malicious software that was found on computer servers at nearly 300 of the company's stores.[34] The fraud was detected by banks and credit card companies. Once on the network, the hackers installed back doors to provide them with continued access. They tested their malware

---

30. Heartland Payment Sys., Heartland Q4 2008 Earnings Call Transcript, *available at* http://seekingalpha.com/article/122440-heartland-payment-systems-q4-2008-earnings-call-transcript?page=2.

31. Letter from Emily Dickinson, Hannaford Senior Vice President and General Counsel, to Martha Coakley, Massachusetts Attorney General, and the Massachusetts Office of Consumer Affairs and Business Regulation (description of breach), Ellen Messmer, *Malware Loaded onto Hannaford Servers Let Attackers Intercept Credit Card Data,* NETWORK WORLD, Mar. 28, 2008, http://networkworld.com/news/2008/032808-hannaford.html?frsc=netflash-rrss; *see also* Press Release, Hannaford Announces Containment of Data Intrusion (Mar. 17, 2008), *available at* http://datalossdb.org/primary_sources/651; J. Vjayan, *Hannaford Says Malware Planted on Its Store Servers Stole Credit Card Data,* COMPUTERWORLD, March 28, 2008, http://computerworld.com/s/article/9073138 (description of breach).

32. *Id.*

33. R. Westervelt, *Data Breach Study Ties Losses to Hannaford,* TJX, FINANCIAL SERVICES SECURITY NEWS, January 20, 2009, http://searchfinancialindustrytechtarget.com/news/article/o,289142,sid185_gci1345455mem1,00html.

34. Hannaford Web site, http://www.hannaford.com.

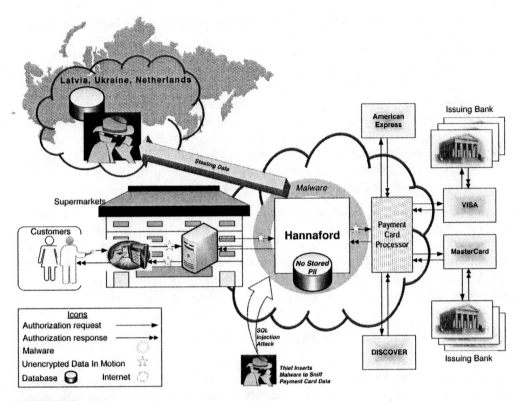

FIGURE 5.2
Breach of the Hannaford Computer Network

against 20 different antivirus programs to make sure they would not be detected, and also programmed the malware to erase evidence from the hacked networks to avoid forensic detection.

Malware on Hannaford servers allowed attackers to intercept card data stored on the magnetic stripe of payment cards as customers used them at the checkout counter. That information was taken in transit from the point-of-sale.

Albert Gonzalez and two other hackers were indicted for conducting a SQL injection attack on the Hannaford corporate computer network that resulted in malware being placed on its network.[35]

Figure 5.2 depicts the flow of a payment card authorization transaction and illustrates the vulnerable points that lead to the Hannaford breach.

1. Card information is captured from the magnetic stripe by swiping the card through a point-of-sale terminal in a grocery store, or by entering the card and payment information into the payment device. Information from the card (e.g., card type, account number, expiration date) is combined with information about the transaction (e.g., dollar amount), to create the authorization request.

---

35. United States v. Gonzalez, No. 09-cr-626 (D.N.J. 2009).

The payment device transmits the authorization request to the payment processor's system.

2. *Breach Part 1:* Malicious software was found on computer servers at Hannaford stores. The malware picked up credit card numbers and expiration dates as they were in transit between the store and the credit card companies.[36] The software may have intercepted credit card data during checkout.[37]

3. *Breach Part 2:* The intruders used sophisticated hacker tools to take data out of Hannaford's system. They broke the data into "batches" suitable for wholesale distribution over the Internet and transmitted it to remote locations in encrypted data streams. The hackers also programmed the malware to erase evidence from the hacked networks to avoid forensic detection.

At Hannaford stores, hackers exploited vulnerabilities at the store level. Attackers intercepted card data as customers swiped them at the checkout counter and as the information that was in transit between the store and the credit card company. The attack resulted in card data being transferred overseas. At critical junctures, security failed, notwithstanding that the data were encrypted, because the system, as a whole, was not secure.

RBS WORLDPAY: VULNERABLE NETWORK

RBS WorldPay, with headquarters in Atlanta, Georgia, processes credit and debit card transactions for financial institutions around the world. The U.S. payment processing arm of The Royal Bank of Scotland Group, it is the second largest ATM processor in the United States. One service provided by RBS WorldPay is processing prepaid payroll card transactions. Employers pay their employees through direct deposits to prepaid payroll card accounts, instead of using paychecks or direct deposits into employees' bank accounts. Cash may be withdrawn by presenting the prepaid payroll card to an automated teller machine (ATM) and entering the card's PIN code.

What Sensitive Information Was Stolen?

Hackers stole personal information (name, address, date of birth) of 1.5 million cardholders of prepaid payroll cards and open-loop gift cards,[38] including the Social Security numbers of 1.1 million people.[39] Actual fraud was committed on approximately 100 accounts through the use of the stolen credit card data.

Anatomy of the Breach

Transactions associated with prepaid payrolls cards are processed by RBS WorldPay on behalf of its client financial institutions: RBS Citizens, N.A., The Bankcorp, Inc., First

---

36. *Id.*
37. *Id.*
38. "Open loop" gift cards are issued by banks or credit card companies and can be redeemed by different establishments (compared with "closed loop" cards, which are issued by a specific store or restaurant and may be redeemed only by the issuing provider).
39. Press Release, RBS WorldPay, RBS WorldPay Announces Compromise of Data Security and Outlines Steps to Mitigate Risk (Dec. 23, 2008), *available at* http://www.rbsworldpay.us/media/news_media25.htm.

Bank of Delaware, and Palm Desert National Bank. Information related to these transactions was maintained on the RBS WorldPay computer network.[40]

Four hackers based in Russia, Estonia, and Moldova exploited vulnerabilities in the RBS WorldPay computer network and obtained access on November 4, 2008. For the next three weeks they executed a massive scheme that demonstrated not only a high degree of technical skill, but also an extraordinary level of international coordination to successfully execute a targeted strike on key aspects of the global financial infrastructure.

Eight hackers were charged with wire and computer fraud, access device fraud, computer intrusion, aggravated identity theft and conspiracy in a 16-count indictment returned on November 10, 2009, in the Northern District of Georgia.

Figures 5.3a and 5.3b depict the flow of a prepaid payroll card transaction and illustrate the vulnerable points that lead to the RBS WorldPay breach. The breach took place in two phases.

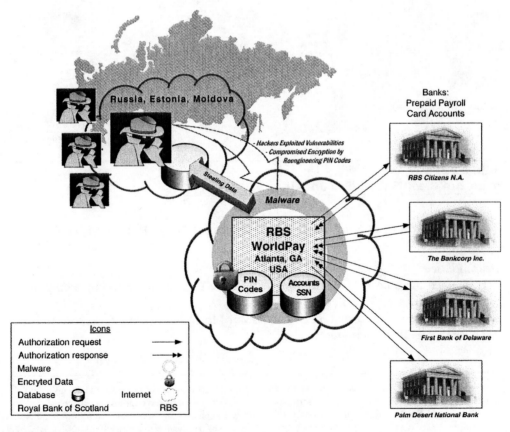

FIGURE 5.3A
Phase 1 of the Breach of the RBS WorldPay
Prepaid Payroll Card Transaction Process

40. United States v. Pleshchuk, Criminal Indictment No. 1:09-CR-491 (Nov. 10, 2008), at 3.

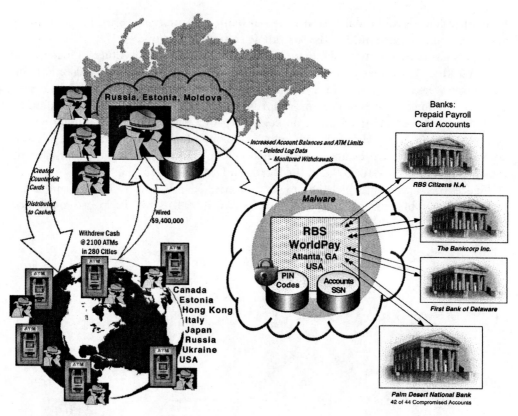

FIGURE 5.3B
Phase 2 of the RBS WorldPay Breach

Hackers identified and exploited vulnerabilities (or "bugs")[41] in the RBS WorldPay computer network and:

Breach Phase 1
1. Gained unauthorized access from outside the United States into the computer network of RBS WorldPay.
2. Obtained login information and a password to access a computer server on the RBS WorldPay computer network.

---

41. Because the specific vulnerabilities in the RBS WorldPay computer network are not identified in the Indictment and have not otherwise been described publicly, security experts have speculated on what those vulnerabilities might be. *See, e.g.,* Byron Acohido, *RBS WorldPay: How a Gang Stole $9.4 Million from 280 ATMs in 12 Hours,* LAST WATCHDOG ON INTERNET SEC. (Nov. 13, 2009), *available at* http://lastwatchdog.com/rbs-worldpay-anatomy-9-million-global-atm-cyber ("They very well may have used a SQL injection attack on one of RBS's public facing Web pages."); Chris Wysopal, *We Need to Learn More About the RBS WorldPay ATM Attack,* VERACODE (Nov. 11, 2009), *available at* http://www.veracode.com/blog/2009/11/we-need-to-learn-more-about-the-rbs-worldpay-atm-attack ("It is not clear how the attackers are accessing the SQL server, whether it is a command-line on the server itself, another machine, or perhaps through SQL Injection. It is clear that it is game over once an attacjer can modify your database tables.").

3. Inside the system, gained information without authorization, including pre-paid payroll card numbers and PIN codes.
4. Developed a method for reverse engineering PIN codes from the encrypted data on the RBS WorldPay computer network.
5. Manipulated the data on the RBS WorldPay computer network, including raising the limits (available account balance) on the amount of cash that could be withdrawn from ATMs on certain of the prepaid payroll cards.
6. Cloned 44 cards embedded with the account details and PIN codes and distributed them to cashers located around the world; 42 of the 44 cards were issued by the Palm Desert National Bank (PDNB).[42]

Breach Phase 2
1. Distributed the fraudulent cards to cashers who used the cards over and over to make substantial cash withdrawals from 2,100 ATM machines in 280 cities around the world.
2. Directed the cashers to keep 30 to 50 percent of the money before transmitting the remainder of the more than $9 million back to the hackers in Eastern Europe through Western Union and Web Money, a Russia-based digital currency service.
3. Accessed the RBS WorldPay computer network from outside the United States and observed the withdrawals taking place at the ATMs on the cards they fraudulently obtained and distributed, tracking the proceeds of the fraud.
4. Deleted information on the RBS WorldPay network in order to conceal their activities.

The indictment charges that the hackers "compromised the data encryption" that RBS WorldPay used on payroll debit cards to raise the amount of funds available on the cards, as well as withdrawal limits. In some cases the hackers raised the limits to $500,000. There appears to be a vulnerability in the way banks store PIN codes. The older PIN storage algorithms have weaknesses. "Like password hash storage in Windows, backwards compatibility with older encryption formats can be a grave weakness."[43]

TJX: SENSITIVE DATA IN THE CLEAR, WEAK ENCRYPTION, UNPROTECTED ENCRYPTION KEY

TJX is an off-price retailer selling family apparel and home fashions in over 2,500 stores worldwide, including T.J. Maxx, Marshall's, A.J. Wright, Bob's Stores, and HomeGoods

---

42. Established in 1981, Palm Desert National Bank (PDNB) is a locally owned, independent bank with four locations in California. According to its Web site, its Electronic Banking Solutions (EBS) division was established in 1994 "with a mission to provide premier electronic banking services throughout the United States for a variety of product line services. EBS has taken the lead in a number of electronic products and continues to lead the industry in electronic banking." PDNB, About Us, https://www.pdnb.com/web/aboutus/aboutus.html. An unanswered question is why 42 of the 44 fraudulent cards used in the breach were issued by PDNB.

43. Wysopal, *supra* note 41. See Australian Inst. of Criminology, The Unbearable Lightness of PIN Cracking, paper delivered at the Financial Cryptography and Data Security 2007 conference, *available at* http://www.aic.gov.au/documents/9/3/6/%7B936C8901-37B3-4175-B3EE-97EF27103D69%7Drpp78.pdf.

stores in the United States; Winners and HomeSense in Canada; and T.K. Maxx stores in the United Kingdom, Ireland, and Germany.[44]

What Sensitive Information Was Stolen?

In early 2007 an "unauthorized computer intrusion" resulted in the theft of customer data.[45] TJX collected from customers: (1) account number, expiration date, and an electronic security code for payment card authorization; (2) bank routing, account, and check numbers and, in some instances, driver's license number and date of birth for personal check verification; and (3) name, address, and drivers' license, military, or state identification number ("personal ID numbers") for unreceipted returns.[46] In some cases, the personal ID numbers may have been the same as customers' Social Security numbers.[47] This information is particularly sensitive because it can be used to facilitate payment card fraud and other consumer harm.[48]

The company announced that 45.6 million credit and debit card numbers were stolen by intruders over a period of more than 18 months. In addition, personal data provided in connection with the return of merchandise without receipts by about 451,000 individuals in 2003 was also stolen.[49] This personal information included personal ID numbers, which in some instances were also consumers' Social Security numbers.[50]

TJX stated in its SEC filing, "To date, we have been able to identify only some of the information that we believe was stolen. Deletions in the ordinary course of business prior to discovery of the computer intrusion and the technology used by the intruder have, to date, made it impossible for us to determine much of the information we believe was stolen, and we believe that we may never be able to identify much of that information."[51] Thus, remarkably, and contrary to appropriate business practices, it appears that TJX could not account for the sensitive personal information it had collected, processed, and stored. It could not even identify what data had been stolen.

Anatomy of the Breach

TJX customer information was stolen from a portion of the TJX computer system in Framingham, Massachusetts, that processes and stores information related to payment card, check, and unreceipted merchandise return transactions for customers of certain of its stores, and from a portion of their computer system in Watford, United Kingdom,

44. The TJX Cos., Inc., SEC Form 10-K (FY ended Jan. 31, 2009), *available at* http://www.sec.gov/Archives/ edgar/data/109198/000095013509002399/b73492tje10vk.htm#002 [hereinafter TJX 2009 SEC Form 10-K]; and (FY ended Jan. 27, 2007), *available at* http://www.sec.gov/Archives/edgar/data/109198/000095013507001906/b64407tje10vk.htm [hereinafter TJX 2007 SEC Form 10-K].
45. TJX 2007 SEC Form 10-K, at 13; J. Abelson, THE BOSTON GLOBE, *Canadian Officials Fault TJX Safeguards*, September 26, 2007, http://www.boston.com/business/globe/articles/2007/09/26canadian_officials_faultTKX_safeguards.
46. Fed. Trade Comm'n, *In re* The TJX Cos., Inc., No. 072-3055, Complaint, para. 5, *available at* http://www.ftc.gov/os/caselist/0723055/080327complaint.pdf [hereinafter FTC TJX Complaint].
47. *Id.* at 11.
48. *Id.* at para. 5.
49. TJX 2007 SEC Form 10-K, *supra* note 45, at 17.
50. FTC TJX Complaint, *supra* note 46, at para. 11.
51. TJX 2007 SEC Form 10-K, *supra* note 45, at 17.

that processes and stores information related to payment card transactions at certain stores there and in Ireland.[52]

Figure 5.4 depicts the flow of a payment card authorization transaction and illustrates the vulnerable points that lead to the TJX breach.[53]

1. TJX operated corporate computer networks in the United States ("central corporate network") and internationally, as well as networks in each store. These networks linked worldwide corporate headquarters in the United States with each store and were used to process sales transactions and provide wireless access to the networks for wireless devices, such as for marking down prices.[54]

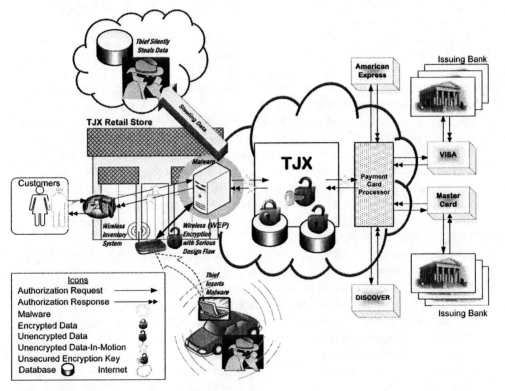

FIGURE 5.4
Breach of the TJX Computer Network

---

52. TJX 2007 SEC Form 10-K, *supra* note 45, at 14–15.

53. FTC TJX Complaint, *supra* note 46, at para. 4. The FTC concluded that since at least July 2005, TJX engaged in a number of additional practices that failed to provide reasonable and appropriate security for personal information on its networks. TJX (1) did not require network administrators and other users to use strong passwords or to use different passwords to access different programs, computers, and networks; (2) failed to use readily available security measures to limit access among computers and the Internet, such as by using a firewall to isolate card authorization computers; and (3) failed to employ sufficient measures to detect and prevent unauthorized access to computer networks or to conduct security investigations, such as by patching or updating antivirus software or following up on security warnings and intrusion alerts.

54. FTC TJX Complaint, *supra* note 46, at para. 4.

2. Consumers paid for purchases at the stores with credit and debit cards ("payment cards"), cash, or personal checks. In selling its products, TJX routinely used its computer networks to collect personal information from consumers to obtain authorization for payment card purchases, verify personal checks, and process merchandise returned without receipts ("unreceipted returns").

3. To obtain payment card authorization, TJX formatted personal information from the card into an authorization request. It typically transmitted authorization requests from in-store networks to designated computers ("card authorization computers") on the central corporate network, and from there to the payment card processor and the banks that issued the cards ("issuing banks"). TJX received responses authorizing or declining the purchase from issuing banks over the same networks.[55]

4. Until December 2006, TJX stored authorization requests and personal information obtained to verify checks and process unreceipted returns in "clear text" (unencrypted) on its in-store and corporate networks. TJX transmitted authorization requests and responses in clear text between and within its in-store and corporate networks.[56]

5. Intruders had undetected access to TJX's database by intercepting wireless signals in two Marshall's stores in Miami, Florida.[57] They exploited wireless networks of the retail stores to gain unauthorized access to the TJX network.

6. Between July and November 2005, an intruder connected to the TJX computer networks without authorization, installed hacker tools, found personal information stored in clear text including track 2 data and encrypted PIN blocks (personal identifier numbers associated with debit cards), and downloaded it over the Internet to remote computers.[58]

7. The intruders used sniffer programs to monitor and steal (a) password and account information, and (b) track 2 data as it was moving across a network.[59]

8. Between May and December 2006, an intruder periodically intercepted payment card authorization requests in transit from in-store networks to the central corporate network, stored the information in files on the network, and transmitted the files over the Internet to remote computers.[60]

9. Data were transmitted to payment card issuers without encryption.[61] Intruders had unprotected access to the decryption algorithm for the encryption software utilized by TJX.[62] This gave the hackers the ability to unscramble information stored digitally on the stolen cards.

---

55. *Id.*, para. 6.
56. *Id.*, para. 7.
57. Indictment at 4d., United States v. Gonzalez, No. 1:08-cr-10223-PBS-1 (D. Mass. 2008).
58. *Id.*
59. On December 23, 2009, Stephen Watts of New York was sentenced in U.S. District Court in Massachusetts for providing a sniffer program used to monitor and capture data including customers' credit and debit card information as it traveled across the TJX corporate computer networks. Press Release, U.S. Atty's Office, Dist. Mass., Hacker Sentenced For Providing Data Theft Tool in National Identity Theft Case (Dec. 23, 2009), *available at* http://www.justice.gov/criminal/cybercrime/wattSent.pdf.
60. Indictment, United States v. Gonzalez, No. 1:08-cr-10223-PBS-1 (D. Mass. 2008).
61. *Id.*
62. *Id.*

10. Hackers sold personal information (track 2 data) in Eastern Europe. They created fraudulent payment cards that they used to withdraw cash from ATMs.

The efforts of TJX to provide security for the credit card and other personal data it collected from consumers were seriously flawed. TJX used wired equivalent privacy (WEP) for wireless encryption, which has a serious design flaw that allows hostile entities to derive the encryption key and see all traffic with relative ease. There are problems and limitations with some of the encryption deployments for wireless technologies.[63] "With advances in cryptanalysis, software for analyzing wireless network traffic and deriving encryption keys and passwords has become commonplace. Assigning a complex encryption key for WEP still allows an attacker to find out what the key is within a matter of minutes using software such as Aircrack and WepLab. Using stronger encryption algorithms with weak keys leaves networks vulnerable to dictionary attacks that use lists of words and permutations to try to guess encryption keys."[64]

The TJX breach exploited vulnerabilities in the TJX information system at the store level and in the software used to manage large business databases. Security "failed" at multiple points, including TJX's use of wireless technology with a weak encryption mechanism that could be hacked and its transmission of authorization requests in clear text between and within its in-store and corporate networks made its information system vulnerable to attack. Intruders also had access to the TJX decryption algorithm through the use of an unsecured key or password that defeated any protection encryption might have provided on its information system. During the payment approval process, TJX transmitted payment card data (including the track 2 data on the magnetic stripe) without encryption to payment card issuers.

DSW: UNSECURED NETWORK, WEAK PASSWORDS

Discount Shoe Warehouse, DSW Inc., is a Columbus, Ohio-based retailer that operates 190 stores in 32 states. In 2004, DSW sold approximately 23.7 million pairs of shoes. It generates over $100 billion in revenue annually.[65]

What Sensitive Information Was Stolen?

In 2005, DSW discovered a data security failure that allowed hackers to gain access to sensitive credit and debit card information (name, card number, expiration date, and security code), and checking account information (bank routing number, account number, check number, and driver's license number and state) for more than 1.4 million customers.[66]

---

63. Johnny Cache & Vincent Liu, Hacking Exposed Wireless: Wireless Security Secrets and Solutions 8 (2007).

64. *Id.*

65. *In re* DSW, Inc., FTC Complaint, Docket No. C-4157, *available at* http://www.ftc.gov/os/caselist/0523096/0523096c4157DSWComplaint.pdf [hereinafter FTC DSW Complaint].

66. *Id.*; Decision and Order, *available at* http://www.ftc.gov/os/caselist/0523096/0523096c4157DSWDecisionandOrder.pdf; DSW SEC Form 10-K (FY ended Jan. 31, 2009), *available at* http://www.sec.gov/Archives/edgar/data/1319947/000095015209003376/l35986ae10vk.htm.

Anatomy of the Breach

Hackers gained access to the DSW computer networks through wireless access points on the networks. Intruders intercepted wireless signals and connected wirelessly to in-store networks without authorization. This information was transmitted wirelessly to a computer network located in the store and then sent to the bank or check processor.[67] Albert Gonzalez, along with three coconspirators, was indicted for this breach of the DSW computer system.[68]

Figure 5.5 depicts the flow of a payment card authorization transaction and illustrates the vulnerable points that lead to the DSW breach.

1. DSW used its computer networks to obtain authorization for credit card, debit card, and check purchases at its stores and to track inventory.[69] Cash registers in DSW stores were connected to the in-store computer networks through wireless access points. Other wireless access points were used to transmit information about DSW's inventory from in-store scanners to the in-store computer networks.[70]

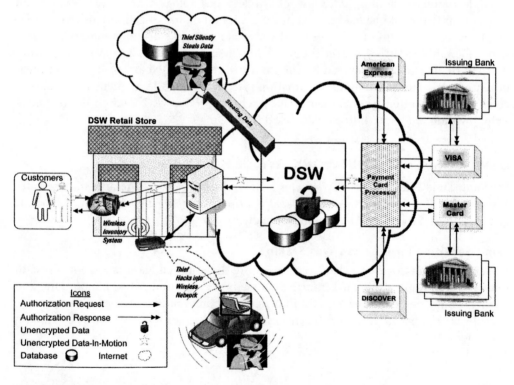

FIGURE 5.5
Breach of the DSW Computer Network

---

67. *In re* DSW, Decision and Order, *supra* note 66.
68. FTC DSW Complaint, *supra* note 65. United States v. Gonzalez, No. 1:08-cr-10223-PBS-1 (D. Mass. 2008).
69. FTC DSW Complaint, at para. 4.
70. *Id.* at para. 6.

2. DSW collected customer information at the cash register and transmitted it wirelessly, formatted as an authorization request, to a computer network located in the DSW store. The authorization request was then transmitted to the appropriate bank or check processor, which sent a response back to DSW through the same networks. Until at least March 2005, DSW stored personal information used to obtain credit card, debit card, and check authorizations, including magnetic stripe data, on in-store and corporate computer networks.[71]

3. Hackers gained access to the DSW computer networks through wireless access points on the networks. Intruders intercepted wireless signals and connected wirelessly to in-store networks that processed and stored credit and debit card transactions. They located and stole sensitive data on these networks, including track 2 data and encrypted PIN blocks (personal identifier numbers associated with debit cards). The hackers decrypted the encrypted PIN numbers.[72]

4. An intruder connected to the DSW computer networks without authorization, installed hacker tools, found personal information stored in clear text, and downloaded it over the Internet to remote computers.

5. Hackers sold personal information (track 2 data) in Eastern Europe. They created fraudulent payment cards that they used to withdraw cash from ATMs.

The breach exploited a number of vulnerabilities in the DSW information system. The FTC concluded that until at least March 2005, DSW engaged in a number of practices that, taken together, failed to provide reasonable and appropriate security for personal information collected at its stores. Among other things, DSW (1) created unnecessary risks to the information by storing it in multiple files when it no longer had a business need to keep the information; (2) did not use readily available security measures to limit access to its computer networks through wireless access points on the networks; (3) stored the information in unencrypted files that could be accessed easily by using a commonly known user ID and password; (4) did not sufficiently limit the ability of computers on one in-store network to connect to computers on other in-store and corporate networks; and (5) failed to employ sufficient measures to detect unauthorized access.

As a result, a hacker could use the wireless access points on one in-store computer network to connect to, and access personal information on, the other in-store and corporate networks. Security "failed" at multiple points, including the use of a wireless system that could be hacked, and storing the sensitive customer information in unencrypted files that could be easily accessed using a commonly known user ID and password.

WEB NEWSROOM: UNPROTECTED ENCRYPTION KEY

Web Newsroom develops new markets for content providers and advertisers around the world by distributing and promoting news from more than 200 content sources.[73] The goal is to have individual providers' news content found, played, and paid for by the millions of Web sites and blogs that compose the "long tail" of the Web. The Web Newsroom provides access to hundreds of thousands of fully licensed news stories that

---

71. *Id.* at para. 5.
72. United States v. Gonzalez, No. 1:08-cr-10223-PBS-1 (D. Mass. 2008).
73. Voxant Newsroom, About Us, http://www.thenewsroom.com/about_us.

can be published, or embedded, on customers' Web sites, including CBS, the *Wall Street Journal*, the Associated Press, and Reuters.

What Sensitive Information Was Stolen?

Hackers breached the e-commerce server of Web Newsroom, a Reston, Virginia, provider of news and ad syndication for the Web, stealing credit card numbers from approximately 4,500 customers in the United States.[74] Encrypted credit card numbers could have been accessed during the incident.

Anatomy of the Breach

The Voxant online e-commerce store server was hacked using what appeared to be a typical phishing scheme.[75] Although the credit card numbers were encrypted, the encryption key was not well protected in the application database.[76]

Figure 5.6 depicts the flow of sensitive information from a computer used by an advertiser or content provider to the e-commerce Web site of the Web Newsroom for an online transaction.

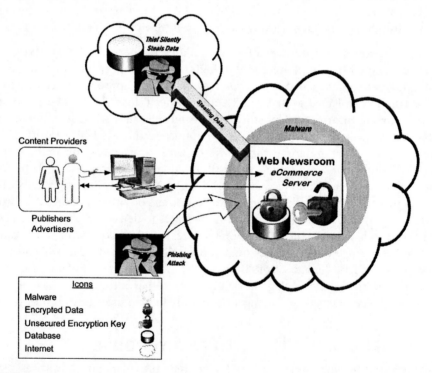

FIGURE 5.6
Breach of the e-Commerce Web Newsroom Site

---

74. Letter to the New Hampshire Attorney General from the "Voxant Management Team" (Aug. 31, 2007), *available at* http://doj.nh.gov/consumer/breaches.

75. SC Magazine, The Data Breach Blog, http://breach.scmagazineblogs.com/2007/09/14/server-hack-compro mises-voxant-online-store/.

76. Letter to the New Hampshire Attorney General, *supra* note 74.

1. Advertisers or content providers access the Web Newsroom e-commerce site through the Internet from a business or home computer.
2. Secure transactions can take place between the customer and the Web Newsroom.
3. The Web Newsroom collected customer data, including credit card numbers, in connection with the sale of news stories. The Web Newsroom stored sensitive information encrypted on its network.
4. Through a phishing scheme, a hacker gained access to the Web server and found that the encryption key was not well protected. The hacker used the unprotected encryption key to decrypt the customer records data base and steal credit card numbers.

Security "failed" because even though Web Newsroom encrypted sensitive customer data on its computer system, it did not protect the encryption key. No information system that attempts to protect sensitive date with the use of encryption can be secure unless the encryption key is fully protected.

GUIDANCE SOFTWARE: UNENCRYPTED DATABASE RECORDS

Guidance Software sells software and related training materials that customers use, among other things, to investigate and respond to computer breaches and other security incidents.[77] The company's Web site states that its software solutions provide the foundation for organizations to conduct computer investigations, including intellectual property theft, incident response, compliance auditing, and responding to eDiscovery requests.[78]

What Sensitive Information Was Stolen?

Guidance collected sensitive personal information from customers, including credit card information, through its Web site, sales representatives, and telephone and fax orders and stored the information on its computer network.[79] The information included name, address, e-mail address, telephone number, and, for customers paying with a credit card, the card number, expiration date, and security code number.[80]

Anatomy of the Breach

From September through December 2005, a hacker used SQL injection attacks[81] on the Web site and Web application to install common hacking programs on the Guidance corporate network. As a result, the hacker obtained unauthorized access to credit card

---

77. Matter of Guidance Software, Inc., File No. 062 3057, Complaint, *available at* http://www.ftc.gov/os/caselist/0623057/0623057%20-Guidance%20complaint.pdf [hereinafter FTC Guidance Software Complaint]; Agreement containing consent order, *available at* http://www.ftc.gov/os/caselist/0623057/0623057%20-Guidance%20consent%20agreement.pdf.

78. Guidance Software, Company Overview, http://www.guidancesoftware.com/computer-forensics-ediscovery leader.htm.

79. *Id.*; FTC Guidance Software Complaint, *supra* note 77, at para 5.

80. *Id.*

81. *Id.*

information for thousands of customers.[82] Until December 2005, Guidance employed SSL encryption[83] but stored sensitive customer information in clear text. It did not adequately assess the vulnerability of its Web application and network to commonly used SQL injection attacks.

"SQL injection is one of the many Web attack mechanisms used by hackers to steal data. It is the type of attack that takes advantage of improper coding of a Web application and allows hackers to inject SQL commands into, for example, a login form to allow them to gain access to the data held within the database."[84]

Figure 5.7 depicts the flow of sensitive customer information in an e-commerce business transaction and illustrates the vulnerable points that lead to the Guidance breach.

1. Guidance Software operated a Web site to sell software and related training materials to customers.[85]
2. It operated a computer network that customers used, in conjunction with the Web site and Web application program, to obtain information and to buy Guidance products and services (the "corporate network").[86]
3. Guidance protected sensitive information, including credit card numbers, sent from a customer's computer to the Guidance Web site with SSL encryption, the protocol over which the majority of secure e-commerce transactions occur on the Internet today.
4. Guidance stored sensitive personal information obtained from customers on the corporate network on a computer accessible through its Web site.[87] The information was stored unencrypted in clear readable text.[88]
5. Guidance stored user credentials in clear readable text network that facilitated access by a hacker to sensitive personal information on the network.[89]
6. In 2005 a hacker used SQL injection attacks on the Guidance Web site and Web application to install common hacking programs on the Guidance corporate network. The hacking programs were used to find sensitive personal information, including credit card numbers, expiration dates, and security code numbers, stored on the corporate network.[90]
7. The hacker transmitted the information over the Internet to computers outside the network.[91]

---

82. *Id.*

83. SSL (Secure Sockets Layer) is a protocol developed by Netscape for transmitting private documents via the Internet. SSL uses a cryptographic system with two keys to encrypt data—a public key known to everyone and a private or secret key known only to the recipient of the message. When used with a browser client, SSL establishes a secure connection between the client browser and the server. It sets up an encrypted tunnel between a browser and a Web server over which data packets or data streams can travel. The majority of secure e-commerce transactions use this protocol.

84. C.A. Mackay, SQL *Injection Attacks*, THE PROJECT CODE, January 25, 2005, http://www.codeproject.com/KB/database/sqlinjectionattacks.aspx.

85. http://www.guidancesoftware.com.

86. FTC Guidance Software Complaint, at para. 4.

87. *Id.* at para 6.

88. *Id.* at para 9.

89. *Id.*

90. *Id.* at para. 9.

91. *Id.*

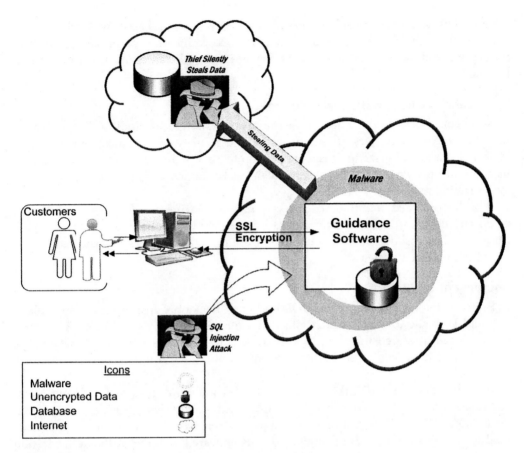

FIGURE 5.7
Breach of the Guidance Software Computer Network

Even though Guidance employed SSL encryption to protect communications over the Internet, it stored customer information in clear readable text. Until December 2005, Guidance "failed to provide reasonable and appropriate security for sensitive personal information stored on its corporate network," including not using readily available security measures to monitor and control connections from the network to the Internet and failing to employ sufficient measures to detect unauthorized access to sensitive personal information.[92]

CARDSYSTEMS: FAILURE TO APPLY A FIREWALL, MAINTAIN VIRUS DEFINITIONS, AND USE STRONG PASSWORDS

CardSystems operations center in Tucson, Arizona, processed more than $15 billion in credit card and online transactions each year on behalf of more than 105,000 small to

92. *Id.* at para. 8.

medium businesses.[93] In October 2005 the company was purchased by Pay By Touch, a payment processor that specialized in biometric verification of purchases, such as fingerprint reading at checkout counters. Pay by Touch filed for bankruptcy in November 2007.

What Sensitive Information Was Stolen?

CardSystems stored information from the magnetic stripe of credit and debit cards, including account numbers, expiration dates, and security codes. Since 1998, CardSystems had stored authorization responses for up to 30 days in one or more databases on its computer network. Each day, these databases contained as many as several million authorization responses.[94]

A hacker obtained unauthorized access to magnetic stripe data for tens of millions of credit and debit cards. Information on at least 68,000 MasterCard accounts was taken from CardSystems' database, potentially affecting one out of every seven credit cards issued in the United States.

Anatomy of the Breach

In September 2004 a hacker used a SQL injection attack on CardSystems' Web application and Web site to install a malicious script on the company's network.[95] The script was designed to search for records with track data—the data on the magnetic stripe of credit and debit cards—including account numbers, expiration dates, and security codes.

In early 2005, issuing banks discovered several million dollars in fraudulent credit and debit card purchases that had been made with counterfeit cards. The counterfeit cards contained complete and accurate magnetic stripe data, including the security code used to verify that a card is genuine, and thus appeared genuine in the authorization process. The magnetic stripe data matched the information CardSystems had stored on its computer network. In response, issuing banks cancelled and reissued thousands of credit and debit cards. Consumers holding these cards were unable to use them to access their credit and bank accounts until they received replacement cards.[96]

Figure 5.8 depicts the flow of a payment card authorization transaction and illustrates the vulnerable points that lead to the CardSystems breach.

1. Card information is captured from the magnetic stripe by swiping the card through a point-of-sale terminal. The payment device transmits the authorization request to CardSystems, which sends it to a computer network operated by or for a bank association (such as Visa or MasterCard) or another entity (such as American Express), which transmits it to the issuing bank.[97]
2. *Breach Part I:* In September 2004, a hacker used an SQL injection attack on CardSystems' Web application and Web site to install hacking programs. The

---

93. *In re* CardSystems Solutions, Inc., FTC Complaint, Docket No. C-4168, para. 3, *available at* http://www.ftc .gov/os/caselist/0523148/0523148CardSystemscomplaint.pdf.
94. *Id.* at para. 5
95. *Id.* at para. 7.
96. *Id.* at para. 4.
97. *Id.* at para. 7.

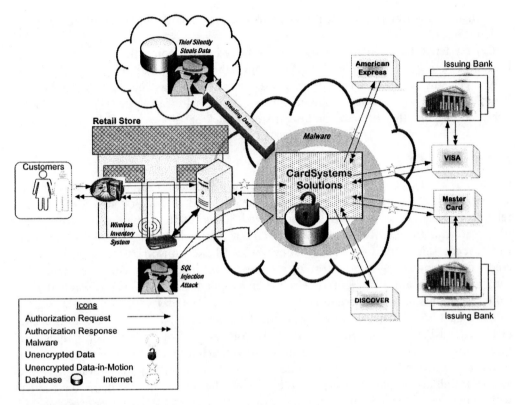

FIGURE 5.8
Breach of the CardSystems Payment Card Processing Network

programs collected and transmitted magnetic stripe data stored on the network every four days to computers located outside the network, beginning in November 2004.[98]

3. *Breach Part 2:* The hacker exported data and succeeded in stealing files containing thousands of consumer account records.

The FTC concluded that CardSystems (1) did not adequately assess the vulnerability of its Web application and computer network to commonly known or reasonably foreseeable attacks, including SQL injection attacks; (2) failed to use strong passwords to prevent a hacker from gaining control over computers on its computer network and access to personal information stored on the network; (3) did not use readily available security measures to limit access between computers on its network and between such computers and the Internet; and (4) failed to employ sufficient measures to detect unauthorized access to personal information or to conduct security investigations.[99]

Security "failed" at multiple points, including CardSystems' failure to encrypt customer data, which was intercepted when it was unencrypted on the company network

---

98. *Id.*
99. *Id.* at para. 6.

and when it was transmitted in the clear to the card brands and member banks that issued the cards.

CardSystems disclosed that it should not have been keeping the records that were breached, saying that it had improperly retained them for "research purposes." "As we have repeatedly acknowledged, our error was that the data was kept in readable form in violation of Visa and MasterCard security standards," said CardSystems president John Perry, adding that the company no longer stores track data.[100]

CRIMINAL PROSECUTIONS

On September 11, 2009, Albert Gonzalez of Miami pleaded guilty to 19 counts of conspiracy, computer fraud, wire fraud, access device fraud, and aggravated identity theft relating to hacks into numerous major United States retail companies including TJX, BJ's Wholesale Club, OfficeMax, Boston Market, Barnes & Noble, and Sports Authority.[101] According to the indictment, Gonzalez and his coconspirators broke into retail credit card payment systems through a series of sophisticated techniques, including "wardriving" (locating unsecured wireless networks from a car) and installation of sniffer programs to capture credit and debit card numbers used at these retail stores.

In August 2009 Gonzalez was indicted in New Jersey for the massive data breaches of Heartland Payment Systems, Hannaford Brothers, and other large companies. The indictment charged that Gonzalez conspired with two hackers from Russia and an unindicted coconspirator to use SQL injection attacks to penetrate the corporate networks and steal millions of payment card numbers and other card data.[102] They were charged with violations of the federal conspiracy statute, 18 U.S.C. § 371, for acts prohibited by the Computer Fraud and Abuse Act, 18 U.S.C. § 1030. The indictment alleges that the defendants used interconnected computers in the United States, Latvia, the Netherlands, and the Ukraine to store malware, stage the attacks, and receive payment card numbers and card data from the networks they penetrated. Gonzalez pleaded guilty on December 29, 2010, to conspiring to hack into computer networks supporting major American retail and financial organizations, and to stealing data relating to tens of millions of credit and debit cards.[103]

Gonzalez was sentenced on March 26, 2009, to 20 years and a day, and fined $25,000 for his role in the breaches into Heartland Payment Systems, Hannaford Brothers, 7-Eleven, and other companies. The sentence will run concurrently with a 20-year sentence he received in two other cases involving hacks into TJX, Office Max, Dave & Busters restaurants, and others. Restitution will be decided at a future hearing.

Eight hackers led by Victor Pleshchuk of Russia and Sergei Tsurikov of Estonia were indicted for wire fraud, computer fraud, access device fraud, computer intrusions,

---

100. *Credit Card Data Processing: How Secure Is It?: Hearing Before the U.S. House of Representatives,* 109th Cong. (July 21, 2005) (statement of John M. Perry, President and CEO, CardSystems Solutions), *available at* http://financialservices.house.gov/media/pdf/072105jmp.pdf.

101. News Release, U.S. Dep't of Justice, Major International Hacker Pleads Guilty for Massive Attack on U.S. Retail And Banking Networks (Dec. 29, 2009), http://www.justice.gov/criminal/cybercrime/gonzalezPlea.pdf.

102. United States v. Gonzalez, Hacker 09-cr-626 (D.N.J.).

103. News Release, U.S. Dep't of Justice, *supra* note 101.

aggravated identity theft, and conspiracy in a 16-count indictment returned on November 10, 2009, in the Northern District of Georgia. The hackers exploited vulnerabilities in the RBS WorldPay computer network and attacked key aspects of the global financial infrastructure that resulted in the theft of $9.5 million. Because the United States has no extradition treaty with Russia, Pleshchuk pleaded guilty in a Russion court. He received four years probation and was ordered to pay $8.9 million in restitution. Tsurikov was extradited from Estonia to the United States in August 2010. Two other suspects were arrested in Hong Kong and face criminal charges there.[104] Because the United States has no extradition treaty with Russia, Pleshchuk pleaded guilty in a Russian court. In a secret proceeding, he received four years probation and was ordered to pay $8.9 million in restitution Tsurikov was extradited from Estonia to the United States in August 2010.[105] Two other suspects were arrested in Hong Kong and face criminal charges there.[106]

BETTER SECURITY PRACTICES?

Since suffering massive data breaches, several of the companies have taken significant steps to improve their security and proactively combat the compromise of their information systems.

End-to-End Encryption

In May 2009, Heartland executives announced plans to introduce a "fully encrypted end-to-end terminal solution" designed to offer merchants the "highest level of data security in the marketplace."[107] The data would be encrypted from the moment a payment card is swiped until it leaves Heartland's possession. They issued a challenge to the payment card brands to allow them to send data in encrypted form and outlined improvements to the payment card authorization process they believe should be undertaken by the card brands.[108]

Heartland CEO Robert Carr also commented on inadequacies in the payment card industry data security standards (PCI DSS), professional standards designed to ensure information system security, and pledged to implement measures exceeding their requirements:

> While I continue to support the PCI standard as driving necessary improvements in the security of cardholder data, Heartland is committed to going beyond this standard in

104. U.S. Department of Justice Press Release, International Hacker Arraigned After Extradition, Elaborate Scheme Stole Over $9.4 Million from Credit Card Processor (August 6, 2010), *available at* http://atlanta-fbi.gov dojpressrel/pressrel09/atl111009.htm.

105. U.S. Dep't. of Justice Press Release, International Hacker Arraigned After Extradition, Elaborate Scheme Stole Over $9.4 Million from Credit Card Processor (August 6, 2010), *available at* http://atlanta.fbi.gov/dojpressrel/pressrel10/at080610.htm.

106. Linda McGlasson, RBS WorldPay Extradition, BankInfo Security (August 9, 2010), *available at* http://www.bankinfosecurity.com/articles.php?art_id=2830.

107. Statement of Bob Baldwin, President and CFO, Heartland Payment Sys., Inc. Q1 2009 Earnings Call Transcript, *available at* http://seekingalpha.com/article/136164-heartland-payment-systems-inc-q1-2009-earnings-calltranscript?page=2.

108. Digital Transaction News, May 7, 2009, http://www.digitaltrasactions.net/newstory.cfm?newsid=2206.

order that both merchants and cardholders can have the highest possible confidence in the security of their payment card data.

This is what they expect and deserve and Heartland intends to be a leading voice in persuading the payment card industry to accept this challenge. We are undertaking this investment primarily because the increasing sophistication of attacks on the payment systems requires a more than appropriate response for both our protection and our merchants' protection.

We are in a cyber crimes arms race, and we need to stay ahead of the bad guys who never rest and do not call committee meetings to update their malicious tools and attack vectors. This is good, not only for the system but we also believe it will be good for our business as security concerns grow among merchants large and small, we are optimistic that our solutions will be well received in the marketplace so there is also the prospect of financial benefit from our encryption solutions.[109]

Payment Processors Information Sharing Council

A newly formed group under the umbrella of the Financial Services Information Sharing and Analysis Center (FS-ISAC), the Payment Processors Information Sharing Council provides a forum for sharing information about fraud, threats, vulnerabilities, and risk mitigation in the payments industry.[110] FS-ISAC, a nonprofit organization, is the only industry venue for collaboration on critical security threats facing the financial services sector.

"Military Industrial Strength" Security

Hannaford executives are working with IBM, General Dynamics, Cisco Systems, and Microsoft security on a program aimed at putting "military and industrial strength" security controls in place to plug vulnerabilities and prevent future attacks.[111]

Hannaford expects to spend "millions" on IT security upgrades including the installation of new intrusion-prevention systems that will monitor activities on its network and the individual systems at its stores, plus the deployment of PIN pad devices in store checkout aisles featuring Triple DES encryption.[112] Company officials said the new measures include encryption of all card numbers during the entire time they are within the supermarket chain's data network.[113] Hannaford also said it has installed a "24/7-managed security monitoring and detection service" to detect intrusions.[114]

Security Lessons Learned

These case studies suggest the following lessons:

---

109. Statement of Bob Baldwin, *supra* note 105.

110. Payment Processors Information Sharing Council, http://www.ppisc.com/.

111. Ron Hodge, president and CEO and CIO Bill Homa press conference, April 28, 2009, http://www .atwcorp/downloads/itn/Grocery-Headquartrts-PCI-DSS-Article.pdf.

112. Jaikumar Vijayan, *Hannaford to Spend "Millions" on IT Security Upgrades After Breach,* COMPUTERWORLD, Apr. 22, 2008, http://www.computerworld.com/action/article.do?command=viewArticleBasic&articleId=9079652.

113. *Id.*

114. *Id.*

- Encryption is an important tool for securing information—but only one factor in the overall information security system.
- If encryption is to be effective, it must be implemented from end to end: sensitive data must be protected during its use or transmission from one part of the system to another, including transmission over the Internet.
- A comprehensive information security program must be developed, including the conduct of a risk assessment, development of security measures for access control and appropriate encryption, system monitoring and development of measures for both intrusion detection and data leakage prevention, staff training to ensure consistent implementation of security requirements, and overall, continuous maintenance of the system. Chapter 2 contains an action plan to prevent data breaches.[115]
- Compliance with all generally accepted professional standards for information security must be ensured. For example, payment processors should meet or exceed the PCI DSS standards.
- Prompt notification of consumers and other entities of any breaches of information systems containing sensitive personal data is required in order to ensure that steps may be taken in a timely manner by consumers to protect against identity theft and fraud.
- The payment card industry should continue—through the support of professional associations and otherwise—to meet, confer, and share their experiences in developing "best practices" for protecting information systems from cyber crime and unauthorized access.

---

115. NIST Special Publications provide comprehensive lists of security procedures and controls that should be implemented.

PART III

Law

CHAPTER 6

Ambiguities in State Security Breach Notification Statutes

Thomas J. Smedinghoff

During the past several years, we have witnessed a nationwide rush to enact laws and regulations that impose an obligation on businesses to *disclose* security breaches involving personal information to the persons whose data was compromised. Most of these laws do not impose a duty to provide security for that data.[1] Instead, they typically require only that companies disclose security breaches to affected persons.[2]

Designed as a way to help protect persons who might be adversely affected by a security breach of their personal information, these breach notification laws impose on companies an obligation similar to the common law "duty to warn" of dangers. Such a duty is often based on the view that a party who has a superior knowledge of a danger of injury or damage to another that is posed by a specific hazard must warn those who lack such knowledge. By requiring notice to persons who may be adversely affected by a security breach (e.g., persons whose compromised personal information may be used to facilitate identity theft), these laws seek to provide such persons with a warning that their personal information has been compromised, and an opportunity to take steps to protect themselves against the consequences of identity theft.[3]

---

1. In addition, several states have enacted laws requiring companies to provide reasonable security for personal data in their possession. *See, e.g.,* Arkansas, ARK. CODE ANN. § 4-110-104(b); California, CAL. CIV. CODE § 1798.81.5(b); Connecticut, Conn. Pub. Act No. 08-167; Maryland, MD. CODE ANN., COM. LAW § 14-3503; Massachusetts, MASS. GEN. LAWS ch. 93H, § 2(a) and regulations at 201 MASS. CODE REGS. 17.00 et seq.; Nevada, NEV. REV. STAT. § 603A.210; Rhode Island, R.I. STAT. 11-49.2-2(2) and (3); Oregon, OR. REV. STAT. § 646A.622; Texas, TEX. BUS. & COM. CODE ANN. § 48.102(a); and Utah, UTAH CODE ANN. § 13-44-20. There are also laws that impose on businesses an obligation to provide appropriate security for other corporate information. These include, for example, the Electronic Signatures in Global and National Commerce Act, 15 U.S.C. § 7001(d); the Sarbanes-Oxley Act at 15 U.S.C. §§ 7241 and 7262; the Uniform Electronic Transaction Act; and IRS Regulations at Rev. Proc. 97-22, 1997-1 C.B. 652, 1997-13 I.R.B. 9; Rev. Proc. 98-25; IRS Announcement 98-27, 1998-15 I.R.B. 30, and Tax Regs. 26 C.F.R. § 1.1441-1(e)(4)(iv).

2. Pisciotta v. Old Nat'l Bancorp., 2007 U.S. App. Lexis 20068, at *13 (7th Cir. Aug. 23, 2007).

3. *See, e.g.,* CAL. DEP'T OF CONSUMER AFFAIRS, OFFICE OF PRIVACY PROT., RECOMMENDED PRACTICES ON NOTICE OF SECURITY BREACH INVOLVING PERSONAL INFORMATION 6 (June 2009), *available at* http://www.privacy .ca.gov/res/docs/pdf/COPP_Breach_Reco_Practices_6-09.pdf; Interagency Guidance on Response Programs for Unauthorized Access to Customer Information and Customer Notice, Part III of Supplement A to Appendix, at 12 C.F.R. pt. 30 (OCC), 12 C.F.R. pt. 208 (Federal Reserve System), 12 C.F.R. pt. 364 (FDIC), and 12 C.F.R. pt. 568 (Office of Thrift Supervision) (Mar. 29, 2005), 70 Fed. Reg. 15,752 (Mar. 29, 2005) [hereinafter Interagency Guidance].

For the most part, laws imposing an obligation to disclose security breaches are a direct reaction to a series of well-publicized security breaches involving sensitive personal information over the past few years,[4] and an effort to address the problem of identity theft. Yet the concept of such laws is not new, nor is it limited to personal information. In 1998, for example, the Internal Revenue Service (IRS) imposed a disclosure requirement on all taxpayers whose electronic tax records were the subject of a security breach. In a Revenue Procedure that sets forth its basic rules for maintaining tax-related records in electronic form, the IRS requires taxpayers to "promptly notify" the IRS District Director if any electronic tax records "are lost, stolen, destroyed, damaged, or otherwise no longer capable of being processed . . . , or are found to be incomplete or materially inaccurate."[5]

With respect to personal information, a total of 46 states in the United States, plus the District of Columbia, Puerto Rico, and the U.S. Virgin Islands, have enacted security breach notification laws as of June 2010, all generally based on a 2003 California law.[6] In addition, the federal banking regulatory agencies issued final interagency guidance for financial institutions regarding this duty to disclose breaches,[7] and the HITECH Act (part of the American Recovery and Reinvestment Act of 2009) amended the Health Insurance Portability and Accountability Act of 1996 (HIPAA) to impose a duty to disclose security breaches on HIPAA-covered entities and business associates.[8]

These laws generally require that any business in possession of computerized sensitive personal information about an individual must disclose a breach of the security of such information to the person affected.[9]

THE BASIC OBLIGATION

Taken as a group, the state and federal security breach notification laws generally require that any business in possession of certain sensitive personal information about a covered individual must disclose any breach of such information to the person affected. The laws are generally similar in structure, approach, content, and terminology. The key requirements of the breach notification laws, which vary from state to state, include the following:

- *Type of information.* The sensitive personal information covered by the breach notification laws is typically defined as information consisting of (1) a person's first name or initial and last name, plus (2) any one of the following: Social Security number, driver's license or state ID number, or financial account

---

4. For a chronology of such breaches in the United States, and a running total of the number of individuals affected, see Privacy Rights Clearinghouse, Chronology of Data Breaches, http://www.privacyrights.org/ar/Chron DataBreaches.htm.

5. IRS Rev. Proc. 98-25, § 8.01.

6. See list of statutes in Appendix A.

7. Interagency Guidance, *supra* note 3.

8. *See* American Recovery and Reinvestment Act of 2009 § 13402 (ARRA); 42 U.S.C.S. § 17932. This portion of ARRA is part of the Health Information Technology for Economic and Clinical Health Act, or HITECH Act.

9. Except where the business maintains computerized personal information that the business does not own, in which case the laws require the business to notify the owner or licensor of the information, rather than the individuals themselves, of any breach of the security of the system.

number or credit or debit card number (along with any PIN or other access code where required for access to the account). In some states this list is longer, and may also include medical information, insurance policy numbers, passwords by themselves, biometric information, professional license or permit numbers, telecommunication access codes, mother's maiden name, employer ID number, electronic signatures, and descriptions of an individual's personal characteristics.[10] The federal HITECH Act covers unsecured protected health information.[11]

- *Definition of breach.* Generally, the statutes require notice to affected individuals following the unauthorized acquisition of unencrypted computerized data that compromises the security, confidentiality, or integrity of personal information about such individuals. In some states, however, notice is not required unless there is a reasonable basis to believe that the breach will result in substantial harm or inconvenience to the affected individual.

- *Who must be notified.* Notice of the breach must be given to any residents of the state whose unencrypted personal information was the subject of the breach. In addition, several states require notice to a designated government agency (e.g., the state attorney general) and/or to the major credit reporting agencies.

- *When notice must be provided.* Generally, persons must be notified in the "most expedient time possible and without unreasonable delay," although some statutes impose specific time limits. In most states the time for notice may be extended for the following:
  - Legitimate needs of law enforcement, if notification would impede a criminal investigation; and
  - Taking necessary measures to determine the scope of the breach and restore reasonable integrity to the system.

- *Form of notice.* Notice may be provided in writing (e.g., on paper and sent by mail), in electronic form (e.g., by e-mail, but only provided the provisions of E-SIGN[12] are complied with), or by substitute notice.

- *Substitute notice options.* If the cost of providing individual notice is greater than a certain amount (e.g., $250,000) or if more than a certain number of people would have to be notified (e.g., 500,000), substitute notice may be used, consisting of:
  - E-mail when the e-mail address is available, and
  - Conspicuous posting on the company's website, and
  - Publishing notice in all major statewide media.

---

10. *See, e.g.,* Cal. Dep't of Consumer Affairs, Office of Privacy Prot., Recommended Practices on Notice of Security Breach Involving Personal Information 6 (June 2009), *available at* http://www.privacy .ca.gov/res/docs/pdf/COPP_Breach_Reco_Practices_6-09.pdf; Interagency Guidance on Response Programs for Unauthorized Access to Customer Information and Customer Notice, Part III of Supplement A to Appendix, at 12 C.F.R. pt. 30 (OCC), 12 C.F.R. pt. 208 (Federal Reserve System), 12 C.F.R. pt. 364 (FDIC), and 12 C.F.R. pt. 568 (Office of Thrift Supervision) (Mar. 29, 2005), 70 Fed. Reg. 15,752 (Mar. 29, 2005) [hereinafter Interagency Guidance].

11. 42 U.S.C.S. § 17932.

12. 15 U.S.C. §§ 7001 *et seq.* This generally requires that companies comply with the requisite consumer consent provisions of E-SIGN at 15 U.S.C. § 7001(c).

Several of these issues vary from state to state, however, and some have become controversial. One of the most debated issues revolves around the nature of the event that triggers a duty to notify. In California, for example, notification is required whenever there has been an unauthorized access that compromises the security, confidentiality, or integrity of the electronic personal data. In other states, however, unauthorized access does not trigger the notification requirement unless there is a reasonable likelihood of harm to the individuals whose personal information is involved[13] or unless the breach is material.[14]

While the general approach outlined above may seem relatively straightforward, it is important to note that the breach notification statutes collectively raise numerous novel and undecided issues,[15] that there is no available legislative history to provide ready guidance, and to date, none of the statutes have been the subject of any significant interpretation by any court or regulator.[16] Accordingly, there is no direct precedent on which to rely on for guidance in interpreting these statutes, making analysis of any set of facts with respect to a specific breach much more difficult and subject to potentially differing conclusions.

Determining the applicability of state breach notification laws to a particular factual situation, and determining a company's compliance obligations, is frequently made difficult by a variety of ambiguities that appear in many of the state breach notification laws. Several of those ambiguities are summarized below.

WHAT IS COVERED PERSONAL DATA?

Most state breach notification laws define covered personal data as (1) a person's first name or initial and last name, plus (2) one of the following data elements: Social Security number, driver's license number, or financial account or credit or debit card number. Other states add additional information to the list, such as medical information[17] and biometric information.

Notwithstanding this definition, there are certain categories of personal information that raise questions about coverage. One example is Social Security numbers. In some cases, a security breach involves Social Security numbers without the corresponding individual's name. Are they covered by the breach notification statutes? While there are a few states that cover breach of Social Security numbers alone,[18] most require a

---

13. Arkansas, Connecticut, Delaware, and Louisiana are examples of states in this category.

14. Montana and Nevada are examples of states in this category.

15. *See, e.g.*, Pisciotta v. Old Nat'l Bancorp, 499 F.3d 629 (7th Cir. 2007) (noting "the novelty of the legal questions posed by information exposure and theft").

16. The few decided cases that address the breach notification laws add little to the analysis. *See, e.g.*, Ponder v. Pfizer, Inc., 2007 U.S. Dist. Lexis 83129 (M.D. La. Nov. 7, 2007) (noting that the Louisiana breach law provides for a private right of action); *Pisciotta*, 499 F.3d 629 (noting that the Indiana breach law requires only that a database owner disclose a security breach to potentially affected consumers, that it does not require the database owner to take any other affirmative act in the wake of a breach, and that if the database owner fails to comply with the duty to disclose, the statute provides for enforcement *only* by the Attorney General of Indiana—i.e., it creates no private right of action against the database owner by an affected customer and imposes no duty to compensate affected individuals for inconvenience or potential harm to credit that may follow); Parke v. CardSystems Solutions, Inc., 2006 U.S. Dist. Lexis 77241 (N.D. Cal. Oct. 11, 2006) (noting that there appears to be no reported appellate decisions interpreting the California breach law).

17. The federal HITECH Act focuses on "unsecured protected health information." 42 U.S.C.S. § 17932.

18. Examples include Indiana and New York.

combination of an individual's name plus Social Security number before the duty to notify is triggered. Thus, in most states it would appear that a breach of Social Security numbers, without more, is not covered, although given the sensitivity of these numbers it is not clear that this should be the result.

A similar problem arises in cases involving a breach of an individual's name and credit card numbers, but without any additional information relating to those credit card numbers, such as address, card verification value (CVV) code, access code, or password that would permit access to the financial account. The breach notification laws in approximately 30 states include credit or debit card numbers in the definition of covered personal data only when "in combination with any required security code, access code, or password that would permit access to the financial account." In those states, does a security breach involving an individual's name and credit card number without more, trigger the duty to notify?

Some have argued that credit card numbers can be used to make purchases without knowledge of the expiration date, address, CVV number, or other information. To the extent that is true, it would appear that theft of such credit card information should be covered. However, that is not always clear.

WHAT IS A SECURITY BREACH?

An event that triggers the obligation to provide individuals with notice of a breach involving their personal information is typically referred to in the breach statutes as a "breach of the security of the system." This term is often defined as "unauthorized acquisition of unencrypted computerized data that compromises the security, confidentiality, or integrity of personal information maintained by the person or business."[19] The requirements of this definition, in combination with certain other exclusions available in many states (e.g., an exclusion for security breaches that the custodian of the exposed data determines will not likely cause harm),[20] allows for more than one approach to determining when factors are present that impose an obligation to notify under the breach notification statutes.

Under most state breach notification laws, the foregoing definition appears to require two elements for a security breach:

- An "unauthorized acquisition" of computerized data,
- "That compromises" the security, confidentiality, or integrity of personal information maintained by the business.

This leaves open the possibility that there may be an unauthorized acquisition of computerized data that does *not* compromise the security, confidentiality, or integrity of the personal information maintained by the business. There are two common examples of this scenario.

---

19. *See, e.g.,* CAL. CIV. CODE § 1798.82(d).

20. For example, Iowa's Breach Notification Statute stipulates that notification is not required if, "after an appropriate investigation or after consultation with the relevant federal, state, or local agencies responsible for law enforcement, the person determined that no reasonable likelihood of financial harm to the consumers whose personal information has been acquired has resulted or will result from the breach. Such a determination must be documented in writing and the documentation must be maintained for five years."

The first is an unauthorized acquisition of personal information by trusted persons—e.g., persons subject to an obligation of confidentiality. Numerous security incidents have involved an erroneous transfer of personal information to the wrong party, but in such situations the recipient is also obligated to the sender under an obligation of confidentiality. In such situation, there has clearly been an unauthorized acquisition of the data, but one may argue that such an unauthorized acquisition does not compromise the security, confidentiality, or integrity of the personal information involved. At least such would be the case if one presumes that the recipient honors its obligation of confidentiality.

A second scenario involves the theft of a laptop containing personal information by someone with a malicious motive (e.g., either to steal the hardware to resell it or perhaps to get the data). Is notice required if the laptop is recovered shortly after the theft, while the company is still investigating and before it has given any notice, if the forensic investigation is able to establish that the data has not been accessed or copied? In such a case there has clearly been an unauthorized acquisition of the data, and by a person with an improper or illegal motive. Nonetheless, the forensic examination establishes that the acquisition did not compromise the security, confidentiality, or integrity of the personal information on the laptop.

An example of such a situation is the Veterans Administration security breach of 2006. In that case, a laptop containing the names, Social Security numbers, dates of birth, and in many cases phone numbers and addresses of 26 million veterans was stolen from a VA employee's home. Thereafter the laptop was recovered, and a detailed forensic examination by the FBI concluded that the data on the laptop was never accessed. One may ask whether notice is necessary in such situation. In those states that use a likelihood of harm standard (discussed below), it may be relatively easy to conclude that, notwithstanding the breach, notice is not required because there is no significant likelihood of harm. But in states requiring notice for any breach, regardless of the likelihood of harm, the question is a more difficult one.

WHAT IS ENCRYPTED DATA?

Most of the breach notification statutes provide an exemption if the data is encrypted.[21] That is, notification of data subjects is not required if the security breach involved

---

21. The breach notification statute in Wyoming does not recognize the encryption exception. The statute in the District of Columbia does not mention encryption, but does focus on the likelihood that the exposed information could be misused by providing that "[a]cquisition of data that has been rendered secure, so as to be unusable by an unauthorized third party, shall not be deemed to be a breach of the security of the system." Additionally, the federal Interagency Guidance in the financial sector does not recognize the encryption exception, although it requires notice only "If the [financial] institution determines that misuse of its information about a customer has occurred or is reasonably possible." The federal regulators took the position that "a blanket exclusion for all encrypted information is not appropriate, because there are many levels of encryption, some of which do not effectively protect customer information." See Interagency Guidance, supra note 3, at 36. Conversely, the federal HITECH Act focuses on "unsecured protected health information," which it defines as "protected health information that is not secured through the use of a technology or methodology specified by the Secretary [of HHS]," or alternatively, "protected health information that is not secured by a technology standard that renders protected health information unusable, unreadable, or indecipherable to unauthorized individuals and is developed or endorsed by a standards developing organization that is accredited by the American National Standards Institute." 42 U.S.C.S. § 17932(h).

encrypted data. The manner in which the statutes address the encryption issue, however, varies widely.

Almost half of the breach notification statutes provide no definition of encryption whatsoever. They simply require notice only if the stolen data is "unencrypted" or "not encrypted," without any further definition or explanation of what qualifies as encrypted.[22] The remaining statutes define encryption, but do so in a variety of different ways.

Some statutes focus on a requirement that the data be "unreadable" or "unusable." For example, several state breach laws expressly define encryption as an algorithmic process to transform data into a form in which the data is *rendered unreadable or unusable* without the use of a confidential process or key.[23] Other statutes impliedly define encryption in a similar manner. This might occur, for example, by defining "breach of security" as "unauthorized access to or acquisition of electronic files, media, databases or computerized data containing personal information when access to the personal information has not been secured by encryption or by any other method or technology that renders the personal information unreadable or unusable."[24] Since most encryption techniques can be broken, given sufficient time and effort, the issue may become one of determining how strong the encryption is, and whether that is sufficient to qualify.

Conversely, some state breach laws appear to expressly recognize that encryption is not completely unbreakable, and focus instead on a likelihood of compromise standard. These states often define encryption as "the use of an algorithmic process to transform data into a form in which there is a *low probability of assigning meaning* without use of a confidential process or key."[25]

The difference between the "unreadable or unusable" standard and the "low probability of assigning meaning" standard is not entirely clear. Some might argue that the "unreadable or unusable" standard is an absolute test, one that requires the encryption to be unbreakable.[26] But if that interpretation is followed, all but the very strongest encryption techniques will likely fail to qualify. On the other hand, if a lesser standard is applied, the question has to focus on determining exactly how strong the encryption must be. For example, must it render the data unreadable or unusable to the average person, to the average data thief, or to the average cryptologist? The same issue also arises when interpreting the "low probability of assigning meaning" standard—that is, low probability to whom? No courts have yet addressed these issues.

While these two approaches appear to differ in the strength of the encryption required, it is also worth noting that they all define encryption in terms of the use of an "algorithmic process." While it is not clear what is required to qualify as an algorithmic

---

22. See, e.g., statutes in Alaska, Arkansas, California, Delaware, Florida, Georgia, Idaho, Illinois, Louisiana, Maine, Montana, New York, Puerto Rico, Rhode Island, Tennessee, Virgin Islands, and Washington listed in the Appendix.
23. See, e.g., Arizona, Hawaii, North Carolina, Oregon, and Vermont statutes listed in the Appendix.
24. CONN. GEN. STAT. § 36a-701b(a). See also Colorado, Minnesota, Nebraska, New Jersey, North Dakota, South Carolina, and Utah statutes listed in the Appendix.
25. See, e.g., MD. CODE § 14-3501, OHIO REV. CODE § 1349.19, and 73 PA. CONS. STAT. § 2303 statutes listed in the Appendix.
26. In fact, the New Hampshire statutes uses the phrase "*completely* unreadable or unusable." N.H. REV. STAT. § 359-C:19.

process,[27] several statutes recognize that there may be "another method" to achieve the same goal. Thus, there is a group of statutes that define encryption as the "transformation of data through the use of an algorithmic process into a form in which there is a low probability of assigning meaning without the use of a confidential process or key, *or* securing the information by *another method* that renders the data elements unreadable or unusable."[28] Interestingly, in these statutes the use of an algorithmic process must transform data into a form with "a low probability of assigning meaning without the use of a confidential process or key," whereas the use of "another method" must "render the data elements unreadable or unusable."

Adding to the debate, one state has gone further than most, and defined encryption as the "transformation of data through the use of a *128-bit or higher algorithmic process* into a form in which there is a low probability of assigning meaning without use of a confidential process or key."[29] Yet the regulations adopted to enforce that law have eliminated the 128 bit requirement. They simply define encrypted as "the transformation of data through the use of an algorithmic process, or an alternative method at least as secure, into a form in which meaning cannot be assigned without the use of a confidential process or key, unless further defined by regulation by the Office of Consumer Affairs and Business Regulation."[30]

The most recent legislation (the HITECH Act addressing notification of breaches involving protected health information covered by HIPAA) takes yet another approach by leaving the issue to the regulators. That statute does not reference encryption. Instead, it requires notification in the event of a breach of "unsecured protected health information," where that term is defined as "protected health information that is not secured through the use of a technology or methodology specified by the Secretary" of Health and Human Services. And if the Secretary does not specify any technology, the statute provides, as a default definition, that unsecured protected health information "shall mean protected health information that is not secured by a technology standard that renders protected health information unusable, unreadable, or indecipherable to unauthorized individuals *and* is developed or endorsed by a standards developing organization that is accredited by the American National Standards Institute."[31]

---

27. For example, a Captain Crunch decoder ring would appear to use an algorithmic process, since it works by taking each letter in a string and adding 13 to it, so that, e.g., "a" becomes "n," "b" becomes "o," "z" becomes "m," and so on. It also arguably renders data "unreadable," although deciphering the data is a trivial task.

28. See, e.g., K.S.A. § 50-7a01, Ind. Code § 24-4.9-2-5, N.H. Rev. Stat. 359-C:19, 24 Okla. Stat. § 162, Va. Code § 18.2-186.6, and W. Va. Code § 46A-2A-101 statutes listed in the Appendix.

29. *See* Mass. Gen Laws ch. 93H, § 1(a) (emphasis added).

30. 201 Mass. Code Regs. § 17.02.

31. On April 17, 2009, HHS issued proposed guidance specifying how entities may safeguard such information in a manner that renders it unusable, unreadable, or indecipherable to unauthorized individuals. *See* "Guidance Specifying the Technologies and Methodologies that Render Protected Health Information Unusable, Unreadable, or Indecipherable to Unauthorized Individuals for Purposes of the Breach Notification Requirements," 74 Fed. Reg. 19,006, *available at* http://www.hhs.gov/ocr/privacy/hipaa/understanding/coveredentities/federalregisterbreachrfi .pdf.

Thus, of the breach notification statutes that do define encryption, the term is generally defined to include one or more of the following:

- An algorithmic process that renders the data unreadable or unusable;
- An algorithmic process that results in a low probability of assigning meaning to the data;
- A 128 bit or greater algorithmic process that results in a low probability of assigning meaning to the data;
- Another method that renders data unreadable or unusable; or
- A method specified by a regulator.

Finally, it is also worth noting that some (but less than half) of the states recognize that no matter how good the encryption is, if the encryption key is compromised the protection is lost. Thus, for example, the New Hampshire breach law provides that "Data shall not be considered to be encrypted for purposes of this subdivision if it is acquired in combination with any required key, security code, access code, or password that would permit access to the encrypted data."[32] Several other states contain provisions that have a similar effect.[33]

Thus, in almost all circumstances, reliance on the encryption exemption essentially becomes a judgment call. Presumably in some cases the strength of the encryption is so weak that a court would find that it does not reasonably qualify as encryption under the statutes. But conversely, the mere fact that a form of encryption can be broken, as most can with enough effort, does not necessarily mean that such encryption does not qualify as encryption under the statutes.

WHEN DOES A BREACH TRIGGER THE OBLIGATION TO NOTIFY?

Several states require notice in the event of a breach regardless of the risk to the affected individuals.[34] In a majority of jurisdictions however, notice is not required if a determination can be made that there is no reasonable likelihood of harm (or some variation thereof) to the individuals whose personal information was acquired as a result of the breach. Unfortunately, determining whether this standard has been met requires a judgment call based on largely unknown facts. And the difficultly of making such a determination is further complicated by the differing statutory approaches to the "likelihood of harm" exception.

Based on a review of the various breach notification statutes, the approaches used in the "likelihood of harm" exception can be categorized as follows:

- *Focus on likelihood of loss or injury.* Notification is not required where the security breach is not reasonably likely to cause substantial economic loss (Arizona); not

---

32. N.H. Rev. Stat. § 359-C:19.

33. See, e.g., Arkansas, Hawaii, Indiana, Massachusetts, Michigan, Minnesota, New York, North Carolina, Oklahoma, Oregon, Pennsylvania, Puerto Rico, and Virginia statutes listed in the Appendix.

34. See California, District of Columbia, Georgia, Illinois, Minnesota, Nevada, New York, North Dakota, Oklahoma, Puerto Rico, Tennessee, Texas, Virgin Islands, and Washington statutes listed in the Appendix.

likely to cause substantial loss or injury to, or result in identity theft (Michigan); not reasonably believed to cause loss or injury (Montana and Pennsylvania); and creates no reasonable likelihood of harm (Arkansas, Connecticut, Florida, Louisiana, and Oregon).

- *Focus on likelihood of misuse of the information.* Notification is not required where misuse of information is not reasonably likely to occur (Colorado, Delaware, District of Columbia, Idaho, Kansas, Maryland, New Hampshire, Utah, and Wyoming); misuse of the information is not reasonably possible (New Jersey, Vermont, and Maine); use of information for an unauthorized purpose is not reasonably likely to occur (Massachusetts and Nebraska); and illegal use of the personal information is not reasonably likely to occur and presents no material risk of harm (North Carolina and Hawaii).
- *Focus on likelihood of identity theft.* Notification is not required where (or unless) the security breach could result in identity deception, identity theft, or fraud (Indiana); will not likely result in a significant risk of identity theft (Rhode Island); will not cause a material risk of identity theft or other fraud (Ohio and Wisconsin); and does not create a substantial risk of identity theft or fraud, or used for unauthorized purpose (Massachusetts).

These three different approaches are further complicated by the fact that the standard applied to each of them varies widely from state to state. The different standards can be summarized as follows:

- Not likely
- Not reasonably likely
- Not reasonably believed
- Not reasonably possible
- Will not cause
- Does not create substantial risk.

The breach notification statutes do not articulate what is meant by their respective versions of the likelihood of harm standard beyond language similar to that quoted above, leaving it to businesses to make a determination on the basis of the often limited factual information available to them.

WHO IS AN EMPLOYEE OR AGENT?

Most breach notification statutes also contain a so-called "good faith" exception. Under that exception, a good-faith acquisition of the information by an unauthorized employee or agent is not considered to be a breach of the security of that information, so long as certain other criteria are present. While the criteria differ from state to state, one key threshold issue involves who qualifies for the exception—that is, who is considered to be an employee or an agent.

While it is generally clear who qualifies as an employee, the question of who qualifies as an agent for purposes of the good-faith exception is a more difficult one. Specifically, is the definition limited to the standard common-law definition of an agent—that is, one who has authority to act on behalf of the principal? Or does it include mere contractors and service providers providing services for the company that suffers the breach? Or for that matter does it include any trusted person (e.g., someone who has signed a confidentiality agreement).

The Restatement (Third) Agency defines "common-law agency" or "true agency" as "the fiduciary relationship that arises when one person (a 'principal') manifests assent to another person (an 'agent') that the agent shall act on the principal's behalf and subject to the principal's control, and the agent manifests assent or otherwise consents so to act."[35] In this relationship, the agent "acts as a representative of or otherwise acts on behalf of another person *with power to affect the legal rights and duties of the other person.*"[36] Thus, "the common-law definition requires that an agent hold power."[37] However "a relationship is not one of agency within the common-law definition unless the agent consents to act on behalf of the principal, and the principal has the right throughout the duration of the relationship to control the agent's acts."[38]

The fact that the breach notification statutes generally require good-faith acquisition by an "employee or agent" of the owner of the personal information does not, however, necessarily meant that the term "agent" in the breach notification statutes is limited to a common-law agent. The Restatement (Third) Agency acknowledges that: "*some statutes and many cases* use agency terminology when the underlying relationship falls outside the common-law definition."[39] In other words, there is not an automatic presumption that when used in a statute the term "agent" always means common-law agent. As one court has noted, "[t]he term agent is thrown around in many legal contexts and often without great precision."[40]

Accordingly, when the term "agent" is used in a statute the legislative intent is critical. As the Restatement (Second) Agency notes:

> *Statutory Use.* Whether the word "agent" as used in a statute corresponds to the meaning given here [i.e., a common-law agent] depends, with other factors, upon the purpose of the statute.[41]

---

35. RESTATEMENT (THIRD) AGENCY § 1.01, cmt. a.

36. *Id.* cmt. b (emphasis added).

37. *Id.* cmt. c.

38. *Id.*

39. *Id.* cmt. a (emphasis added).

40. Fasciana v. Elec. Data Sys. Corp., 829 A.2d 160, 168 (Del. Ch. Ct. 2003). *See also* RESTATEMENT (THIRD) AGENCY § 1.01, cmt. a (noting that "Moreover, the terminology of agency is widely used in commercial settings and academic literature to characterize relationships that are not necessarily encompassed by the legal definition of agency. In philosophical and literary studies, 'agency' often means an actor's capacity to assert control over the actor's own intentions, desires, and decisions. In economics, definitions of principal-agent relations encompass relationships in which one person's effort will benefit another or in which collaborative effort is required. In commercial settings, the term 'principal' is often used to designate one who benefits from or is affected by the acts of another, or one who sponsors or controls another. It is also common usage to refer without distinction to parties who serve any intermediary function as 'agents.' Not all such situations, however, meet the legal definition of an agency relationship.").

41. RESTATEMENT (SECOND) AGENCY § 1, cmt. f. *See also* Home Fed. Sav. & Loan Assoc. v. Peerless Ins. Comp., 197 F. Supp. 428, 439 (N.D. Iowa 1961) (citing *Restatement Second* and noting that "the question to be determined is whether [the individual] was an agent within the meaning of the particular statute involved").

As one court stated, "the key question that must be addressed . . . is what definition of agent did the General Assembly intend to use in drafting [the statutory section]."[42] Similarly, another court called upon to interpret the term "agent" in a statute specifically rejected the common-law definitions of the term "agent" proposed by the litigants, noting that "[t]hese definitions are rejected as not probative and incongruent with the statutory framework underlying this action."[43] It then undertook what it described as "the amorphous task of defining the term 'agent' as intended by [the statute]."[44] In doing so, it noted that "in the absence of contrary legislative intent an overly restrictive common-law definition of agent which would subvert the purpose of the statutory framework in which it is employed *is to be avoided*."[45]

Unfortunately, there is no legislative history or case law precedent that indicates whether the reference to an "agent" in the breach notification statutes refers to a common-law agent or more generally to someone such as a service provider retained by the data owner to provide services. In this age of outsourcing where a company's personal data is often processed by an outsourced third-party service provider, it may be appropriate to assume that the various legislatures that enacted the breach notification statutes recognized that economic reality and intended that the term "agent" would apply to the conduct of such companies and consultants. But no court has yet examined that issue.

WHAT ASSUMPTIONS CAN/SHOULD YOU MAKE?

In the world of security breaches, there are a number of fact situations that raise questions about which presumptions, if any, are reasonable to make under the circumstances.

For example, when a backup tape is sent to offsite storage via a delivery service, but never arrives, what assumptions are reasonable under the circumstances? Specifically, should the company assume that there has been an unauthorized acquisition and provide notice to the individuals named on the tape? Or is the company entitled to assume that in the absence of evidence of malicious conduct, the tapes are merely lost and there should be no presumption of unauthorized acquisition?

A similar question arises when computers are missing in circumstances where no one has any knowledge of the circumstances of their disappearance. For example, what assumptions are appropriate when a corporate inventory of its equipment reveals that several computers are missing, but the company has no information whatsoever regarding whether the computers were stolen, destroyed, simply misplaced and unaccounted for, or in use with a different inventory identification tag? In such situations, should the

---

42. *Fasciana*, 829 A.2d at 168 (interpreting the term "agent" in Section 145 of the Delaware General Corporation Law and ultimately concluding that its use in that statute was intended by the General Assembly to be the common-law definition).

43. United States v. Dix Fork Coal Co., 692 F.2d 436, 439 (6th Cir. 1982) (interpreting the term "agent" in the Surface Mining Control and Reclamation Act of 1977, 30 U.S.C. § 1271(c)).

44. *Id.* at 439.

45. *Id.* at 440 (emphasis added) (ultimately using the definition of "agent" that appeared in 30 U.S.C. § 802(e) of the Coal Mines Health and Safety Act, and noting that the Act "parallels in purpose, policy, and structure the instant Act").

company assume that the computers were stolen and provide notice to the individuals whose data may have been on those computers, or in the absence of any evidence of any wrongdoing, is it entitled to assume that whatever happened to the computers does not rise to the level of a security breach? Is substitute notice required?

A related question arises when laptops or other computer devices are actually stolen, but the company has absolutely no idea what information was on those devices. Does the law require notice under such circumstances, and if so, who should receive notice?

CHAPTER 7

State Data Breach Notification Laws and the Duty to Provide Information Security

Lucy L. Thomson

States have been active in recent years in enacting data breach notification laws. California was the first state to enact a data breach notification law and other states have followed its lead. Although some 46 states, the District of Columbia, Puerto Rico, and the U.S. Virgin Islands have notification laws, most of these statutes do not impose a duty to provide security for that data.[1] As of July 2010, there were no data breach notification laws at all in Alabama, Kentucky, New Mexico, and South Dakota.

More recently, in response to massive data breaches, states have acted to keep personal information secure by expanding the laws to protect data—not merely to report when it has been hacked or stolen.

Massachusetts, California, Maryland, Nevada, and New Jersey have passed laws that include requirements to provide at least some type of information security to protect sensitive personal information.

Nevada and Massachusetts have enacted statutes requiring substantial security measures to protect personal information. Massachusetts requires any firm conducting business with state residents to employ encryption, adopt a risk-based approach to ensuring security, and protect against data leakage. Nevada has taken the additional step of requiring holders of credit card and other personal information in computerized information systems to comply with the professional standards promulgated by the Payment Card Industry Council.

NEVADA: PROFESSIONALLY BASED SECURITY STANDARDS

Beginning in January 2010, the State of Nevada has mandated PCI DSS compliance for businesses accepting credit cards. Though Minnesota law currently codifies certain select PCI DSS requirements, the new Nevada law is significantly more comprehensive,

---

1. Appendix A provides a summary of key federal and state statutes providing security measures.

as it adopts the PCI DSS in its entirety by reference. In doing so, Nevada became the first state to transform these standards into state law. Commentators have suggested that a domino effect may result as states seek ways to protect consumers and businesses from the damages caused by massive data breaches.

The credit card industry has been grappling with the issue of what standards are adequate to reduce risks of data breaches. A number of the leading credit card companies have taken the lead in developing such standards.

The Payment Card Industry Security Standards Council has developed professional standards to set baseline requirements for the security of information systems holding credit card information. These data security standards (PCI DSS) are incorporated by the major credit card processing companies in contracts as a means of ensuring that retailers properly safeguard cardholder accounts.[2] The Council was formed by American Express, Discover Financial Services, JCB, MasterCard Worldwide, and Visa International.

Overall, these standards mandate businesses with computerized information systems to

- build and maintain a secure network
- protect credit card data
- maintain a vulnerability management system
- implement strong access control measures
- regularly monitor and test networks
- maintain an information security policy

There are two sets of standards: Payment Application Data Security Standard (PA-DSS), which applies to software applications, and PCI DSS, which applies to merchants that accept payment cards. Compliance requirements vary by business transaction volume.

The PCI Security Standards Council serves as an advisory group and manages the underlying PCI security standards. Each payment card brand is responsible for its own compliance programs and has set different deadlines for compliance for software providers and merchants. Visa's final security deadline for its merchants is July 1, 2010. If this deadline is not met, merchants risk customers not being able to use credit cards. The goal of the credit card processing companies is to ensure that all their merchants use only PA-DSS-compliant applications and PCI DSS policies and procedures.

The standard was created to help organizations that process card payments prevent credit card fraud through increased controls around data and its exposure to compromise. The standard applies to all organizations that hold, process, or pass cardholder information from any card branded with the logo of one of the card brands.

Validation of compliance can be performed either internally or externally, depending on the volume of card transactions the organization is handling, but regardless of the size of the organization, compliance must be assessed annually.

---

2. *See* Gretchen McCoy, *How Should You Ensure PCI DSS Compliance?*, SC Magazine, Mar. 9, 2009, http://www .scmagazineus.com/how-should-you-ensure-pci-dss-compliance/article/128484/.

Noncompliant companies that maintain a relationship with one or more of the card brands, either directly or through an acquirer, risk losing their ability to process credit card payments and being audited and/or fined.[3]

Commentators have suggested that even these standards are just the beginning of an ongoing effort to develop effective standards. A number of businesses have suffered massive breaches although they were in compliance with the PCI-DSS standards. Clearly, more discussion and work is needed here.

MASSACHUSETTS: RISK-BASED APPROACH

Massachusetts General Law Chapter 93H was passed to safeguard the personal information of residents of the Commonwealth of Massachusetts and to address the problems of identity theft and fraud. This statute is discussed at length because it was the first to require security for information systems and is more detailed than other state statutes. As such, it is one attempt in the ongoing conversation about how to protect information systems containing credit card data and other personal information from massive data breaches resulting in harm to both consumers and businesses alike.

The law imposes a duty on any person (a natural person, corporation, association, partnership, or other legal entity) who owns, licenses, stores, or maintains personal information about a resident of the Commonwealth of Massachusetts[4] to provide notice of a security breach to the affected individual, and to develop, implement, maintain, and monitor a comprehensive information security program for the records. The requirement for a comprehensive security system sets the Massachusetts statute apart from many other state laws.

Regulations implement the provisions of Massachusetts General Law Chapter 93H and define the standards to be met by persons who own, license, store, or maintain personal information about a resident of the Commonwealth of Massachusetts. They became effective on March 1, 2010.

The purposes of the regulation are to:

1. Establish minimum standards to be met in connection with the safeguarding of personal information contained in both paper and electronic records;
2. Ensure the security and confidentiality of such information in a manner consistent with industry standards;
3. Protect against anticipated threats or hazards to the security or integrity of such information; and
4. Protect against unauthorized access to or use of such information in a manner that creates a substantial risk of identity theft or fraud against such residents.[5]

---

3. *See generally* PCI Sec. Standards Council, http://www.pcisecuritystandards.org.

4. 201 Mass. Code Regs. 17.01(b) (Scope).

5. 201 Mass. Code Regs. 17.01(a) (Purpose and Scope); Mass. Gen. Laws ch. 93H, § 2. Massachusetts law directs the Office of Consumer Affairs and Bus. Regulation to adopt regulations that are "designed to safeguard the personal information of residents of the commonwealth." Mass. Gen. Laws ch. 93H, § 2(a). The statute directs that the regulations ensure the security and confidentiality of personal information; provide real protection against anticipated threats to the security or integrity of such information; and protect against unauthorized access to or use of such information. *Id.*

This is the first data breach notification law in which a state has attempted to define information security requirements specifically. The new Massachusetts regulations go further than other states by requiring companies to implement a risk-based, process-oriented, comprehensive, written information security program in accordance with a detailed list of requirements *and* also encrypt all "personal information" on laptops or other portable devices, all records and files containing personal information transmitted over public networks to the extent technically feasible, and all data containing personal information transmitted wirelessly.

The regulations reflect lessons learned from over 300 breach notifications received pursuant to Massachusetts General Law Chapter 93H, Section 3. These notifications demonstrate that wireless transmissions of personal information must be encrypted in order to ensure their security. The proliferation of thefts of laptops and other portable devices with personal information stored on them indicate that the information must be encrypted to have meaningful protection. Massachusetts was involved with several of the largest data breach cases, including TJX, an off-price retailer, and DSW, a retail shoe outlet, whose sensitive electronic consumer records were stolen by hackers who accessed the computer networks through their wireless systems.

What Personal Information Is Covered?

"Personal information" has a particular meaning under the Massachusetts statute.[6] It includes a Massachusetts resident's first name and last name or first initial and last name in combination with any one or more of the following data elements that relate to such resident:

- Social Security number
- Driver's license number or state-issued identification card number
- Financial account number or credit or debit card number, *with or without* any required security code, access code, personal identification number, or password that would permit access to a resident's financial account

The Massachusetts statute provides for the protection of personal information as it has been commonly defined and includes all of the key pieces of information that are associated with identity theft and other information, for example credit and debit card numbers, that, once breached, can lead to fraud.

What Is a Security Breach?

A "breach of security" has two elements under the Massachusetts law:

1. The unauthorized acquisition or unauthorized use of (a) unencrypted data or (b) encrypted electronic data and the confidential process or key that is capable of compromising the security, confidentiality, or integrity of personal information

---

6. Information that is publicly available, or obtained from federal, state, or local government records that are lawfully made available to the general public, is excluded from "personal information." Mass. Gen. Laws ch. 93H, § 1(a); 201 Mass. Code Regs. 17.02 (Definitions).

2. That creates a substantial risk of identity theft or fraud against a resident of the commonwealth.[7]

The statute protects data containing personal information regardless of physical form or characteristics, thus covering paper files as well as electronic information.[8]

The definition of security breach in the Massachusetts statute is broad. It includes unauthorized acquisition and use of both unencrypted and encrypted data with the access key. Unlike the new federal HITECH breach notification statute, it does not exempt encrypted data from the requirements of the statute. The breach must create a "substantial risk" of harm; the trend is to dismiss harmless or technical data breaches—although many questions loom here as it will be a factual matter in each breach as to whether there is a risk, including how serious it might be.

What Is Encrypted Data?

Massachusetts and Nevada both require that certain types of sensitive personal information be encrypted, but their definitions of encryption are different.

Nevada defines "encryption" as

the use of any protective or disruptive measure, including without limitation, cryptography, enciphering, encoding or a computer contaminant, to:

1. Prevent, impede, delay or disrupt access to any data, information, image, program, signal or sound;

2. Cause or make any data, information, image, program, signal or sound unintelligible or unusable; or

3. Prevent, impede, delay or disrupt the normal operation or use of any component, device, equipment, system or network.[9]

The Massachusetts regulation defines "encrypted" to mean the transformation of data through the use of an algorithmic process, or an alternative method at least as secure, into a form in which meaning cannot be assigned without the use of a confidential process or key, unless further defined by regulation by the office of consumer affairs and business regulation.[10]

Massachusetts links encryption to the use of an algorithmic process, the "core element" of encryption, or another equally secure "method." Nevada's definition includes the notion of "delay," that is, delay in access to the information. It is unclear how

---

7. A good faith but unauthorized acquisition of personal information by a person or agency, or employee or agent thereof, for the lawful purposes of such person or agency, is not a breach of security unless the personal information is used in an unauthorized manner or subject to further unauthorized disclosure. MASS. GEN. LAWS ch. 93H, § 1(a); 201 MASS. CODE REGS. 17.02 (Definitions).

8. "Data" is defined as "any material upon which written, drawn, spoken, visual, or electromagnetic information or images are recorded or preserved, regardless of physical form or characteristics." MASS. GEN. LAWS ch. 93H, § 1(a).

9. NEVADA REV. STAT. § 597.970.

10. The statute provides that the department of consumer affairs and business regulation may adopt regulations, from time to time, to revise the definition of "encrypted," as used in this chapter, to reflect applicable technological advancements. *Id.* § 1(b). MASS. GEN. LAWS ch. 93H, § 1(a).

delaying access precludes access, the obvious goal of any encryption process. States are struggling to find ways to define a proper security methodology.

What Data Must Be Encrypted?

Massachusetts requires encryption of all data-in-transit "to the extent technically feasible" when it travels "across public networks," or is transmitted wirelessly. Stored data must be encrypted when it contains personal information on laptops or other portable devices.[11] A combination of a person's name and Social Security number, bank account number, or credit card number must be encrypted when stored on portable devices or transmitted wirelessly on public networks, according to the new law. Encryption of personal information on portable devices carrying identity data like laptops, PDAs, and flash drives must also be completed by March 1, 2010. Nevada requires businesses to encrypt all transmissions of personal customer information (other than a facsimile) outside of the secure system of the business.[12]

These provisions leave a number of unanswered questions. The Massachusetts statute originally defined "encrypted" as the "transformation of data through the use of a 128-bit or higher algorithmic process into a form in which there is a low probability of assigning meaning without use of a confidential process or key, unless further defined by regulation of the department of consumer affairs and business regulation." The regulation subsequently eliminated the 128-bit requirement. The current regulation does not require any particular type of encryption; it does not specify how strong an encryption algorithm must be. It does not explain what qualifies as an "algorithmic process," what "an alternative method at least as secure" is, nor what is meant by the phrase "to the extent technically feasible."

In Nevada, would a password-protected document sent in an e-mail comply with that law? Under either state law, could the information be put in a zipped archive with a password and sent over the Internet?

What Is the Duty to Report a Known Security Breach or Unauthorized Use of Personal Information?

Massachusetts law has specific reporting requirements when a person or agency knows or has reason to know of a breach of security or that the personal information of a Massachusetts resident was acquired or used by an unauthorized person or used for an unauthorized purpose. A person or agency that owns or licenses data must notify the Massachusetts Attorney General, the Office of Consumer Affairs and Business Regulation, and any affected residents of the Commonwealth of Massachusetts; a person or agency that maintains or stores, but does not own or license data, must notify and cooperate with the owner or licensor of such information. The statute requires notification of applicable parties and entities "as soon as practicable" and "without reasonable delay."[13] The parameters of these standards will be filled out as cases arise.

The issue of prompt notification of data breaches to consumers has been an issue in several of the major data breaches experienced by American corporations. It appears

---

11. 201 MASS. CODE REGS. 17.04(3) (Computer System Security Requirements).
12. NEV. REV. STAT. §§ 603A.010 et seq.
13. MASS. GEN LAWS ch 93H § 1.

that several knew of significant data breaches and delayed notification. This delay is the focus of several lawsuits filed against the corporations and businesses to collect damages. Consumers are not fully equipped to act to protect themselves from identify theft and fraud if they are unaware of the breaches.

What Are the Requirements for Security Breach Notifications?[14]

Under Massachusetts law, "Notice" shall include

1. Written notice;
2. Electronic notice, if notice provided is consistent with the provisions regarding electronic records and signatures set forth in 15 U.S.C. § 7001(c) and Massachusetts General Law 110G; or
3. Substitute notice, if the person or agency required to provide notice demonstrates that the cost of providing written notice will exceed $250,000, or that the affected class of Massachusetts residents to be notified exceeds 500,000 residents, or that the person or agency does not have sufficient contact information to provide notice.[15]

"Substitute notice" shall consist of all of the following:

1. Electronic mail notice, if the person or agency has electronic mail addresses for the members of the affected class of Massachusetts residents;
2. Clear and conspicuous posting of the notice on the home page of the person or agency if the person or agency maintains a website; and
3. Publication in or broadcast through media or medium that provides notice throughout the commonwealth.[16]

Notice requirements reflect considerations of cost and the need to provide for an array of substitute notices to advise all affected persons in the event of a data breach that will place them at risk. There are similar provisions in breach notification statutes in many states.

What Is a Comprehensive Information Security Program?

Every person who owns, licenses, stores, or maintains personal information about a resident of the Commonwealth shall develop, implement, maintain, and monitor a comprehensive information security program for any records containing personal information.[17]

This security program must

- be written
- be reasonably consistent with industry standards, and

---

14. The requirements are summarized at Commonwealth of Mass., Consumer Affairs and Bus. Regulations, Requirements for Security Breach Notifications Under Chapter 93H, http://www.mass.gov/?pageID=ocaterminal&L =3&L0=Home&L1=Bus.&L2=Identity+Theft&sid=Eoca&b=terminalcontent&f=idtheft_notification_reqs&csid= Eoca.

15. Mass. Gen. Laws ch. 93H, § 1(a).

16. *Id.*

17. 201 Mass. Code Regs. 17.03 (Duty to Protect and Standards for Protecting Personal Information).

- contain administrative, technical, and physical safeguards to ensure the security and confidentiality of the records.

The safeguard must be consistent with the safeguards for protection of personal information and information of a similar character set forth in any state or federal regulations by which the person who owns, licenses, stores, or maintains such information may be regulated.

Unanswered questions arise about what industry standards apply: How are inconsistencies to be resolved with other state or federal regulations? Nonetheless, the requirement for a security program is, in the eyes of many commentators, an advance forward to ensuring that entities that maintain computerized information systems containing personal data maintain proper security of financial and personal data of consumers. It means that businesses need to look at their entire security program—as a whole. They cannot simply encrypt sensitive data. They must assess risks, employ security standards, train staff, monitor and maintain their systems, and manage their information systems in a manner to minimize the risk of data breaches.

Written Information Security Plan

The Massachusetts statute is more far-reaching than the data breach notification laws of other states because it requires the preparation of a written information security plan (WISP). The entities' security program must include a comprehensive plan to implement all security requirements. The WISP must contain

- a designated person to maintain the WISP
- provisions for the conduct of a risk assessment
- security policies for employees
- disciplinary measures for violation
- termination of system access for employees who have left employment
- assessments of third-party service providers
- limitations on the collection, retention, and access to personal information
- locating and assessing personal information provisions for
- physical access controls
- measures to monitor implementation of the WISP
- annual review of security measures
- data breach incident reporting and assessment[18]

Computer Security System Requirements

A person who stores or transmits personal information electronically must include in the WISP the following elements about its computers, including any wireless system:

1. Secure user authentication protocols including
   a. Control of user IDs and other identifiers;
   b. A reasonably secure method of assigning and selecting passwords, or use of unique identifier technologies, such as biometrics or token devices;

---

18. 201 Mass. Code Regs. 17.03(a).

    c. Control of data security passwords to ensure that such passwords are kept in a location and/or format that does not compromise the security of the data they protect;

    d. Restricting access to active users and active user accounts only; and

    e. Blocking access to user identification after multiple unsuccessful attempts to gain access or the limitation placed on access for the particular system.

2. Secure access control measures that

    a. Restrict access to records and files containing personal information to those who need such information to perform their job duties; and

    b. Assign to each person with computer access unique identifications plus passwords that are not vendor-supplied default passwords and that are reasonably designed to maintain the integrity of the security of the access controls.

3. To the extent technically feasible, encryption of all transmitted records and files containing personal information that will travel across public networks and encryption of all data to be transmitted wirelessly.

4. Reasonable monitoring of systems for unauthorized use of or access to personal information.

5. Encryption of all personal information stored on laptops or other portable devices.

6. For files containing personal information on a system that is connected to the Internet, there must be reasonably up-to-date firewall protection and operating system security patches, reasonably designed to maintain the integrity of the personal information.

7. Reasonably up-to-date versions of system security agent software, which must include malware protection and reasonably up-to-date patches and virus definitions, or a version of such software that can be supported with up-to-date patches and virus definitions and is set to receive the most current security updates on a regular basis.

8. Education and training of employees on the proper use of the computer security system and the importance of personal information security.[19]

    Unanswered questions about the WISP include what "reasonable methods" are for assigning and selecting passwords, monitoring of systems for unauthorized use of or access to personal information, providing firewall protections and operating system security patches, and system security agent software and other security elements set forth in the state regulation.

    This regulatory provision appears to move away from a risk-based approach and prescribes technology and procedures that must be included for every information system, regardless of its use and the risks posed by the specific information system. In some cases, particular technology will not be applicable to the system. For example, databases that are not connected to the Internet need not have virus protection. The regulation does not clearly recognize that specific security steps, methods, and procedures need to be individually developed to meet the security needs of the data that is contained in the information system—and the risks posed by maintaining such information.

---

19. 201 Mass. Code Regs. 17.04 (Computer System Security Requirements).

Records Disposition

Paper or electronic records (including records stored on hard drives or other electronic media) containing personal information shall be disposed of in a manner that complies with Massachusetts General Law 93I.[20]

Verification of Third-Party Service Providers[21]

The regulations require persons to take reasonable steps to verify that third-party service providers with access to personal information have the capacity to protect such personal information. Among other things, persons should select and retain service providers that are capable of maintaining safeguards for personal information, and should contractually require the service providers to maintain such safeguards.

The regulations require that entities ensure their vendors act to protect information by contract. However, they do not address whether vendors have an independent requirement to protect information consistent with the state statute and regulations.

Compliance

Compliance with the regulations will be evaluated taking into account the

1. Size, scope, and type of business of the person obligated to safeguard the personal information under such comprehensive information security program;
2. Amount of resources available to such person;
3. Amount of stored data; and
4. Need for security and confidentiality of both consumer and employee information.[22]

The regulations provide in Section 17.03(2) that the evaluation considerations concerning size, scope, and type of business apply both to Section 17.03 and Section 17.04 (Computer System Security Requirements).

Are these standards specific enough to provide a standard for compliance? The standards do not appear to contain any "bottom line." As with many provisions of the statute and regulations, state officials are struggling to balance being prescriptive with affording discretion to businesses to develop information systems consistent with their needs—and protect the security of the data.

---

20. The statute provides:

> When disposing of records, each agency or person shall meet the following minimum standards for proper disposal of records containing personal information:
>> (a) paper documents containing personal information shall be either redacted, burned, pulverized or shredded so that personal data cannot practicably be read or reconstructed;
>> (b) electronic media and other non-paper media containing personal information shall be destroyed or erased so that personal information cannot practicably be read or reconstructed.

MASS. GEN. LAWS ch. 93I, § 2.

21. 201 MASS. CODE REGS. 17.03(f) (Duty to Protect and Standards for Protecting Personal Information).

22. 201 MASS. CODE REGS. 17.03 (Duty to Protect and Standards for Protecting Personal Information); Commonwealth of Mass., Office of Consumer Affairs & Bus. Regulation, A Small Bus. Guide: Formulating a Comprehensive Written Information Security Program, *available at* http://www.mass.gov/Eoca/docs/idtheft/sec_plan_smallbiz_guide.pdf.

MARYLAND AND NEW JERSEY: INFORMATION SECURITY STATUTES

Several states have developed statutes that require some measure of information security.

The Maryland Personal Information Protection Act contains a general requirement for information security. It provides that a business that owns or licenses personal information must implement and maintain reasonable security procedures and practices appropriate to the nature of the personal information and the nature and size of the business.[23]

The New Jersey Identity Theft Protection Act limits disclosure of Social Security numbers and prohibits their transmission over the Internet or use to access a website unless the connection is secure, the number is encrypted, or authentication is required.[24]

BREACH OF HEALTH INFORMATION

In enacting a data breach notification law in July 2009, Missouri joined California, Arkansas, and Texas in requiring notification of breaches of medical and health insurance information, including an individual's medical history, mental or physical condition, treatment or diagnosis, health insurance policy number, and any other unique identifiers used by a health insurer.

AFFIRMATIVE SECURITY MEASURES

The trend exhibited by states shows an increasing awareness of the need to protect personal information, including health information, in electronic information systems from intrusion.

The states are moving from merely requiring the notification of individuals in the event of breaches to affirmatively requiring security measures, such as encryption, and mandatory compliance with professional standards of the Payment Card Industry Security Standards Council.

---

23. Md. Attorney Gen., Guidelines for Businesses to Comply with the Maryland Personal Information Protection Act, http://www.oag.state.md.us/idtheft/businessGL.htm.

24. N.J. STAT. ANN. §§ 56:11-44 *et seq.*

CHAPTER 8

HITECH: The First Federal Data Breach Notification Law

Arthur E. Peabody, Jr. and Lucy L. Thomson

OVERVIEW

Information technology is transforming the way health professionals and the health care industry provide care to individuals and to the entire population. Privacy and information security are at the center of a sea change in the way individual health records are created, managed, and shared. Embedded in the Obama administration's 2009 stimulus package, Congress enacted the first federal data breach notification law as part of the Health Information Technology for Economic and Clinical Health Act, known as the HITECH Act,[1] a law whose primary purpose is to promote health information technology, including electronic medical records.

Health care is delivered by a wide variety of individuals, organizations, and entities, including health care providers, plans, and clearinghouses. In addition, many other entities work with providers and plans—with full access to records containing individually identifiable health information, for a variety of purposes, including the provision of medical care and treatment. HITECH and the Health Insurance Portability and Accountability Act (HIPAA) were designed to protect personal health records from unauthorized access. Pursuant to the statutory scheme, reasonable efforts must be made to protect this individually identifiable health information by encrypting it. And if unauthorized access occurs, to notify individuals of the breach in a timely manner.

In enacting HITECH, Congress has endeavored to respond to the need to protect electronic medical records and address widespread invasions of privacy caused by breaches of medical and other individually identifiable health information. HITECH requires entities covered by the statute to notify individuals whose protected health information (PHI) has been breached. Generally, PHI includes all medical records, including electronic medical records, and other information reflecting individually identifiable health

---

1. Title XIII of the American Recovery and Reinvestment Act of 2009 (ARRA), Pub. L. No. 111-5, 123 Stat. 115 (2009).

information maintained by an entity or its business associates. Terms used in HITECH are generally defined consistent with the definitions found in the HIPAA Privacy Rule promulgated by the Department of Health and Human Services (HHS). The HITECH statute and regulations do not focus on the prevention of breaches of individually identifiable health information, but rather on notification of affected individuals should a breach within the coverage of the statute and regulations occur.

This chapter provides a broad overview of the new HITECH Act and will assist in understanding the scope of the statute, how it relates to similar laws and newly proposed or issued regulations, and the use of encryption as a means of preventing lapses of security and the potential widespread invasions of privacy that may result. Finally, this chapter identifies and discusses perceived weaknesses in the approach adopted by the government's decision makers.

Both HHS and the Federal Trade Commission (FTC) have issued interim final rules or regulations designed to implement the requirements of HITECH. Many businesspeople who will be required to implement the statute will be confronted with a complex regulatory scheme. For example, a multiple-step analysis is required to determine whether a "breach" has occurred. In important areas, the regulations contain intricacy and detail that obscure the fundamental requirements. There is little doubt that as a result many covered entities will provide notifications that are unnecessary and, conversely, will fail to notify individuals and other entities when required.

Breach of Protected Health Information

HHS has issued an interim final rule that defines "breach" as the acquisition, access, use, or disclosure of protected health information in a manner not permitted under the HIPAA Privacy Rule that compromises the security or privacy of the protected health information.[2] Under this rule, the first question in any breach is whether the breach violates HIPAA. Pursuant to the interim final rule, HHS has defined "compromise" in a manner that narrows the notification requirement. Not all breaches will trigger the statute's notification requirements. Only breaches that "pose a significant risk of financial, reputational, or other harm to the individual" require notification.[3] As such, the interim final rule contemplates a "harm threshold." HHS states that a risk assessment will be needed to determine what, if any, harm may result from each breach of PHI.

Concept of a "Safe Harbor"

The HHS interim final rule provides a "safe harbor" that, if followed, nullifies the notification requirement. Covered entities that encrypt PHI consistent with standards promulgated by the National Institute of Standards and Technology (NIST) or destroy the information need not comply with the notification requirement should a breach occur. The manner and extent of notification required varies depending on the extent of the breach, that is, the number of individuals whose PHI has been breached. In some cases, only the individuals whose information was subject to the breach must be notified; in

---

2. 74 Fed. Reg. 42,740 at 743 (August 24, 2009).
3. *Id.* at 42,744.

"larger" breaches affecting more than 500 people, the media and the HHS Secretary must also be notified.

Standards Issued by NIST

NIST standards are cited in the regulations as a vehicle to ensure the security of individually identifiable health information, including encryption. The standards present guidance that a covered entity may utilize in encrypting individually identifiable health information. However, the HHS regulations fail to recognize that encryption must be implemented properly, and steps in addition to encryption are required to secure an information system adequately. No single NIST "standard" will ensure the security of an information system absent an appropriate security design, effective means of access control, other critical security controls, and timely maintenance and periodic monitoring of the system. Little notice is given in the HHS interim final rule to the security of the encryption "key" or the means of access to encrypted material. Likewise the regulations give scant attention to the need to ensure that individuals with access to encrypted material are properly trained initially and receive periodic follow-up training, as needed.

Role of the Federal Trade Commission

The FTC has also issued regulations pursuant to HITECH. As the FTC's jurisdiction is limited to non-HIPAA covered entities, its regulations do not cover electronic health records created and utilized in a physician's office or in a hospital. The primary focus of the regulations is the security of personal health records maintained by individuals on vendor Web sites.

WHAT IS A BREACH?

General Definitions

The definition of "breach" is the heart of the statute since it triggers the notification requirement of HITECH. HITECH Section 13400 (Definitions) of subtitle D (Privacy) defines "breach" as "(1) the unauthorized acquisition, access, use, or disclosure of protected health information, (2) which compromises the security or privacy of such information."[4]

HITECH Section 13402 (Notification in the Case of a Breach) of subtitle D (Privacy) provides that in the case of a "breach" of "unsecured protected health information," a "covered entity" shall notify each individual whose unsecured protected health information "(1) has been accessed, acquired, or disclosed as a result of the breach, or (2) is reasonably believed to have been accessed, acquired, or disclosed as a result of the breach."

The two definitions must be read together in order to arrive at a single standard. The notification provision in Section 13402 omits the word "unauthorized" from the concept of access and disclosure. However, the notion of "unauthorized" is captured or

---

4. "Protected health information" has the meaning given to the term in 45 C.F.R. §160.304 of HIPAA and is addressed later in this chapter. The statute and regulations assume that the "protected health information" will be contained in electronic medical records. It is interesting to note that there are very few references to electronic medical records in either the statute or implementing regulations.

defined in the use of the word "breach." The failure to use consistent terminology in the definition and notification provisions of the statute may lead to confusion. Some might argue that the notification provision in Section 13402 imposes a requirement of notification for all breaches—not merely those premised on unauthorized access.

The HHS interim final rule defines "breach" consistent with Section 13400, thereby harmonizing the language of Sections 13400 and 13402, and it incorporates HIPAA standards. In brief, the interim final rule defines "breach" as the "acquisition, access, use, or disclosure of protected health information in a manner not permitted under Subpart E of this part [the HIPAA Privacy Rule] which compromises the security or privacy of the protected health information."[5] As formulated by HHS, the first question in any breach is whether the breach violates HIPAA. Not all violations of HIPAA will trigger the notification requirements of HITECH.

Under a mandate to issue rules for breach notification by vendors of personal health records, the FTC issued proposed rules incorporating the concepts contained in Section 13424(b)(1)(A)(ii)–(iv) of HITECH, applicable to vendors of personal health records (PHR), related entities, and third-party service providers.[6]

The scope of coverage of "vendors" under the FTC regulation differs from the coverage of "entities" under HITECH. The proposed FTC final rule does not apply to HIPAA-covered entities or to an entity's activities as a business associate of a HIPAA-covered entity. Moreover, the rule does not apply to electronic health records created by hospitals or physicians; it does apply to PHRs created by individuals. The major focus of the rule is vendors of personal health records, related entities, and third-party service providers.

The proposed FTC rule defines "breach of security" as the acquisition of unsecured identifiable health information of an individual in a personal health record without the authorization of the individual. This language is identical to the definition of "breach of security" in HITECH Section 13407(f)(1) (Temporary Breach Notification Requirement for Vendors and Other Non-HIPAA Covered Entities).[7] Defining terms under both agency regulations similarly responds to comments from the public urging HHS and the FTC to work together to adopt common standards and to ensure that each consumer "receives a single notice for a single breach."[8]

In addition, the proposed FTC rule requires notification to individuals whose information was "acquired," while HITECH uses the terms "accessed, acquired, or disclosed." This change is intended to harmonize the proposed FTC rule with the other provisions of the HITECH Act, making clear that the notification standard for FTC-regulated entities, including third-party service providers, is "acquired." The FTC rule has the effect

---

5. 45 C.F.R. § 164.402.

6. *See* HITECH § 318.3 (Breach Notification Requirements), 74 Fed. Reg. 17,923–24 (proposed); 74 Fed. Reg. 42,962 (Final Rule).

7. 74 Fed. Reg. 17,917; 74 Fed. Reg. 42,962, at 67.

8. 74 Fed. Reg. 42,963. Throughout the literature on privacy and security, the impact of notification on the individual whose information has been breached is repeatedly assessed. There appears to be some consensus that the more notifications an individual receives, the less effective the notices will be. *See, e.g.,* OMB Memorandum M-07-16, at 12 (May 22, 2007).

of narrowing the notification standard to those situations where the unauthorized access resulted in the acquisition of PHI.

Rebuttable Presumption of Unauthorized Access

The regulations create a rebuttable presumption that if a breach of PHI has occurred, it has resulted in unauthorized access. In some cases, it will be fairly easy to determine whether unsecured individually identifiable health information has been acquired without authorization. Several examples of such cases are cited in the proposed FTC rule and its proposed HHS final rule. These examples include

- Theft of a laptop containing unsecured personal health records
- Theft of hard copies of health records
- Unauthorized downloading or transfer of PHR by an employee
- Electronic break-in and remote copying of such records by a hacker
- Placement of a PHR on an "obscure" Web site
- Sending and subsequent retraction of an e-mail containing a PHR

In other cases, there may be unauthorized access to data, but it is unclear, without further investigation, whether the data also has been acquired. Unauthorized persons may have access to information if it is available to them. The term "acquisition," however, suggests that the information is not only available to unauthorized persons, but in fact it has been obtained and/or retained by them for some further use.

In the situations described above where there has been unauthorized access to unsecured individually identifiable health information, the FTC states that it believes the entity that experienced the breach is in the best position to determine whether unauthorized acquisition has taken place. Thus, the rule creates a presumption that unauthorized persons have acquired information if they have access to it, thus creating the obligation to provide breach notification. This presumption may be rebutted with reliable evidence showing that the information was not or could not reasonably have been acquired. Such evidence may be obtained by, among other things, conducting appropriate interviews of employees, contractors, or other third parties; reviewing access logs and sign-in sheets; and/or examining forensic evidence.[9]

For example, if an entity's employee loses a laptop containing unsecured health information in a public place, the information would be accessible to unauthorized persons, giving rise to a presumption that unauthorized acquisition has occurred. The entity may rebut this presumption by showing that the laptop was recovered and that forensic analysis revealed that the files were never opened, altered, transferred, or otherwise compromised.[10]

Accordingly, the initial proposed FTC rule added a second sentence to the definition of breach of security as follows:

> Unauthorized acquisition will be presumed to include unauthorized access to unsecured PHR identifiable health information unless the vendor of personal health records, PHR related entity, or third party service provider that

---

9. 74 Fed. Reg. 17,915–16.
10. *Id.*

experienced the breach has reliable evidence showing that there has not been, or could not reasonably have been, any unauthorized acquisition of such information.[11]

Some may ask how workable a notification system is that turns on the ability of a vendor whose data has been breached to show that, nonetheless, the information has not been "acquired."

Limiting PHI and Access to the "Minimum Necessary"

Under the HIPAA Privacy Rule, a covered entity must make reasonable efforts to limit protected health information to the minimum necessary to accomplish the intended purpose of the use, disclosure, or request. In promulgating the interim final rule, HHS notes that "uses and disclosures that impermissibly involve more than the minimum necessary information in violation of §§ 164.502(b) and 164.514(d) may qualify as breaches under this subpart."[12] What does this language mean? How will an entity know what the minimum necessary is? Is this standard objective? Does the mere use of protected health information that exceeds the minimum necessary to meet a legitimate request for individually identifiable health information by a covered entity constitute a breach in and of itself? In other words, does an authorized disclosure become unauthorized— and a breach—if the disclosure includes more information than the minimum necessary to meet the otherwise legitimate request for information? Does the statutory definition of "breach" contemplate such a result? And if an unauthorized disclosure constitutes a breach, does it matter if the improper release includes more information than the minimum necessary?

On the other hand, HHS states that the use or disclosure of protected health information that is incident to an otherwise permissible use or disclosure that occurs "despite reasonable safeguards and proper minimum necessary measures would not be a violation of the Privacy Rule" and, therefore, not a "potential breach" of HITECH. What does this mean? Should this disclosure be evaluated consistent with other requirements of the regulation and the statute itself? Does this "standard" square with the concept of minimum necessary? If additional information is disclosed beyond that which is appropriate in the circumstance, is the disclosure of this information beyond the "minimum necessary"?

Indeed, the HIPAA Privacy Rule contains exceptions to the minimum necessary standard, including requests by a health care provider for treatment purposes.[13] Required policies pursuant to HIPAA include identification of individuals or classes of persons within the covered entity who need access to carry out their duties. Moreover, the Privacy Rule permits a covered entity to rely on the judgment of the party requesting the information that is needed.[14] In fact, an entire medical record may be released only "if justified." The agency incorporated the requirement apparently due to its view that "it is

---

11. 74 Fed. Reg. 17,916. *See also* 74 Fed. Reg. 42,966 (similar commentary).
12. 74 Fed. Reg. 42,744.
13. *See* 45 C.F.R. § 164.502(b)(2).
14. *Id.* § 164.514(d)(3)(iii).

sound practice not to use or disclose private medical information that is not necessary to satisfy a legitimate request for the information."

For example, a hospital may not be able, consistent with HIPAA, to grant nurses access to all patient records, but "a hospital could implement a policy that permitted nurses access to all protected health information of patients in their ward while they are on duty." A health plan could permit its underwriting analysts unrestricted access to aggregate claims information for rate-setting purposes, but require documented approval from its department manager to obtain specific identifiable claims records of a member for the purpose of determining the cause of unexpected claims that could influence renewal premium rate setting."[15] However, "for non-routine disclosures, a covered entity must develop reasonable criteria for determining, and limiting disclosure to, only the minimum amount of protected health information necessary to accomplish the purpose of the disclosure. They also must establish and implement procedures for reviewing such requests for disclosures on an individual basis in accordance with these criteria."[16]

In brief, as a factor to be evaluated as a potential breach under HITECH, the minimum necessary standard serves to incorporate yet another level of complexity for practitioners and others to address in determining whether a breach has occurred.

Finally, we note that the agency observes that not all violations of the HIPAA Privacy Rule will be violations of this subpart, notably omitting a reference to the statute.[17] Since the definitions of "protected health information" are the same in both HIPAA and HITECH, we can only assume that the agency is distinguishing HIPAA from HITECH based on its regulatory interpretations of HITECH's requirements. Furthermore, not all violations of the HIPAA Security Rule "constitute a potential breach under this subpart," because the HIPAA Security Rule provides for the administrative, physical, and technical safeguards and organizational requirements for electronic protected health information, but does not govern uses and disclosures of protected health information.[18] However, the HIPAA statute itself provides, "Each person . . . who maintains or transmits health information shall maintain reasonable and appropriate administrative, technical, and physical safeguards . . . to protect against any reasonably anticipated . . . unauthorized uses or disclosures of the information."[19]

When is a breach of the security rule not a breach of HITECH? And if the agency's proposition is true, is their explanation fully accurate?

The Concept of "Harm" and Risk Assessments

The HHS interim final rule implementing HITECH further defines "breach" as the acquisition, access, use, or disclosure of protected health information that *compromises* the security or privacy of the protected health information. It defines "compromise" as "poses a significant risk of financial, reputational, or other harm to the individual."[20] As such, the HHS interim final rule contemplates a "harm threshold." Although the agency

---

15. *See* 65 Fed. Reg. 82-462–01 at 544.
16. *Id.*
17. 74 Fed. Reg. 42,744.
18. *Id.*
19. 65 Fed. Reg. *supra* at 544.
20. 74 Fed. Reg. 42,767.

has employed a principle limiting the statute's notification requirement to breaches resulting in harm, neither the word "harm" nor that concept appears in the statute. Indeed, HHS commented that covered entities "will need to perform a risk assessment to determine "the likely risk of harm caused by a breach."[21] Apparently, the words "will need to" are obligatory in the regulator's mind. Covered entitles are referred to OMB Memorandum M-07-16 for the factors that need to be considered in determining whether the breach at issue poses a risk of harm to affected individuals.[22] On the contrary, the FTC final rule view of harm is more limited, that is, only accidental breaches that do not result in any harm are exempted from a notification requirement. Its commentary suggests the agency may study this issue in the future.[23]

The regulatory imposed standard of "harm" has given rise to serious criticism of the interim final rule promulgated by HHS. Both HHS and the Federal Trade Commission (FTC) have issued interim final rules or regulations designed to implement the requirements of HITECH. In addition, on July 10, 2010, HHS issued an additional proposed regulation to the HIPAA's Privacy and Security Rules to reflect the requirements of HITECH. Significant changes to the rules include expanding individuals' rights to access their information and restrict information to health plans; imposing a direct requirement that business associates of HIPAA covered entities comply with HIPAA's privacy and security requirements, setting new limitations on the use and disclosure of protected health information; and prohibiting the sale of protected health information without patient consent.[24] Abruptly, on August 1, 2010 HHS withdrew a proposed final breach notification rule from OMB review prior to publication "to allow for further consideration, given the Department's experience to date in administering the regulations."[25] Until such time as a new final rule is issued, the HHS Interim Final Rule remains in effect.

In withdrawing it final breach notification rule—apparently modeled after its interim final rule—HHS may be responding to criticism received from Congressional committees and privacy advocates that the agency's "harm standard," appearing nowhere in HITECH narrowed the requirement to notify individuals of breaches of protected health information too greatly and inconsistent with the intent of Congress.[26]

Under the agency created harm standard, only breaches of PHI posing a significant risk of financial, reputational, or other harm to individuals require notification.[27] As of this writing, however, the Interim Final Rule—and the harm standard—remains

---

21. 74 Fed. Reg. 42,744.

22. *Id.* at n.7.

23. Commentary accompanying the FTC final rule suggests that the agency believes that its standard already takes harm into account, e.g., accidental breaches when PHI is viewed inappropriately yet without harm to the individual do not warrant notification. In addition, the FTC notes that due to the sensitivity of information contained in PHRs, companies need proper incentives to implement policies to safeguard such information, i.e., the broader the notification standard, the more incentive for the company to safeguard sensitive PHRs and the information set forth there. *Id.* 74 Fed. Reg. 42,966. *See* 42 Fed. Reg. 42,967.

24. *See* www.hhs.gov/ocr/privacy/hipaa/understanding/coveredentities/hitechprm.html.

25. Announcement *available at* www.hhs.gov/ocr/privacy/hipaa/administrative/breachnotificationrule/finalrule update.

26. *See, e.g.,* D. Rath, HHS Withdraws Breach Notification Rule (citing criticism of the harm standard), *available at* www.healthcare-informatics.com.

27. 45 CFR § 164.402(1)(i).

in effect. The reader should show particular attention to how the harm standard narrows the notification requirement and complicates the implementation of a statute that promises the American people on its face that each will be notified when their PHI is breached. Congress intended in enacting HITECH that citizens whose PHI was breached to be notified so that could take immediate steps to protect themselves from identity theft and other fraud.

On October 1, 2009, the chairmen of the House committees that drafted the breach notification provisions of HITECH wrote to the Secretary of HHS criticizing the imposition of a harm standard.[28] The letter states directly that "ARRA's statutory language does not imply a harm standard." In fact, during deliberations by the House Committee on Energy and Commerce, a harm standard was considered and explicitly rejected. The letter indicates that Congress intended a "black and white" standard, that is, all individuals subject to a breach of their electronic medical records or other medical information are to be notified. The committee chairmen stated, "The primary purpose for mandatory breach notification is to provide incentives for health care entities to protect data. . . ." These views were echoed by the advocacy group Watchdog in a strongly worded letter condemning the "harm standard."[29] The group wrote that it was "outrageous" to allow health care providers to decide when to notify consumers of data breaches.[30] On the other hand, Premier, a provider alliance and group purchasing organization, wrote to the HHS Secretary urging that the "harm standard" be kept, citing penalties for violations as the best means of ensuring compliance with HITECH's breach notification requirements.[31]

Risk Assessment

The regulations contemplate the conduct of a risk assessment when a breach occurs within the meaning of the statute. The commentary accompanying the HHS interim final rule states that in performing a risk assessment, covered entities "may need to consider a number or combination of factors, including several identified by the agency, as well as the aforementioned OMB Memorandum."[32]

The covered entity needs to consider "who impermissibly used the information and to whom the information was impermissibly disclosed."[33] If, for example, a covered entity discloses the information to another entity covered by the HIPAA Privacy and Security Rules or to a federal agency obliged to comply with statutes protecting privacy

---

28. Letter dated October 1, 2009, to Kathleen Sebelius, Secretary, Department of Health and Human Services, signed by Henry Waxman, Chairman, Committee on Energy and Commerce; John Dingell, Chairman Emeritus, Committee on Energy and Commerce; Charles Rangel, Chairman, Committee on Ways and Means; Frank Pallone, Chairman, Subcommittee on Energy and Commerce; Pete Stark, Chairman, Subcommittee on Health, Committee on Ways and Means; and Joe Barton, Ranking Member, Committee on Energy and Commerce.

29. Letter dated October 29, 2009 to Sebelius, Secretary, HHS, signed by J. Simpson, Consumer WatchDog, *available at* www.consumerwatchdog.org/resources/ltrSebelius102209.pdf.

30. *Id.*

31. Letter dated October 22, 2009 to Sebelius, Secretary, HHS, signed by B. Childs, Vice-President for Public Affairs, Premier, *available at* www.premierinc.com/advocacy/issues/09/HIT/HITECHbreachcomment_ltr10-22-09 .pdf.

32. 74 Fed. Reg. 42,745.

33. 74 Fed. Reg. 42,744.

and information security,[34] the risk of harm may be low. On the other hand, a disclosure to an entity without these obligations may pose a greater risk of harm. The regulators also indicate that the type and amount of protected health information involved in the impermissible disclosure is a factor. In addition, the risk assessment must be "fact specific" and keep in mind that many forms of health information, not merely information about sexually transmitted diseases or mental health, "should be considered sensitive."[35]

These factors are reflective of many of the elements found in OMB's Memorandum M-07-16. To assess the risk of harm, the OMB Memorandum outlines a risk assessment focused on five factors:

1. Nature of the data elements breached (consider the data elements in their context and the broad range of potential harms from their disclosure to unauthorized individuals).
2. Number of individuals affected (may determine the method for notification, but should not be the determining factor in whether notification should be provided).
3. Likelihood the information is accessible and usable (likelihood the information will be or has been used by unauthorized individuals).
4. Likelihood the breach may lead to harm (consider a broad range of potential harms, and the likelihood harm will occur).
5. Ability of the agency to mitigate the risk of harm (act to contain the breach, take appropriate countermeasures, such as monitoring system(s) for misuse of the personal information and patterns of suspicious behavior). "Such mitigation may not prevent the use of the personal information for identity theft, but it can limit the associated harm."[36]

The OMB Memorandum references several possible harms associated with the loss of personal indentifying information. In the words of the Memorandum: "Such harms may include the effect of a breach on confidentiality or fiduciary responsibility, the potential for blackmail, the disclosure of private facts, mental pain and emotional distress, the disclosure of address information for victims of abuse, the potential for secondary uses of information which could result in fear or uncertainty, or the unwarranted exposure leading to humiliation or loss of self-esteem." A "list of recipient patients at a clinic for the treatment of contagious disease" is also listed as an example.[37]

"Risk Assessment" as a Tool for Determining Harm—A Critique

First, risks assessments are necessarily complex. How much risk equals harm? How useful are the OMB factors in determining whether notification is required based on the specific facts of a particular breach? Risks assessments are more commonly conducted as the basis for developing security plans for information systems as a whole; not to evaluate specific breaches of information after they occur.

---

34. Such statutes include the Privacy Act of 1974, 5 U.S.C. § 552a, and the Federal Information Security Management Act of 2002, 44 U.S.C.A. §§ 3541 *et seq.*
35. 74 Fed. Reg. 42,745.
36. OMB Memorandum M-07-16, at 14 (May 22, 2007).
37. *Id.* at 15.

Second, the OMB "factors" are very broad and fail to establish any objective standards. The agency commentary accompanying the HHS interim final rule is not much more helpful. At best, it identifies factors "to be considered." Reasonable individuals can come to different conclusions based on the same facts—even after giving them full consideration. Significantly, in addressing the ability of an entity to mitigate the risk of harm, the authors of the OMB Memorandum acknowledge that "where the potential injury is more individualized [the harm] may be difficult to determine."[38] Indeed, HHS officials acknowledge that a risk assessment can properly reach the conclusion that the "risk of identifying a particular individual is so small that the use or disclosure poses no significant risk of harm to any individuals."[39] All these "standards" are subjective; no one is given more weight than another; covered entities are invited to make judgments.

Third, the OMB memorandum references "guidance from the Identity Theft Task Force" for an assessment as to whether the loss of the information might result in identity theft—yet another source of information that a covered entity would be obliged to consider in reaching any judgment as to whether the breach resulted in harm.

In sum, the HHS interim final rule reflects the requirements of the HITECH statute as embellished by HIPAA and the agency's concept of harm, guidance for which may be found in the commentary accompanying the interim final rule, OMB Memorandum M-07-16, and the Identity Theft Task Force established by Federal Executive Order 13,402.

Exceptions to the "Breach Rule"

Section 13400 of subtitle D (Privacy) of HITECH sets forth the following exception to the meaning of "breach": [It is not considered a breach] "where an unauthorized person to whom such information is disclosed would not reasonably have been able to retain such information."

The current HHS guidance exempts from "breach" situations in which a covered entity or business associate has a "good faith belief" that the unauthorized person to whom disclosure of PHI was made would not reasonably be able to retain the information. What is a "good faith belief"? Is it likely that reasonable individuals could come to different judgments based on the same facts albeit in good faith?

In addition, a "breach" does not include—

    (i) any unintentional acquisition, access, or use of protected health information by an employee or individual acting under the authority of a covered entity or business associate if—

        (I) such acquisition, access, or use was made in good faith and within the course and scope of the employment or other professional relationship of such employee or individual, respectively, with the covered entity or business associate; and

        (II) such information is not further acquired, accessed, used, or disclosed by any person; or

38. *Id.* at 15.
39. 74 Fed. Reg. 42,746.

(ii) any inadvertent disclosure from an individual who is otherwise authorized to access protected health information at a facility operated by a covered entity or business associate to another similarly situated individual at same facility; and

(iii) any such information received as a result of such disclosure is not further acquired, accessed, used, or disclosed without authorization by any person.[40]

This exception raises questions. For example, does the phrase "would not reasonably have been able to retain such information" preclude coverage where a person browsed through personal health records, did not copy them, but passed on but one fact, inadvertently or otherwise, to a third party? Or if an authorized person, such as a nurse, properly accessed the medical record of a celebrity, did not retain the records, but talked about the celebrity with a nurse at a different branch of the same organization in a telephone conversation that is overheard by a visitor who passes the information along to a tabloid? The latest guidance suggests that the further use or disclosure of the information takes the disclosure out of the exception.[41] However, the guidance does not specifically address the nuances cited in the examples above, for example, the inadvertent further disclosure of information by individuals. There are probably hundreds of different examples not contemplated by the regulatory language. How will each of these play out?

In addition, the guidance in clarifying "similarly situated individual" and "same facility" has broadened these concepts to narrow notification requirements in response to comments.[42] "Similarly situated individuals" are those in the same organization who are authorized to have access to the information; "same facility" includes "organized health care arrangement," irrespective of size or location. "Breaches" caused by these individuals do not trigger notification requirements.

Limitations of Notification Requirements

The HHS guidance otherwise seeks to limit the scope of the statute's notification requirements by various interpretations of the statute.

HHS suggests that there may be circumstances where the covered entity can take immediate steps to mitigate impermissible use or further disclosure of the PHI when it appears a breach has occurred. If, for example, the recipient of the information disclosed by a breach can give assurances that the information will not be further used or disclosed—or even destroyed, the agency "interprets" that the statute has not been violated because the information has not been compromised—notwithstanding the breach.[43] Another example of a breach that is not a "breach" is the return of the material obtained by the unauthorized recipient prior to its use for an improper purpose.[44]

---

40. The most recent HHS guidance changes the terms "employee or individual" in paragraph (i) to "workforce members" in order to cover individuals under the direct control of an employer irrespective of whether the individual is being paid or not, *e.g.,* volunteers. 74 Fed. Reg. 42,747.
41. *Id.*
42. *Id.*
43. 74 Fed. Reg. 72,745.
44. *Id.*

These "opinions" suggest that the agency finds "minor" breaches unworthy of the statute's protections.

In addition, the agency advises that in the performance of a risk assessment, covered entities and business associates should take into consideration the amount and type of information involved in the breach or impermissible use or disclosure.[45] The guidance suggests that release of the identity of a person and a statement that he or she had been hospitalized would violate the Privacy Rule but not result in significant risk of harm, financial or reputational, to the person—and would not meet the agency's interpretation of "breach." On the other hand, disclosure of information that the person had been hospitalized and received a specific type of service, for example, oncology, might result in the requisite harm contemplated by the regulators.[46] Would the disclosure of the identity of a patient admitted to a treatment facility well known for the treatment of cancer violate the regulations contemplated by the agency? There are an infinite number of types of information created about any person who is hospitalized. The concept of harm may differ greatly from person to person depending on their professional and personal circumstances. Expectations of privacy vary greatly from person to person. At what point does the requisite degree of harm contemplated by the regulators obtain? And how should consensus be reached as to what disclosures are harmful?

HHS has rejected some suggestions for exceptions to the notification rule or modified them. In light of the risk of reidentification of information in a limited data set,[47] the HHS determined, following the receipt of comments, not to use the concept as a method for rendering PHI unusable, unreadable, or indecipherable. However, the agency removed from the definition of "breach" the disclosure of PHI that constitutes a limited data set so long as date of birth and zip code are not included because "we believe that impermissible uses or disclosures of this information . . . would pose a low level of risk."[48] In the words of the agency, "A covered entity that impermissibly uses or discloses data that is stripped of the 16 direct identifiers . . . , zip codes, and dates of birth, may take advantage of the exception to what is a breach, regardless of the intended purpose of the use or disclosure or whether a data use agreement was in place."[49] To demonstrate coverage within the "narrow exception," a covered entity need only show that the lost information lacked the identifiers.[50]

---

45. *Id.*

46. *Id.*

47. The issue of "re-identification" is very current. A *New York Times* article reported that researchers were able to reidentify formerly anonymous Netflix users by comparing film preferences of some customers on the Internet Movie Database (http://www.imdb.com), and by using e-mails and other distinguishing information. In addition, a researcher was able to identify the medical records of William Weld, then governor of Massachusetts, by correlating birthdays, ZIP codes, and gender in voter registration rolls and information published by the state's insurance department. Natasha Singer, *When 2+2 Equals a Privacy Question*, N.Y. TIMES, Oct. 18, 2009.

48. 74 Fed. Reg. 42,746.

49. *Id.*

50. *Id.*

Heightened HIPAA Enforcement Under HITECH

HITECH contains a number of provisions that increase the potential sanctions that may be imposed under HIPAA. On October 30, 2009, HHS published an interim final rule to conform the HIPAA enforcement regulations to the penalty provisions of HITECH.[51] This new rule revises the HIPAA enforcement regulations with respect to the imposition of civil penalties by incorporating the HITECH categories of violations and tiered ranges of civil monetary penalties for violations of the new HIPAA rules. On February 22, 2010, the federal government, through the HHS Office for Civil Rights, began enforcement of the HITECH breach notification provision—and its accompanying penalties.

HITECH establishes a tiered system of civil penalties based on the nature of the improper conduct. Violation categories are set forth in Section 1176(a)(1) of the statute. The interim final rule provides for four categories of penalties based on the degree of culpability.

TABLE 8.1
HITECH Enforcement Provisions

	Each violation	All such violations of an identical provision in a calendar year
(A) Did Not Know	$1,000–50,000	$1,500,000
(B) Reasonable Cause	$1,000–50,000	$1,500,000
(C)(i) Willful Neglect— Corrected	$10,000–50,000	$1,500,000
(C)(ii) Willful Neglect— Not Corrected	$50,000	$1,500,000

Pursuant to the statute, the Government Accountability Office (GAO) is directed to prepare a report within 18 months of the enactment of HITECH recommending a methodology to allow affected individuals to share in civil monetary penalties imposed under HIPAA. HHS must adopt such a methodology within three years of HITECH's enactment. Once implemented, this provision is intended to increase the incentive for individuals to file privacy and security complaints with HHS.[52]

- State attorneys general are granted authority to bring civil actions to enforce HIPAA. HHS has been directed to evaluate how to enable affected individuals to share in penalties collected for violating HIPAA.[53]
- HITECH "clarifies" that criminal penalties may be imposed under HIPAA on any individual or entity that wrongly obtains or discloses protected health

---

51. 76 Fed. Reg. 56,123.
52. *See* HITECH § 13410(c)(2), (3).
53. *See* HITECH § 13410(e).

information maintained by a covered entity. This provision is intended to end the debate over whether HIPAA authorizes the imposition of criminal penalties only on covered entities, expanding coverage to vendors and others acting as "business associates."

- HHS is directed to conduct periodic audits of covered entities and business associates to evaluate HIPAA compliance. In the past, HHS enforcement, at best, consisted of responding to complaints.[54]

Summary

The most recent HHS guidance suggests that in order to determine whether a breach occurred, a covered entity or business associate must evaluate the following issues:

1. Whether there has been an impermissible use or disclosure of PHI under the HIPAA Privacy Rule;
2. Whether the impermissible use or disclosure compromises the security or privacy of PHI, that is, when there is significant risk of financial, reputational, or other harm to the individual; and
3. Whether the otherwise impermissible use or disclosure of PHI falls within one of the exceptions enunciated in the statute or regulations.

WHAT IS UNSECURED PROTECTED HEALTH INFORMATION?

Encryption and Destruction

"Unsecured protected health information" means protected health information that is not secured through the use of a technology or methodology to be specified by the HHS Secretary in guidance to be issued in the future, and annually thereafter.[55]

However, the initial HHS guidance provided an interim definition:

> Unsecured protected health information shall mean protected health information that is not secured by a technology standard that renders protected health information unusable, unreadable, or indecipherable to unauthorized individuals and is developed or endorsed by a standards developing organization that is accredited by the American National Standards Institute.[56]

On April 27, 2009, HHS issued guidance that identified two methods for rendering PHI "unusable, unreadable, or indecipherable" to unauthorized individuals: encryption and destruction.[57] This guidance was formalized on August 24, 2009, when HHS issued its interim final rule (with request for comments).[58] No changes were made to the

---

54. *See* HITECH § 13411.

55. HITECH §§ 13401(c), 13402(h)(1)(A).

56. HITECH § 13402(h)(1)(B). A standards-developing organization must be accredited by the American National Standards Institute (ANSI), including the National Council for Prescription Drug Programs, which develops standards for information transactions, data elements, or any other standard. ANSI, About ANSI, *available at* http://www.ansi.org.

57. 74 Fed. Reg. 19,006.

58. 74 Fed. Reg. 42,740, at 42.

standard enunciated in the April interim rule in the subsequent agency's August 2009 guidance.

The HHS guidance states that by using the encryption and/or destruction methods it describes, covered entities and business associates may determine which breaches require compliance with the notification requirement.[59] If a breach does not involve "unsecured" PHI, that is, PHI that has been rendered unusable, unreadable, or indecipherable by unauthorized individuals by one of the prescribed methods, the covered entity or business associate is not required to provide notification in the event of a breach. As such, the guidance proffered by HHS offers an approach by which a covered entity or business associate may protect itself, insofar as the breach notification requirements are concerned, from addressing any breaches of "secured" information. Covered entities and business associates would, of course, still be obligated under the HHS Privacy Rule and Security Rule to adopt measures designed to prevent such breaches.

The HHS guidance stated:

> Encryption is one method of rendering electronic PHI unusable, unreadable, or indecipherable to unauthorized persons. The successful use of encryption depends upon two main features: The strength of the encryption algorithm and the security of the decryption key or process. The specification of encryption methods in this guidance includes the condition that the processes or keys that might enable decryption have not been breached.[60]

More specifically, the guidance provides that protected health information (PHI) is rendered unusable, unreadable, or indecipherable to unauthorized individuals only if encrypted or destroyed.

The HHS guidance clearly specifies encryption and defines the concept.

Electronic PHI has been encrypted as specified in the HIPAA Security Rule by "the use of an algorithmic process to transform data into a form in which there is a low probability of assigning meaning without use of a confidential process or key" and such confidential process or key that might enable decryption has not been breached.[61]

The guidance amplified by both HHS interim final rules further states that encryption processes identified below have been tested by the National Institute of Standards and Technology (NIST) and judged to meet this standard:

> Valid encryption processes for data-at-rest are consistent with NIST Special Publication 800–111, *Guide to Storage Encryption Technologies for End User Devices* [for example, computers].

> Valid encryption processes for data-in-motion are those that comply, as appropriate, with NIST Special Publications 800-52, Guidelines for the Selection and Use of Transport Layer Security (TSL) Implementations; 800-77, Guide to IPsecs VPNs; or 800-113, Guide to SSL VPNs, or others that are Federal Information Processing Standards (FIPS) 140–2 "validated."[62]

---

59. *See* 74 Fed. Reg. 42,741.
60. 74 Fed. Reg. 19,006 (Apr. 27, 2009).
61. *Id.*
62. *See* 74 Fed. Reg. 42,742.

The HHS August interim final rule clarifies the definitions of "data in motion," "data at rest," "data in use," and "data disposed" in response to comments.[63]

As well, the HHS guidance sets forth plainly the requirements for destruction.

> The media on which the PHI is stored or recorded has been destroyed in one of the following ways:
>
> > Paper, film, or other hard copy media have been shredded or destroyed such that the PHI cannot be read or otherwise cannot be reconstructed.
> >
> > Electronic media have been cleared, purged, or destroyed consistent with NIST Special Publication 800–88, *Guidelines for Media Sanitization*, such that the PHI cannot be retrieved.[64]

This HHS guidance also addresses the destruction of PHI in both paper and electronic form as a method for rendering such information unusable, unreadable, or indecipherable to unauthorized individuals. If PHI is destroyed prior to disposal in accordance with the guidance, no breach notification is required following access to the disposed hard copy or electronic media by unauthorized persons. Query—what data could anyone find if the material has been "destroyed" properly?

"Safe Harbor"

The guidance creates what is essentially a "safe harbor." At its core, the guidance establishes criteria for the encryption and destruction standard for health information. If met, covered entities and business associates will not be subject to HITECH's data breach notification requirements for breaches of data that are encrypted or destroyed in accordance with the NIST technologies and methodologies specified in the HHS guidance. The FTC adopts the HHS guidance in its proposed final rule[65] with little comment.

The HHS interim final rule recognizes that covered entities may adopt "a method other than encryption or an encryption algorithm that is not specified in this guidance."[66] However, the agency warns that even if the covered entity is in compliance with its Security Rule,[67] the entity will be required to notify affected individuals of any breaches within the meaning of HITECH and its guidance. In this manner, the agency reminds readers that in implementing the HITECH statute, the safe harbor applies only to a breach involving records that are encrypted.[68]

---

63. 74 Fed. Reg. 42,742. These definitions represent the only significant change from the initial guidance to the HHS April interim final rule.

64. *See id.* at 72,743.

65. 74 Fed. Reg. 42,969

66. 74 Fed. Reg. 42,742.

67. HIPAA, 45 C.F.R. § 164.

68. In issuing its April 27, 2009, guidance regarding acceptable methodologies that render PHI unusable, unreadable, or indecipherable to unauthorized individuals, HHS indicated an interest in receiving comments on other methodologies, e.g., fingerprint-protected Universal Serial Bus (USB) drives, and, more generally, whether there are other methods for rendering PHI, both in electronic and paper form, unusable, unreadable, or indecipherable to unauthorized individuals. The interim final rule does not address any of these methodologies. Finally, the HHS Office for Civil Rights asked whether any of its recommended measures creating the specified safe harbor would fail to render information unusable, unreadable, or indecipherable to unauthorized individuals. The subsequent August 2009 interim final rule is silent here.

At the outset, it should be noted that NIST is changing its encryption guidance in the special publications specified by HHS as providing the safe harbor for data breach notification. The Recommendation in draft Special Publication 800-131 provides more specific guidance for transitions to stronger cryptographic keys and more robust algorithms.[69] This will no doubt provide confusion and potential litigation about whether the safe harbor applies in the event of a breach.

Furthermore, a review of the professional standards cited in the HHS guidance indicates that the NIST publications do not provide prescriptive standards or a series of prescribed steps to accomplish a goal. Instead, the cited NIST materials consist of descriptions of various steps that may be taken to mitigate risks. For example, NIST Special Publication 800-111, Guide to Storage Encryption Technologies for End User Devices (personal computers, PDAs, or removable storage media) provides an "overview" of "recommendations to facilitate more efficient and effective storage, encryption solution design, implementation, and management." In general, it describes security controls for storage and common types of storage encryption technologies. While this guidance provides helpful hints about issues that should be considered, it does not specify a minimum level of encryption that would be considered for an organization to be in compliance. Thus, it contains no system that an information security manager might adopt—it suggests the "pieces" that, if properly linked, might afford the necessary security.

It is noteworthy that these NIST guidelines emphasize that "authentication" of the user is a critical component of any adequate security system, suggesting that encryption is only one component of an appropriate information security system. The concepts associated with the encryption key or access mechanism to the encrypted material referenced in the NIST guidelines receive little attention in the HHS guidance. In the interim final rule, HHS states that access controls are "not included" in the guidance. The agency merely emphasizes the "benefit of strong controls."[70] Finally, the NIST guidelines note that any system must be implemented and properly maintained or "some files that should be protected may not be."[71] The concepts of authentication, security of the access key, and proper implementation and maintenance of the information system are merely referenced or not included in the HHS guidance.

Likewise, the NIST Guidelines for the Selection and Use of Transport Layer Security (TLS) Implementations provides a brief introduction to computer communications architecture concepts. While some specific approaches are specified, flexibility is granted.[72] While only TLS may be used for the protection of federal data, there is an exception for the transfer of non-federal data that permits the "use of SSLv3." Clients are directed not to use any protocol less than SSLv3.[73] Does this suggest that private health entities need not meet the federal standard?

---

69. NIST Recommendation for the Transitioning of Cryptographic Algorithms and Key Sizes, Draft Special Pub. 800-131 (Jan. 12, 2010) [hereinafter NIST Recommendation].
70. 74 Fed. Reg. 42,742. The discussion of access controls is framed in terms of whether strong access controls ought to be viewed as a means of rendering PHI unusable, unreadable, or indecipherable to unauthorized individuals. See id. Although the agency recognizes the importance of strong access controls, none of the guidance articulates a clear understanding of the relationship of the security of the encryption key to the vitality of the encryption process. Id.
71. NIST Recommendation at 3–4.
72. See, e.g., § 2.2.2 describing various symmetric encryption algorithms.
73. NIST Recommendation at 21.

In any event, the NIST guidelines are general in nature rather than prescriptive. If the covered entity is free to pick and choose among the many options, the availability of the safe harbor to a particular entity in a specific situation will almost assuredly quickly become a matter of dispute; did the covered entity comply with the HHS guidance by implementing appropriate NIST "standards," and, if so, which ones and to what extent?

It is unclear how adherence to the approaches identified in the NIST materials merits the safe harbor referenced in the HHS guidance. It appears that an entity could devise a proper system for the encryption of data-at-rest using the concepts identified in the guidelines—but the wide variations in methods and approaches referenced by NIST, together with the complexities associated with the varied needs of different organizations, will not necessarily ensure a successful outcome in every case. The HHS guidance says nothing about the implementation of the encryption. Chapter 5 presents a number of cases in which massive data breaches occurred even though sensitive personal records were encrypted. In each case, at crucial points, the information was not protected, or an important security control was not implemented properly.

The degree to which covered entities currently encrypt PHI remains a matter of some speculation. In a November 2009 security survey, Symantec noted that only 35 percent of survey respondents, which consisted primarily of hospitals and multihospital delivery systems, utilize network encryption; 67 percent implement encryption of data in transmission; fewer than half of the entities encrypt stored data. One third of the participants reported that their organization had had at least one known case of identify theft. These facts raise questions as to the preparedness of entities to implement HITECH's data breach notification requirements.[74]

WHEN DOES A BREACH TRIGGER NOTICE OBLIGATIONS?

A breach is "discovered" as of the first day on which the breach is:

- Known to such entity or associate, respectively (including any person, other than the individual committing the breach, that is an employee, officer, or other agent of such entity or associate, respectively), or
- Should reasonably have been known to such entity or associate (or person) to have occurred.[75]

Moreover, the FTC follows this approach in its rule.[76] Section 318.3(c) provides that a breach "shall be treated as discovered as of the first day on which such breach is known to a vendor of personal health records, PHR related entity, or third party service provider, respectively (including any person, other than the individual committing the breach, that is an employee, officer, or other agent of such a vendor of personal health records, PHR related entity, or third party service provider, respectively) or should reasonably have been known to such vendor of personal health records, PHR related entity, or third party service provider (or person) to have occurred.

Section 13407(c) of HITECH specifies the standard for the "discovery of a breach." FTC-regulated entities are covered by the same standard.

---

74. Second Annual HIMSS Security Survey, sponsored by Symantec.
75. HITECH § 13402(c); *see also* 74 Fed. Reg. 42,749.
76. 74 Fed. Reg. 17,923–24.

Regarding the "reasonably should have been known" standard, the FTC expects entities that collect and store unsecured individually identifiable health information to maintain reasonable security measures, including breach detection measures, which should assist them in discovering breaches in a timely manner. If an entity fails to maintain such measures, and thus fails to discover a breach, such failure could constitute a violation of the rule because the entity "reasonably" should have known about the breach. The FTC recognizes, however, that certain breaches may be very difficult to detect, and that an entity with strong breach detection measures may nevertheless fail to discover a breach. In such circumstances, the failure to discover the breach would not constitute a violation. It is entirely unclear what the FTC might find to be a breach that falls within the broad, generalized "definition" of "difficult to detect."

The HHS interim final rule modifies the statutory language by incorporating the phrase "by exercising reasonable diligence" to clarify the statute's "reasonably have known" standard. The agency deems it "important" for covered entities to implement systems for discovering breaches and to train employees to be aware of the need to timely report privacy and security "incidents."

In any event, an entity is required to act whenever a breach comes to its attention and where the entity should have reasonably known of the breach by exercising reasonable diligence.

WHAT ARE THE REQUIREMENTS FOR BREACH NOTIFICATION?
Who Must Be Notified?
A business associate must notify

- the covered entity
- the individual
- next of kin of the individual (if the individual is deceased)
- the HHS Secretary

When Must Notice Be Provided?
- As of the first day on which such breach is known.
- Without unreasonable delay and in no case later than 60 calendar days after the discovery of a breach.[77]

---

77. 74 Fed. Reg. 42,749. The FTC notes that the standard for timely notification is "without unreasonable delay," with the 60-day period serving as an outer limit. Thus, in some cases, it may be an "unreasonable delay" to wait until the 60th day to provide notification. For example, if a vendor of personal health records or PHR-related entity learns of a breach, gathers all necessary information, and has systems in place to provide notice, it would be unreasonable to wait until the 60th day to send the notice. There may also be circumstances where a vendor of personal health records or PHR-related entity discovers that its third-party service provider has suffered a breach (e.g., through a customer or whistleblower) before the service provider notifies the vendor or entity that the breach has occurred. In such circumstances, the vendor or entity should treat this breach as "discovered" for purposes of providing timely notification, and should not wait until receiving notice from the service provider to begin taking steps to address the breach.

- Notice may be delayed if authorized for law enforcement purposes—if a law enforcement official determines that a notification, notice, or posting required under this section would impede a criminal investigation or cause damage to national security.

What Form of Notice Is Required?
Individual notice:

- Written notification by first-class mail at the last known address of the individual or the next of kin.
- Electronic mail (if the individual has indicated e-mails as a preference for receiving communications). The notification may be provided in one or more mailings as information is available.
- Telephone or other means, as appropriate (if there is urgency because of possible imminent misuse of unsecured protected health information).

Substitute notice options:

- Web site home page of the covered entity—Conspicuous notice if 10 or more individuals were involved in a breach.
- Major print or broadcast media, including major media in the geographic areas where the individuals affected by the breach likely reside, including establishing a toll-free phone number.
- Media notice is required if the unsecured individually identifiable health information of more than 500 residents of a state or jurisdiction is involved.

Notice to the HHS Secretary:

- 500 or more individuals: Notice must be provided immediately.
- Less than 500 individuals: A covered entity must maintain a log of any breach that has occurred, and annually submit to the Secretary a report documenting breaches that have occurred during the year.

HHS public Web site:

- Post a list that identifies each covered entity involved in a breach in which the unsecured protected health information of more than 500 individuals is acquired or disclosed.

What Is the Content of the Notification?
Notice of a breach shall include, to the extent possible, the following:

1. A brief description of what happened, including the date of the breach and the date of the discovery of the breach, if known.
2. A description of the types of unsecured protected health information that were involved in the breach (such as full name, Social Security number, date of birth, home address, account number, or disability code).

3. The steps individuals should take to protect themselves from potential harm resulting from the breach.[78]
4. A brief description of what the covered entity involved is doing to investigate the breach, to mitigate losses, and to protect against any further breaches.
5. Contact procedures for individuals to ask questions or learn additional information, which shall include a toll-free telephone number, an e-mail address, Web site, or postal address.

Who Is Covered by the Breach Notification Requirements?

Health care is delivered by a wide variety of individuals, organizations, and entities. Under HIPAA and HITECH, a "covered entity" and a "business associate" are subject to the data breach notification provision.

A covered entity is defined by the HIPAA Privacy Rule as:

1. A health plan.
2. A health care clearinghouse.
3. A health care provider who transmits any health information in electronic form in connection with a transaction covered by this subchapter.[79]

HITECH adopts this definition.[80]

With respect to a covered entity, 45 C.F.R. § 160.103 defines a HIPAA business associate as a person who:

(i) On behalf of a covered entity or of an organized health care arrangement . . . in which the covered entity participates, but other than in the capacity of a member of the workforce of such covered entity or arrangement, performs, or assists in the performance of:

(A) A function or activity involving the use or disclosure of individually identifiable health information, including claims processing or administration, data analysis, processing or administration, utilization review, quality assurance, billing, benefit management, practice management, and pricing; or

(B) Any other function or activity regulated by this subchapter; or

(ii) Provides, other than in the capacity of a member of the workforce of such covered entity, legal, actuarial, accounting, consulting, data aggregation . . . , management, administrative, accreditation, or financial services to or for such covered entity, or to or for an

---

78. It is not entirely clear whether the covered entity is always in a position to advise an individual whose PHI has been breached as to steps needed to afford protection from harm. For example, if an individual's electronic medical record has been breached, an array of different information may be disclosed that may vary from person to person. How can a covered entity adequately address these individual situations? Will they have the necessary information to do so?
79. 45 C.F.R. § 160.103.
80. HITECH § 13400(3).

organized health care arrangement in which the covered entity participates, where the provision of the service involves the disclosure of individually identifiable health information from such covered entity or arrangement, or from another business associate of such covered entity or arrangement to the person.[81]

HITECH adopts the definition of "business associate" under HIPAA.[82]

In light of the increased number of entities possessing or having access to individually identifiable health information, both lawyers and medical professionals are engaged in a debate as to what entities fall within the current definitions of "business associate." Those urging greater coverage of the statute's notification provisions argue that many entities, for example, companies operating Web sites that collect and store large amounts of individually identifiable health care information, are already covered by the present definitions. Others argue that it is the intent of HITECH to broaden coverage.

HITECH requires HHS to conduct a study on privacy and security for vendors of personal health records "that are not covered entities or business associates" under the present HIPAA Privacy Rule, 45 C.F.R. 160.103.[83] This study will address potential privacy, security, and breach notification requirements for entities that are not HIPAA-covered entities (1) that offer products or services through the Web site of a vendor of personal health records, (2) that offer products or services through the Web sites of HIPAA-covered entities that offer individuals personal health records (this category differs from the first category in that it covers entities whose applications are offered through the Web sites of HIPAA-covered entities, as opposed to non-HIPAA covered entities; entities may fall into both categories if they offer their applications through both HIPAA-covered Web sites and non-HIPAA covered Web sites) and (3) that access information in a personal health record or send information to a personal health record.

Notwithstanding the requirement for a "study," HITECH expands the notification requirement to these entities through a "Temporary Breach Notification" provision in Section 13407. This "temporary" provision may render any study meaningless.

Under the mandate to issue rules requiring vendors of personal health records to notify individuals when the security of their individually identifiable health information has been breached, the FTC issued proposed rules that would cover the entities identified for study in HITECH Sections 13424(b)(1)(A)(ii)–(iv), that is, vendors of personal health records, PHR-related entities, and third-party service providers.[84] The FTC is not

---

81. "Business associate" has the meaning given in 45 C.F.R. § 160.103.

> A covered entity participating in an organized health care arrangement that performs a function or activity as described by paragraph (1)(i) of this definition for or on behalf of such organized health care arrangement, or that provides a service as described by paragraph (1)(ii) of this definition to or for such organized health care arrangement, does not, simply through the performance of such function or activity or the provision of such service, become a business associate of other covered entities participating in such organized health care arrangement.

45 C.F.R. § 160.103 (Definitions).

82. HITECH § 13400(2).

83. HITECH § 13424(b)(1)(A)(ii)–(iv). Although a study is mandated, HITECH contains a notification provision that applies to each "vendor of personal health records." *See id.* § 13407.

84. Breach Notification Requirements, 74 Fed. Reg. 17,923–24 (proposed April 20, 2009).

waiting for the HHS study commissioned by HITECH prior to taking action to "cover" these entities; it makes the HITECH "temporary" breach notification provisions part of its proposed rule.

The FTC rule recognizes that there are new types of Web-based entities that collect or handle consumers' sensitive health information. Some of these entities offer personal health records which consumers may use as an electronic, individually controlled repository for their medical information. Others provide online applications through which consumers may track and manage different kinds of information in their personal health records. These innovations have the potential to provide numerous benefits for consumers, which can only be realized if they have confidence that the security and confidentiality of their health information will be protected—so the FTC is acting to ensure its views of HIPAA and HITECH privacy and security requirements are immediately applied to these entities.

The FTC rule is significant in light of Google's, Microsoft's, and Revolution Health's Web-based portals with systems of electronic patient health records through which individuals may organize their health records. Through partnerships with HMOs and leading health providers, Google and Microsoft have also established arrangements to serve as repositories for the patient health records created and/or used by these entities. Google has established a pilot project with the Cleveland Clinic to create a system of electronic patient health records called Google Health. Kaiser Permanente, the nation's largest HMO, is conducting a pilot to link its health records system to Microsoft's consumer health storage platform, HealthVault. Revolution Health, founded by AOL cofounder Steve Case, is a "consumer-centric health company" that allows consumers to make "informed choices and offers more convenience and control over their individual healthcare decisions." Companies such as Surescripts are electronic prescribing networks for medications.[85]

After HITECH was enacted—and even before the FTC issued its proposed rule—these companies quickly took the position that they are not covered by the definition of business associates. Google Health product manager Roni Zeigler said: "Our understanding is that HITECH . . . did not change the definition for a covered entity or a business associate, so our service is offered directly to the consumer. Our understanding is that we are neither a covered entity nor a business associate. We're providing a service directly to the consumer or a patient." In short, Google Health has taken the position that it is not covered by HIPAA—and is attempting to escape coverage under the FTC interpretation of HITECH.[86]

---

85. *Google, Microsoft Say HIPAA Stimulus Rule Doesn't Apply to Them*, iHEALTHBEAT, Apr. 8, 2009, *available at* http://www.ihealthbeat.org.

86. Google Health explains its position on its Web site:

> Unlike a doctor or health plan, Google Health is not regulated by the Health Insurance Portability and Accountability Act (HIPAA), a federal law that establishes data confidentiality standards for patient health information. This is because Google does not store data on behalf of health care providers. Instead, our primary relationship is with you, the user. Under HIPAA, you have a right to obtain a copy of your medical records. If you choose to use Google Health, we'll help you store and manage your medical records online.

David Cerino, general manager of Microsoft's Health Solutions Group, said, "We're still outside" of HIPAA. The Microsoft Web site contains a statement that explains the company's position that Microsoft HealthVault is not a covered entity or business associate as defined by HIPAA and is outside of HIPAA.[87]

What Personal Information Is Covered?

The HITECH Act seeks to protect individually identifiable health information.

At the outset, it should be noted that the HITECH Act sets as a national goal the utilization of an electronic record for every American by 2014.[88] In this circumstance, detractors of the legislation fear that privacy rights of citizens may be jeopardized. At least one lawsuit is pending in [federal court] seeking an injunction to adequately protect personal health information and to enjoin federal agency defendants from disbursing the $22 billion budgeted for the electronic health records system contemplated by the HITECH Act.[89]

The definitions in the Act and proposed FTC rules are similar, if not exact, in substance. The definitions of health information and individually protected information in HITECH are borrowed from the Social Security Act, 42 U.S.C. § 1320d (4) and (6), and are found in the HIPAA Privacy Rule.[90]

> "Health information" means any information, whether oral or recorded in any form or medium, that—
>
> (A) is created or received by a health care provider, health plan, public health authority, employer, life insurer, school or university, or health care clearinghouse; and

---

Although Google Health is not covered by HIPAA, we are committed to protecting your privacy. Our Google Health privacy policy governs what information Google Health collects and how we use it, and any violation of that policy can be enforced by the Federal Trade Commission, which takes action against companies that engage in unfair and deceptive trade practices—including violations of their privacy policies.

Google Health, Is Google Health Covered by HIPAA?, http://www.google.com/intl/en-US/health/about/privacy.html.

87. Microsoft HealthVault's HIPAA statement:

> The Microsoft HealthVault team is often asked about our approach to the privacy and security requirements of the Health Insurance Portability and Accountability Act (HIPAA). Microsoft HealthVault is not a covered entity or business associate as defined by HIPAA. The "lay" explanation is quite simple. HIPAA was designed to regulate the flow of health information when it is out of the patient's direct control—for example, when it is forwarded to third-party billing services by a healthcare provider. At the same time, the HIPAA authors clearly recognized that patients have a right to a copy of their own health information, and built into the legislation an explicit mechanism that allows for patients to request and receive that copy. The obligations that HIPAA places on covered entities and business associates do not apply to the copy under the patient's control, because patients are in the best position to decide which parts of their information they want to share, and with whom they share it. HealthVault is, very simply, a tool for individual patients to manage health information that is under their control.

Microsoft HealthVault and HIPAA, *available at* http://clients.metia.com/2877/files/HIPPA_Microsoft_Health Vault.pdf.

88. § 3001 (a)(3).

89. *Available at* http://www.courthousenews.com/2009/07/01/Class_Action_Raises_Privacy_Concerns.

90. *See* 45 C.F.R. 160.103.

(B) relates to the past, present, or future physical or mental health or condition of an individual, the provision of health care to an individual, or the past, present, or future payment for the provision of health care to an individual.

"Individually identifiable health information" means any information, including demographic information collected from an individual, that—

(A) is created or received by a health care provider, health plan, employer, or health care clearinghouse; and

(B) relates to the past, present, or future physical or mental health or condition of an individual, the provision of health care to an individual, or the past, present, or future payment for the provision of health care to an individual, and—

(i)   identifies the individual; or

(ii) with respect to which there is a reasonable basis to believe that the information can be used to identify the individual.

The FTC rule follows these definitions.[91]

Protected health information as defined in HIPAA means individually identifiable health information that is transmitted by electronic media, maintained in any medium described in the definition of electronic, or transmitted or maintained in any other form or medium.[92]

Employment records maintained by a covered entity in its capacity as an employer are excluded from the definition of protected health information. The modifications do not change the fact that individually identifiable health information created, received, or maintained by a covered entity in its health care capacity is protected health information.

PHI includes references not only to the patient, but also their relatives, employers, or household members. It covers personal health records in both electronic as well as paper form.[93]

Electronic protected health information means information that is contained on electronic storage media or transmission media used to exchange information already in electronic storage media.[94] HITECH and the proposed FTC rule adopt this formulation.[95] An electronic health record means an electronic record of health-related information on an individual that is created, gathered, managed, and consulted by authorized health care clinicians and staff.[96]

In sum, the statute, regulations, and proposed FTC rule cover records in electronic form that contain individually identifiable health care information.

---

91. § 318.2 (Definitions), para. (e), 74 Fed. Reg. 17,915 (proposed April 20, 2009).
92. 45 C.F.R. § 160.304. Certain education records are excluded, *e.g.*, student records of psychiatric treatment. *See* 20 U.S.C. § 1232g(a)(4)(B)(iv).
93. S.C. Med. Ass'n. v. Thompson, 327 F.3d 346 (4th Cir. 2003), *cert. denied*, 540 U.S. 981 (2003).
94. 45 C.F.R. § 160.103.
95. 79 Fed. Reg. 17,916.
96. HITECH § 13400 (5).

HEALTH CARE BREACH CHALLENGES REMAIN

To implement HITECH, HHS relies on encryption and data destruction as a means of protecting individually identifiable health care information and provides for timely notification of any breaches of unsecured individually identifiable health information Encryption or destruction provide a "safe harbor" from the statute's notification provisions. Only further experience will allow both medical and legal practitioners to determine whether health care providers will use these tools effectively to protect individually identifiable health care information, including electronic medical records, from unauthorized access and improper use.

CHAPTER 9

Breach Notification and Encryption: A Global Perspective

Ruth Hill Bro

The security breach legislative phenomenon, and corresponding front-page media coverage, started in the United States but now is spreading to the rest of the world. Although privacy laws throughout the world impose obligations to protect personal data, they do not necessarily contain the express obligations found in U.S. state laws to notify data subjects in the event of a breach. As other countries see repeated media reports about data breaches and legislative responses in the United States, and are witnessing data breaches in their own countries in both the private and public sectors, calls for legislation outside the United States are increasing. At the same time, more attention is being paid to limiting the impact of data breaches, specifically by use of encryption—especially where sensitive personal data is concerned.

Increasingly, two of the most pressing questions internationally are these:

1. Is there an obligation to notify data subjects and/or data authorities in the event of a data security breach?
2. Are encryption or any other special measures required to protect sensitive personal data?

These questions and related concerns are explored below.

NOTIFICATION OBLIGATIONS: OVERVIEW

It is not a matter of if, but rather when, data security breach legislation will be enacted outside the United States. Germany updated its federal data protection law in 2009 to include data security breach notification obligations. Japan and Hong Kong impose breach notification obligations through sector-specific "guidance." Other jurisdictions, including Australia, Canada, New Zealand, and the United Kingdom, have actively considered legislative approaches. More countries will join them.

A major force in this regard is likely to be the European Commission, which has developed proposals to reform the EU telecoms regulatory framework, including the ePrivacy Directive (Directive 2002/58/EC on privacy and electronic communications). On November 24, 2009, the European Parliament formally approved the telecom reform package, including the new ePrivacy Directive, which contains an obligation to notify data subjects and competent national authorities in the event of information security breaches. It was published in the Official Journal of the European Union on December 18, 2009.[1] Such notification obligation, however, only applies to providers of electronic communication services such as telecom operators, mobile phone communication services providers, Internet access providers, providers of transmission of digital TV contents (not the content provider), and other providers of electronic communication services. The amended ePrivacy Directive must be implemented into national laws of the EU Member States by May 25, 2011.

As a prelude to legislation, governments are issuing guidance to assist organizations in determining how to respond to data security breaches (including when to notify data subjects and government entities). Jurisdictions outside the United States that provide such guidance include

- Australia: *Guide to Handling Personal Information Security Breaches* (Aug. 2008), *available at* www.privacy.gov.au/materials/types/download/8628/6478.
- Canada: *Key Steps for Organizations in Responding to Privacy Breaches* (includes link to Privacy Breach Checklist) (Aug. 2007), *available at* www.priv.gc.ca/information/guide/2007/gl_070801_02_e.cfm.

    Alberta:
    - Key Steps in Responding to Privacy Breaches (2007), *available at* www.oipc.ab.ca/Content_Files/Files/Publications/Key_Steps_in_Responding_to_a_Privacy_Breach.pdf
    - *Reporting a Privacy Breach to the Office of the Information and Privacy Commissioner of Alberta* (2007), *available at* www.oipc.ab.ca/Content_Files/Files/Publications/Reporting_Privacy_Breaches_to_OIPC_2007.pdf.

    British Columbia:
    - *Key Steps in Responding to Privacy Breaches* (June 2008), *available at* www.oipc.bc.ca/pdfs/Policy/Key_Steps_Privacy_Breaches(June2008).pdf.
    - *Privacy Breach Checklist* (June 2008), *available at* www.oipc.bc.ca/pdfs/Policy/Privacy_Breach_Checklist(June2008).pdf.
    - *Breach Notification Assessment Tool* (Dec. 2006), *available at* www.oipc.bc.ca/pdfs/Policy/ipc_bc_ont_breach.pdf.

---

1. (Directive 2009/136/EC of the European Parliament and of the Council (of 25 November 2009) amending Directive 2002/22/EC on universal service and users' rights relating to electronic communications networks and services, Directive 2002/58/EC concerning the processing of personal data and the protection of privacy in the electronic communications sector and Regulation (EC) No 2006/2004 on cooperation between national authorities responsible for the enforcement of consumer protection laws), at http://eur-lex.europa.eu/LexUriServ/LexUriServ.do?uri=OJ:L:2009:337:0011:0036:EN:PDF.

Ontario:

- *What to Do If a Privacy Breach Occurs: Guidelines for Government Organizations* (Dec. 2006), *available at* www.ipc.on.ca/images/Resources/priv-breach-e.pdf.
- *What to Do When Faced with a Privacy Breach: Guidelines for the Health Sector* (June 2006), *available at* www.ipc.on.ca/images/Resources/up-hprivbreach.pdf.
- *Breach Notification Assessment Tool* (Dec. 2006), *available at* www.oipc.bc.ca/pdfs/Policy/ipc_bc_ont_breach.pdf.

- New Zealand: *Key Steps for Agencies in Responding to Privacy Breaches, and Privacy Breach Checklist* (which together make up the New Zealand Office of the Privacy Commissioner's Privacy Breach Guidance Material) (Feb. 25, 2008), *available at* www.privacy.org.nz/privacy-breach-guidelines-2/.
- United Kingdom: *Guide on data security breach management* (March, 27, 2008), *available at* www.ico.gov.uk.

Sector-specific requirements—not only laws but also official guidance—must also be taken into account when evaluating how to respond to a data breach, including whether to notify data subjects or government authorities. For example, both Hong Kong and Japan have issued official guidance regarding data security breaches with respect to financial institutions. Although such guidance might be characterized as nonbinding or best-practice, the reality is that if an organization falls within that sector and does not adhere to the guidance in these countries, there could be significant consequences, including government investigations with the potential for administrative sanctions.

Even absent specific data security breach notification laws or official government guidance (as discussed above), however, businesses will need to take the following factors into account in deciding whether to notify:

- Notification obligations may stem from contractual arrangements (e.g., the EU Model Processor Clauses, other contracts executed by the company).
- Notification obligations may also arise from registration of a database with a data protection authority (e.g., as in Argentina).
- In many jurisdictions, it is considered best practice to be proactive in the event of a data security breach, including notifying the data subjects affected. Taking proactive steps might be relevant in determining the outcome of any complaints arising as a result of the breach, especially where notification would permit data subjects to take their own steps to avoid or limit the potential harm.
- Virtually all jurisdictions recognize a general obligation, whether under statutory law or otherwise, to take reasonable steps to implement appropriate physical, technical, and organizational measures to protect personal data from misuse or loss and from unauthorized access, modification, or disclosure. Notification of data security breaches may, in some circumstances, be considered to be a reasonable step in such protection of personal information (e.g., notifying data subjects or authorities may help to limit the harm).
- In some jurisdictions, there may be an implied obligation to provide notification regarding a suspected data breach by virtue of the more general requirement under data protection laws that the data subject be notified as to third

parties with whom the personal data is shared and how such information might be used.

- Commercial considerations (particularly the damage to brand reputation from any negative media coverage associated with not warning data subjects of a suspected breach so they can take steps to protect themselves) should also be assessed in determining the organization's risks and the approach it will take.

DATA PROTECTION REQUIREMENTS: OVERVIEW

In the United States, at least a dozen states have enacted legislation that imposes obligations on businesses to protect the personal data they hold, and many more states are considering legislative approaches. Such legislative activity is occurring in large measure in reaction to the steady stream of corporate data security breaches—all too often involving sensitive personal data—being reported by the media. Attention is increasingly shifting in the United States and elsewhere to limiting the impact of data breaches, including through encryption.

As noted above, virtually all jurisdictions recognize a general obligation, whether under statutory law or otherwise, to implement appropriate physical, technical, and organizational measures to protect personal data. Such implementation usually would entail comprehensive periodic risk assessments. These assessments, in turn, would be designed to identify all reasonably foreseeable internal and external threats to the security, confidentiality, and integrity of the data that could result in loss, misuse, unauthorized access, disclosure, alteration, or destruction of the data or the hardware or software on which the data resides. Then, the organization would need to put appropriate controls in place in response to gaps (vulnerabilities) identified in such assessments.

The security measures an organization undertakes must be responsive to the particular threats the organization faces and must address its specific vulnerabilities. The following factors are relevant in deciding what steps to take:

- The sensitivity of the personal information that the organization holds (the more sensitive the data, the greater the level of security likely to be needed).
- The harm that is likely to result to individuals if there is a breach of security (the greater the harm and the likelihood of it occurring, the greater the level of security likely to be needed).
- How the organization stores, processes, and transmits the information (different rules may apply for different media).
- The size, complexity, capabilities, and public profile of the organization (e.g., organizations that are large or have a high profile can be more visible targets for a wider range of bad actors, and additional precautions may thus be warranted).
- The financial heft and sophistication of the organization. For example, failure to undertake legally required steps may be subject to greater scrutiny and censure by the public and regulators where the company is a financial giant that could readily afford the security steps or is sophisticated and knew better or should have known better; perception is everything.
- The industry category of the organization (industry-specific laws or guidelines could affect the organization's obligations).

- The industry standard (if something bad were to happen, the organization could have a hard time defending the fact that it did not do what most in the industry do). For example, as suggested by at least one of the U.S. Federal Trade Commission consent decrees (i.e., Ziff-Davis), failure to at least comply with industry standard practice may be evidence of inadequate security.
- Whether the industry standard is sufficient. For example, the mere fact that most others in the industry are not encrypting would not insulate a company from scrutiny or liability; if great harm could have been averted by encrypting and the cost would not have been prohibitive, a court or government official would likely reject the argument that the company did not need to encrypt simply because most other companies were not encrypting. As the *T.J. Hooper* case[2] pointed out years ago, even the industry standard might not be enough in certain circumstances. In that case, an inexpensive weather radio (though not the industry standard for tugboats towing barges then) was available for relatively little cost and likely could have been used to provide adequate warning of the unexpected storm and thereby avoid a great harm (in this case, a coal shipment was lost when the storm sunk the barge carrying the coal). As Judge Learned Hand noted in that case: "Indeed in most cases reasonable prudence is in fact common prudence, but strictly it is never its measure. A whole calling may have unduly lagged in the adoption of new and available devices. . . . Courts must in the end say what is required; there are precautions so imperative that even their universal disregard will not excuse their omission."[3]
- Whether the burden (B) of the contemplated measure is less than the probability (P) multiplied by the injury (L), otherwise known as the BPL test. Judge Learned Hand articulated the BPL test in another tugboat case, *United States v. Carroll Towing Co.*,[4] 15 years after the *T.J. Hooper* decision: "Since there are occasions when every vessel will break from her moorings, and since, if she does, she becomes a menace to those about her; the owner's duty, as in other similar situations, to provide against resulting injuries is a function of three variables: (1) The probability that she will break away; (2) the gravity of the resulting injury, if she does; (3) the burden of adequate precautions. Possibly it serves to bring this notion into relief to state it in algebraic terms: if the probability be called P; the injury, L; and the burden, B; liability depends upon whether B is less than L multiplied by P: i.e., whether $B < PL$."[5]

Requirements to use encryption to protect sensitive personal data can vary by jurisdiction. In addition to considering the more general security factors identified above, companies should consider the following factors with respect to encryption in particular:

- In many jurisdictions, although appropriate measures are required to protect personal data (as discussed above), no particular encryption requirements may yet apply. Generally speaking, however, the more sensitive the personal data, the higher the level of protection that should be provided.

---

2. *In re* Eastern Transp. Co. v. Northern Barge Corp., 60 F.2d 737 (2d Cir. 1932) (T.J. Hooper case).
3. *Id.* at 740.
4. United States v. Carroll Towing Co. 159 F.2d 169 (2d. Cir. 1947).
5. *Id.* at 173.

- In some jurisdictions, local law prohibits the use of sensitive personal data except in special cases, as enumerated in local law. In cases where some use of sensitive personal data is permitted, it should be treated as confidential and be deleted as soon as it is not required for the specific purpose for which it was collected.
- Requirements to protect sensitive personal data, and to use encryption in particular, may vary by the type of data (health data, credit card information, and the like) or the type of entity (e.g., there may be industry-specific requirements).
- Data protection authorities in some jurisdictions (particularly where the laws are strict, such as those in Italy, Poland, and Spain) have issued regulations or guidance expressly requiring or recommending the use of encryption or similar techniques.
- In many jurisdictions, particularly in the EU, sensitive data may be processed only if the data subject has explicitly consented to such processing and only if such data is necessary for the specific purpose defined by the data controller.
- In some countries, protecting sensitive data by a specific measure (e.g., encryption) recommended under applicable guidelines may exempt an organization from the obligation to notify data subjects of a data security breach or to announce corrective actions being taken to prevent future security breaches.
- Special requirements might apply depending on the medium—for example, encryption is more likely required where portable or mobile devices are used to store and transmit personal information, and where Web sites are collecting the data.

Even where not legally required, encryption can be a practical and proactive way to limit the damage that a data breach would do, especially when it comes to "sensitive" and other special categories of personal data, which tend to be the focus of data breach notification statutes.

The definition of what is "sensitive," or otherwise constitutes a special category of personal data, can present difficult issues in several respects:

- The definition can vary statutorily from jurisdiction to jurisdiction.
- Other types of information could be viewed as "sensitive," notwithstanding what the law says (e.g., although the EU Data Protection Directive does not include financial data on the list of "sensitive" data, most people would view financial data to be sensitive data).
- Likewise, the definition of healthcare/medical data (which is typically sensitive data under most jurisdictions' data protection laws) can be quite expansive in some jurisdictions so that even more ordinary data can become "sensitive" where, for example, it is being collected by a healthcare Web site.

Outside the United States, specific categories of personal data that are "sensitive" vary, depending on the local data protection law at issue, but often include data about racial or ethnic origin, political opinions, religious or philosophical beliefs, trade union membership, health or sex life, and criminal convictions.

Ultimately, there is no definitive list of what kind of data may be considered to be "sensitive" beyond what is defined as such by the data protection regulations. Indeed, the

French data protection authority (the CNIL) prefers more general guidelines measuring adequate means of security based on the nature of the data.[6] Taking that approach, financial information is sensitive even if it does not literally fall within the statutory language of the data protection laws. Likewise, profiles that result from processing personal data might in some cases be considered to be sensitive and thus may not be used without taking specific measures.

Similar approaches can be found outside of the EU. Although there may be no distinction under local law between sensitive and nonsensitive personal data, determining the adequacy of the data protection measures should—as noted above—take into account the nature of the information and the damage that may result in the event of loss or misuse. Again, sector-specific guidance may come into play here, as it does in deciding whether to provide notification in the event of a data breach.

Even within the EU, it is likely that one will find differing approaches to this issue. Although the same general principles and rules have been implemented at the EU level, data security is an aspect on which the EU Member States have been left some room for localization. For example, the Italian encryption requirement is a peculiarity of Italian law that specifies the general security requirements established by the EU Directives. Likewise, Spain imposes very specific security obligations, depending on the nature of the data processed. Ultimately, one is unlikely to find a prescription at the local level for a specific encryption protocol, standard, or technology, even where encryption is required or recommended, given that legal provisions as a matter of principle generally avoid discriminating against or outlawing certain standards or technology. Instead, legal provisions are generally viewed as setting the minimum required level of security.

How, then, does a multinational business approach the difficult task of developing policies and procedures to protect personal data in every jurisdiction in which it operates? One approach is to define the term "sensitive" expansively to include anything that could be seen to be health-related, financial-related, or otherwise sensitive if it were to be the subject of an interception or other data security breach (though the organization may need to adjust its conduct significantly to comply with this higher bar, and thus apply encryption and other measures to a wider range of data). In setting policy, an organization would be well advised to ask how it would play in the court of public opinion if there were to be a breach and it came to light that the organization did not view the information in question to be important enough to encrypt or to take certain other precautionary steps. At the same time, it is important that the company not set the bar so high that it cannot, practically speaking, keep the promises it has made. Likewise, companies will need to determine if certain contemplated uses of encryption will trigger other obligations (e.g., many countries have rules regarding the importation and use of encryption products, software, and technology).

Even after navigating all of these issues associated with data security breaches and encryption/protection of sensitive data, another difficulty is that this is an area that is rapidly changing. New data protection laws (and other laws with data protection implications)

---

6. From the French data protection Authority ("CNIL") recommendation of July 21, 1981, relating to the security measures of an information system.

could be on the horizon that will dramatically change the requirements for businesses. Thus, it is prudent for organizations to keep track of these developments.

NOTIFICATION AND ENCRYPTION REQUIREMENTS BY COUNTRY

As noted previously, jurisdictions can vary in the way they approach such issues. Below are high-level perspectives from 32 jurisdictions regarding the two primary questions discussed above:[7]

1. Is there an obligation to notify data subjects and/or data authorities in the event of a data security breach?
2. Are encryption or any other special measures required to protect sensitive personal data?

Argentina

Obligation to Notify

In Argentina, companies that have had a data security breach are obligated to provide notification. If the data security breach affects information that has been registered with the Data Protection Authority as a database, then such incident must be reported to the Data Protection Authority. The Data Protection Authority typically requests the company to clearly explain the details of the security methods that have been implemented to prevent third parties from using private information. The company may be sanctioned if the Data Protection Authority concludes that the company has not implemented an appropriate security method.

If the incident affects information related to any password or similar private information used by employees, then the company should report the incident to the affected employees to allow them to take the appropriate course of action (e.g., change the password).

Databases that store sensitive data must comply with security requirements according to the levels defined by the Authority as "basic," "medium," and "critical." Such requirements include the following:

- The security policy must detail the corresponding procedures and security measures and must be continuously updated. The policy must include (1) a job description of the individuals working on the database; (2) a description of the quality-control process; (3) a security breach protocol, including reporting, management, and solutions; (4) a description of backup procedures; and (5) a description of the procedures to identify and authenticate authorized users.
- In addition, the company must (1) adopt preventive measures to avoid viruses; (2) conduct internal or external audits to verify fulfillment of the required procedures; (3) implement access controls that allow identification of the user, date, and time of access (reports should be kept for three years); (4) implement a data recovery procedure; (5) implement a mechanism to avoid breaches

---

7. As of April 2009, all contributors identified in this section were affiliated with Baker & McKenzie International, a Swiss Verein with member law firms around the world.

(where information is distributed in hard copy); and (6) keep backup copies in different and fireproof premises.

Compliance with "critical measures" is not required if personal data is kept in order to comply with legal obligations or for administrative purposes.

Requirement for Encryption or Other Special Measures

Although appropriate measures are required to protect personal data (as referenced above), no particular encryption requirements apply.

Contributed by Roberto Grane and Guillermo Cervio.

Australia

Obligation to Notify

There is currently no formal requirement in Australia to notify data subjects or data authorities in the event of a data security breach. The Privacy Commissioner has indicated, however, that it is best practice for organizations to be proactive in the event of a data security breach and to notify the data subjects affected. The Privacy Commissioner might consider such proactive steps to be relevant when determining the outcome of any complaints arising as a result of the breach. Furthermore, organizations and government agencies are required to take reasonable steps to protect the personal information they hold from misuse and loss and from unauthorized access, modification, or disclosure; notification may, in some circumstances, be considered a reasonable step in such protection of personal information.

In August 2008, the Australian Law Reform Commission (ALRC) recommended a number of reforms to Australia's privacy laws, including that organizations and government agencies be required to notify data subjects and the Privacy Commissioner when specified personal information has been, or is reasonably believed to have been, acquired by an unauthorized person, and when the organization, agency, or data authority believes that the unauthorized acquisition may raise a real risk of serious harm to any affected individual. One of the factors that may be taken into account in determining whether the unauthorized acquisition may pose a real risk of serious harm is whether the information had been adequately encrypted.

The government has indicated that it will consider the ALRC's recommended reforms to Australia's privacy laws in two stages, and that the recommendation regarding data breach notification will fall within the second stage. The government's response to the first stage was released in late 2009, and its response to the second stage is not likely to be released before late 2010 or 2011.

In August 2008, the Privacy Commissioner also published a voluntary guide to assist organizations and agencies in responding effectively to a data breach. The guide is similar to guidelines developed by the Privacy Commissioner of Canada and the Privacy Commissioner of New Zealand. The guide outlines what steps an organization or agency should consider taking when responding to a data breach, including the factors it should consider when determining whether it would be appropriate in those circumstances to notify data subjects or the Privacy Commissioner.

Requirement for Encryption or Other Special Measures

Organizations must take reasonable steps to protect all personal information (including sensitive information) they hold from misuse and loss and from unauthorized access, modification, or disclosure. What constitutes reasonable steps will depend on the circumstances, and Australia's privacy laws do not prescribe any specific measures that must be taken to satisfy this obligation.

The Privacy Commissioner has indicated that taking reasonable steps may include taking measures to protect the physical security, computer and network security, and communications security of the information and that good-practice computer and network security would include systems such as firewalls, routers, network intrusion detection systems, host intrusion detection systems, appropriate encryption, and expert monitoring.

Contributed by Patrick Fair, Jane Williams, Anne-Marie Allgrove, and Adrian Lawrence.

Austria

Obligation to Notify

Effective January 1, 2010, there are now express legal requirements in the DSG (Datenschutzgesetz, the Austrian data protection law), under Sec. 24 para 2a, that require the data controller to inform data subjects about systematic and profound illegal use of data, if such breach may cause damage to the data subjects. Such notification is not required if the threat of damage is insignificant or if disproportionate costs would arise in providing such information to all data subjects concerned. Furthermore, providers of electronic communication services must inform subscribers of such services of the risk of a breach of the security of the network. Information obligations also may stem from contractual arrangements (*e.g.,* the EU Model Processor Clauses).

Requirement for Encryption or Other Special Measures

No express legal requirements as to encryption or any other special measures apply to the protection of personal data. In general, the DSG requires the data controller to ensure that data is protected against accidental or intentional destruction or loss and that it is not accessible to unauthorized persons. The assessment in each individual case will depend on the kind of data used as well the extent and purpose of the use and will have to consider the state of technical possibilities and economic justifiability. Especially with regard to sensitive personal data or data such as credit card details, use of special measures (such as encryption of transfer lines or the data itself) are strongly recommended.

Contributed by Andrea Grubinger.

Belgium

Obligation to Notify

There is no express general legal requirement under Belgian law for a data controller or a data processor to notify data subjects or government authorities about the hacking of personal data or, more generally, to notify them about a security failure allowing unauthorized access to such data.

The Belgian Act of March 11, 2003, concerning certain legal aspects of the Information Society, however, makes it an obligation for transport, caching, and hosting service providers to report to the public prosecutor alleged illegal activities on their systems of which they become aware. This requirement might then apply to the hacking of personal data or to the unauthorized access to data that such service providers are transporting, caching, or hosting.

It is worth noting, however, that the new ePrivacy Directive (which must be implemented into national laws by May 25, 2011) imposes an obligation to inform individuals and competent national authorities in case of information security breaches (under certain circumstances). This obligation applies to providers of electronic communication services (*e.g.* telecom operators, mobile phone communication service providers, Internet access providers). It is therefore to be expected that a legal obligation to notify regarding security breaches will at least be imposed on Belgian electronic communication service providers.

It also could be argued that informing data subjects about a potential data security breach falls within the scope of the data controller's obligation of loyalty (in Article 4 of the Belgian Data Protection Act), and also its obligation to inform data subjects about the "recipient(s)" of their data (Article 9 of the Act).

Moreover, in accordance with the Belgian civil law principles of good faith and fairness in contractual relationships between parties and in accordance with the Belgian law on torts, it is in any case advisable for a data controller to inform data subjects about a potential data security breach so that the latter can take any appropriate measures to mitigate their risks or prejudice.

Because there is no specific text on this issue, the scope of the notification should not be too limited and should allow the data subjects to take any measure they may find appropriate to mitigate the risks. The likelihood of a claim to be filed against a data controller will indeed increase if it appears that the data controller did not warn the data subjects about a potential or actual security breach of their personal data where the former had the opportunity to do so.

Requirement for Encryption or Other Special Measures

To guarantee the confidentiality and security of personal data, the EU Data Protection Directive 95/46 of 24 October 1995 and the Belgian Data Protection Act (of December 8, 1992, as amended in 1998 and supplemented by the Royal Decree of February 13, 2001) require, in substance, that the controller implement appropriate technical and organizational measures to protect personal data against accidental or unlawful destruction or accidental loss, alteration, unauthorized disclosure, or access, in particular where the processing involves the transmission of data over a network, and against all other unlawful forms of processing.

Such measures must ensure a level of security appropriate to the risks presented by the processing and the nature of the data to be protected, taking into account the state of the art and the cost to implement such measures. The Belgian Privacy Commission has issued guidelines with respect to general security measures.

Although no specific technical measures are imposed by law, the Belgian Privacy Commission stated, in an opinion of November 22, 2000, relating to the protection of privacy in the frame of electronic commerce, that "as part of the appropriate technical measures, encryption technology should be used to protect confidentiality of certain messages, and their integrity should be guaranteed by using electronic signature."[8]

---

8. Belgian Privacy Commission. Opinion 34/2000 of November 22, 2000 relating to the protection of privacy in electronic commerce.

In addition, in a recommendation of May 17, 2001, on certain minimum requirements for collecting personal data online in the European Union, the EU Article 29
Data Protection Working Party recommended taking "the steps necessary to ensure data
security during processing including transmission (for example restrict and define the
persons authorized to have access to the data, use strong encryption etc. Article 17 of
Directive 95/46/EC)."[9]

In light of the preceding, the online collection of sensitive data should at least be protected by appropriate encryption methods. Moreover, the use of encrypted forms to collect sensitive data is in line with common practice.

Beyond this, any processing of sensitive data must comply with additional precautionary measures:

First, health-related personal data may be processed only under the supervision of a
health professional, except with the data subject's written consent or where the processing is necessary for the prevention of an actual danger or for the prosecution of a specific criminal offense. The health professional and his agents must be subject to secrecy
with respect to the so-processed personal data.[10]

Second, when processing sensitive data, the data controller must implement the following complementary measures:[11]

- The categories of persons having access to the personal data must be designated by the data controller or, as the case may arise, by the subcontractor,
with a detailed description of their functions as to the relevant processing.
- The list of the categories of the so-designated persons must be held at the disposal of the Belgian Privacy Commission by the data controller or, as the case
may arise, by the subcontractor.
- The data controller must ensure that the designated persons are obliged, under
a legal or statutory obligation, or under any equivalent contractual provision,
to keep the relevant data confidential.
- When informing data subjects, the data controller must mention the legal or
statutory basis authorizing the processing of the sensitive personal data.

Third, the data controller must provide the data subjects with the purposes for which
their sensitive data is being processed, as well as the categories of persons having access
to that data.[12]

Fourth, the processing of sensitive data may not be authorized by the data subject's
written consent where the data subject is in a relationship of dependence vis-à-vis the
data controller, which would prevent the data subject from giving consent freely, unless
the processing at stake aims at granting the data subject a benefit.[13]

Contributed by Daniel Fesler and Elisabeth Dehareng.

---

9. Article 29—Data Protection Working Party. Recommendation 2/2001 on certain minimum requirements
for collecting personal data on-line in the European Union (WP 43).
10. Belgian Data Protection Act of December 8, 1992, art. 7, § 4.
11. Royal Decree of February 13, 2001, art. 25 (implementing the Data Protection Act of December 8, 1992).
12. *Id.* art. 26.
13. *Id.* art. 27.

Brazil

Obligation to Notify

There is no data authority in Brazil. Furthermore, there are no express legal requirements under Brazilian law to notify data subjects or data authorities in the event of a data security breach. Nevertheless, because data controllers are generally liable for any data security breach, it is highly advisable to inform the affected data subjects as soon as the data controller becomes aware of a data security breach. This is especially important in situations where early notice could help to mitigate possible damage to the data subjects (e.g., by allowing the data subjects to change passwords or take other precautionary measures to avoid damage). Accordingly, data controllers may be able to reduce their liabilities for damages that can be mitigated by means of early notification of the breach.

Requirement for Encryption or Other Special Measures

In general terms, and except for certain regulated areas (e.g., the banking sector), there is no express requirement under Brazilian law to use encryption or any other special measures to protect certain types of data. It should be noted that there is no specific legal definition of sensitive personal data in Brazil. Notwithstanding the absence of specific legislation, in order to reduce the liability for data security breaches, data controllers should expressly inform data subjects of the security measures adopted to protect their personal data against unauthorized access or use, and should use all reasonable technology and procedures to reduce the risks of possible security breaches.

Contributed by Bruno C. Maeda, Esther M. Flesch, and M. Cristina Cortez.

Canada

Obligation to Notify

Data breach notification is required in certain circumstances in Canada. Although the Personal Information Protection and Electronic Documents Act ("PIPEDA," the federal private sector privacy law) currently does not expressly mandate data breach notification, there are circumstances when notification is necessary in order to comply with PIPEDA. In this regard, the Office of the Privacy Commissioner of Canada ("OPC") has published guidelines entitled "Key Steps for Organizations in Responding to Privacy Breaches" ("Guidelines") to help organizations identify situations where notification of an affected data subject, the OPC, and/or other parties may be required.

Some Canadian provinces have provided additional guidance to organizations. The Office of the Information and Privacy Commissioner for Alberta has issued a document entitled "Key Steps in Responding to Privacy Breaches," while the Office of the Information & Privacy Commissioner for British Columbia has published two documents, "Breach Notification Assessment Tool" and "Key Steps in Responding to Privacy Breaches."

Beyond issuing guidance, Alberta has enacted a privacy law that includes mandatory data breach notification provisions.[14] In Ontario, subject to certain exceptions, a health information custodian that has custody or control of personal health information about

---

14. Personal Information Protection Act, S.A. 2003, c. P-6.5, at http://pipa.alberta.ca/index.cfm?page=legislation/act/index.html.

an individual shall notify the individual at the first reasonable opportunity if the information is stolen, lost, or accessed by unauthorized persons.

More data breach notification requirements are coming. On May 27, 2010, the federal government of Canada introduced the Safeguarding Canadians' Personal Information Act ("Bill C-29"),[15] which proposes numerous amendments to PIPEDA. The proposed amendments include mandatory data breach notification as well as a newly defined carve-out from personal information for "business contact information," criteria for valid consent, an exemption allowing personal information to be used and disclosed for business transactions, an "insurance exception," and an exemption for certain disclosures of personal information to legal authorities. While some amendments are of a "housekeeping nature" (they clarify ambiguities and address inconsistencies in PIPEDA), other amendments (notably data breach notification and the standard for obtaining valid consent) could result in additional obligations for organizations that collect and process personal information in Canada. If Bill C-29 is passed, companies will have to create or update internal policies and procedures for responding to data breach scenarios and review and update, as required, their privacy policies and processes for obtaining consent from data subjects.

Bill C-29 would require organizations that suffer a material data breach to report such a breach to the OPC "as soon as feasible" after the discovery of a breach. The obligation to determine whether a breach constitutes a "material breach of security safeguards" rests with the organization, which must consider specific criteria, including the sensitivity of the information, the number of individuals affected, and whether the breach is indicative of a systematic failure of security. Organizations would also be required to notify individuals who are affected by a data breach if it is reasonable under the circumstances to believe that the breach poses "a real risk of significant harm to the individual." "Real risk" includes but is not limited to "bodily harm, damage to reputation or relationships, loss of employment, business or professional opportunities, financial loss, identity theft, negative effects on the credit record and damage to or loss of property." Again, the onus would be on the organization to determine whether there is a real risk, taking into consideration the sensitivity of the information and the probability that the information has been, is being, or will be misused by third parties.

Requirement for Encryption or Other Special Measures

Personal information shall be protected by security safeguards appropriate to the sensitivity of the information. More sensitive information should be safeguarded by a higher level of protection. The methods of protection should include technological measures such as the use of passwords and encryption.

In Alberta and British Columbia, an organization must protect personal information that is in its custody or under its control by making reasonable security arrangements against such risks as unauthorized access, collection, use, disclosure, copying, modification, disposal, or destruction. Encryption is one way to comply with this requirement.

In Ontario, a health information custodian must take steps that are reasonable under the circumstances to ensure that personal health information in the custodian's custody

---

15. *Available at* www2.parl.gc.ca/HousePublications/Publication.aspx?Docid=4547739&file=4.

or control is protected against theft, loss, and unauthorized use or disclosure, and the records containing the information are protected against unauthorized copying, modification, or disposal. Encryption is one way to comply with this requirement.

Quebec has no specific requirement for encryption.

Contributed by Theo Ling.

Chile

Obligation to Notify

In Chile, there is currently no express requirement to notify data subjects or data authorities in the event of a data security breach. Under the Computing Criminal Conduct Act N°19.223, however, the unlawful intended disclosure of personal data constitutes a criminal offense in Chile and is punishable with imprisonment. The crime may be aggravated where the person responsible for the custody of the information made the unlawful release. Unlawful access to the information by a third party is also a crime. As in the case of any public prosecution crime, there is generally no obligation to inform the authorities of the occurrence of a crime, but the company should not take actions tending to hide, aid, or burden the prosecution of such crime.

Finally, under the Data Protection Act, the entity responsible for the data collection would remain liable for the breach of the data security vis-à-vis the data subjects.

Requirement for Encryption or Other Special Measures

Chilean data protection law imposes a duty of care on the data collector but does not specify how this should be done. There are no references to encryption or other technologies in the law.

Contributed by Diego Ferrada.

China (PRC)

Obligation to Notify

There are currently no "data authorities" in China, and current laws in China do not specify any duty of data breach notification with regard to data subjects.

Requirement for Encryption or Other Special Measures

Generally, all entities in China should maintain the security of their communications network and should ensure the security of data collected, but there is no legal requirement to use encryption or any other special measures to protect sensitive personal data. There are, however, industry-specific regulations that impose special duties on certain types of data carriers.

Contributed by Nancy Leigh.

Colombia

Obligation to Notify

The Statute for the Protection of Personal Data was recently enacted in Colombia, and it contains no express obligations to report data security breaches. The government is currently working on a new bill that would likely increase obligations, including with regard to data breaches; the government hopes such a law would be in place by the end of 2010.

Requirement for Encryption or Other Special Measures

The Statute for the Protection of Personal Data regulates the collection, use, and transfer of personal data as well as the management of databases related to the commercial and financial information of data subjects. According to the statute, "personal data" is defined as any piece of information that allows the identification of the data subject. Protection is afforded to both private and semiprivate personal information. "Private personal information" refers to data that is only relevant to the data subject. "Semiprivate personal information" is information that refers to the data subject but is relevant not only to the data subject but also to third parties that need to use it to make informed decisions about the data subject (e.g., commercial establishments and financial institutions). As a general rule, the statute does not protect public information (i.e., information regarding the data subject that is contained in public documents). Nevertheless, protection will be afforded to public information when other regulations impose a duty to protect such information.

According to the statute, personal data cannot be accessed via the Internet or mass media unless appropriate technical measures of control are implemented to restrict such access only to data subjects and other authorized users. Technical measures should be appropriate to guarantee that the security of the records containing personal data are not altered, lost, used, or consulted without the required authorizations. No particular technology or method is referenced with regard to such measures.

The statute appointed the Superintendent of Industry and Commerce as the authority in charge of controlling the activities of databases containing personal data. The Superintendent can order data managers (i.e., collectors of information and operators) to conduct periodic audits in order to verify that the data managers have adopted adequate security measures to protect personal data. We cannot rule out the possibility of the Superintendent requiring databases to report data security breaches.

Contributed by María Carolina Pardo Cuéllar.

Czech Republic

Obligation to Notify

If a data security breach in the Czech Republic affects information that had been registered with the Office for Personal Data Protection, then such incident must be reported to the Office. Moreover, if the incident affects information related to any password or similar private information used by the data subjects, then the company should report the incident to the data subjects to allow them to take the appropriate course of action (e.g., change their password).

Requirement for Encryption or Other Special Measures

The Czech Data Protection Act defines sensitive personal data as data relating to nationality, racial or ethnic origin, political attitudes, membership in trade unions, religious and philosophical beliefs, criminal convictions, health conditions and sexual life, and genetic or biometric data that enables the direct identification or authentication of the data subject. Subject to a few exemptions stipulated in the Act, sensitive data may be processed only if the data subject has given explicit (namely, written) consent to such processing and only if such data is necessary for a specific purpose defined by the controller and covered by the data subject's consent. Nevertheless, the Act does not require that the data controller encrypt such sensitive personal data or adopt any additional technical measures beyond those adopted in relation to processing nonsensitive personal data.

Contributed by Patrik Kastner.

Egypt

Obligation to Notify

There are no laws in Egypt that specifically address obligations to notify data subjects or data authorities with respect to certain categories of data in the event of a data security breach.

Requirement for Encryption or Other Special Measures

Generally, all entities in Egypt should maintain the security of their communications network and should ensure the security of data collected, but there is no legal requirement to use encryption or any other special measures to protect sensitive personal data. There are, however, industry-specific regulations that impose special duties on certain types of data carriers, such as in banking activities.

Contributed by Hazim Rizkana.

France

Obligation to Notify

In France, there is no legal requirement for the data controller to notify the data protection authority or the data subjects about a security breach. Nevertheless, because the data controller may be liable in the event of a security breach, the French data protection authority (CNIL) generally advises that the data controller should promptly inform the data subjects concerned to allow them to take appropriate measures to mitigate the consequences of the security breach and thus limit the liability. Once notified, the victim of a data security breach may notify such breach to the CNIL, which may exercise its investigative powers or file a complaint with the French attorney general (Procureur de la République) on the ground of noncompliance with the data controller's obligation to take appropriate security measures to protect the data. We are not aware, however, of any case in France on this issue.

The EU Article 29 Data Protection Working Party issued an opinion on February 10, 2009, on the proposal amending Directive 2002/58/EC on privacy and electronic communications that supports strengthening Article 4 of the ePrivacy Directive by requiring providers of publicly available communication services to provide notification regarding security breaches. The opinion recommends the approach for providing such notification (including informing the data protection authority, informing the users, maintaining records, and so on). Therefore, it is likely that this position should be followed in most of the EU countries, including France.

Requirement for Encryption or Other Special Measures

There is no express requirement as such for encryption or other measures in French law. Nevertheless, in light of the CNIL recommendation of July 21, 1981, relating to the security measures of an information system (which recommends implementation of security measures in accordance with the sensitivity and nature of the data, the risks to which the information system may be confronted, etc.), encryption measures or other appropriate technical measures should be used for sensitive data such as banking details, health data, and so on. It is the CNIL view that security measures must be determined on a case-by-case basis.

According to the CNIL's last Annual Report, n°30:

- In 2009, the CNIL, for the first time, used the urgency procedure to stop data processing because of a security breach. A notary public's office that specialized in fee and debt collection (*Huissier*) had been informed of a security breach in its IT system enabling unauthorized access to its database. Although warned of this breach, the notary public did not correct the breach. Therefore, the CNIL triggered the urgency procedure under French law, in order to request that the processing stop and to require the notary public to correct the breach within a 15-day deadline, which the notary public did.
- Since 2010, the CNIL has changed its strategy and is developing its investigation actions to ensure that companies are complying with French data protection law. The CNIL's actions include ensuring that security measures are satisfactory.
- Since 2008, the CNIL and the EU Article 29 Data Protection Working Party are working with the French standardization organization (AFNOR), and with the International Organization for Standardization (ISO), on a standard norm for security.
- The CNIL is particularly interested in the security measures implemented by health data hosting providers, because health data is regarded as sensitive data.

Contributed by: Denise Lebeau-Marianna and David Charlot.

Germany

Obligation to Notify

In September 2009, new sections to the BDSG (the Federal Data Protection Act, Bundesdatenschutzgesetz), the TKG (the Telecommunications Act, Telekommunikationsgesetz), and the TMG (the Telemedia Act, Telemediengesetz) came into effect that impose the entirely new duty to notify the competent data protection authority (DPA) and the data subjects (and, in some instances, the public as well) about a security breach. Each of these laws describes a security breach as the unlawful transfer or disclosure of personal data to a third party. A third party is any person/entity other than the data controller itself (i.e., the person/entity lawfully collecting, processing, and/or using the data for its own purposes). Even the disclosure of personal data to another entity within the same group of companies may, therefore, constitute a security breach, unless the disclosure is justified. A notification obligation only applies if the incident involves the following types of data and if the illegal access or transfer could have severe adverse effect on the rights or protection-worthy interests of the relevant data subjects: sensitive personal data (being defined as personal data revealing racial or ethnic origin, political opinions, religious or philosophical beliefs, trade-union membership, health, or sex life); personal data that is subject to professional confidentiality obligations (e.g., confidentiality obligations applicable under statutory law to attorneys, doctors, etc.); personal data related to criminal acts or public offenses or suspicion regarding the same; personal data related to bank accounts or credit card accounts; or contract data or traffic data related to telecommunication and online services (e.g., Internet use, telephone connections, etc.).

Requirement for Encryption or Other Special Measures

Section 9 of the BDSG specifies that technical and organizational measures to protect personal data shall be required if the effort involved is reasonable in relation to the desired level of protection. Also, the Annex to Section 9 BDSG in a very generic way requires adequate technical and organizational measures to be adopted in light of the type of personal data or data categories to be protected. Since the 2009 reform of the BDSG, the Annex to Section 9 BDSG for the first time expressly mentions "state of the art encryption" as one of the means to address the following controls: (i) access control to data processing systems, (ii) access control to specific areas of processing systems, and (iii) transmission control of personal data.

In a nutshell, encryption will often be required to adequately protect sensitive data or other types of high-risk data, but the specifics of the individual case may allow for lesser protection.

In the legislative memorandum regarding the new provisions on security breaches, the German Government outlined its interpretation that no "severe adverse effect on the rights or protection-worthy interests of the relevant data subjects" (which is one of the elements triggering a notification obligation) will be present if the relevant data had been encrypted by state-of-the-art encryption technology.

Contributed by Christoph Rittweger.

Hong Kong

Obligation to Notify

There is no express legal obligation in Hong Kong to notify data subjects or the Privacy Commissioner in the event of a data security breach. If, however, the data user is a bank, a deposit-taking company, or another "authorized institution" under the Banking Ordinance and is therefore supervised by the Hong Kong Monetary Authority (HKMA), the nonbinding guidelines issued by the HKMA through its circulars are relevant. Under these "best practice" guidelines, HKMA expects that any loss or leakage of customer data by an authorized institution will be reported to the HKMA as quickly as possible and that the affected customers will be notified as soon as practicable.

Requirement for Encryption or Other Special Measures

There is currently no distinction in Hong Kong between sensitive and nonsensitive personal data. There are no special measures required to protect personal data in Hong Kong.

Contributed by Jennifer Van Dale and Anna Gamvros.

Hungary

Obligation to Notify

There is no specific obligation in Hungary to inform data subjects or authorities about a data security breach. If, however, the authorities discover such a breach during an inspection, the data controller could be subject to sanctions; a data subject discovering a breach can claim damages as a result of the breach. (The data controller may be exempted from liability if it can prove that the damage was due to reasons beyond its control.) If the data subject requests information about the data processing (given that the data subject is entitled to know who acquired the personal data), the data controller may inform the data subject about the security breach. In any case, it may be advisable to inform data subjects if their involvement could have mitigated the damages.

Requirement for Encryption or Other Special Measures

The Data Protection Act does not differentiate between security measures required to protect personal data or sensitive personal data. Instead, the Act contains a general reference to appropriate technical measures, particularly if personal data is transferred through IT equipment. Although the rules do not refer to encryption, in certain cases the appropriate security measure may be the application of encryption technology.

   Contributed by Tamás Kaibinger, Zoltán Hegymegi-Barakonyi, Ines K. Radmilovic, and Emese Szitási.

Indonesia

Obligation to Notify

Under Indonesian Law No. 11 of 2008 on Electronic Information and Transaction (EIT Law), before personal data can be used through electronic media, the consent of the owner of such personal data must first be obtained. Although this provision under the EIT Law does not specifically require notification to data subjects in the event of a data security breach, the prudent course would be to notify the data subject.

   There is no regulatory obligation (including under the EIT Law) to notify certain data protection authorities in the event of data security breaches.

Requirement for Encryption or Other Special Measures

Encryption or other special measures for protecting sensitive personal data are not a regulatory requirement, but such measures are recommended as a prudent course of action. Encrypting, anonymizing, or de-indentifying sensitive personal data could, to a certain extent, minimize possible claims of violations of a data subject's rights to privacy.

   Contributed by Alvira M. Wahjosoedibjo.

Italy

Obligation to Notify

The Italian Code does not specifically require disclosure to data subjects or the Italian Data Protection Authority (or other authorities) in the event of a security breach. Under the Code, however, the data controller is liable to compensate for monetary and moral damages caused by the security breach and claimed by data subjects.

Under a specific provision applicable to the provider of a publicly available electronic communications service (Art. 32, paragraph 3 of the Code), where there is a particular risk of a breach of network security, the provider of a publicly available electronic communications service must inform subscribers and, if possible, users about the risk; when the risk lies outside the scope of the measures to be taken by the provider, notice must be provided regarding all of the possible remedies, including an indication of the likely costs involved. This information also must be provided to the Italian Data Protection Authority and the Italian Authority for Communications Safeguards.

Requirement for Encryption or Other Special Measures

Article 34(h) of the Code requires implementation of encryption techniques or identification codes for specific processing operations performed by healthcare bodies with respect to data disclosing health and sex life. Article 24 of Annex B to the Code (regarding technical specifications on minimum security measures) also provides for encryption of the electronic data transfer.

Article 22, paragraph 6, of the Code and Article 9 of Annex A II to the Code (the latter containing the code of conduct and professional practice applying to processing of personal data for statistical and scientific purposes) provide that when sensitive and judicial data are contained in lists, registers, and/or databases that are kept with the help of electronic means, they shall be processed by using either encryption techniques or identification codes and/or other solutions that, in the light of the number and type of the processed data, make the data temporarily unintelligible to those entities that are authorized to access them and allow identifying data subjects only if this is necessary.

Furthermore, the Italian Data Protection Authority has issued different regulations in which (for security and confidentiality purposes) it expressly requires or recommends the use of encryption or similar techniques. Examples of this include the guidelines for data processing within the framework of clinical drug trials;[16] the general regulation on mandatory security measures for lawful interceptions;[17] and the general regulation on electrical and electronic waste and data protection,[18] requiring adoption of encryption technology solutions whenever it is necessary to protect a piece of data and/or a dataset (e.g., files or file collections) in case of reuse and/or recycling of waste electrical and electronic equipment to prevent unauthorized access and allow the data to be erased or else made unintelligible.

Contributed by Francesca Gaudino.

Japan

Obligation to Notify

Japan's Personal Information Protection Law (PIPL) does not create an obligation to notify data subjects or data authorities in the event of a data security breach. There are, however, a number of sets of guidelines issued by government ministries that provide guidance on the means for compliance with the PIPL within specific fields or industries. Some of these guidelines create an obligation to notify data subjects and/or governmental

---

16. July 24, 2008; 190 Gazz. Uff. (Aug. 14, 2008).
17. Dec. 15, 2005; 67 Boll. (Dec. 2005).
18. Oct. 13, 2008; 287 Gazz. Uff. (Dec. 9, 2008).

authorities in the event of a data security breach, and some guidelines also provide recommendations for data security measures. Where the guidelines apply to a specific industry (e.g., the guidelines issued by the Financial Service Agency apply to entities in the banking business), affected entities should undertake the recommended measures for data security or in the event of a data security breach. Although compliance with the guidelines is not strictly mandatory under the PIPL, noncompliance can lead to ministerial investigations with the potential for administrative sanctions in addition to a public finding that the entity in question has violated the PIPL.

If sensitive data is protected by a specific measure recommended under applicable guidelines (e.g., encryption, etc.), the entity may be exempt from the obligation to notify data subjects of a data security breach or from the obligation to announce corrective actions it is taking to prevent future security breaches.

Requirement for Encryption or Other Special Measures

The PIPL does not expressly require entities to take specific data security measures such as encryption or other special measures to protect sensitive personal data.

Contributed by Nobuko Narita and Timothy Griffiths.

Malaysia

Obligation to Notify

Malaysia recently introduced laws on personal data and privacy with the Personal Data Protection Act 2010 ("PDPA"). The Personal Data Protection Bill was passed by the Lower House and Upper House of Parliament in April and May 2010 respectively and subsequently gazetted in June 2010. It is presently anticipated that the PDPA will come into force by the end of 2010 or early 2011.

The key objective of the PDPA is to regulate the processing of personal data by data users in the context of commercial transactions, with the intention of safeguarding the data subject's interest. At present, apart from certain sectoral secrecy obligations, information of a personal nature is protected as confidential information through contractual obligations or the common law.

The PDPA provides that when processing personal data, a data user shall take practical steps to protect the personal data from any loss, misuse, modification, unauthorized or accidental access or disclosure, alteration, or destruction by having regard to: (a) the nature of the personal data and the harm that would result from such loss, misuse, modification, unauthorized or accidental access or disclosure, alteration, or destruction; (b) the place or location where the personal data is stored; (c) any security measure incorporated into any equipment in which the personal data is stored; (d) the measures taken to ensure the reliability, integrity, and competence of personnel having access to the personal data; and (e) the measures taken to ensure the secure transfer of the personal data. Where processing of personal data is carried out by a data processor on behalf of the data user, it is the responsibility of the data user to ensure that the data processor provides sufficient guarantees with respect to the technical and organizational security measures governing the processing to be carried out and takes reasonable steps to ensure compliance with those measures.

The PDPA does not, however, provide for any mandatory notification requirements to data subjects and/or data authorities in the event of a data security breach. It remains to be seen whether subsidiary legislation or guidelines/codes of practice will be enacted/issued by the Minister of Information, Culture and Communications ("Minister") or the Personal Data Protection Commissioner in this regard.

Pending the coming into force of the PDPA, the common law duty of confidentiality would prevent the unauthorized use of information of a "confidential" nature to the prejudice or detriment or the data subject. The law does not impose any affirmative obligation to notify the data subject when a data security breach occurs. Nevertheless, in the event of a security breach of the data subject's information, there will be an obligation to minimize such security breach, which may include informing the data subject of such breach/loss of data if this minimizes or resolves the security breach.

Requirement for Encryption or Other Special Measures

The PDPA includes special provisions with respect to the processing of "sensitive personal data," which is defined as any personal data consisting of information as to the physical or mental health or condition of a data subject; his political opinions, religious beliefs, or other beliefs of a similar nature; the commission or alleged commission by him of an offense; or any other personal data as the Minister may determine by order published in the gazette.

Apart from requiring the explicit consent of a data subject before processing sensitive personal data, the PDPA does not require any encryption or other special measures for protection. Therefore, the security provisions discussed above in relation to ordinary personal data (which do not specifically require encryption or other special security measures) would likewise apply to sensitive personal data unless specific subsidiary legislation or guidelines/codes of practice are later introduced to cover such data.

However, until the PDPA comes into force, the common law duty of confidentiality may extend to requiring data users to adopt such measures where, for example, it is the industry standard and it would be reasonable to expect data users to do so.

Contributed by Adeline Wong and Sonia Ong.

Mexico

Obligation to Notify

On July 5, 2010, the Mexican Ministry of the Interior published the Mexican Federal Law for the Protection of Personal Data in Control of Private Persons ("Data Protection Law"), which came into effect on July 6, 2010. This is the first federal law of its type in Mexico and creates a new set of obligations and compliance challenges for any private person or company that collects, uses (including accessing, handling, profiting from, transferring, disposing), stores, manages, or otherwise processes personal data in Mexico. In general, all data collectors must provide a privacy notice (containing specified content) to all data subjects; appoint a responsible person or group; process personal data only for purposes specified in the law; adhere to data transfer requirements; and take various other steps under the new Data Protection Law.

Personal data is considered to be information that refers to an identified or identifiable individual, regardless of the location, nationality, or other aspects of the data subject (whether a customer, prospect, employee, supplier, vendor, business partner, competitor, or other third party). Under the Data Protection Law, sensitive personal data (which can trigger additional obligations, including express consent of the data subject and greater penalties for noncompliance) refers to data that affects the most intimate personal sphere of its owner, which undue use could result in discrimination or which creates a risk for the data subject; examples include data regarding racial or ethnic origin; present or future health conditions; genetic information; religious, philosophic, or moral beliefs; union affiliation; political opinions; and sexual preference.

According to article 20 of the Data Protection Law, any breach to the security of personal data that affects the patrimonial or moral rights of data subjects in a material manner must be immediately notified to the data subjects.

Although effective on July 6, 2010, some of the Data Protection Law's effects are set to be implemented at later times, including certain requirements for data collectors, the ability for data subjects to request correction of their data, and the publication of regulations to the Law (to be published no later than July 6, 2011), among others. Such regulations will provide further details regarding processes and procedures, may clarify certain general aspects of the law, and could include additional provisions regarding breach notification obligations.

Requirement for Encryption or Other Special Measures

The Data Protection Law does not specifically require the use of encryption to protect sensitive data. Instead, all data processors must implement and maintain the administrative, technical, and physical measures that will protect personal data from damage, loss, alteration, destruction, and unauthorized use, access, and treatment. Security measures implemented shall not be less than those used by data collectors to protect their own information and shall also take into account existing risks, the sensitivity of the data, and relevant technical developments. It is possible that the regulations to be published by July 6, 2011 could require encryption or other special measures.

Contributed by: Sergio Legorreta Gonzalez and Fernando Godard Perez.

Netherlands
Obligation to Notify

Where there is a security breach in the Netherlands, the data controller should inform the data subjects based on the general obligation to inform them as to how their personal data has been processed. There is, however, no legal obligation to inform or notify the Dutch Data Protection Authority.

Requirement for Encryption or Other Special Measures

As to whether encryption or any other special measures are required to protect sensitive personal data, the following rule applies, based on the Dutch Data Protection Act: "The responsible party shall implement appropriate technical and organizational measures to secure personal data against loss or against any form of unlawful processing. These measures shall guarantee an appropriate level of security, taking into account the state of the art and the costs of implementation, and having regard to the risks associated with the processing and the nature of the data to be protected. These measures shall also aim at preventing unnecessary collection and further processing of personal data."

Which "appropriate technical and organizational measures" will be taken is left to the discretion of the data controller. Encryption is one of the security measures that can be taken. Nevertheless, there are no further specific measures in the Dutch Data Protection Act regarding the protection of sensitive data.

Contributed by Remke Scheepstra and Annika Sponselee.

Philippines
Obligation to Notify
There is no explicit requirement in the Philippines to notify data subjects of a security breach.

Requirement for Encryption or Other Special Measures
Because data subjects have a legitimate expectation of privacy with respect to any personal data that is collected, data collectors must implement reasonable safeguards to avoid unauthorized access. Under the Electronic Commerce Act of the Philippines, parties to any electronic transaction shall be free to determine the type and level of electronic data message or electronic document security needed, and to select and use or implement appropriate technological methods that suit their needs.

Contributed by Christopher Lim and Joseph Lyle Sarmiento.

Poland
Obligation to Notify
There is no express general legal requirement under the Polish personal data protection law for a data controller to notify data subjects or government authorities (i.e., the Inspector General for the Protection of Personal Data) about a security breach.

Requirement for Encryption or Other Special Measures
Data controllers must apply special security measures when processing sensitive data.

Where the database contains "sensitive data" (personal data revealing racial or ethnic origin, political opinions, religious or philosophical beliefs, or religious, party, or trade union membership, as well as the processing of data concerning health, genetic code, addictions, or sex life or data relating to convictions, penalty decisions, fines, and other decisions issued in court or administrative proceedings), the data controller must apply at least a "medium level" of security for the protection of such a database. The specific requirements are specified in the Regulation of April 29, 2004, by the Minister of Internal Affairs and Administration regarding personal data processing documentation and technical and organizational conditions that should be fulfilled by devices and computer systems used for personal data processing. According to this regulation, the "medium level" of security includes at least the following measures:

- Where the password is used for user authentication, the password must consist of at least eight characters, including small and capital letters, numbers, and special characters;
- Any devices and information media containing personal sensitive data being transferred outside of the area where the personal data is processed must be secured in such a way as to ensure confidentiality and integrity of the data. A description of the applied measures must be documented by the data controller.
- The data controller must also fulfill all of the obligations at the "basic level" of data security.

Contributed by Tomasz Koryzma, Radosław Nożykowski, and Magdalena Kogut—Czarkowska.

Russia

Obligation to Notify

Russian law requires the operator (processor) of personal data to notify the data subjects about any illegal actions with respect to the personal data, which arguably should include notification of a data security breach. The data authorities must be informed about the same if they submitted an inquiry about the possible breaches. It should be noted that processing of personal data generally requires advance filing of a notice with the Russian data authorities.

Requirement for Encryption or Other Special Measures

Recently the statutory requirement for encryption for personal data processing was lifted. Now, Russian law requires the data operator (processor) or other person with access to personal data to maintain confidentiality and nondisclosure of the data. The operator must undertake organizational and technical measures to secure nondisclosure of personal data and to exclude unauthorized access to it. Although appropriate security is required, encryption is not necessarily required for all data systems containing personal data. It is for the operator to decide what instruments to apply in order to secure personal data. At the same time, Russian law is developing extensive regulations that govern special requirements and levels of security that apply to data systems containing personal data.

Contributed by Evgeny Reyzman, Ekaterina Kobrin, and Edward Bekeschenko.

Singapore

Obligation to Notify

Singapore's Model Data Protection Code for the Private Sector (the "Model Code") does not impose an obligation to notify in the event of a data security breach. Other specific requirements may apply with respect to data held by organizations in certain sectors (e.g., banks).

Requirement for Encryption or Other Special Measures

Under the Model Code's Principle 7—Safeguards, all personal data should be protected by appropriate security safeguards, including technological measures like encryption. The nature and extent of the security safeguards to be deployed would depend on the sensitivity of the data collected and should be commensurate with the risk and consequences of disclosure. Compliance with the Model Code, however, is voluntary, as the Model Code does not have the force of law.

Contributed by Ken Chia and See Khiang Koh.

Spain

Obligation to Notify

Notice to data subjects or data authorities regarding data security breaches is not legally required in Spain. From a practical perspective, however, it may sometimes be worthwhile to inform data subjects of an incident, as this could provide an argument that any eventual damages award should be reduced.

From an internal perspective, however, a data security breach or any anomaly that does, or might, affect data security must be reported to the security officer (for medium- or high-level security measures). The security officer will then take the proper steps to address the security incident and record the following details: (1) the kind of incident; (2) the time at which it occurred; (3) the person reporting it; (4) to whom it was reported; and (5) the effects of the incident.

Requirement for Encryption or Other Special Measures

Sensitive data is described under Law 15/1999 as data revealing ideology, trade union membership, religion, beliefs, racial origin, health, sex life, or criminal or administrative offenses. Note, however, that only public entities are allowed to process data on criminal or administrative offenses.

Spanish data protection regulations, mainly Title VIII of Royal Decree 1720/2007 (which implements Law 15/1999 on Personal Data Protection), foresee additional requirements (including specific security measures) for processing sensitive personal data.

For instance, sensitive personal data falls in the category for high-level security measures, which means that in addition to the low- and medium-level security measures, data controllers/data processors processing sensitive data shall comply with supplementary measures (an exemption to the foregoing rule would be employee health-related personal data strictly necessary for the accomplishment of legal duties, which do fall within the low-level category).

The following primary high-level security requirements are to be observed by automated databases containing sensitive data:

- Sensitive data shall be distributed only if it has previously been encrypted or an alternative mechanism has been used that ensures that the information is neither intelligible nor manipulated during transmission. In addition, processing of data through portable devices outside the data controller's premises must be accomplished through encryption; otherwise the processing must not occur.
- Backup and recovery copies must be stored outside the place where the information systems are located.
- A record of access shall indicate (1) user name, (2) date and time of access, (3) files accessed, (4) kind of access, and (5) acceptance or rejection of such access by the system. The record must be under the control of a security officer.

No one should be authorized to deactivate the recording mechanism. Records should be kept for a minimum period of two years.

- Sensitive data may be transmitted through public electronic communications networks or wireless networks only if it has been previously encrypted or made illegible to any unauthorized third party.

The primary security requirements for nonautomated databases (i.e., paper files) containing sensitive data are as follows:

- Sensitive data must be stored in areas where access is limited by doors that are kept locked when access to sensitive data is not required. When such measures cannot be implemented, the data controller/data processor must adopt alternative measures as described in the security document.
- Sensitive data may be copied and reviewed only under the control of the persons appointed in the security document. Copies must be deleted to avoid recovery.
- Access to sensitive data must be limited to authorized personnel. Appropriate mechanisms must be implemented to identify access by different users to sensitive data.

Contributed by Norman Heckh and Jordi Masdevall.

Sweden

Obligation to Notify

Although the law is somewhat unclear, it is the view of the Swedish Data Inspection Board that the data controller usually must inform the data subjects of the breach. The information must include details about the anticipated effects of the breach. Moreover, the data controller must inform other institutions that might be affected (e.g., banks). Although there is no obligation to notify the Swedish Data Inspection Board, it might be advisable to contact the authority if a large number of people are affected.

Requirement for Encryption or Other Special Measures

Under Swedish law, there are no explicitly stated mandatory measures that need to be taken with respect to the protection of personal data. Nevertheless, the data controller must implement appropriate technical and organizational measures to protect the personal data that is processed. The measures must provide a level of security that is appropriate, having regard to (1) the technical possibilities available, (2) what it would cost to implement the measures, (3) the special risks that exist with the processing of personal data, and (4) the sensitivity of the personal data. Sensitive data would require a higher level of security. Encryption could thus be one of many measures that must be implemented. For example, encryption or similar protection may be advisable when the sensitive personal data is transferred via a network or when portable IT equipment (e.g., mobile units and removable storage media) is used.

Contributed by Stefan Brandt and Åsa Nelhans.

Switzerland

Obligation to Notify

There is no explicit provision in the Swiss FLDP (the Federal Data Protection Act) that would require the data controller to notify either the Data Protection Commissioner or the data subjects affected by the security breach. One of the aims of recent revisions to the FLDP, however, was to enhance transparency in the processing of personal data. A provision introduced as part of the new law requires that the data subject be notified regarding any collection of data and the corresponding purpose. One could argue that this requirement also applies to security breaches where the data may have been collected by a third party.

Requirement for Encryption or Other Special Measures

No particular encryption requirements apply.

Contributed by Nicolas Passadelis.

Taiwan

Obligation to Notify

In Taiwan, the data controller has no express legal obligation to notify data subjects of a security breach. Nevertheless, Taiwan's sole data protection law, the Computer Processed Personal Data Protection Law (CPPDPL), requires public agencies and covered nonpublic institutions (principally financial institutions, credit agencies, and data management firms) to take proactive measures to protect computerized personal data. The CPPDPL carries statutory penalties for the unauthorized use, disclosure, alteration, or destruction of such personal data. In addition, data controllers are subject to tort claims under the Civil Code.

Both data encryption and a policy of notifying data subjects of security breaches might be seen as data protection measures that could mitigate statutory penalties. In addition, such policies could minimize damage to the data subject and thereby avert tort litigation, or at least lessen its effects.

Note that a new Personal Data Protection Law (PDPL) has been passed, but the effective date is subject to further announcement. The earliest effective date may be in the middle of 2011. The PDPL will replace the CPPDPL and will cover public agencies and all nonpublic institutions. The descriptions under this Taiwan section do not change even under the new PDPL.

Requirement for Encryption or Other Special Measures

There are no encryption requirements under the current laws in Taiwan.

Contributed by H. Henry Chang and Thomas E. Hand.

Thailand

Obligation to Notify

No specific requirements apply in Thailand. Under the Privacy Notification statute, however, if there is a breach of the subscribers' rights in relation to personal information, privacy, or the right to communicate through telecommunications means, the telecommunications operators must notify the subscribers without delay.

Requirement for Encryption or Other Special Measures

No specific requirements apply.

Contributed by Dhiraphol Suwanprateep and Pattarakorn Tangkaravakun.

United Kingdom

Obligation to Notify

There is presently no legal obligation on data controllers to notify either individual data subjects or the U.K.'s Information Commissioner's Office (ICO) in the event of a data security breach, although companies operating in particular industries (e.g., firms regulated by the U.K.'s Financial Services Authority) may be subject to specific legal or regulatory requirements or codes of practice that include obligations that approach a notification duty or obligation.

Notwithstanding the absence of a specific legal obligation, the ICO issued in 2008 a Good Practice Note (a form of guidance) indicating that serious data security breaches should be brought to the ICO's attention. The ICO has stated that the overriding consideration in determining whether a breach should be reported is the potential harm to individuals. From November 1, 2007 until May 15, 2010, there were 1011 security breaches notified to the ICO.

In addition, the Data Protection Act 1998 (DPA) requires data controllers to process personal data fairly and to notify data subjects about the data controllers' data processing activities. Processing is defined broadly and includes "disclosing" data, which can include any type of disclosure, whether accidental or otherwise. Accordingly, while the DPA does not specifically require a data controller to notify data subjects of a security breach, the accidental disclosure of data could arguably be considered "processing" for which notice must normally be provided (i.e., having the effect of imposing on a data controller an obligation to notify data subjects of data security breaches in certain circumstances).

Requirement for Encryption or Other Special Measures

The DPA requires data controllers to adopt appropriate technical and organizational measures to protect personal data. There are no specific legal obligations on data controllers to use encryption to protect sensitive personal data, but in certain circumstances it will be appropriate to use encryption.

The ICO has stated that portable and mobile devices used to store and transmit personal information should be protected using approved encryption software. The ICO has warned that enforcement action will be taken in cases where encryption software has not been used to protect data and losses occur. The ICO currently recommends that data controllers meet Federal Information Processing Standards (FIPS) 140-2 and 197.

In regard to the processing of sensitive personal data and credit card information through a Web site, the ICO has indicated that it would be difficult to meet the security requirements of the DPA without having a secure, encryption-based transmission system. It is common practice for merchants and service providers that transmit, process, or store payment card details to be contractually required to adhere to the Payment Card Industry Data Security Standard (PCI DSS), which requires the use of strong cryptography and security protocols to safeguard sensitive cardholder data during transmission over open, public networks.

Those organizations subject to the regulation of the FSA should be aware of the significant fines that can be imposed by the FSA for not taking appropriate security measures. For example, in August 2010, the FSA fined Zurich Insurance £2,275,000 for failing to have adequate systems and controls in place to prevent the loss of customers' confidential information. In this particular case, Zurich had outsourced the processing of some of its general insurance customer data to a South African affiliate, which then lost an unencrypted back-up tape containing 46,000 customers' personal data during a routine back-up to a data storage facility.

Contributed by Charlotte Story, Ilana Saltzman, and Ross McKean.

Vietnam
Obligation to Notify
(1) Specific Obligation for Online Social Service Providers
Vietnam has a notification obligation for "online social service providers." These agencies must (1) at the request of competent State management agencies, provide information on any violations of certain enumerated prohibited acts with respect to the use of personal information; and (2) provide periodic reports of any such violation.

Such prohibited acts include disclosing state secrets, and military, security, economic, foreign relations and other secrets prescribed by law, which include personal information and photographs. The reports must include, among other things, data on blogs violating the online service provider's privacy rules.

(2) Obligation to Notify Authorities
Under a 2004 decision (Decision No. 71) governing security in management, provision, and use of Internet Services in Vietnam,[19] agencies, organizations, and individuals participating in Internet activities must "detect, and notify in time to the police offices of, activities of violating information safety and security, attacking or destroying the equipment systems, thus obstructing activities of providing Internet services, and other lawbreaking acts; to closely coordinate with the police agencies in verifying and clarifying the details of the violations, to supply necessary information and documents related to the cases when so requested."[20]

While this provision does provide a technical obligation to notify the "police offices" in the event of a security breach, Decision No. 71, on close reading, appears to require some level of intent, or at least bad faith, on the part of the violator.

In addition, if a network owner's (or online social service provider's) server is located outside Vietnam, and its domain name is not registered as ".vn", these entities arguably are not governed by Vietnamese law. In the event of a security breach, therefore,

---

19. Decision No. 71/2004/QD-BCA(A11) of 29 January 2004 Promulgating the Regulation of Ensuring Safety and Security in Activities of Managing, Providing and Using Internet Services in Vietnam ("Decision No. 71").
20. Article 10 of Decision No. 71.

the authorities likely would not require the website or online social service "owner" to report such a breach.

(3)   Obligation to Notify Users

There are no provisions of law (or known practice or precedent) that specifically address this issue. However, if the laws are conservatively interpreted and applied (of which there is no known precedent), then it would be prudent to notify users in order to mitigate the risk of being considered noncompliant. In addition, individuals are entitled to claim compensation (including damages and/or a public apology) for loss caused by a breach during the provision of personal information.

Requirement for Encryption or Other Special Measures

There is no specific obligation to use encryption or other special measures to protect sensitive personal data. There is only a general obligation that organizations storing or using data must ensure the security of the same.

  Contributed by Yee Chung Seck, Elizabeth Nightingale, Alyssa Worsham, and Thanh Tung Le.

PART IV

Technology

CHAPTER 10

Encryption: The Basics

Eric A. Hibbard

Over the past several years, companies, along with their customers and consumers, have been subjected to the headaches associated with data compromises or exposures. Whether through malicious attacks against computer systems or inadequate data handling procedures, the financial toll for all parties involved has been significant. With cybercrime surpassing the profitability of illegal drug trafficking, governments have been obliged to force public disclosure as well as to levy penalties on organizations responsible for some of these data indiscretions.

All too often, encryption is identified as the cure-all for these data woes. However, encryption is nothing more than a way of obscuring data to prevent unauthorized access. Sometimes it can introduce more problems than it solves, and it can lead to a false sense of security.

This chapter provides a short introduction to encryption and key management, as well as a discussion of their relevance to data security.

ENCRYPTION OVERVIEW

Data encryption is rarely implemented by itself, but rather in conjunction with authentication, which ensures that entities are who they say they are, and access control, which limits data access to explicitly authorized entities. In many applications, a combination of cryptographic services (confidentiality, data integrity, authentication, authorization, and nonrepudiation) is desired. The National Institute of Standards and Technology (NIST) notes that designers of secure systems often begin by considering which security services are needed to protect the information contained within and processed by the system.[1] After these services have been determined, the designer then considers what mechanisms will best provide them. Cryptographic mechanisms consisting of algorithms, keys, and other keying material often provide the most cost-effective means of protecting the security of information. This is particularly true in applications in which the information would otherwise be exposed to unauthorized entities.

---

1. NIST Special Publication 800-57 Recommendation for Key Management—Part 1: General (Revised), March 2007, *available at* http://csrc.nist.gov/publications/PubsSPs.html, p. 31.

Encryption can be used as a preventative control (protect data from disclosure to unauthorized parties), a detective control (discovery of unauthorized changes to data), or both. There are multiple considerations that need to be taken into account when evaluating the deployment of an encryption process, including, but not limited to, the following:

- Properly used, encryption can strengthen an organization's systems.
- Encryption has the potential to weaken other security controls/mechanisms (such as inspection of data).
- Although necessary, encryption carries the risk of making data unavailable should anything go wrong with data handling, key management, or the actual encryption.
- Encryption may potentially have significant overhead cost/impact on hosts and networks.

According to the Information Systems Audit and Control Association (ISACA), "The most critical aspect of encryption is the determination of what data should be encrypted and where and when it should be encrypted."[2]

Cryptographic Algorithms

In cryptography, encryption is a means of transforming data from a readable form (known as plaintext or cleartext) to one that is unintelligible (referred to as ciphertext). Encryption functions must, by definition, be reversible.

There are three basic classes of cryptographic algorithms (or ciphers): hash algorithms, symmetric key algorithms, and asymmetric key algorithms. The classes are defined by the number of cryptographic keys that are used in conjunction with the algorithm; hash algorithms use no keys, symmetric key algorithms use a single secret key, and asymmetric key algorithms use two related keys (key pair).

The following is a short summary of each of the classes of cryptographic algorithms:

Symmetric key ciphers (secret key cryptography)
- Use the same key to encrypt and decrypt the data
- Two types: block ciphers and stream ciphers
- Block ciphers are commonly used for storage
- Symmetric key algorithms are generally much less computationally intensive than asymmetric key algorithms

Asymmetric key ciphers (public key cryptography)
- Use a pair of keys with a mathematical association that allows any data encrypted by one key to be decrypted only by the other
- Commonly used for authentication and digital signatures rather than encrypting data

Hashing algorithms
- Do not encrypt data, but provide a one-way (nonreversible) transformation used to store data securely as well as to verify data integrity
- Do not require the use of keys
- The size of the value output by the hashing process is fixed (SHA-1 is 20 bytes)

---

2. ISACA IT Standards, Guidelines, and Tools and Techniques for Audit and Assurance and Control Professionals, *available at* http://www.isaca.org, March 2010, p. 294, Section 1.3.1.

For protecting data, especially at-rest, symmetric key encryption is the primary approach, so this class of algorithms will be emphasized throughout the remainder of this chapter.

Symmetric key algorithms can be divided into stream ciphers and block ciphers. Stream ciphers encrypt the bits of the message one at a time, and block ciphers take a number of bits (often called a block) and encrypt them as a single unit. Blocks of 64 bits have been commonly used; the Advanced Encryption Standard (AES) algorithm approved by NIST in December 2001 uses 128-bit blocks. Some examples of popular and well-respected symmetric algorithms include Twofish, Serpent, AES (aka Rijndael), Blowfish, CAST5, RC4, Triple DES, and IDEA.[3]

With a symmetric key block cipher algorithm, the same plaintext block will always encrypt to the same ciphertext block when the same symmetric key is used. If the multiple blocks in a typical message (data stream) are encrypted separately, an adversary could easily substitute individual blocks, possibly without detection. Furthermore, certain kinds of data patterns in the plaintext, such as repeated blocks, would be apparent in the ciphertext. To address this problem, different cryptographic modes of operation have been developed to provide additional protections.[4]

As noted earlier, symmetric key ciphers are generally much less computationally intensive than asymmetric key ciphers. In practice, this means that a quality asymmetric key cipher is hundreds or thousands of times slower than a quality symmetric key cipher. The disadvantage of symmetric key ciphers is the requirement of a shared secret key, with one copy at each end. Since keys are subject to potential discovery by a cryptographic adversary, they need to be changed often and kept secure during distribution and in service. The consequent requirement to choose, distribute, and store keys without error and without loss is difficult to reliably achieve.

Key Management

The use of all types of encryption relies on the management of cryptographic keys. All ciphers, both symmetric and asymmetric, require all the parties using the cipher to have access to the necessary keys. This gives rise to the need for key management. It is, in actual practice, the most difficult aspect of cryptography generally, for it involves system

---

3. The definition and specification of the more common cryptographic algorithms can be found in ISO/IEC 18033-2:2006, INFORMATION TECHNOLOGY—SECURITY TECHNIQUES—ENCRYPTION ALGORITHMS—PART 2: ASYMMETRIC CIPHERS (2006-05-08), *available at* http://www.iso.org; ISO/IEC 18033-3:2005, INFORMATION TECHNOLOGY—SECURITY TECHNIQUES—ENCRYPTION ALGORITHMS—PART 3: BLOCK CIPHERS (2005-07-01), *available at* http://www.iso.org; ISO/IEC 18033-4:2005, INFORMATION TECHNOLOGY—SECURITY TECHNIQUES—ENCRYPTION ALGORITHMS—PART 4: STREAM CIPHERS (2005-07-15), *available at* http://www.iso.org; and NIST FIPS 197, ADVANCED ENCRYPTION STANDARD (2001-11-26), *available at* http://csrc.nist.gov/publications/PubsFIPS.html.

4. The definition and specification of the more common modes of operation can be found in ISO/IEC 10116:2006, INFORMATION TECHNOLOGY—SECURITY TECHNIQUES—MODES OF OPERATION FOR AN N-BIT BLOCK CIPHER (2006-02-03), *available at* http://www.iso.org; NIST SPECIAL PUBLICATION (SP) 800-38A, RECOMMENDATION FOR BLOCK CIPHER MODES OF OPERATION—METHODS AND TECHNIQUES (December 2001), *available at* http://csrc.mist.gove/publications/PubsSPs.html; NIST SP 800-38C, RECOMMENDATION FOR BLOCK CIPHER MODES OF OPERATION: THE CCM MODE FOR AUTHENTICATION AND CONFIDENTIALITY (May 2005), *available at* http://csrc.nist.gov/publications/PubsSPs.html; and NIST SP 800-38D, RECOMMENDATION FOR BLOCK CIPHER MODES OF OPERATION: GALOIS/COUNTER MODE (GCM) AND GMAC (November 2007), *available at* http://csrc.nist.gov/publications/PubsSPs.html.

policy, user training, organizational and departmental interactions in many cases, coordination between end users, and so on.[5]

Keys are analogous to the combination of a safe. If a safe combination becomes known to an adversary, the strongest safe provides no security against penetration. Similarly, poor key management may easily compromise strong algorithms. Ultimately, the security of information protected by cryptography directly depends on the strength of the keys, the effectiveness of mechanisms and protocols associated with keys, and the protection afforded to the keys. All keys need to be protected against modification, and secret and private keys need to be protected against unauthorized disclosure. Key management provides the foundation for the secure generation, storage, distribution, and destruction of keys.

The problem of key management is rather different depending on whether the keys are for symmetric or asymmetric ciphers. For symmetric ciphers it is necessary to arrange for secret keys to be generated and shared among pairs (or larger groups) of entities. For asymmetric ciphers it is necessary for key pairs to be generated and for public keys to be distributed in such a way that their authenticity is guaranteed.

The NIST SP 800-57 Part 1 identifies 19 different types of cryptographic keys, each used for a different purpose. Of the NIST-identified key types, the following are particularly important to symmetric encryption:

- *Symmetric data encryption key.* Used with symmetric key algorithms to apply confidentiality protection to information.
- *Symmetric key-wrapping key.* Used to encrypt other keys using symmetric key algorithms; key-wrapping keys are also known as key-encrypting keys.

Keeping keys secret is one of the most difficult problems in practical cryptography. To prevent a key from being guessed, keys need to be generated truly randomly and contain sufficient entropy. The problem of how to safely generate truly random keys is difficult, and it has been addressed in many ways by various cryptographic systems. Common approaches include "collecting" entropy from the timing of unpredictable operations, such as disk drive head movements, as well as using a password-based key derivation function like those of the RSA Laboratories' Public-Key Cryptography Standards (PKCS) series, specifically PKCS #5 v2.0.[6]

---

5. Overall frameworks for key management are given in ISO/IEC 11770-1:2008, INFORMATION TECHNOLOGY—SECURITY TECHNIQUES—KEY MANAGEMENT—PART 1: FRAMEWORK (2006-02-03), *available at* http://www.iso .org; ISO/IEC 11770-2:2008, INFORMATION technology—SECURITY techniques—KEY management—PART 2: MECHANISMS USING SYMMETRIC TECHNIQUES (2006-02-03), *available at* http://www.iso.org; NIST SP 800-57, RECOMMENDATION FOR KEY MANAGEMENT—PART 1: GENERAL (REVISED) (2007-03-08), *available at* http://csrc.nist .gov/publications/PubsSPs.html; and NIST SP 800-57, RECOMMENDATION FOR KEY MANAGEMENT—PART 2: BEST PRACTICES FOR KEY MANAGEMENT ORGANIZATION (March 2007), *available at* http://csrc.nist.gov/publications/ PubsSPs.html.

6. *See* IETF RFC 2898, PKCS #5: PASSWORD-BASED CRYPTOGRAPHY SPECIFICATION (Version 2.0, September 2000), *available at* http://www.ietf.org.

APPLYING ENCRYPTION

The way encryption is applied can afford very different protections, depending on how and where it is integrated. For example, encrypting files or shares within a file system can offer user-aware protections that are not possible with encryption of drive-level storage. It is also important to understand why encryption should be considered (that is, what threat is to be mitigated).

In-Flight Versus At-Rest Encryption

Inevitably, any encryption discussion associated with protecting data will include a differentiation between in-flight and at-rest encryption. Although difficult to define—even the Storage Networking Industry Association (SNIA) has had challenges agreeing on a single definition for each—it is important to understand the concepts, which can be summarized as:

- *At-rest encryption.* Encryption that protects data while it resides on the media. It involves encrypting data that will be decrypted when those data flow through the same point (or an equivalent) in the opposite direction. The point of encryption may be within a storage device (tape drive encryption), or within the entity in which the data is created and/or consumed (end-to-end encryption).
- *In-flight encryption.* Encryption that protects data while it is being transferred over a physical link (media) between two communicating entities (for example, a host bus adapter and a switch). Either the two entities have negotiated and implemented some form of communications encryption or the data is encrypted before it is transmitted.

As one can see in the descriptions above, an at-rest encryption mechanism has the potential of protecting the confidentiality of the actual data as it traverses all of the down-stream communications links. Communications-based encryption (for example, IPsec, TLS, SSH) results in the communicating parties having access to the plaintext data, but it can also include integrity checks to ensure the ciphertext is not changed while it is in flight.

SNIA Position on Encryption

The SNIA security position on encrypting data, especially primary data, is one of a measure of last resort. That said, SNIA strongly recommends that appropriate encryption be used when sensitive data leaves the direct control of the organization owning or having responsibility for these data. In this context, sensitive data is data that has legal and/or regulatory requirements for confidentiality protection as well as data that requires protection as part of the organization's due care (trade secrets, intellectual property, etc).

SNIA refers to data that leaves the control of the custodian organization as externalized data. When these externalized data are also sensitive data, SNIA recommends the following:

- Data stored on removable media (like backup tapes), which potentially leaves the control of the organization, must be protected while at rest.
- Data stored in third-party data centers must be protected both in flight and at rest within these "untrusted" data centers.
- Data transferred between "trusted" data centers (controlled by the organization) must be protected.

Point of Encryption

All at-rest encryption is dependent on the placement on an encryption/decryption mechanism within the data flow path, which is known as the point of encryption. The placement of the point of encryption is critical because it defines where in the information and communications technology (ICT) infrastructure that the plaintext data must be routed to be turned into ciphertext, and conversely, it represents the point in the ICT infrastructure that the ciphertext must traverse before it can become usable plaintext data.

Independent of the cryptographic implementation, the placement of the point of encryption within the ICT has a major impact on the protection the encryption can offer. From a simplistic perspective, the following are the major point of encryption categories (see Figure 10.1):

- *Application level.* Under the control of specific application or database; finest granularity of control and maximum insight into the data (type, users, sensitivity).
- *Filesystem level.* Under the control of the operating system (OS) or OS-level application; control at file level with insights into the users and groups.

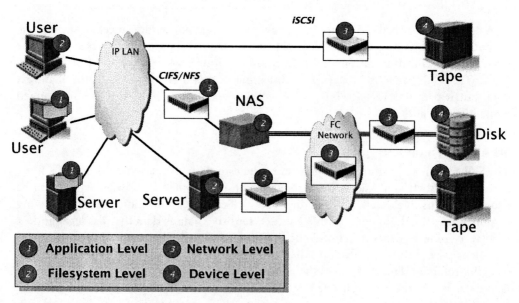

FIGURE 10.1
Point of Encryption Options

- *Network level.* Under the control of a network-based system.
  - *File-based (NAS).* Control at the share/filesystem level (possibly file level) with moderate insights into the users.
  - *Block-based.* Control at the logical volume level with limited insights into the "community of users."
- *Device level.* Under the control of the end device; control at the logical volume level and/or the media level with limited insights into the "community of users."

The general position of security professionals on the use of encryption is that it should be applied as close to the source of data (the generating application) as possible. Doing so maximizes the protection (in-flight and at-rest protection), and it allows characteristics/attributes of the data to be factored into the protection. Unfortunately, this general guidance often proves impractical because of mitigating circumstances and factors.

Factors to Consider

Architecturally, there may be multiple viable point-of-encryption options. In such situations, the following factors and impacts should be considered as part of the selection process:

- *Usability.* User experiences a change in the interface, process, and/or storage mechanism, which may hamper its acceptance.
- *Availability.* The degree to which the overall availability (resiliency and redundancy) of the system/solution will be restricted, diminished, or eliminated.
- *Infrastructure.* The degree to which networking, systems and storage infrastructure must be changed.
- *Performance/Throughput.* Negative impact compared to existing (low=10 percent, moderate=20 percent, significant=35 percent, extreme=50 percent+).
- *Scalability.* The degree to which the overall scalability of the existing system will be restricted, diminished, or eliminated.
- *In-flight confidentiality.* Characterization of in-flight confidentiality protection from the user system/application to the storage device or media.
- *Disaster recovery/business continuity (DR/BC).* The degree to which the overall DR/BC will be restricted, diminished, or eliminated.
- *Proof of encryption.* Characterization of the proof of encryption aspects (functionality, integration into existing infrastructure, evidence).
- *Environmentals.* Characterization of the environmental aspects (power, cooling, space).

When each of these factors is compared and contrasted for the four point-of-encryption categories (see Table 10.1), there is no clear winner. In other words, each organization's unique requirements (for example, on compliance), data sensitivity, and existing infrastructure have to be carefully considered to arrive at an acceptable solution.

That said, some organizations are looking to encryption at the network level (to a lesser degree) and device level as a safety net. The primary objective is to ensure that storage media (tapes and disks), used in conjunction with sensitive data, are encrypted. If these protected media are mishandled (lost, incomplete, transferred to unauthorized parties, etc.) or returned to a vendor or supplier, the organization is often able to avoid the cost and/or embarrassment associated with a security incident.

184   DATA BREACH AND ENCRYPTION HANDBOOK

TABLE 10.1
FACTORS INFLUENCING ENCRYPTION

Impact	Application	Filesystem	Network	Device
Usability	Low	Low-moderate	None	None
Availability	Can be significant	Can be significant	Low-moderate (redundancy)	Low-moderate
Infrastructure	Can be significant	Can be significant	Low-moderate	Low
Performance/ Throughput	Can be severe	Can be significant	Low	Low-moderate
Scalability	Can be significant	Can be significant	Can be moderate	Minimal
In-flight Confidentiality	Excellent	Low-moderate (NAS); Excellent (Host)	Low-moderate	None
DR/BC	Can be extremely complicated	Can be complicated	Can be extremely complicated	Can be extremely complicated
Proof of Encryption	Can be complicated	Relatively easy	Low-moderate	Can be complicated
Environmentals	Low-moderate	Low-moderate	Can be significant	Low

ENCRYPTION AND KEY MANAGEMENT GUIDANCE

According to NIST, cryptography should be considered for data that is sensitive, has a high value, or is vulnerable to unauthorized disclosure or undetected modification during transmission or while in storage.[7] However, there are many details and issues that must be addressed to ensure that the cryptographic methods provide appropriate protection against intentional and accidental compromise and alteration of data. This section offers pragmatic guidance for implementing and using cryptographic solutions.[8]

---

7. NIST SP 800-21, GUIDELINE FOR IMPLEMENTING CRYPTOGRAPHY IN THE FEDERAL GOVERNMENT (2d ed. December 2005), *available at* http://csrc.nist.gov/publications/PubsSPs.html.

8. Much of this guidance is derived from the documents identified in *supra* notes 3–7 as well as STORAGE NETWORKING INDUSTRY ASSOCIATION (SNIA) TECHNICAL PROPOSAL, SNIA STORAGE SECURITY—BEST CURRENT PRACTICES (BCPs) (Version 2.1.0, Sept. 4, 2008), http://www.snia.org/forums/ssif/programs/best_practices/.

Encryption

The protection provided by encryption is very dependent on the quality of the algorithm selected and how it is used. Consider the following when selecting algorithms and establishing appropriate parameters for their use in protecting information:

- Cryptographic algorithms should be both publicly known and widely accepted (e.g. RSA, SHA, Triple DES, Blowfish, Twofish) or banking industry standard algorithms; for the latter, avoid DES.
- Choose a key size or key length (usually measured in bits or bytes) that ensures the key space (set of all possible keys) is extremely large.
- When a symmetric key block cipher algorithm is selected, it is also important to select a mode of operation that provides the required information service such as confidentiality or authentication.
- Consider meeting or exceeding the NIST (SP 800-57 Part 1) recommended minimum security levels, defined as bits of strength (not key size):
    - 80 bits of security until 2010 (128-bit AES and 1024-bit RSA).
    - 112 bits of security through 2030 (3DES, 128-AES and 2048-bit RSA).
    - 128 bits of security beyond 2030 (128-AES and 3072-bit RSA).

Not all data/information are ideal candidates for encryption, so the actual determination should be based on the business needs (the justifiable business need given the cost versus benefit or risk reduction) and the risk appetite of the organization. Avoid treating encryption as some form of crypto fairy dust, which is expected to cure all of the organization's data security issues. Consider the following when encryption is used as an appropriate risk mitigation mechanism:

Identify and classify sensitive/regulated data.
- Document what data is considered sensitive and require encryption as well as requirements for when and how the encryption is to be applied.
- Document the sensitive data's characteristics, including an estimate of the financial value of each data item to be protected.

Analyze risks and protection options.
- Analyze data flows cradle-to-grave (disaster recovery/business continuity infrastructure as well as archives are often overlooked).
- Perform a risk assessment on all data to understand what data (or group of data) is sensitive and whether it should be protected.
- Understand potential operational issues and their effects on availability, performance, scalability, and proof of encryption (evidence that encryption is in place and operational).
- Understand the costs of protection.
- Define a rollback plan at the same time as defining the encryption scheme.

Mitigate risks with encryption.
- Ensure that the chosen algorithm protects at the desired level (according to the risk analysis) as well as being cost-effective and convenient.
- Ensure that the chosen algorithm has a sufficient attacker work factor (the cost of circumventing the mechanism) to deter cryptanalytic attack.

- Ensure that all applicable local and international laws and regulations (where applicable) have been considered and respected.

Challenges—The use of encryption technology introduces certain challenges that cannot be ignored. These challenges may include identifying the appropriate point of encryption, aligning the encryption with data reduction mechanisms, and creating appropriate audit trails. Consider the following guidance to help address these challenges:

Point of encryption.
- Select the location of at-rest encryption such that it minimizes the impacts to users, data availability, information and communications technology (ICT) infrastructure, performance and throughput, scalability, DR/BC, and environmentals (heat, power, and space).
- Implement the in-flight and at-rest encryption mechanisms such that they provide end-to-end protections.
- If undecided between two potential points of encryption, pick the one closest to the application generating the data.

Alignment with data reduction services.
- Ensure that compression is performed before encryption to realize the maximum data reduction benefits; compressing ciphertext results in an expansion of data.
- Ensure that deduplication is performed prior to encryption (and compression) to realize the maximum data reduction benefits.

Proof of encryption.
- Ensure that the encryption mechanisms create appropriate audit log entries (activation, verification, integrity checks, rekeying, etc.).
- Agree in advance what audit log material will be necessary for the legal department to accept that encryption was properly performed.
- Perform regular and audited checks that encryption was properly performed; consider outside accreditation.

Comply with import/export controls.
- Understand and obey government import and export regulations associated with encryption and key management.

Guidance for Key Management

Successful use of cryptography is dependent on adhering to basic principles associated with keying material as well as implementing key management. The widespread use of cryptographic mechanisms places increased importance on the management and protection of cryptographic parameters (e.g., the key). The secure management of these keys is critical to the integration of cryptographic functions into a system, since even the most elaborate cryptographic system will be ineffective if its keying materials are poorly managed. Consider the following guidance on the administration and use of the services of generation, distribution, storage, archiving, derivation, and destruction of keying material in accordance with a security policy. Consider the following guidance on basic aspects of keys and key management.

Observe important properties of keys.

- Use a cryptographic key for only one purpose; specifically, do not use key-encrypting keys (also known as key-wrapping keys) to encrypt data or use data-encrypting keys to encrypt other keys.
- Randomly choose keys from the entire key space.
- Check for and avoid use of known weak keys.
- Limit the amount of time a key is in plaintext form and prevent people from viewing plaintext keys.

Implement and use key management safely.

- Fully automate key management whenever possible.
- Limit the use of data encryption keys to a finite amount of time (known as a key lifetime or cryptoperiod) or to a maximum amount of data processed.
- Sparsely use keys with a long life.
- Separate the key-encrypting keys from the data encryption keys.
- Document the authorization and protection objectives and constraints that apply to the generation, distribution, accounting, storage, use, and destruction of cryptographic keying material.
- Enforce strict access controls to limit user capabilities and separation of duties constraints for key generation, change, and distribution.

Establish keys securely.

- Generate symmetric keys by using either an approved random number generation method, a key update procedure that creates a key from the previous key, or an approved key derivation function that derives a key from a master key.
- Avoid concatenating split-key or multikey components as the combination function used to generate keys.
- Limit the distribution of data encryption keys to backups or to other authorized entities that may require access to the information protected by the keys.
- Protect keys using either encryption or an appropriate physical security mechanism/procedure throughout the distribution process.

Ensure proper operational use.

- Ensure that the installation of a key within the device or process that is going to use it does not result in leakage of the key or information about the key.
- Provide confidentiality for keying material in storage, using either encryption with an approved algorithm or physical protection (i.e., cryptographic module or secure storage with controlled access).
- Use reasonable measures to prevent modifications, to use methods to detect (with a very high probability) any modifications that occur, and to restore the keying material to its original content when modifications have been detected.
- Store symmetric data encryption keys in backup storage during the cryptoperiod of the keys in order to allow key recovery, and store in archive storage after the end of the key's cryptoperiod, if required.
- Replace a key when it may have been compromised, its cryptoperiod is nearing expiration, or to limit the amount of data protected with any given key.

Key disposition.
- Remove keying material and other related information from backups when no longer needed for operational use.
- Destroy keying material as soon as it is no longer required (e.g., for archival or reconstruction activity) in order to minimize the risk of a compromise.

Plan for problems.
- Have a compromise recovery plan in the event of a key compromise.
- Consider escrowing keying material used to protect business/mission critical information; the loss on an encryption key with no key recovery capability renders all of the data encrypted under the lost key unusable.

AN APPROACH TO IMPLEMENTING ENCRYPTION

It is easy to underestimate the issues and complexities associated with implementing encryption solutions. To help address this problem, SNIA developed the Encryption of Data At-Rest—Step-by-Step Checklist whitepaper.[9] This whitepaper outlines a set of steps that organizations can use as a basis to implement their own encryption approach for securing data at-rest. The outlined steps offer a comprehensive view of the elements that should be addressed, but it is recognized that organizations may only need to use a subset of the steps. The following is a summary of the major steps.

Step 1: Understand Confidentiality Drivers

Understanding the reasons for pursuing an encryption strategy is important from the outset. Failure to capture the full set of drivers can result in an inadequate and/or unusable solution. Consequently, this step includes identifying the relevant regulator and legal obligations, identifying all relevant executive management concerns, reviewing organizational policies associated with data protection, reviewing organizational IS/IT strategic plans, and reviewing recent information systems audit results/findings to identify data privacy/confidentiality deficiencies.

Step 2: Classify the Data Assets

In some instances, it is reasonable to encrypt all of an organization's data; however, a more likely scenario is one in which a subset of the data is encrypted, due to cost constraints, the sheer volume of data, geopolitical reasons, and so on. In these situations, both the data sensitivity and criticality must be considered. As such, this step identifies the organizational categories of mission critical data and sensitive data worthy of data protection measures. From these, the organization must determine its confidentiality categories (e.g., most confidential, competitively sensitive, personally identifiable information, top secret, restricted financial, cafeteria menu) to be subjected to encryption measures.

---

9. *Available at* http://www.snia.org/forums/ssif/knowledge_center/white_papers.

Step 3: Inventory Data Assets

Once the encryption drivers are understood and a classification scheme has been established, it is time to chase the data. Specifically, the data associated with each of the confidentiality categories must be identified along with the underlying technology/media on which it resides and its locations. In addition, this step includes performing a risk assessment (with an eye to unauthorized disclosure) on the identified data and adjusting the encryption priorities to reflect the findings.

Step 4: Perform Data Flow Analysis

Simply knowing where the data resides is not enough to ensure adequate confidentiality. Often, the data will go through multiple transitory locations before arriving at its final resting point. In addition, the data may be mirrored, replicated, copied, backed up, and so on as part of the organization's data availability/resiliency strategy. Each of these must be considered as part of the encryption approach.

Step 5: Determine the Appropriate Points of Encryption

Eventually, a basic decision has to be made as to where the encryption should be applied. To do this, the organization must determine the actual risks to be mitigated by the encryption solution, the granularity needed for the encryption, and the importance of access control (e.g., specific user, workgroup, communities of users) to be used in conjunction with encryption for the confidentiality categories. In addition, a variety of technology-related issues should be factored into this decision.

Step 6: Design the Encryption Solution

Systems design can be thought of as the process or art of defining the hardware and software architecture, components, modules, interfaces, and data for a computer system to satisfy specified requirements. Designing an encryption solution is no different, but it does require attention to compliance, export controls, and industry standards. For this step, the organization should document its encryption strategy, architecture/framework, and the specific encryption requirements to be addressed. After validating the encryption requirements with the organization's stakeholders and business units, the hardware and software architecture, components, modules, and interfaces necessary to protect the confidentiality of the organization's data must be specified.

Step 7: Begin Data Realignment

In some situations, the design makes certain assumptions about the ICT infrastructure and locations of the data. In addition, cost constraints may limit the full use of the design. To address these issues, data may need to be migrated or realigned to take full advantage of the expected encryption solution. This step concludes with any necessary data alignments.

Step 8: Implement Solution

Implementing the encryption solution is where the rubber hits the road. The specified components are acquired and/or developed, end-to-end tests are conducted, the systems are deployed, and the roll-back plan must be developed and documented. Note, however, the solution is not put into full operational use at this stage.

Step 9: Activate Encryption

The final step is focused on those activities that transition the encryption solution into operational use. At a minimum, it should include management acceptance of the solution and approval to proceed to a production state (e.g., management accreditation).

SUMMARY

Encryption can be used as a preventative control (protect data from disclosure to unauthorized parties), a detective control (discovery of unauthorized changes to data), or both. There are multiple considerations that need to be made when evaluating the deployment of an encryption process, including, but not limited to:

- Properly used, encryption can strengthen an organization's systems.
- Encryption has the potential to weaken other security aspects (e.g., inspection of data, antivirus protection).
- Although necessary, encryption carries the risk of making data unavailable should anything go wrong with data handling, key management, or the actual encryption.
- Encryption can potentially include significant overhead cost/impacts on hosts and networks.

According to the ISACA, "The most critical aspect of encryption is the determination of what data should be encrypted and where and when it should be encrypted."[10] To reinforce this point, ISACA has developed a specific procedure that an information systems auditor should use when evaluating an organization's management controls over encryption methodologies. Likewise, the Federal Financial Institutions Examination Council and the Payment Card Industry Security Standards Council have developed their own guidance on encryption.

The bottom line for encrypting data at-rest is that all data should be evaluated from a risk perspective for unauthorized viewing and from a business perspective given the cost versus benefit or risk reduction.

---

10. ISACA IT Standards, Guidelines, and Tools and Techniques for Audit and Assurance and Control Professionals, *available at* http://www.isaca.org, March 2010, p. 294, Section 1.3.1.

CHAPTER 11

Encryption Best Practices

Robert Thibadeau

Encryption hides information. But what counts as reasonable encryption, reasonable hiding of information? It does not take much technical knowledge to watch out for what is reasonable and what is not. It is also comforting to know what encryption really is, what keys really are, and how the pieces of the encryption puzzle fit together. With the knowledge of how modern encryption is done, it becomes relatively easy to understand how to think about good and bad practices in using encryption.

It is good to require "encryption" to protect sensitive information and ensure privacy, but simply requiring "encryption" without a measure of reasonableness in the keys and how they are used can provide little, if any, significant data protection. Without much effort, encryption can ensure privacy to a high degree.

With modern encryption technology, digital information is almost perfectly hidden. Understanding how encryption is done on the eight-bit bytes of information, and why it is so good at hiding, is straightforward. How encryption works is described in the next few paragraphs. Much less straightforward, and usually the Achilles heel of data encryption, is how people use encryption technology. Bad practices may allow the "bad guys" to decrypt the information, and, sometimes just as serious, bad practices may allow them to maliciously or accidentally alter the private information.

ENCRYPTION FUNDAMENTALS

We begin with a short and simple primer on how encryption works its magic. For encryption to be generally useful, it must allow encryption and decryption of a large amount of information. The medical records of a thousand patients can easily be millions of bytes, and if they include digital x-rays and other imagery, additional billions of pixel bytes. For now, let us begin with an imaginary patient, Amy, with about 5,000 words, or about 30,000 bytes, of personal information and another 20 million bytes of pixel imagery. The "plaintext" version of Amy's medical record is the version that is not hidden, and can be read with database, word processing, or image viewing tools.

Here is how encryption works. Encryption is perfect if the result of encrypting Amy's medical record turns it into exactly the same number of bytes, 20,030,000, but now the bits inside the bytes are indistinguishable from perfectly random noise. In other words,

191

the bytes now appear to contain no information whatsoever using any tool that anyone has ever invented. A good encryption algorithm will give this result. This can be achieved easily with a computer operation that performs an "exclusive-or" (XOR) of the bytes in Amy's record with exactly the same number of bytes that are known to have no information. The XOR of two identical bits is always zero, and the XOR of a one and a zero bit is always one.

The result is that Amy's encrypted record will look perfectly random because the random bits were perfectly random. It is perfectly encrypted and no tools have ever been invented that can decrypt it. The magic of the XOR is that if you do the XOR operation a second time, but now with the encrypted version of Amy's record and the original random bits, you will now decrypt the record and be able to read it again. In other words, the key that encrypts the data will decrypt it. Table 11.1 shows a simple example of encrypting and decrypting one byte.

All encryption algorithms that are good for encrypting and decrypting large bulks of data use exactly this reversing "XOR" trick with a random number. There is really only one more step to understanding bulk encryption. In thinking through how to do perfect encryption, it was necessary to come up with a huge number of perfectly random bytes, 20,030,000 in Amy's case. A 20-megabyte key is quite large. It doubles the size of Amy's medical record, but worse, if the "bad guy" obtains the key, he has her record, so where and how do you keep this key?

The answer is in cryptology. Modern technological advances have enabled us to use very short keys to perform bulk encryption with hardly any practical loss of encryption strength. For example, a single key of 16 random bytes, or 128 bits, is considered as strong as is imaginable.

TABLE 11.1
Simple Example

XOR Step	Bit 0	Bit 1	Bit 2	Bit 3	Bit 4	Bit 5	Bit 6	Bit 7
1, Original Plaintext	0	1	1	0	1	1	0	0
2, Random Key	1	0	0	1	1	0	0	1
3, Encrypted Data	1	1	1	1	0	1	0	1
4, Random Key	1	0	0	1	1	0	0	1
5, Decrypted Plaintext	0	1	1	0	1	1	0	0

The basic ways this works is that the short random key does indeed provide the random bits that are XORed with the plaintext, but the plaintext also has its bytes substituted and mixed around and around, back and forth, in a block of bytes. Cryptographers are crafty people. They also use other tricks across blocks of bytes to make the encrypted data look even more random, but these are details. The essence is that the crafty operations are reversible but the essential protection is the XOR of the random key material with the information in the medical record. The essence is the XOR operation.

It is relatively simple to understand why merely 16 bytes can nearly perfectly encrypt or decrypt Amy's 20 megabytes. A 128-bit random number is much larger than it first appears. In fact, it is likely that no random 128-bit number has ever been produced twice by a good random number generator. To get a feeling for how big this number is, a "bad guy" trying to guess the key would require an average of 1.7×10^{38} tries. This works out to about 50 million billion centuries guessing a trillion keys a second. If you began at 128 ones, and proceeded to count down to all zeros, it would take about twice that long, or about a hundred million billion centuries counting down at the rate of a trillion counts a second. That is a very long time.

We are now finished with the fundamentals of encryption for bulk data protection. Fortunately, there are internationally recognized standards that help us get further details right.

NIST AND THE AES ENCRYPTION STANDARD

Computers are becoming faster all the time, and the number of computers is increasing apace. Even so, the U.S. certification body for good encryption, the National Institute of Standards and Technology (NIST), says that 128-bit encryption should be good at least through the year 2031. In fact, 256-bit encryption (32-byte keys), which is 2128 times as strong as 128 bit, is also rated the same, as good to at least 2031. No one can know for sure, but NIST officials will tell you this is as far ahead as they can look. 128 bits might be solid for another 20 years or more, and so will 256 bits. There is not much practical difference, just as there is not much practical difference today, and for the foreseeable future, between a 128-bit key, a 256-bit key, and a 20-megabyte key.

Several years ago, NIST sought to replace the U.S. standard for encryption, and created an international standard by sponsoring an open global competition for the new standard. This is called the Advanced Encryption Standard (AES).[1] Because all the strength of the hiding is in the key, the AES algorithm is published and available for anyone in the world to inspect. NIST also will certify it is done correctly and has given it a "FIPS 197" approval.[2]

When referring to AES, often the key length is also given, as in AES 128, AES 192, or AES 256. Other key lengths are possible, but these three are the NIST-approved AES standard options. Some of the other little tricks used by the crafty cryptographers refer to "modes" of AES. A well-known NIST-approved mode, for example, is "counter

---

1. http://csrc.nist.gov/publications/fips/fips197/fips-197.pdf.
2. *Id.*

mode" where you also XOR in the count of each successive block of 128 bits in a record. AES is called a block cipher and the block size is 128 bits. In AES, when the bytes are shuffled, they are shuffled inside each block, not across blocks. AES is used in every country of the world and is highly regarded. There are certainly other good ciphers, but AES is well recognized as a safe bet that can be certified to be correct.

WHAT CAN GO WRONG WITH ENCRYPTION?

Short Encryption Key Lengths

We begin with what we have learned about how encryption works. While 128-bit keys are strong, a too-short key is a significant problem. An older encryption standard called DES (for Data Encryption Standard) commonly uses a 40-bit key. Forty bits is a much smaller number. In fact, with modern computers, it is a dangerously short key length to protect Amy's medical record. It takes about nine minutes to guess the key at a billion guesses a second. A number of forensic companies will claim they can crack encryption in a matter of a few minutes. But in the fine print, they are quoting cracks for 40-bit keys. This weak encryption is still in use in laptop and desktop operating systems, such as Windows, which is why the forensic companies have success. This situation is changing. There is no good excuse for vendors not to use AES 128 or stronger with a NIST-approved mode of operation.

The Key Itself Is Not a Completely Random Number

Regular computer programs are notoriously difficult to program to produce random numbers. The random number generator in computer software is usually what is called a pseudo-random number generator. It will produce what looks like random numbers, but they are not. NIST provides standards for pseudo-random number generators, but these must be started with what are called hardware sources of entropy to give good completely unpredictable, results.[3] There are no standards for the random hardware starting points, or seeds, but there are many known ways to get good ones from various noise sources. Testing the quality of a random number generator may require generating billions of test keys to make sure that no bits in the keys appear to be predictable in any way, and experts are needed to do this work.

The Encryption Key Is Compromised

The last major way that encryption fails in hiding Amy's medical record is that an unauthorized person gets control of the encryption key. Now his work is very short; he simply decrypts the record because he either knows the key or can use it.

Sophisticated key management technologies exist for making sure the "bad guy" will not achieve control of the key, but we can speak to the essential components and how they are put together. Typically, key management is a much larger part of the encryption puzzle than the encryption itself. For example, usually a good policy is to encrypt the

---

3. http://csrc.nist.gov/groups/ST/toolkit/rng/index.html.

medical records of each patient with a different key. This means that an unauthorized person who obtains Amy's key can decrypt only Amy's records.

Layered Encryption

It is always possible that an insider can get through one layer of encryption. A natural property of encryption is layered defense. A device can protect all its contents with one key, and each medical record in the device can also be encrypted with different keys. There is no limit to the number of times a block of bytes can be encrypted as long as they are decrypted in the opposite order of encrypting.

Having multiple layers allows for orderly control over access to data. For example, a data center may protect large amounts of data with just a few device keys, while a particular application may protect individual records with a key for every record. Both ensure that the data is protected, and one layer of encryption takes care of some unauthorized persons while another takes care of others. It is usually prudent to have multiple layers. One layer actually protects another layer because it is difficult to know when a key has actually decrypted one layer since there is no plaintext to look at.

Encrypting the Keys

Most data thieves will go after control of the keys rather than even try to do a brute force crack of the encrypted medical record. To keep intruders from obtaining the keys, the keys are also stored in an encrypted form or in protected hardware, but the keys have to be used at some points. When a key is being used, it is necessarily in plaintext and therefore is most likely to be stolen. Software encryption has the problem that an operating system bug can read all the keys being used. This is why hardware encryption is preferable unless the computer doing the encryption can be proven to be safe. "Safe" typically means it is completely isolated from other computers, and particularly from the Internet. With layered protection, it may be reasonable to accept exposure of some keys because other keys may not have that exposure.

Hardware Encryption Protection

There are many examples of hardware encryption protection. The oldest type is called a hardware security module (HSM). An HSM is typically a few thousand dollars and is built just to perform a handful of cryptographic operations and prevent any unauthorized access to the keys. The most advanced HSM will also destroy any keys it is holding if there is an attempt to physically tamper with the HSM.

Another type of hardware encryption protection is the self-encrypting disk drive.[4] Since most data worldwide is stored on disk drives, the self-encrypting disk does not typically allow the data encryption key to be read off the drive, and can also generate high-quality random numbers for new keys. The Trusted Computing Group's Storage Workgroup is composed of all the hard-drive makers who have agreed on standards for self-encrypting drives.[5] Properly configured, a self-encrypting drive never exposes the keys that operate it to an unsafe operating system.

---

4. This new technology is discussed in chapter 14.
5. http://www.trustedcomputinggroup.org/developers/storage.

Networks may also be encrypted for data-in-transit, and the network hardware often provides encryption in well-known standards such as Internet Protocol Security (IPsec),[6] but it should be checked if the encryption keys are ever available to an unsafe operating system environment.

ACCESS TO THE ENCRYPTION KEYS

The largest and most complex aspect of key management is the technology for granting and denying use of the keys, even if they are solidly stored behind a hardware shield. The size and complexity of granting access to the keys is due to the huge range of reasonable possibilities, and not particularly in any single approach. The best way to explain key access is to describe different families of techniques and the benefits and pitfalls in each.

A Key Protects Other Keys

Often the user sees this as a password system. The user types in a password, or logs in with his password, and is granted access. Clearly it is a rare human who can remember a 128-bit random string like "00010203050607080A0B0C0D0F101112" (16 bytes in hexadecimal), which is required if you want protection against using a 128-bit key to be as strong as the strength of the data encryption.

Multi-Factor Authentication

A small USB dongle or a smart card may need to be inserted. If this contains a full-strength random secret, then the protection of the use of the keys is strong, as long as the dongle is not lost. The second factor, the password you can remember, could be reasonably strong and provide some protection. A third factor, for example a fingerprint reader or iris scanner, can provide a bit more. But a password that a person can remember or his biometrics are hardly a fraction as strong as a random authentication password that is 128 or 256 bits in length. Multi-factor authentication is like layered encryption. Each factor deals with a different set of threats, but only a good long random number will be as strong as the cipher and this usually requires another device. A password limited to bytes that a user can type easily from a keyboard must be about 24 characters long to match the cryptographic strength of a 128-bit key.

The device that is doing the encryption can protect the data encryption key by using the strong authentication password to encrypt the data encryption key when it is not in use. A common technique, called somewhat incongruously "a split," is to XOR the strong authentication key, the password, and the biometric signature, and then use the mix as the encryption key for the data encryption key when the data encryption key is not in use. For even greater safety against misuse of a key, two cryptographically strong authentication keys may be used, similar to the use of two keys on a safe-deposit box in a bank.

These techniques are what are called "shared secret" solutions to authentication and authorization to use the data encryption keys. An inherent security problem with such

---

6. http://en.wikipedia.org/wiki/IPsec.

solutions is that at some point you have to copy the shared secret around. Typically, the published procedures around copying shared secrets will say that the operator must be careful to prevent the shared secrets from being read by unauthorized persons.

Public Key Cryptography

An alternative to a shared secret system that is better, but involves another type of cryptography, is public key cryptography. It works without key sharing because there are always two keys, one that encrypts and the other that decrypts. The key that can encrypt the data cannot decrypt it. The key that can decrypt it cannot encrypt it. This is called "public" key because one of the two keys may be made publicly available, and is not particularly secret. The other key of the key pair must be hidden, preferably behind a hardware shield.

Depending on whether the encrypting or the decrypting key is hidden, two different use cases result. If you hide the encrypting key, then you can "sign" and prove who you are. The way this usually works is that the bulk-encrypting device will give you a random number called a nonce. Your signing device now encrypts the nonce and hands it back to the bulk-encrypting device. The bulk-encrypting device may now use your public key to decrypt the encrypted nonce and confirm it is the nonce that it originally sent out. It has proved that you know the private encrypting key without ever knowing what that key is or exposing that key to an unsafe operating system environment.

The math is not the simple XOR math, and is not suited to bulk data encryption, but it is highly suited to encrypting data encryption keys. In the second use, the private key is the decrypting key. In this use case, your dongle or smart card encrypts the shared secret with the public key of the bulk encryption device, and that device gets both the shared secret and the shared secret is never exposed. This second technique is essentially how secure credit card purchases are done on the Internet. Your browser obtains the server's public encrypting key, encrypts a new random data encryption key, and sends the key to the server. The server uses this to hide the rest of the transaction.

Public Key Cryptosystems

There are basically two high-profile, well standardized and accepted public key cryptosystems, one called RSA (for its inventors Ron Rivest, Adi Shamir, and Leonard Adleman) and the other known as "elliptic curve." The keys in both systems are fabricated through a random number generator, just like symmetric keys, and therefore have the same questions about random number quality. However, these keys must be much larger than 128 bits to have the same strength as a 128-bit symmetric cipher. This can be quite confusing to someone who does not understand that public key ciphers are based on math that requires larger keys. For example, with RSA, the random number generator is asked to generate two large prime random numbers. Since only a fraction of numbers are prime, the random numbers are not as random as the numbers used for AES, for example. There is no way to know with certainty, but it has been estimated that to equal the strength of a 128-bit AES key, an RSA key size of 3,072 bits would be required, and an elliptic curve key size of 256 bits. The United States and most other governments are now preferring elliptic curve because it is much more efficient to compute and requires smaller keys to achieve the same strength.

Public key cryptography is used for key management and not for bulk data encryption. But there is another facet of hiding and selectively revealing Amy's medical record that also involves encryption. It has been said that the three legs of the evidence stool are time, integrity, and identity, and this may be said to apply to Amy's medical record. How do we know who certifies the information in the record and who may have access to it? Clearly an unauthorized person should not be allowed to change the record and reencrypt it. There are a number of technologies that help solve this puzzle. The most highly preferred way is to use cryptographic hashes and public key signing. Again, this is not difficult to understand having now understood encryption.

Cryptographic hashing takes a large number of bytes of information and computes a unique small key for that data, usually 128 bits or 256 bits. Again, XOR operations and substituting and moving bytes left and right figure prominently, but now the purpose is to collapse all the bytes of information into a "hash" that looks perfectly random. Furthermore, if even one bit in all of the bulk information is changed, the hash will look like a completely different random number.

So far so good. If an unauthorized person alters Amy's record, the hash will be different. But how can we make sure that he does not also change the hash? Enter public key cryptography, but now we use the signing and verification where the public key is the decryption key and the private encrypting key is held only by a certifier. The public key can be in the plaintext version of Amy's record. The computer reading Amy's record hashes the decrypted record, decrypts the signed hash to reveal the hash made by the certifier, and checks to make sure these two hashes match perfectly. Work done.

Now the question is, how do we know that the public key itself is really the certifier's public key? The answer is the same, and the standard for it is called the X.509 certificate standard.[7] An X.509 certificate contains plaintext identifying the name and address of the certifier and his public key that are hashed and signed by the certifier of the certifier. The trick here is that just as it was possible to layer bulk encryption, public key cryptography lends itself to signing chains. This hashing and signing operation allows users to know who certified the certifier. X.509 certificates form the basis for certifying public keys for all credit card commerce on the Internet and also, significantly, for all interbank money transfers worldwide. The public key cryptosystem has sufficient strength to be trusted in the movement of literally trillions of dollars a day on a global basis.

CRITICAL ENCRYPTION MEASURES

Encryption begins with bulk data encryption but, at some point, it is important to ask about how the encryption keys are managed. Bulk data encryption may be very strong, but if the key methodology that provides access to using the encryption is weak, then strong data encryption does no good. Any evaluation of reasonableness in encryption must look in detail at the key management side of encryption to find the weak links.

---

7. http://en.wikipedia.org/wiki/X.509.

With public key cryptography, many known weak links in key management may be readily and easily solved.

The things to watch for in encryption are these:

- Use NIST-approved AES for bulk data encryption. The encryption keys should be at least 128 bits, or 16 bytes, and should be created with a proven source of real random noise.
- The encryption keys should be used where they cannot readily be stolen or copied. It is good, not bad, to layer encryptions on top of one another.
- Managing the encryption keys provides the means for controlling who can use them. The best way is to make sure at least one of the ways of authenticating a proper user is also a random number of the same strength as the AES cipher. This may be done with a shared secret, but this risks that an unauthorized person may obtain this shared secret.
- The best way, in use in all credit card transactions on the Internet and in all interbank transfers for over a decade, is public key cryptography such as NIST-approved RSA or elliptic curve.
- Care must be taken to make sure these key-access keys are also used in hardware-protected environments such as dedicated servers, HSM, or self-encrypting hard disk drives.
- Most cracks of encryption are actually cracks of poor key management, not the encryption itself. To make sure an unauthorized person, or even Amy herself, does not maliciously or accidentally alter Amy's medical record, a system of public key certifiers may be readily established. Public key cryptography invites third-party certification to certify the certifiers.

CHAPTER 12

Circumventing Data Encryption: Password Vulnerabilities

Serge Jorgensen

Controls on electronic data can be generally compared to those on physical data—doors, walls, locks, and keys. Ultimately, data must be accessible in order to be used. While this seems like common sense, changing the state of data from protected, to unprotected, and back to protected is a complex process and often creates a weakness in data protection. Locks, keys, and algorithms all require some means for changing state—providing and removing data access, or opening and closing doors. The common thread across techniques, and the weakest point, is the password requirement.

Passwords have long formed the most basic level of security for allowing or preventing access to information. Before implementing any data-protection strategy, significant thought should be given to password creation and management. This chapter explores encryption as it relates to various password concepts, implementations, and options, along with some of the associated strengths and weaknesses.

PASSWORDS AND DATA ENCRYPTION

The premise of data encryption is to scramble data so that it is unreadable without a key. In basic terms, there are three main parts to the process:

1. The data to be encrypted
2. The encryption engine
3. The key used to activate the engine

In an effort to provide additional security, recent advances have split the key into two pieces, providing a form of two-factor authentication. The meshing of data, engine, and key is shown in Figure 12.1. The physical key is protected (or augmented) by a known password that, when combined, allow the engine to operate. The interrelated components make

FIGURE 12.1
VALC Encryption Components

the encryption engine place a heavy reliance on proper application of password practices. Failure of the key/password combination allows "running" of the engine by anyone.

A complex key, applied to a properly tested encryption algorithm, secured by an as yet uncompromised password, can adequately protect almost any data just like a very thick door with a good lock. This same system can be instantly compromised by leaving the password exposed on a sticky note, or leaving the key in the door lock.

Passwords are the most difficult point for encryption vendors to control, since the ability to create, change, and use the password must remain in the hands of the end user. Regardless of the strength of the mechanism, control of the key that works that mechanism is critical.

SHARED SECRETS

Passwords remain at the root of access control and, despite many efforts to the contrary, most solutions implemented today ultimately include a user-generated password. Password design has gone through many phases, but most often involve a word, phrase, or number created by the user and then remembered or recorded. Some basic password techniques and a comparison of effectiveness to complexity is included in Table 12.1.

Three primary uses of a password are authorization, authentication, and encryption. Using a password for authorization is different from authentication, which in turn is much different from using a password for encryption. Outlined in Table 12.2, these uses share the common requirement of protecting the password from misuse and the common purpose of making data available to the end user while shielding it from others.

TABLE 12.1
Password Techniques and Their Effectiveness

	Easy to Remember	*Hard to Guess*	*Replaceable*	*Overall Effectiveness*
Common words & numbers (names, birth dates . . .)	✓	✗	✓	✗
Combinations of words (name + birth date)	✓	✗	✓	✗
Random strings of characters	✗	✓	✓	✗
Pass phrases (long collections of words that mean something to the end user)	✓	✓	✓	✓
Biometrics	✓	✓	✗	✗

BIOMETRICS, TWO-FACTOR AUTHENTICATION, AND ONE-TIME PASSWORDS

Ultimately, passwords represent a means of authorization—proving that the person making the access request is permitted to view the data. Depending on the methodology used, authorization can be extended to include authentication, verifying that the person making the request is who he says he is through the use of biometrics or similar mechanisms.

There is a growing trend toward one-time passwords. These passwords are auto-generated on demand based on some predefined relationship between provider and requester (e.g., RSA SecurID). Common one-time password implementations use an initial, predetermined value held on a remote server to validate the one-time code generated at the moment access is requested. A password is created by the user, sent to

TABLE 12.2
Password Uses

Uses	*Effect*
Authorization	Manage ability to use or take advantage of something (e.g., e-mail account, computer, stored files)
Authentication	Provide some verification of identity, usually in conjunction with access control
Encryption	Scrambles the data instead of denying access to information; protects data regardless of success/failure of access control and authentication procedures

the authorization device, verified, and then expires and is no longer valid. While some of these devices are used as stand-alone solutions, most are combined with a user-known password, thus creating two-factor authentication.

Two-factor authentication is easily explained as "something you have, and something you know." In the case above, you *know* a PIN or password, and you *have* the device generating a one-time code. The combination of two items adds some additional security, at the cost of additional complexity. Beyond adding some complexity to defeat the malicious user, end users would likely notice if the device they have (or had) was suddenly stolen or misplaced. Finally, two-factor methods provide some (limited) amount of authentication as well as authorization because it is less likely that multiple people might possess both items necessary to submit valid credentials.

Biometric passwords are also growing in popularity. This concept creates a mathematical model of an individual characteristic (e.g., fingerprint, iris, face, and signature) and uses it as the password. Biometric passwords are generally seen as more secure since they are difficult to share, guess, or replicate. However, if the hash value is compromised, a fingerprint or face scan is far more difficult to change than a more traditional password. Biometric passwords are also just as vulnerable to sniffing and capturing attacks.

Table 12.3 provides a comparison of some of the functions of various password methodologies and rates their effectiveness on a scale of one to three stars, with the understanding that there are many different implementations and uses. These concepts are all vulnerable to one attack or another, making the two-factor authentication concept a very desirable methodology to implement where possible.

PASSWORD ATTACKS

The "purpose" of the password is often combined in a mix-and-match pattern to meet the specific needs of an application, but it is best to consider each use as a separate function. Passwords blurring across usage lines (i.e., using the same password to provide

TABLE 12.3
Functions and Effectiveness of Password Methodologies

Technique	Setup	Sniffing Resistant	Brute-Force Resistant	Theft Resistant	Effective for Authentication
Password/phrase	☆☆☆	☆	☆	☆☆☆	☆
Biometric	☆☆	☆☆	☆☆☆	☆	☆☆☆
Software key (certificate)	☆☆	☆	☆☆☆	☆	☆☆
One-time code	☆	☆☆☆	☆☆☆	☆	☆☆
Hardware key (dongle)	☆☆☆	☆☆☆	☆☆☆	☆	☆☆

authorization *and* decrypt data) often creates problems with data compartmentalization when one password is compromised. However, since it is difficult for people to keep track of many different passwords, common practice is that a single password (or slight variations thereof) is used across many sites and for multiple purposes. A password exposed, captured, or guessed in one location can then be applied directly to more heavily protected locations. The process of compromising passwords takes many forms, but sniffing, brute-forcing, and hash-matching are some of the more popular methods.

Password sniffing is the practice of capturing passwords as they move over the path from user to device. Every time a password is used, some data must be transmitted to verify the password information. Usually, these are hashes and encrypted data, but some programs (e.g., POP e-mail through Microsoft Outlook) still send passwords in clear text. Users may not even realize that their passwords are broadcast without protection and can be captured by anyone listening. It is relatively easy to encrypt passwords moving between devices or to implement a one-time password strategy so that a password cannot be reused even if captured.

Brute-forcing a password, or repetitively guessing random combinations of letters and numbers as well as dictionary-based words, is another common technique applied to cracking passwords. Many password-protected resources now offer some defense against brute-forcing through the following techniques:

- Locking an account after a defined, low number of failed access attempts
- Captcha requirements to verify that a human is behind the request
- Time outs between guesses to extend the time an attack would take

Finally, hashed passwords can be attacked by comparing and compromising the hashes—thus revealing the original password or at least allowing transmission of the "correct" hash. In this process, the hashing engine is fed many different values. Depending on the hash process used, if Hash 1 matched Hash 2, then Password 1 may match Password 2. The most widely recognized lookup tables (e.g., Rainbow tables) can contain millions of valid hashes and the associated passwords for various hashing algorithms, including those used to encrypt passwords in common operating systems such as Microsoft Windows NT/2000, Linux, and BSD. There are a number of solutions that prevent successful implementation of these attacks but, like encrypting passwords in transit, the solution must be used in order to be effective.

A common failing of authorization-based protection is moving information outside of the protection area without the awareness that the information is now exposed to malicious access. The value of encryption-based protection is that lost or stolen data remains protected. In addition, encryption

- is more resistant to many techniques that typically circumvent authorization-style controls (i.e., login passwords and boot passwords);
- can also be placed on data without constraint by the operating system; and
- is easily moved between types of media.

A well-tested encryption algorithm (the "engine" in Figure 12.1) is typically open to public inspection since there will be no way to reverse-engineer the mathematical algorithm used. Such an algorithm only allows proper decryption of data if the correct key is known. Vulnerabilities in algorithms often involve determining a method of predicting the key or decrypting data based on faults in the original encryption algorithm. Algorithm and key strength is often a much-touted sales factor, with key lengths of 128 and 256 bits now standard. Such key lengths applied to an effective algorithm make brute-forcing the algorithm virtually impossible. The Advanced Encryption Standard (AES) is an adaptation of the Rijndael cipher, and has rapidly become the common-use standard for data encryption.

Proper implementation of the full AES cipher (and noting that there are more than a few improper and partial implementations) is a very secure way of protecting data while stored and in transit. The most successful and easiest attack vector remains recovering the key from the end user. This brings us back to the basic discussion of password security. The key is safe until the moment it is used, at which point it becomes immediately vulnerable to interception, sniffing, cracking, and replaying. Beyond this, the key is unsafe if it can be easily guessed, or acquired from another less-protected source and then applied to the engine.

PREVENTION

As expected, many manufacturers are adding components to their encryption engines meant to limit the attacks that can be mounted. The most popular of these protections is to limit the number of times that an incorrect password or key can be tried against an encrypted data set before the data set self-destructs or is rendered unusable. Similarly, many tricks have been used to prevent password guessing, and techniques to avoid password sniffing, cache recovery, and session replays are constantly evolving. From biometrics to one-time passwords, there are many options that can provide the safety and security necessary for most applications, if correctly deployed.

Accepting permanent loss of data (due to a forgotten password) is often an unacceptable risk. Instead of effective security measures, this often results in simple passwords, recorded passwords, or unencrypted data backups. It is *these* weaknesses that are identified and exploited first, since these are so much easier (often faster and more effective) than mounting an attack against properly created methodologies and well-implemented strategies.

Ultimately, preventing data breaches rests in the hands of each user with the ability to access or decrypt the data. There are longer-term solutions that replace current password concepts with a more resilient form of authentication. Until that time, users must ensure that passwords are protected against the exploits and attacks explored above. Some simple concepts to prevent data breaches include:

- Monitor access controls to provide some detection from password guessing and hash capture attempts.
- Utilize available resources to create attack-resistance passwords.
- Employ compartmentalization and segmentation methods to prevent any one breach from expanding and causing multiple problems.

Given available authentication techniques and encryption algorithms, there is no reason for data to be exposed unnecessarily.

CHAPTER 13

Managing Cryptographic Keys

Benjamin L. Tomhave

The evolution of compliance initiatives, such as the Payment Card Industry Data Security Standard (PCI DSS), has brought forward numerous requirements for properly managing cryptographic keys, such as for data encryption and digital signatures (hashes). Requirement 3 of the PCI DSS, for example, provides detailed requirements for key strength, key generation, key handling, and protecting the key in production. Requirements include split knowledge and separation of duties such that no one person has full control of the key or encryption system, preventing a malicious person from introducing a key that can then be used to compromise sensitive data.

Unfortunately, despite the prescriptive nature of the PCI DSS, implementing sound key management is neither straightforward nor trivial. In fact, some of the practices can seem quite obtuse to the most astute observer, becoming quite daunting when questions beyond the basic technical aspects of key management arise, like "How often do you rotate the key?" "What's your encryption policy?" and "Where do you store your backup key?" These types of questions can lead to the realization that homegrown or turnkey solutions only address the technology needs, and do not address the technology management requirements.

This chapter is designed to provide an introduction to the primary aspects of key management, as well as to introduce a few additional considerations. For the most part, the cryptographic systems for which this guidance is applicable will be servers and databases, rather than workstation solutions like whole-disk encryption. That being said, some of these concepts (e.g., key escrow) can be applied to endpoint solutions and may, as such, warrant additional investigation.

ASSOCIATED STANDARDS AND STANDARDS COMMITTEES

Before getting into the details of key management, it is first worth acknowledging the comprehensive guidance published by the U.S. National Institute of Standards and Technology (NIST) under Special Publication 800-57 (SP 800-57). Compared with the eight-step process described herein, the NIST standard describes a four-stage process, with each stage detailing numerous steps, along with supporting documents that provide further detailed guidance on many technical aspects of key management. It is an excellent reference, and one that should be referenced when implementing technical key management procedures. This chapter is intended to provide an introductory survey of concepts and concerns relative to key management, not to be a complete or technical procedural guide.

Beyond the NIST standards, there are also a few organizations working on standards around key management. The Institute of Electrical and Electronics Engineers (IEEE) is currently sponsoring the P1619.3 working group, which is focused on developing standard protocols for generating and distributing encryption keys. Meanwhile, the Organization for the Advancement of Structured Information Standards (OASIS) has two technical committees engaged in protocol development around key management. The Enterprise Key Management Infrastructure (EKMI) technical committee was the first on the scene and has provided the basis for many related efforts. OASIS has also chartered the Key Management Interoperability Protocol (KMIP) technical committee, which is related to both EKMI and P1619.3, sponsored by a consortium of major technical vendors. This new technical committee was chartered with a draft protocol already in-hand and appears headed for de facto status given the vendor representation and noticeable public realtions machine behind it. As a result, the future of the EKMI technical committee is unclear, as is the work of IEEE's P1619.3.

INTRODUCTION TO ENTERPRISE KEY MANAGEMENT INFRASTRUCTURE

An enterprise key management infrastructure is a collection of technology, policies, and procedures for managing cryptographic keys in the enterprise. An EKMI has the following features:

- It consists of two major components:
    - a public key infrastructure (PKI), which is used for managing digital certificates and the escrow/retrieval of asymmetric encryption keys. Digital certificates enable strong authentication, message integrity, and the encryption of small bits of data (typically, symmetric data-encryption keys) using two different parts of a related cryptographic pair of keys.
    - a symmetric key management system, which is used for managing symmetric data-encryption keys. While symmetric keys can be used for authentication, message integrity, and data encryption too, they are more often used for data encryption exclusively, because of their performance benefits.
- It provides a single place to define policy on:
    - who may access cryptographic keys
    - when they may access them
    - from which locations
    - for how long
    - with which applications and
    - for what purposes.
- It provides a single repository for the escrow and retrieval of all keys in the enterprise.
- It enables end-to-end security by empowering applications to easily encrypt data directly in the application.

- It uses a standard protocol for the request and receipt of key-management services.
- It is operating system and application independent.
- It enables the secure availability of data-encryption keys, even during a network failure that makes the key-management service unavailable.
- It is scalable to support millions of clients.
- It is designed to be extremely secure.

THE KEY MANAGEMENT LIFECYCLE

In a general sense, the key management lifecycle comprises eight main stages, as represented in Figure 13.1. Each stage represents a major process group that must be addressed both in documentation and in practice.

Creation

The first step in the key management lifecycle is generating the key. Key creation must be conducted in a secure environment (hardened system), and may include requirements

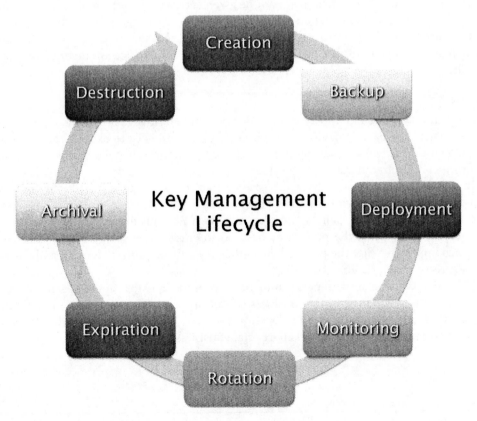

FIGURE 13.1
The Key Management Lifecycle

for dual control and the separation of duties. In most cases, the key in question is a symmetric key (a.k.a. "shared secret key"), which is better able to meet performance requirements. The key generated should be of an adequate size and strength, with its overall quality dependent in part on the base system's ability to generate a random number (see NIST Special Publication 800-57 for detailed recommendations[1]). Key creation should be performed using known good libraries that have been properly reviewed by knowledgeable people. Proprietary algorithms that have not withstood scrutiny should be avoided, instead favoring well-known algorithms such as Advanced Encryption Standard (AES).

Once a key is generated, it may then be desirable to protect it using the public key of an asymmetric key pair (a.k.a. public key cryptography, or PKI). In situations where the encryption key must be distributed to other systems, particularly via a network file transfer, it is often good to follow this practice.

From the standpoint of dual control and the separation of duties, an organization can have one team own and manage the generation of keys, but bar that team access to the encryption system itself, requiring them to instead encrypt the symmetric key with a public key before providing it to the deployment team. The deployment team would then be able to install the key into the production environment. As a further control, it is advisable that the deployment team not be given access to the private key of the asymmetric key pair, instead relying on the application to decrypt the new symmetric key as part of the key installation process. In this manner, neither the key generation team, nor the deployment team, nor the developers will be able to introduce an unauthorized key into the production environment.

Backup

Before a new key is rolled into a production environment, it is vital that a backup of the key be made. The backup could be as simple as writing the key to external media (e.g., CD, DVD, USB drive) and storing it in a physical vault. Or, it may be desired to back it up using existing traditional backup solutions (local or networked).

In either case, but especially in the case of traditional backups, it is highly recommended that a second asymmetric key pair be used to protect the symmetric key. Think of this second public key pair as your "escrow" key. As with the deployment key pair, it is recommended that the public key be used to encrypt the shared key, and then it becomes imperative that the private half of this key pair be protected and readily available for recovery operations.

One other consideration in performing backups is to apply the same disaster recovery plans that you would in any other business continuity planning process. The key should be stored in and retrievable from a location that can be accessed within the recovery time requirements specified by the appropriate business owners.

---

1. NIST SP 800-57, RECOMMENDATION FOR KEY MANAGEMENT (Mar. 2007), *available at* http://csrc.nist.gov/publications/PubsSPs.html.

Deployment

As already mentioned in the discussion of key creation, it is strongly recommended that the symmetric key—used for encrypting sensitive data—be itself encrypted by the public half of an asymmetric key pair prior to being delivered for deployment. This simple step provides a method for separation of duties in an environment where key management activities are not strictly contained within a single system (e.g., encryption appliances).

In all cases, from the perspectives of dual control and the separation of duty, workflow practices should be documented and enforced such that one person is not responsible for or able to perform the creation, backup, and deployment stages of the key management lifecycle.

The purpose of the deployment phase is to introduce the new key into the cryptographic system, but this phase does not include removing the old key from that system. Specifically, it is advisable that the new key first be deployed and tested for a predefined period of time to ensure that key operations are successful before risking a data outage.

With modern appliances, these concerns have decreased, but, from a lifecycle perspective, they are still worth bearing in mind. When working with cryptographic systems, one must tend toward caution, lest a key be lost, effectively removing access to important data. That is to say, errors with cryptographic systems can be quite costly.

Monitoring

The monitoring phase of the lifecycle is arbitrarily placed at this step of the lifecycle, but in reality could just as easily be an area of responsibility that is parallel to the entire key management lifecycle. There are three aspects of monitoring that should be taken into consideration.

First, it is important to monitor for unauthorized administrative access to cryptographic systems to ensure that unapproved keys are not introduced into the system and to ensure that unauthorized key management operations are not performed. Any sort of unauthorized operation could have serious consequences for a cryptographic system, and for the data it's supporting.

Second, monitoring performance on cryptographic systems is important. The performance of cryptographic operations tends to be processor-intensive, which means that systems supporting encryption may be under significant load. Events such as flash popularity can result in a denial of service on its own, but when combined with an overloaded encryption system, the results could be far more serious, including data corruption or unavailability.

Finally, as mentioned in the deployment phase, monitoring of the key in production is also important to ensure that the key has been created and deployed properly. If a corrupt key is deployed too quickly and without proper vetting, then the results could be catastrophic. Similarly, if a fault in the cryptographic system occurs, the result could be an interruption in service, with a negative impact to the business.

Rotation

The concept of key rotation has ties to key deployment, but they are not generally synonymous. In rotating keys, the goal is to not only bring a new encryption key into lead use by the cryptographic system, but to also convert all stored, encrypted data to the new key. This process can be extremely time-consuming and processor-intensive. However, assuming that all previous steps of the lifecycle have been followed, then this phase can be discretely focused on the conversion activity, and less on the activating of the new key for new encryption requests.

Here's how key rotation works: The lifecycle of the first key (K_1) overlaps with the lifecycle of the newer key (K_2) at the rotation (K_2) and expiration (K_1) stages. The trick to understanding these overlapping lifecycles is in realizing that key rotation is as much about the new key as it is about the old key. Rotation represents the turnover of primary cryptographic activities to the new key (K_2), usually in conjunction with the expiration of the old key (K_1).

Note that there may be reasons not to perform a batch rollover of stored data from the old key to the new key. For example, if the data is highly transient (that is, accessed, written, rewritten, or purged/deleted on a very high frequency), then it may be adequate to instead flag a condition where data will be automatically converted to the new key as part of the read/write activity. Using such a capability can reduce some of the load associated with key rotation.

A word of caution: Do not remove an old key from a production system until it can be proven beyond a reasonable doubt that no data in production is still encrypted with the old key. Failing to perform due diligence, such as doing a manual query for the old key ID, may result in data loss or a service outage. Moreover, as will be discussed later, a key should never be completely destroyed until all data encrypted with the key has either been converted to a new key, or deemed ready for destruction itself.

Expiration

The expiration phase of the key management lifecycle represents the beginning of the deprecation period of life for the key. Key rotation for a new key should be completed prior to expiration of the old key, with all data encrypted with that old key converted to the new key. The objective is to have the key replaced within the production system (but not removed) before it expires. In a sense, expiration represents a gating factor for planning and technology management as much as it is a discrete phase in the lifecycle.

Key expiration will be based in part on the strength of the key and its estimated life span. The chosen strength of an encryption key will primarily take into consideration the length of time for which the data may be valid. The goal is to choose a key that is large enough that a brute force attack cannot theoretically succeed while the data is still valid or valuable. For example, if a credit card is valid for four years, then you want to choose a key size such that it will take longer than four years to guess the correct key and thus retrieve the data. NIST Special Publication 800-57 provides in-depth guidance for generating keys of a proper strength.[2]

In addition to key strength, it has also become best practice (and dictated by regulations like the PCI DSS) to require that the key be expired and replaced on a timeframe shorter than the calculated lifespan of the key. The minimum time span that is advocated these days is one year for each key, and preferably more often for keys protecting

---

2. *Id.*

data of the highest sensitivity. Note that this timeframe is typically much shorter than the presumed valid lifespan of the key.

Archiving a Key

The least desirable event when managing cryptographic systems is to destroy a key that still has needed data associated with it. As such, this second-to-last phase in the lifecycle is included, with a potentially open-ended mandate to not proceed to the final phase (destruction).

Archival of expired, decommissioned keys should be based on a determination of whether or not data still exists somewhere in the data ecosystem that may be encrypted with the archived key. The data ecosystem extends beyond "live" data in production to backups that may exist in disaster recovery sites, as well as to all offline backups. If there is a requirement for data to be recoverable, then it is imperative that the keys be archived in parallel to that data.

There are several tips to keep in mind when archiving a key. First, make sure to document and index the key and the data in such a way that if it is necessary to recover data in the future with an archived key, it can be done as effectively and efficiently as possible. Second, ensure that the archived copy of the key has itself been secured. As was recommended in the creation and deployment phases, it may be useful to encrypt a symmetric key with the public half of an asymmetric key pair for safe storage (bearing in mind the importance of then archiving the asymmetric key pair, and particularly the private key). Finally, include a timestamp with the key, as well as an estimated time range that reflects when the key was used for production purposes.

It is worth noting that some cryptographic appliances automatically archive expired keys in a secure fashion and may never progress to the destruction phase. Overall, this is a business risk decision that should be considered on a case-by-case basis. It may be rightfully concluded that encryption keys will never advance from archival to destruction because the risk of such a change, and the associated permanence of data loss, may outweigh the risk of exposing the archived key.

Destruction

The life of a key will truly end when it is destroyed. Key destruction should follow secure deletion procedures to ensure that it is properly obliterated. Be forewarned: Key destruction should not be taken lightly, and should only occur after an adequately long archival phase, and after at least two reviews have been completed to ensure that loss of the key will not correspond to loss of data. NIST Special Publication 800-88 is a useful reference for the sanitation of media, including the secure deletion of sensitive data.[3]

OTHER CONSIDERATIONS

In addition to the key management lifecycle, there are several considerations that organizations should factor into policies, standards, practices, and related business decisions.

---

3. NIST SP 800-88, Guidelines for Media Sanitization (Sept. 2006), *available at* http://csrc.nist.gov/publications/PubsSPs.html.

For example, the loss of an encryption key can represent a catastrophic failure in a cryptographic system. It may then be appropriate to supplement backups by maintaining an escrow key that can be used to recover data in an emergency situation.

Exercise Key Management Processes

Having key management processes documented is a good first step, but it is equally important to test and exercise those processes on a regular basis. An adept emergency response team should be able to execute the first steps of an incident response intuitively and reflexively. Likewise, key management processes and practices should be intuitive in the event that a key change needs to be made in a rapid manner (e.g., under a suspected key compromise scenario). Setting up parallel cryptographic systems in development or test environments may provide a trivial method for regularly testing key management processes and procedures.

Dual Control and Separation of Duties

As mentioned earlier, there may be business or regulatory requirements for dual control and separation of duties. The basic concept is ensuring that no one person or team will have full end-to-end access to cryptographic keys, the cryptographic system, and the data. For this reason, it is often best to implement key creation as described above, where one team generates the key, then hands it off securely to another team for deployment, which in turn uses an installation routine or process that validates the key prior to activation. With respect to the data itself, the developers or operations personnel should not be able to decrypt protected data without proper authorization and monitoring.

Key Escrow

The concept of key escrow has been around for many years (if not a few decades). Much alarm was raised around the U.S. government's idea to hold the recovery key on behalf of users or businesses by way of the Clipper Chip system in the 1990s. Today, key escrow has evolved to be viewed in less alarming and more useful terms.

The most common case for using key escrow is with whole-disk encryption systems. If an end user loses his key (or password), then organizations need to have a backup method to recover the data from the system. However, key escrow also has applicability for data encryption within data storage environments. For example, the backup phase of the lifecycle could make use of an escrow key to provide a safe copy of the primary encryption key in order to prevent against the loss of production data.

Product Interoperability

This is one major problem encountered by organizations when they have two or more cryptographic systems. Due to the requirement for the use of cryptographic protection of sensitive data, it is increasingly likely that mergers and acquisitions will bring together disparate cryptographic systems as part of IT integration. Unfortunately, while many systems will use the same types of keys (e.g., AES), it is not always a given that you will be able to take keys from one system and install them into another. Similarly, the key management interface for one system may not work with the other.

In the end, there are two primary, competing recommendations for addressing this problem. First, organizations may choose to run both cryptographic systems in parallel, so as not to disrupt service. At the same time, documentation and key management processes should be integrated into one streamlined key management program, taking into consideration the competing needs of each line of business.

The other preferred approach is to pick one cryptographic system to become the primary encryption service. However, it is to be noted that, due to archival requirements, the system that is not chosen may still need to be maintained over time until all residual data has been replaced or deprecated.

A third option has also begun emerging by way of the standards mentioned earlier. EKMI, KMIP, and P1619.3 all have protocols proposed or in development to address the secure management of keys. Interoperability is a major goal of each of these initiatives, with the notion that if their protocol is supported by all key management systems, then it will be easier to integrate them under a single key management interface (or system) without having to decommission either system.

Catastrophic Failure

Implementation of cryptographic systems should automatically trigger the revision of disaster recovery plans. What would happen if all encrypted data were to suddenly become unavailable as the result of a failure in the cryptographic system? Implementing a cryptographic system introduces additional failure points and complexity. Use of encryption to protect data means that business continuity and disaster recovery plans need to be actively revised to ensure that organizations can continue to function when faced with a complete failure. All it takes is the loss or corruption of one key to trigger a disaster recovery scenario.

Using Encryption for Virtual Shredding

Traditionally, data has been destroyed by shredding paper or properly disposing of storage media (see NIST SP 800-88 for recommendations on media sanitation[4]). However, there is another alternative, and that is using strong encryption to protect the data, and then securely destroying the key. Without the key, the data will not be useful or accessible, reducing the need for special media sanitation practices. For example, if an organization is storing data for multiple clients and one such client requires that its data be securely deleted from your database when the contract terminates, it would be difficult, if not impossible, to simply destroy the entire database, since this would negatively affect the other customers. Instead, if each client's data were encrypted with a unique key, then just the key could be securely destroyed and attestation could be made to the client that its data is no longer accessible in the system.

---

4. *Id.*

PROPER KEY MANAGEMENT

The management of cryptographic materials (encryption keys) requires robust policies and procedures that are exercised on a regular basis. Following a well-defined key management lifecycle can help reduce the risk involved with encrypting data. It is imperative that all cryptographic functions be properly monitored and that processes be structured to ensure that no one person or team has complete end-to-end access to or control of cryptographic materials and the data it protects. Proper key management will also take into consideration business continuity and disaster recovery planning in order to help defend against massive data loss as a result of a catastrophic failure in the cryptographic system.

CHAPTER **14**

The Self-Encrypting Drive

Robert Thibadeau

About a decade ago, when I was consulting with Phoenix Technologies, a small group of us concluded that hard-disk drives were, in fact, the best end-point for security and privacy. Phoenix makes the BIOS ("basic input/output system") for the overwhelming majority of Windows PCs. With Bob Baldwin,[1] I designed the "Secure Core" system now offered by Phoenix in the BIOS. It does some impressive things that only the computer start-up, the environment before Windows boots, can do. Among other preboot activities, the BIOS powers up and initializes disk drives. The BIOS is also in the background every few seconds even when Windows is running.

Later, the Trusted Computing Group (TCG), a consortium founded by IBM, Intel, Microsoft, and others to develop industry standards, took some of the ideas and defined the Trusted Platform Module (TPM). The TPM is a chip now in over 300 million laptops and servers. Similar to the Phoenix Secure Core preboot software, its main use is to support validating the preboot environment. The motivation for all this was the Chernobyl virus, which had infected the preboot of many hundreds of thousands of PCs.[2] With TCG's and prior Phoenix efforts, the preboot environment is pretty safe nowadays. Windows, on the other hand, remains a rich environment for viruses, malware, and software bugs. That situation is not likely to change, simply because Windows, and other operating systems such as Mac OS X and Linux, permit arbitrary code execution. It is interesting that the iPhone, although running a version of Mac OS X, puts strict limits on code execution precisely to reduce the likelihood of malware creeping into iPhones.

We decided that disk drives were a better place for security precisely because disk drives were in fact complete computers but with strict limits on the code that could run on them. Furthermore, disk drives are where all data is stored. When you power down a PC, the data is only on the drive. When you are running a PC, copies of small regions of the disk drive are on the computer, but the disk drive is still the location for the data. But the disk drive is actually a computer within a computer. A disk drive has a full-blown computer processor, dynamic RAM, and its own much safer preboot, as well as the familiar massive

---

1. Bob Baldwin had a Ph.D. in cryptography from MIT. He tragically died in 2007 of brain cancer. He also assisted me in the cryptographic sections of the self-encrypting drive design.

2. In the past, many hundreds of thousands of PCs were inalterably corrupted by "boot" viruses, which is why you are warned to take your floppy disk out of a machine when you power it up.

amount of nonvolatile storage. A disk drive (flash drive, etc.) can act as any standalone computer can act. It can protect itself.

So, after completing the BIOS security work for Phoenix Technologies, I wrote a proposal at the end of 2001 to Seagate Technology to put security into disk drives. Seagate is the largest supplier of hard drives in the world. The stated goals were ubiquity, utility, and uniqueness. In other words, the goals were to put security on every disk drive (hard-disk drive, flash drive, optical drive, etc.) in the world, achieve clear usefulness and ease of use, and provide a unique grade of security.

The security was to be unique in that it is a level of security that only the primary data storage device protecting its own content can provide. Its trust would begin in the BIOS, not the OS like Windows. In particular, based on a patent I had already filed, I proposed a "cryptographic key [hard-disk security resource] for controlling access and blocking encryption and decryption from multimedia streams under the control of external trust infrastructures."

On behalf of Seagate, I led the effort to standardize self-protecting, self-encrypting disk drives in TCG. It is now a published standard approved by every major disk drive maker in the world, and developed for optical drives and flash drives with inputs from the major producers of those devices as well.

Nearly every disk drive maker has publicly announced self-encrypting disk drives based on the TCG Storage Workgroup standards. These include Seagate, Hitachi, Fujitsu, Toshiba, and Samsung. Today a user can buy self-encrypting disk drives from many sources, although this is not yet widely known. For example, at the time of this writing, one can find self-encrypting disk drives by searching for "full disk or 'hardware' encryption" at Dell's and other manufacturers' websites.

As the Internet and computing has proliferated, more and more people have come to believe that the information in their computers is their property. We are entering an age of information property, or what I have called "infroperty." This makes it natural that all data, in the future, will have data protection layered on it. The self-encrypting drive is a step in that direction.

Self-protecting, self-encrypting disk drives already meet the stated goals of utility and uniqueness, and within a few years they will also meet the third, ubiquity.

Our experience is that self-encrypting disk drives are game changers. This includes both opportunities and challenges for U.S. and international laws, enforcement, and adjudication, particularly in the areas of e-discovery and digital evidence, as well as changes in how we view data privacy and "infroperty."

The term "self-encrypting drive" refers to a hard-disk drive, a flash drive, or other basic storage device that has been enhanced with the capability to protect itself from data theft.[3] The protection can be so good that no Windows virus, no keyboard logger, no amount of physical attack on the powered-off drive can plausibly obtain information from the drive. Self-encrypting drives (shown in the images above, already available commercially, are likely to become universally available in the next few years.

---

3. http://www.trustedcomputinggroup.org/media_room/news/13.

Server Drive   Laptop Drive   USB Drive

Courtesy of Seagate

There are four basic types of self-encrypting disk drives: a boot drive, a USB attached drive (removable drive), an optical disk drive, and an enterprise server drive. There are differences in detail as to how these operate and also in their security profiles. There are also differences in what is available on the market today and what the TCG core storage specification indicates is potentially available on the market tomorrow.

Before getting into all the familial differences, let us study what a self-encrypting disk drive is, no matter what. We assume that this generic drive conforms to the TCG Storage Workgroup specifications in functionality, at the very least. This provides certain guarantees about security and architecture, which are essential to the arguments and the distinctions to be made.

BASIC CHARACTERISTICS

Any storage device interprets commands sent to it over an interface. The commands are of two types: control commands and read/write commands. The control commands communicate with the processor inside the storage device to configure it, and the read/write commands read and write data to the storage media as determined by the state given by the control commands.

Most storage devices, over 99 percent sold, speak one of two command languages (ATA, for Advanced Technology Attachment, or SCSI, for Small Computer System Interface), determined by the ISO/INCITS T13 or T10 committees (ISO is a body of the United Nations).[4] We participated in these committees and extended the ATA and SCSI commands to permit "trusted drive commands" that could control the security subsystem inside the disk drives that we were defining in TCG. This work was completed several years ago.

A first generic aspect of a self-encrypting disk drive is that it speaks the standard language of any disk drive. The security commands can control how the read/write commands are interpreted by the drives, but the read/write commands work just as they have always worked. They are the primary writing and reading of data to and from the disk drive.

The self-encrypting disk drive is preferably always encrypting. The day it comes out of manufacturing, its encrypting circuits are encrypting the writes to its disk (or media)

---

4. InterNational Committee for Information Technology Standards (incits), http://www.incits.org.

and decrypting the reads from its disk. Because this is part of the circuitry in the disk drive and the encryption is not programmed in software, the encryption and decryption add a few billionths of a second delay, which is imperceptible to any user. This is a major claim to utility and uniqueness.

Encryption in a self-encrypting storage device is invisible and imperceptible. It has near-zero cost of ownership on an ordinary basis. This is different from what people widely experience and report with software encryption. In those cases, software encryption can easily, and often does, slow the computer down or cause a conflict with software running on the computer.

As one example, a goal of data encryption is to create data that looks completely random. This is the same as the goal of data compression. Encrypted data therefore, cannot, by definition, be compressed. If data compression follows encryption, it does not work. On the other hand, encryption does not care whether the data looks random or not. So encryption has to be the last thing that happens. Putting encryption into the storage device guarantees it is the last thing that happens. No one has to think about it.

Encryption on self-encrypting disk drives is AES (Advanced Encryption Standard of the National Institute of Standards and Technology), which employs an encryption key that is 128, 192, or 256 bits long (or a short 16, 24, or 32 bytes long).[5] All self-encrypting drives have their own internal random number generator for generating keys. Out of manufacturing, these drives generate their own unique random key and begin AES encryption with that key over every read/write block of data on the drive. There can be no "history" problem.[6] All data is encrypted no matter where the drive was before. The drive is always protecting any content written to or read from the drive.

Because an encrypting drive uses the short cryptographic key to encrypt or decrypt its contents, erasing all the written data on a drive can be nearly instantaneous. Within a few millionths of a second of receiving a command to change the encryption key, the drive will permanently replace the old encryption key with a new one. The drive is cryptographically erased and the drive can now be reformatted and reused. Since all the data on a laptop is on its disk drive, the laptop can be erased and repurposed in a few seconds.

Without encrypting drives, such erasing of the data on the drive normally takes several hours, and even then is not guaranteed to be complete. Most large corporations require that drives be macerated for assurance that data cannot be obtained from them. With self-encrypting drives, the drives do not need to be physically destroyed to ensure the data on them will be protected.

An additional feature of the self-encrypting drive is that different bands or blocks of data on the drive can be encrypted using different encryption keys. In certain trusted computing applications, this permits certain applications to operate on data that is protected from other applications. This can provide additional levels of assurance.

For example, a little-known fact is that viruses often attack virus checker programs. If a virus does not have access to a region of a disk drive, it cannot modify or delete the virus checker components, no matter how privileged it is in the operating system environment. Out of the factory, the disk drive is encrypting every block with one key. With

---

5. http://csrc.nist.gov/publications/fips/fips197/fips-197.pdf.
6. In the security industry, these are called "warehouse attacks."

additional TCG Storage Workgroup control commands, new keys can encrypt block subranges, but the main key is still encrypting every leftover block.

The security subsystem on the self-encrypting drive is designed to manage access to resources inside the drive. This includes access to loading the encryption circuits with encryption keys or access to changing the encryption keys.

Access is controlled in the drive, as in any computing system, with secrets. The secrets may be symmetric secrets such as passwords or cryptographically strong authentication keys, or may be asymmetric proofs of knowledge as with RSA or Elliptic Curve public key cryptosystems. This is where the differences exist in laptop, USB, optical, and enterprise drives, as well as the present and future versions of the drives. But what is common is that the access control is governed by secrets that are held outside the drive and provided to the drive after the drive is powered up.

It is also for this reason that self-encrypting drives are very secure for data-at-rest. When the disk drive is powered off, for whatever reason, the data on the drive is fully encrypted and the encryption keys on the drive are encrypted using the external secrets. No amount of reverse engineering, or physical attack, of the self-encrypting disk drive can get the data off it as long as cryptographically strong external secrets guard access to the data.[7]

The basic self-encrypting drive actually refuses to read or write data normally until the knowledge of the authentication key is proven to the drive. This blocking of normal read/write functions is called "drive locking." Thus, drive locking and drive encryption are the same thing on a basic self-encrypting drive. It not generally feasible to read the encrypted data off a self-encrypting drive, because without proper authentication the self-encrypting drive blocks normal reading and writing.

A common concern about the self-encrypting drive is that users will be locked out of their information if they forget the password. Different vendors may supply additional solutions, but the basic solution is to provide for multiple authentication secrets, including special secrets that can reset all the secrets and some different ones that can erase the drive.

There is very little security risk with more than one authentication secret. It allows users to provide several passwords, for example, so they do not have to remember which password they used for which drive. It should be remembered, though, that the security of the data on the drive is only as strong as the weakest authentication secret.[8]

The last property that all self-encrypting drives have in common is that they exploit the "system" area of storage in all disk drives that is not available to normal read/write operations. This allows self-encrypting drives to store credentials, labels, time-stamps, and other information needed to authenticate the encryption functions; derive effective keys; and provide many other security functions. These are secret hiding areas as well as secret control areas as defined by the TCG specifications.

Generally speaking, access is initially granted through a "root secret," which allows the first owner to change the access controls. Once the owner configures the access to his satisfaction, the drive functions as it was set it up to function. The host can use the

---

7. Chapter 12 discusses password control and important issues about how authentication secrets can be compromised and encryption can be circumvented.

8. *Id.*

system areas to store information that will survive even if the disk is erased and refor-matted. Some uses include putting in disk identification, time stamps, and software license information that can survive disk erasure or reformatting.

VARIATIONS ON THE BASIC SELF-ENCRYPTING DRIVE

The differences among various types of hard drives (flash drives, optical drives, etc.) can be described in simple terms related to the user experience and security. By and large, hard-disk drives and flash drives operate the same way. The differences are between boot drives (e.g., laptop and desktop), nonboot drives (e.g., server), removable drives (e.g., USB drives), and removable media (optical disk or tape) drives.

To begin, it is important to know about the preboot environment in any computer. This is because preboot is the beginning of the chain of trust that can provide the self-encrypting drive such strong security. A self-encrypting drive in a laptop will not boot Windows (or Mac OS X, etc.) until it has been unlocked in preboot. Every Phoenix BIOS, and every other major BIOS, supports hard drive locking using an ATA lock-ing command that predates the TCG specification. Self-encrypting drives out of the box support this.

So, without any new software on the PC, any legacy laptop can use a self-encrypting drive in boot. The user can configure a hard-drive password in the standard Phoenix or other BIOS preboot and have the advantages of an encrypted boot drive. Unlike software encryption, the entire Windows directory is encrypted. Everything that can be written or read using normal read/writes is encrypted. Lenovo has recently introduced network preboot control over secrets that can unlock drives for laptops brought up on networks. Several software vendors, such as Wave Systems, Secude, and WinMagic, provide soft-ware to similarly give improved control over the self-encryption capabilities of the drive by also providing preboot environments. When a self-encrypting drive is locked, it shows a special range of readable blocks to the normal read/write commands. This con-tains the preboot code that can be provided by certified security software vendors.

However, in the simplest use of a self-encrypting drive on a laptop, a user opens the laptop, and it asks for a hard-drive password. The user types in the password, and it boots Windows (or Mac OS X) normally. That is the entire user experience. It is trans-parently safe. A great use at home, for example, is that no matter how smart your teen-ager is about getting into Windows or seeing what is on your hard drive, you can be sure he cannot get to it once the laptop lid is closed. Similarly, closing the laptop protects it from anyone else who may be in the home, office, conference room, or motel room when the user is not there.

The nonboot drive similarly will not read or write normally until a correct authenti-cation code is provided to it. In server environments where there may be dozens or even thousands of disk drives in large storage arrays, typically the central storage controller will manage the distribution of the authentication codes to the drives to unlock them. Several companies, including IBM and LSI, are supporting TCG self-encrypting drives in this way, and more companies will likely follow. The primary benefits include the sure knowledge that if a drive is pulled out of a server, its data can no longer be accessed. It can be put immediately into another controller without ever worrying whether the old data will leak. The legal and regulatory benefits for data privacy are quite obvious. In particular, it is more difficult for an operator to make a mistake. Enterprise self-encrypting drives add considerable cost recovery and security over other encryption methods as drives are moved in and out of enterprise servers.

A removable disk drive, such as a USB drive, operates a third way. In this case, the USB drive, when plugged in, shows up as a drive, but one that is much smaller than its actual capacity. It is using the feature of the boot drive that presents a special restricted range of read-only blocks to the external interface. In this case, double clicking an unlock function in the USB drive will allow the authentication secrets to be sent to the drive. It may be that future versions of Windows or other operating systems will recognize TCG locked drives and unlock them.

This brings up a security problem with USB drives in that if there is an operating system bug or virus, it can monitor the secret sent to the drive and report that secret to an intruder. Most self-encrypting drives in current production have the problem that when the drives are used as removable storage devices, a software virus or keylogger can learn how to unlock the secret. The same problem, of course, exists today with all types of software encryption. In TCG we provide a means for future drives to use public key cryptography that effectively denies any Windows malware from learning the secret. Generally speaking, if both the laptop and the USB drive are self-encrypting, the user can have some assurance, though not perfect. The laptop may have malware that knows how to unlock the USB drive, but until the laptop is booted, that malware is itself encrypted and not readable.

The last use is the optical, or removable media, drive. In all the previous cases, it is technically quite difficult to see the encrypted bits on the drive. The user sees the unlocked drive as a normal disk drive. There is no perceptible difference from any other drive. But in this case users are writing CDs, DVDs or Blu-ray disks with fully encrypted data, protected by the optical disk read/write circuits in the player or burner. The users may archive data on optical disks, but when they try to read them, they are asked to produce a secret or other authentication proof. This means that that no one can go through content on a user's CDs without his explicit permission. The TCG optical drive specification selects encryption modes that are known to be strong even if the user can read all the encrypted bits and can readily read the system areas of the optical media. But like any removable storage, there is a possibility of Windows or other operating systems malware detecting the secrets as they are being passed to the drive.

In the case of removable (USB) or removable media (optical) drives, another scenario is shipping large quantities of data. For example, a user can mail a USB drive with 100 gigabytes of proprietary data on it from Los Angeles to Rome without worrying that any agent can read that data. The drive itself has protected the data. Furthermore, anyone with the proper authentication credentials can read the data.

A self-encrypting USB drive is an inexpensive way to create offsite backups. A user may ship the drive to a friend in another city or country, and if the data needs to be recovered, the friend can just mail the drive back. The user does not have to trust that the drive has been physically protected, as the friend could never have read the data on the drive. These are examples of how the self-encryption drive achieves the goals of uniqueness and utility through transparent and ease of use.

COMMON CONCERNS

One complaint about TCG's efforts is that it is digital rights management (DRM) in disguise. The response, as can be plainly seen with the optical specification, is that it is DRM, but for the masses, not just for the movie or music owners. Nearly everyone now has his own "infroperty" he would like to protect.

A common question for the various manufacturers of self-encrypting drives is whether they contain a "backdoor." Most DRM schemes are purposefully weak in certain ways, and are expected to be cracked by serious crackers. Self-encrypting drives, on the other hand, are designed not to be cracked except by proof of knowledge of the authentication secret. Since the secret can be very strong, and is not selected from a discoverable set (as in DRM), it can be expected that some disk drives will be uncrackable once powered down. Not even a physical attack of the drive by the drive maker can get the unencrypted data off the drive. Every disk drive maker who has been asked about a backdoor has stated there is not one. A backdoor, of a kind, may be created if needed by the user. For example, to allow a corporate IT department access, it is simple to exploit the feature of multiple authentication codes.

FUTURE CAPABILITIES DEFINED BY THE TCG SPECIFICATIONS

The TCG Storage Workgroup specification allows more enhanced security features than simply control over inline read/write encryption circuits. These are potential future features of drives that are optional for the drive makers.[9]

First, there is the ability of different external agents to own, exclusively, different security subsystems inside the drive. There can be only one primary owner of the locking and encrypting subsystem, but other subsystems may be defined with other features, including forensic logging, clock, and cryptographic service features.

The forensic logging and clock features allow a drive to keep track of date/time secure from anything in the external environment. Because drives do not have clock chips or batteries, the clock is a composite of a monotonic counter that counts every time the clock is read. Data fields that hold real-time values increment as normal clocks after the drive is powered up and the clock is set. The forensic logging may be set to log automatically any security changes on the drive (recording both date/time and monotonic counter value). It may also be set to be a write-only forensic log repository for use by external programs.

The cryptographic services can provide symmetric or public key cryptosystem support without exposing any private keys to the host environment. These provide the full capability of a basic Microsoft CSP (Cryptographic Service Provider) or the equivalent PKCS#11 Cyptoki module on the Mac and Linux.

WHAT THE FUTURE OF ENCRYPTED DATA MAY HOLD

Let us now imagine a likely world in which nearly everyone is using self-encrypting drives. All of the data in this world is encrypted, and when the storage devices are pow-

---

9. The full details of these security features may be found in the Storage Workgroup Core specification, *available at* http://www.trustedcomputinggroup.org; *also see* R. Thibadeau, *Trusted Computing for Disk Drives and Other Peripherals*, IEEE SEC. & PRIVACY MAG., Sept.–Oct. 2006.

ered down, the data is unavailable without knowledge of the authentication secrets. If a company is trying to protect medical, tax, or bank records, proprietary data, or its intellectual property, the situation is much improved because the self-encrypting drive provides transparent and easy-to-use data protection.

Of course, there is a two-edged sword for law enforcement in this, but this two-edged sword already exists. If you are an intruder, you power down your computers before the police walk in. If you did not stupidly write the password on a sticky note and post it on the computer screen, the police will have to obtain your password from you, or guess it. If you are a "good guy," you might do the same thing before the police walk in, just to be sure the police do not improperly inspect your computer. But right now the bad or good guys do not actually require self-encrypting drives to use strong data encryption. They may use free software that is readily available on the Internet, with the same result in this situation. Software encryption is more difficult to use routinely, but "bad guys" facing jail are more motivated. So it seems reasonable that the lion's share of the benefit will go to the good guys: protecting their "infroperty."

With ubiquitous self-encrypted storage devices, the world may become simpler, but, even if it does not, most certainly the world will change. Hopefully these devices will make it similarly easier and more straightforward to create and enforce relevant laws and contracts and for every person to protect his "infroperty."

CHAPTER 15

ENCRYPTION TECHNOLOGIES: A PRACTICAL ASSESSMENT

Thomas L. Hahler

One goal of an encryption solution is to hide information from someone who should not see it. Another is that the person who should see the information is able to do that correctly. Factors for making choices about encryption solutions are presented to assist readers in understanding and making appropriate trade-offs for their particular needs.

CHOICES FOR HIDING INFORMATION

In order to allow information to be seen only by those for whom it is intended, various solutions are possible.

1. *The information may be stored securely.* Information may be stored in a vault. The vault can be heavily guarded. Only authorized individuals can access the vault containing the information. The facility can have chain-link fences, additional electronic access to specific rooms, cameras for monitoring, and other such physical control devices and methods. This physical storage solution is very common with objects to be protected. Fort Knox, where gold is stored, would meet those criteria. It also helps that gold is heavy and cannot be transported on a thumb drive.
2. *The information may be hidden entirely.* If someone does not know that information or an object exists, they cannot get to it. If one buries money in a jar in the back yard and plants a tree over it, it is unlikely that someone is going to find it (at least until the tree dies and is replaced).
3. *The information may be disguised as something else.* It has been a common practice to hollow out a book and put household jewels in it. Obviously, there are risks to this approach, as someone who is scanning books on a bookshelf might come upon it and open it.
4. *The information may be encrypted.* In the case of encryption, the information may be seen, put in plain view, does not need to be disguised as something else, and

does not need to be stored securely.[1] Encryption does not solve all of the problems of hiding information, however, since one must figure out how to secure the encryption key. The choices for securing the encryption key are similar to the choices above.

There are various ways that information may be encrypted on computers. Some algorithms that currently exist are SAFER, WAKE, Blowfish, IDEA, Rijndael, Serpent, Twofish RC6, and MARS. There are multiple factors involved in choosing an algorithm. These factors are not only technical but also political. The political factors include legal issues not just in the United States but also in other countries. Some statutes do not allow the export of software with specific encryption algorithms. Some countries have banned encryption entirely. Others have required that encryption keys be put in escrow so that governments can access the information if required.

ENCRYPTION ALGORITHMS: AN HISTORICAL PERSPECTIVE

In a broad historical context, encryption has changed over time. In Athens, Greece, in the fifth century B.C., messages to be kept secret were written on a strip of papyrus wrapped around a rod. When the papyrus was unwrapped, the message was unintelligible. The message could be decrypted by wrapping it around another rod of the same diameter.

In the 15th century, Leonardo DaVinci wrote his journals in mirror writing, preventing casual observers from reading his notes (although this is not a very secure encryption method).

Encryption (and breaking encryptions) was an important activity in the two World Wars. The breaking of the German encryption codes provided invaluable information to the Allies about German activities.

Much of the information being encrypted up to this time could be considered time sensitive, such as about troop movements in the time of war. The encryption did not have to stand up to attempts to break it over long periods of time. Therefore, any encryption system that took a considerable amount of time to break would do the job.

Much has changed in modern times—the use of computers to encrypt or decrypt information and the use of computers and the Internet for electronic commerce. With the use of the Internet (and electronic communications in general), there is now a need to encrypt data to protect financial, medical, and personal information about people, and sensitive information about businesses.

In earlier years, if someone in a restaurant made an extra copy of a credit card charge slip and put it through the payment system, the transaction could be traced back to where the charge was made and it would be contained by geography. However, now credit and debit charges can be made from anywhere in the world and may not necessarily be detected easily. Fraudulent debit card charges can be made rapidly and quickly deplete the owner's bank account; it may be difficult even to determine where the charges were made. Since such things as Social Security numbers, bank account num-

---

1. Assuming the encryption algorithm can be trusted.

bers, and payment card numbers may be used to access financial information, these must be protected from disclosure.

FACTORS TO BE CONSIDERED IN MAKING ENCRYPTION DECISIONS

Since encryption has in the past been costly and time consuming, much effort has been spent attempting to determine what data need to be encrypted and what does not. This is a never-ending exercise and has no satisfactory answer. On a computer or network, consider whether the following types of information should be encrypted:

- The operating system, or the application programs themselves?
- Log files?
- Financial or medical information?
- A photograph collection?
- If financial information itself must be encrypted, does the metadata about the financial system also need to be encrypted?

Encryption is only part of the larger information system design. It is feasible today to consider encryption of both data-in-motion and data-at-rest. It is relatively common to use the Hypertext Transfer Protocol Secure (HTTPS) protocol to encrypt data between a user and a server. This is commonly used for secure access to banks and e-mail servers. HTTPS protects data while it is being transmitted from devices that attempt to read the information on a communication circuit. The data itself may be at the source, at the destination, or in transit. HTTPS protects only the data in transit.

The use of whole disk encryption at a user's computer protects data at that end of the connection. What is left is protection of the data at the server location. This will require both hardware encryption and solutions for such things as backup tapes and their storage.

Additional factors to consider are whether support must be provided for Windows, Mac, Unix, Linux, and virtual machines.

Once the requirements for which operating systems are to be supported and what capabilities are to be provided, a strategy for determination of the encryption solution(s) to be used can be developed.

Media That Can or Should Be Encrypted

Removable media of all types is a good candidate for encryption, as anything that can be easily moved can also be easily lost or stolen. This may vary from 3.5-inch floppy diskettes containing only a megabyte of information to cartridge tapes and computer hard drives containing a terabyte or more of data.

On the low end, although a 3.5-inch diskette doesn't contain much information, one of these diskettes could easily hold the names, addresses, telephone numbers, Social Security numbers, dates of birth, and bank account numbers of 5,000 individuals. A one-terabyte disk in a high end PC could contain the same information on five million people. Such a drive costs only around $100.

Flash drives and thumb drives come in sizes from 1 to 32 or more gigabytes and are small, easily portable, and potentially easily lost. They should be encrypted if the information on them is sensitive.

Advanced Encryption Standard

The encryption solution should use the advanced encryption standard (AES) encryption algorithm with 128- or 256-bit encryption. AES is relatively easy to implement and it is fast when used in hardware or software. Most modern workstations and laptops in 2010 are fast enough to perform software encryption without affecting the performance of the system or slowing things down for the user. It is when one is connected to a server performing multiple encryptions at once that performance may be an issue.

ENCRYPTION WITH WEB BROWSERS

The most common use of encryption is with Web browsers using HTTPS. The browser chooses the encryption algorithm to use. In general, AES 256-bit encryption is being used on newer implementations and with the latest versions of operating systems.

Table 15.1 shows the encryption used for various browsers and operating systems.

TABLE 15.1
Encryption for Various Browsers and Operating Systems

Web Browser	Operating System	Best Cipher	Verdict?
Firefox v3.0.5	Windows XP & Vista	AES 256-bit	Good!
Firefox v3.01	Mac OS X 10.5.5	AES 256-bit	Good!
Safari v3.2.1	Windows XP	RC4 128-bit	Fair
Safari v3.2.1	Windows Vista	AES 128-bit	Good
Safari v3.2.1	Mac OS X 10.5.5	AES 128-bit	Good
Safari	iPhone v2.2	AES 128-bit	Good
Chrome v1.0.154.43	Windows XP	RC4 128-bit	Fair
Chrome v1.0.154.43	Windows Vista	AES 128-bit	Good
Internet Explorer v7	Windows Vista	AES 128-bit	Good
Internet Explorer v8 beta	Windows XP	RC4 128-bit	Fair
Internet Explorer v7	Windows XP	RC4 128-bit	Fair
Internet Explorer v6	Windows XP	RC4 128-bit	Fair
Opera v9.62	Windows XP & Vista	AES 256-bit	Good!

Source: Adapted from LuxSci.com, http://luxsci.com/blog/256-bit-aes-encryption-for-ssl-and-tls-maximum-security.html; Erik Kangas, Ph.D., President, LuxSci.com.blog. Reprinted with permission.

The Web site Fortify (https://www.fortify.net/cgi/ssl_2.pl) may be used to check the encryption on any browser.

LuxSci provided results showing the encryption used when connecting to its own e-mail host. The host offers a range of connection options. Table 15.2 shows how various mail clients connected using their default settings.

TABLE 15.2
Encryption for Various Mail Clients

E-mail Program	Operating System	Verdict?	Results
Mozilla Thunderbird v2.0.0.19	Windows XP & Vista	Good!	256-bit AES
Thunderbird v2.0.0.19	Mac OS X v10.4.11	Good!	256-bit AES
Outlook 2007	Windows XP	Fair	128-bit RC4 is the best supported
Outlook 2007	Windows Vista	Good	128-bit AES chosen (though 256-bit is available, it is not listed first in the program and thus not used)
Outlook 2003	Windows XP	Fair	128-bit RC4 is the best supported
Mail.app	Mac OS X v10.5.5	Good	128-bit AES chosen (though 256-bit is available, it is not listed first in the program and thus not used)
Mail.app	Mac OS X v10.4.11	Good	128-bit AES chosen (though 256-bit is available, it is not listed first in the program and thus not used)
Mail.app	iPhone v2.2	Good	128-bit AES chosen (though 256-bit is available, it is not listed first in the program and thus not used)
Eudora v7.1.0.9	Windows XP	Good	256-bit AES
Eudora v8.0.0b4	Mac OS X v10.4.11	Good	256-bit AES
Entourage v12.1.5	Mac OS X v10.4.11	Fair	DES

Source: Adapted from LuxSci.com, http://luxsci.com/blog/256-bit-aes-encryption-for-ssl-and-tls-maximum-security.html; Erik Kangas, Ph.D., President, LuxSci.com.blog. Reprinted with permission.

HARDWARE VERSUS SOFTWARE ENCRYPTION

Hardware encryption is much faster than software encryption. However, it does require additional computer cards to perform this function. When encryption and decryption are used to be sent over a line to a remote device, hardware encryption can perform at the speeds of the communication links. It is more expensive that software encryption.

In general, hardware encryption should be used at servers and software encryption is fast enough to be used at individual workstations.

Hardware Encryption

The use of hardware encryption is required primarily on servers where multiple users require this capability. Examples of products for IBM mainframes and servers are SSH Tectia Server for IBM z/OS 1.6, 1.7, 1.9, which supports AES 128-bit encryption in hardware and AES 128/192/256-bit in software; and IBM 4758 PCI Cryptographic Coprocessor, which is available for iSeries, pSeries, and xSeries machines, older zSeries servers, and Intel-based machines running Windows 2000. An example from Hewlett Packard is HP StorageWorks LTO Ultrium 1840 Tape Drive. Similar products are available from the major computer manufacturers that provide support for the encryption of such things as backup tapes and virtual tape libraries.

Software Encryption

Some Available Encryption and Decryption Software

Table 15-3 is a partial list of encryption software and provides a comparison of disk encryption software. It shows that there are solutions for Windows, Linux, and Mac OS X individually but there are few single solutions for all three. The literature also does not show "interoperability" between operating systems.

TABLE 15.3
Comparison of Disk Encryption Software

Name	License	Operating System Support
BestCrypt	Commercial, limited source code	Linux 2.6, Windows NT-based
BitLocker Drive Encryption	Commercial, closed source	Windows Vista Enterprise, Windows Vista Ultimate, Windows Server 2008
CGD	Free, open source (BSD)	NetBSD 2.0+
Check Point Full Disk Encryption	Commercial	Linux, Windows, Mac OS X
CryptArchiver	Commercial	Windows NT-based
DiskCryptor	Free, open source (GPL)	Windows 2000, XP, Server 2003, Vista, Server 2008

(continued on next page)

TABLE 15.3 *(continued from previous page)*
Comparison of Disk Encryption Software

Name	License	Operating System Support
DISK Protect	Commercial	Windows NT-based
dm-crypt/ cryptsetup	Free, open source (GPL)	Linux 2.6, Windows 2000, XP, Vista (via FreeOTFE)
dm-crypt/LUKS	Free, open source (GPL)	Linux 2.6, Windows 2000, XP, Vista (via FreeOTFE)
DriveCrypt	Commercial	Windows NT-based
DriveSentry GoAnywhere 2	Commercial	Windows XP, Vista
e-Capsule Private Safe	Commercial	Windows 2000, XP, 2003, Vista
eCryptfs	Free, open source (GPL)	Linux 2.6.19+
FileVault	Commercial	Mac OS X v10.3 and later
FinallySecure	Closed source	Windows XP, Vista
FREE CompuSec	Freeware	Linux 2.4-2.6, Windows 2000, XP, Vista
FreeOTFE	Freeware	Linux (via dm-crypt/LUKS); Windows 2000, XP, Vista, Pocket PC
GBDE	Free, open source (BSD)	FreeBSD 5.0+
GELI	Free, open source (BSD)	FreeBSD 6.0+
Keyparc	Free, closed source	Windows, Linux, Mac OS
n-Crypt Pro	Commercial	Windows NT-based
PGPDisk	Commercial, source available for personal review	Windows NT-based, Mac OS X
Private Disk	Commercial	Windows NT-based, Windows 9x
R-Crypto	Commercial	Windows 2000/XP/2003/Vista (32/64 bit)
Safeboot Device Encryption	Commercial	Windows NT-based, Windows Mobile, Windows Vista 32/64, Symbian, Palm

(continued on next page)

**TABLE 15.3 *(continued from previous page)*
Comparison of Disk Encryption Software**

Name	License	Operating System Support
SafeGuard Easy	Commercial	Windows NT-based[21]
SafeGuard PrivateDisk	Commercial	Windows
Scramdisk 4 Linux	Free, open source (GPL)	Linux 2.4–2.6
SecuBox	Commercial	Windows CE, Windows Mobile Pocket PC, Smartphone [24]
Secude securenotebook	Commercial	Windows XP/2000
SecureDoc	Commercial	Windows 2000/XP/Vista, Mac OS X
Sentry 2020	Commercial	Windows NT-based, Pocket PC
SpyProof!	Commercial	Windows NT4/2000/XP/Vista
TrueCrypt	Free, open source (custom)	Linux 2.4-2.6, Windows 2000, XP, 2003, Vista, Mac OS X

Source: Wikipedia, Comparison of Disk Encryption Software, http://en.wikipedia.org/wiki/Comparison_of_disk_encryption_software. The full listing may be found there.

Examples of File Software Encryption

WinZip

WinZip by WinMagic is a product that allows for the encryption and compression of files within a .zip archive. This product is FIPS 140-2 certified and allows the use of AES 256-bit encryption for versions of WinZip after 9.0. This archive may then be copied to a CD, DVD, thumb drive, external hard drive, and so on.

Since it is an archive, the file name of the archive is not encrypted and the names of the files within the archives are visible in clear text. The contents of the files are encrypted and cannot be read.

This is a Microsoft Windows-only solution although the WinMagic literature indicates that they have published enough information to allow other developers to be able to read their archives.

The advantage of this software is that the encrypted archive may be copied to portable media and then sent safely to its intended recipient. The password should not be sent with the package but rather it should be transmitted to the recipient through another mechanism.

If the file is sent on physical media such as a thumb drive, then the password may be sent by telephone, fax, or e-mail, for example. If the file is sent as an e-mail attachment, then the password should *not* be sent via e-mail (even if it is a separate e-mail.)

Rather, the password should be sent using a different communication path such as fax, telephone, or postal mail.

The disadvantages of this solution are that the filenames are not encrypted and that this is a Windows-only solution (Windows 2000, XP, or Windows Vista). It is not available on a Macintosh running OS X or on Linux.

Vista "Native" Solution

In Vista, a program called BitLocker performs whole-disk encryption of the entire operating system partition. This is available only in Vista Ultimate or Vista Enterprise editions of the operating system. It requires the use of a password stored on a USB drive.

No one can boot the computer at all without the key or the recovery password.

Macintosh OS X "Native" Solution

The Mac has a program called FileVault that encrypts a user's home directory and all of the files under it with AES 128-bit encryption. It does not encrypt the OS or application files. It has the advantage that multiple people may use the computer but no user can view the contents of another user's files.

SecureDoc Encryption by WinMagic, Inc.

SecureDoc offers the ability to encrypt the hard drive entirely on PCs running Windows or Vista operating systems. It provides software encryption and is able initially to encrypt the hard drive at a rate from 20 to 50 gigabytes per hour depending on the processor speed. It can also be configured to support removable media in several ways. It can be configured not to allow access to removable media or to read-only access if the drive is not encrypted, or to allow only read/write access if it is encrypted (with predefined keys).

WinMagic announced a solution for the Macintosh in December 2008 and can now support PCs and Macintosh but does not appear to offer a Linux solution.

Check Point

Check Point software offers a full disk encryption solution for Windows, Linux, and Macintosh systems. It is a FIPS 140-2 compliant solution. The vendor makes the point that any solution that relies on file or folder encryption is subject to human error in not putting sensitive files in the folders where they are encrypted. It uses AES 256-bit encryption.

It has a provision to lock user accounts with an automatic unlock after a certain number of minutes or to remain locked until assisted by a help desk staff member.

The software provides a mechanism to recover from a hard drive failure that requires two administrators to unlock the recovery file.

Pretty Good Privacy

Pretty Good Privacy (PGP) is a program that provides full disk encryption for Windows and Macintosh computers. It provides for both managed and unmanaged users. An unmanaged user is one that is not under the control of a PGP universal server,

236 DATA BREACH AND ENCRYPTION HANDBOOK

which enforces policies on individual workstations. For example, a managed user may be required to use whole disk encryption.

The program contains a full public key encryption solution that focuses on the use of public and private keys and asymmetric encryption in addition to the whole-disk encryption capability. The whole-disk encryption capability uses a symmetric algorithm for speed and uses AES 256-bit encryption.

PGP whole-disk encryption has a license expiration feature that decrypts the data (after notifying the user) so the user will be able to retrieve the files.

RAID disk drives cannot be whole-disk encrypted. Diskettes, CDs, and DVD can also not be whole-disk encrypted. (Encrypted files may be placed on them, however.)

PGP allows Windows-formatted disks that are encrypted by PGP Desktop 9.9 to be moved from one computer to another.

Extra security precautions that PGP Desktop advertises include that passphrases are erased from memory right after entry and are not written to virtual disk space. Also, with whole-disk encryption, the key is stored in two places in RAM with one being the key and the other being a bit-inverted copy of the key. These copies are swapped every few seconds to prevent memory from retaining an imprint of the key.

PGP also allows for the creation of virtual disks that may be exchanged with users of other operating systems.

Truecrypt

Truecrypt allows the encryption of entire hard drives, virtual encrypted disks, and entire storage devices such as a USB drive. It uses AES-256, Serpent, and Twofish encryption algorithms.

TrueCrypt is free and open source. It supports Windows, Macintosh, and Linux and provides the ability to share encrypted disks between Windows and Macintosh systems.

KEY MANAGEMENT

Key management is probably the last major sticking point regarding the encryption of all data. To address this problem and aid IT security, compliance, and data recovery, seven organizations—Brocade, RSA, HP, IBM, LSI, Seagate, and Thales—have announced a joint initiative to develop an interoperability specification for encryption key management. The Key Management Interoperability Protocol (KMIP) is designed to provide a single, comprehensive protocol for communication between enterprise key management services and encryption systems. It should allow companies to reduce risk by removing redundant and incompatible key management processes.

The completed work will be moved to OASIS.[2] Engaging the industry in the formalization of this work as a standard is the critical next step. The area of key management

---

2. OASIS (Organization for the Advancement of Structured Information Standards) is a not-for-profit consortium that drives the development, convergence, and adoption of open standards for the global information society. The consortium produces more Web services standards than any other organization along with standards for security, e-business, and standardization efforts in the public sector and for application-specific markets. Founded in 1993, OASIS has more than 5,000 participants representing over 600 organizations and individual members in 100 countries.

in general has vendor solutions that work only with the vendors' own product lines. What this means at this time is that key management must be well defined prior to starting an enterprise long-term encryption program since the chosen solution may lock the user into one particular system for many years.

When Encryption Fails—Data Is Only as Secure as the Weakest Link

Inconsistent security policies, rules, and procedures among different organizations, environments, and interfaces may result in the compromise of sensitive and personal records. Institutions processing credit card transactions may follow different security rules, leading participants to believe their data has been encrypted when in fact it is not. Here are some examples of what may happen to put the data at risk.

1. *Online purchase*—A payment transaction is encrypted but the password is not secure. A company uses HTTPS; the user creates a user account and chooses a password. The merchant stores the passwords on a server that is not secure. The customer believes his or her transaction and personal information are secure when in fact they are not secure.
2. *Audit logs*—A company stores encrypted audit logs on an unencrypted backup tape. The tape is lost and large amounts of data are stolen.
3. *Public Internet access*—Access to the Internet is gained on a public computer (e.g., hotel) where a keystroke logger has been installed on the computer. The person using the computer for a transaction believes the data is encrypted, but the data are not because they are being logged for later retrieval. Similarly, transactions made with wireless Internet access in a public place may be intercepted easily. What data may be intercepted? Passwords, credit card numbers, and other sensitive data.
4. *Transactions monitored*—The password is encrypted but transactions are being monitored where private and personal information is collected. Revealing information such as purchases, location, and associations may be embarrassing or provide evidence of illegal activity.
5. *Temporary files*—may be viewed, copied, or logged.

   In conclusion, encryption alone is not sufficient to protect sensitive personal information. Comprehensive security policies and procedures must be put into place to ensure that the encryption is performed correctly and adequately protects the information.

PART V

Response

CHAPTER 16

Security Best Practices: The Watchword Is Prioritize!

Lucy L. Thomson

21ST CENTURY INFORMATION SECURITY CHALLENGES

Hackers are increasing in sophistication and determination to penetrate and take control of networks that comprise the critical infrastructure of both government and the private sector. The attacks on Google's e-mail service and corporate infrastructure in China is a recent example of the threat major companies are facing from sophisticated computer network attacks, some of them orchestrated by foreign governments.[1] Dozens of companies in critical sectors such as defense, energy, financial, and technology, as well as key government agencies, have been targeted.

The recent Cyberspace Policy Review by the White House and the Comprehensive National Cybersecurity Initiative emphasized the critical need for a concerted international effort to combat cybercrime.[2] A cyberspace report by the Center for Strategic and International Studies (CSIS) declared that cybersecurity is a strategic issue "on par with weapons of mass destruction and global jihad."[3] Cybersecurity risks pose some of the most serious economic and national security challenges of the 21st century.[4] CSIS concluded that the damage from cyberattack is real, and "a growing array of state and

---

1. Ellen Nakashima, Steven Mufson & John Pomfret, *Google Threatens to Leave China*, WASH. POST, Jan. 13, 2010, at A1.

2. THE WHITE HOUSE, CYBERSPACE POLICY REVIEW: ASSURING A TRUSTED AND RESILIENT INFORMATION AND COMMUNICATIONS INFRASTRUCTURE, at I, *available at* http://www.whitehouse.gov/assets/documents/Cyberspace_Policy_Review_final.pdf. National Security Council, The Comprehensive National Cybersecurity Initiative, *available at* http://www.whitehouse.gov/sites/default/files/cybersecurity.pdf.

3. CTR. FOR STRATEGIC & INT'L STUDIES, SECURING CYBERSPACE FOR THE 44TH PRESIDENCY 15 (Dec. 2008), *available at* http://csis.org/files/media/csis/pubs/081208_securingcyberspace_44.pdf.

4. *Id.*

nonstate actors are compromising, stealing, changing, or destroying information and could cause critical disruptions to U.S. systems."[5]

In targeted attacks around the globe, hackers have stolen the most critical assets of many organizations: information, including proprietary information, trade secrets, computer source code, and personal and other sensitive information. Increasingly stealthy and poised to seize on security lapses as well as persistent vulnerabilities, hackers exploit security weaknesses throughout an enterprise. While the seriousness of data breaches continued to escalate, experts predict that security threats by global organized crime networks and hostile governments, as well as exploits of the vulnerabilities of increasingly complex networked information systems, will increase significantly in 2010 and beyond.[6] Malicious insiders are a formidable threat as well, often misusing administrative privileges to obtain information they are not authorized to access.

Thwarting malicious actors is not the entire extent of the information security challenges facing organizations today. Hundreds of data breaches result from the compromise of information on lost or stolen mobile devices—laptops, thumb drives, PDAs, cell phones, and other devices.[7] Several essential steps must be taken to prevent these types of data breaches; the most obvious is not to store sensitive information on mobile devices. Data and information that are placed on mobile devices should be encrypted. Since encryption is just one important piece of a comprehensive information security program, this must be done so that the encrypted data may be used without being exposed and compromised.[8] Data management is another important aspect of information security—consistent with fair information principles, organizations should not retain personal information that can be readily used for identity theft, such as credit card and Social Security numbers, when it is not required to complete the particular transaction for which it was collected or for legal purposes.[9]

---

5. CSIS Comm'n on Cybersecurity for the 44th Presidency, Threats Posed by the Internet, *available at* http://csis.org/files/media/csis/pubs/081028_threats_working_group.pdf. *See* Cyberspace Policy Review, *supra* note 2, at iii.

6. Linda McGlassen, *Top 8 Security Threats of 2010: Financial Institutions Face Risks from Organized Crime, SQL Injection and Other Major Attacks*, BankInfo Sec., Dec. 21, 2009, *available at* http://www.bankinfosecurity.com/articles .php?art_id=2019 (experts highlight these major security threats to watch in 2010: (1) organized crime targeting financial institutions, (2) assault on authentication, (3) more malware, (4) return to telephone-based fraud, (5) increased insider threat, (6) mobile banking attacks, (7) Web 2.0 and social media attacks, and (8) more SQL attacks). *See* SearchSecurity.com Emerging Information Security Threats, http://searchsecurity.techtarget.com/ topics/0,295493,sid14_tax303581,00.html (emerging security threats include attacks on RFID tags and readers, mobile devices, and hardware devices, and hackers using rootkits and self-morphing Trojans to gain control of PCs); Kelly Jackson Higgins, *The 9 Coolest Hacks of 2009*, Dark Reading, Dec. 23, 2009, *available at* http://www .darkreading.com/vulnerability_management/security/attacks/showArticle.jhtml?articleID=222003008 (review of breaches in 2009 provides a flavor of the broad scope of vulnerabilities that can be exploited). See chapters 1 and 5.

7. See chapter 2.

8. *See* Part IV, Technology (chapters 10–15), for a detailed discussion of the considerations that are important in implementing encryption correctly.

9. For example, in a recent data breach notification letter, a major hotel chain advised individuals that their credit card numbers compromised in the breach were accessible in hotels, spas, gift shops, and restaurants long after their original authorized use. There is no justification for retaining vast amounts of sensitive consumer data for months and even years after individuals' hotel stays are over without the consumers' consent and without any business need for keeping that data.

FAILED SECURITY

Failed security has resulted in massive data breaches that lead to the loss or compromise of millions of personally identifiable individual records, potentially exposing them to identity theft or fraud.[10] More than half of the data breaches have been committed by hackers or malicious insiders.[11] Organized crime and sophisticated international hackers are suspected of being responsible for some of the major breaches.[12]

The attack methodologies profiled in chapter 5 illustrate how hackers used a variety of sophisticated and common attacks to exploit the lack of security controls in a number of unsecured areas of corporate information systems. One of the largest breaches involved Heartland Payment Systems, the sixth largest processor of credit and debit card transactions in the United States.[13] In this breach, security failed at multiple points. Intruders broke into the Heartland networks and stole payment card transaction data. Even though Heartland encrypted some of the sensitive customer data, there were opportunities for these data to be intercepted when they were unencrypted on the company network, and when they were transmitted unencrypted "in the clear" to the card brands and member banks that issued the cards.

In another of the largest breaches of 2009, TJX used wireless technology with encryption with a serious design flaw that could easily be broken and transmitted authorization requests in "clear text" between and within its in-store and corporate networks. These flaws made its information system vulnerable to attack. Intruders had access to TJX's decryption algorithm through an unsecured key or password that defeated any protection encryption might have provided on its information system.

DATA BREACHES CAN AND MUST BE PREVENTED

Business owners, data custodians, and their attorneys in the private sector and in government around the globe must redouble their efforts to understand the risks of collecting, storing, and sharing sensitive and personal information, the many ways data can be breached, and the tools available to protect the data.[14] They must develop the expertise to avoid these breaches, and to address them appropriately if and when they occur. This includes an appreciation of the fact that there is no one solution that is appropriate for every organization. Information security must be tailored based on the type(s) of data to be protected, the potential threats and risks to the data, and the nature of the information system of the organization, including the hardware, software, applications, and interconnections. As well, business owners must understand that implementation, continuous monitoring, and auditing are as important as the initial security controls that are put in place.

---

10. *See* chapter 5.

11. *See* Open Sec. Found., Data Loss Statistics, http://datalossdb.org/statistics.

12. *See Verizon: Organized Crime Caused Spike in Data Breaches*, New Criminologist, Apr. 29, 2009, *available at* http://www.newcriminologist.com/news.asp?nid=2142.

13. Heartland Payment Systems, http://www.heartlandpaymentsystems.com.

14. *See,* Thomas Shaw, Information Security and Privacy—A Practical Guide for Global Executives, Lawyers and Technologists, ABA (2011) (a comprehensive guide to information security and privacy law by the ABA Section of Science & Technology Law).

WHERE TO BEGIN?

National Institute of Standards and Technology Guidelines

Where to Begin highlights the major approaches followed by government and many private sector organizations to create and implement system security plans to protect computer networks and the information in the system.

Pursuant to the Federal Information Security Management Act of 2002 (FISMA)[15] the National Institute of Standards and Technology (NIST) has produced a series of excellent security guidelines.[16] A comprehensive set of security controls may be found in NIST Recommended Security Controls for Federal Information Systems and Organizations, Special Publications 800-53, revision 3 and 800-53, revision 1.[17] While these publications were drafted for government information systems, they contain a wealth of valuable guidance that is equally appropriate for private sector organizations.

NIST Special Publication 800-30 describes how to conduct a risk assessment.[18] NIST designed the guide to provide a "foundation for the development of an effective risk management program, containing both the definitions and the practical guidance necessary for assessing and mitigating risks identified within IT systems."[19]

NIST Special Publication 800-53A, Revision 1, *Guide for Assessing the Security Controls in Federal Information Systems and Organizations,* June 29, 2010, provides guidelines for developing security assessment plans and associated security control assessment procedures that are consistent with Special Publication 800-53, Revision 3, *Recommended Security Controls for Federal Information Systems and Organizations,* August 2009 (including updates as of May 1, 2010). According to information on the NIST website, this publication represents the third in a series of publications being developed under the auspices of the Joint Task Force Transformation Initiative, a partnership that includes NIST, the Intelligence Community (IC), the Department of Defense (DOD), and the Committee on National Security Systems (CNSS).[20] The mission of the Joint Task Force is to develop a unified information security framework for the federal government and its contractors. The updated security assessment guideline incorporates best practices in information security from the DOD, IC, and Civil agencies and includes security control assessment procedures for both national security and non-national security systems.

15. Title III of the e-Government Act, Pub.L. 107-347, 44 U.S.C.A. § 3541 *et seq., available at* http://csrc.nist.gov/groups/SMA/fisma/index.html; see OMB Memorandum M-10-15—FY 2010 Reporting Instructions for the Federal Information Security Management Act and Agency Privacy Management, *available at* http://www.whitehouse.gov/sites/default/files/omb/assets/memoranda_2010/m10-15.pdf.

16. *See* Nat'l Inst. of Standards & Tech., Computer Security Resource Center, Publications, http://csrc.nist.gov/publications/PubsSPs.html. See Guide to NIST Information Security Documents, *available at* http://csrc.nist.gov/publications/CSD_DocsGuide.pdf. See Appendix B, Resources.

17. *Id.*

18. NAT'L INST. OF STANDARDS & TECH., RISKS MANAGEMENT GUIDE FOR INFORMATION TECHNOLOGY SYSTEMS, Special Pub 800-30 (July 2002), *available at* http://csrc.nist.gov/publications/nistpubs/800-30/sp800-30.pdf.

19. *Id.* at 1.

20. NIST CSRC, News & Events, NIST announces the publication of Special Publication 800-53A, Revision 1, Guide for Assessing the Security Controls in Federal Information Systems and Organizations. June 29, 2010, *available at* http://csrc.nist.gov/news_events/index.html#june29.

The guideline for developing security assessment plans is intended to support a wide variety of assessment activities in all phases of the system development life cycle including development, implementation, and operation. The important changes in Special Publication 800-53A, Revision 1, are part of a larger strategic initiative to focus on enterprise-wide, near real-time risk management—that is, managing risks from information systems in dynamic environments of operation that can adversely affect organizational operations and assets, individuals, other organizations, and the Nation. The increased flexibility in the selection of assessment methods, assessment objects, and depth and coverage attribute values empowers organizations to place the appropriate emphasis on the security control assessment process at every stage in the system development life cycle to include a robust continuous monitoring process.

ISO/IEC 27000-series Standards

The International Organization for Standardization (ISO) and the International Electrotechnical Commission (IEC) have joined forces in the Joint Technical Committee 1 (JTC1), *Information technology*, Subcommittee 27 (SC27), *IT Security techniques*, to create an Information Security Management System (ISMS) family of standards. This ISMS series is deliberately broad in scope and is applicable to all types of organizations, independent of their size or focus. A governing principle behind this series is that an organization should design, implement, and maintain a coherent set of processes and systems to manage risks to its information assets, thereby ensuring acceptable levels of information security. It is also important to note that this ISMS is one of the few security frameworks that formally specifies a management system that mandates specific requirements for which an organizations can be formally audited and certified compliant with the standard.

The ISO/IEC 27000-series standards incorporate continuous feedback and improvement activities, summarized by the "plan-do-check-act" (or PDCA) approach,[21] that seek to address changes in the threats, vulnerabilities or impacts of information security incidents. Within the context of the ISO/IEC 27000-series standards the PDCA translates into:

- The **Plan** phase involves establishing the ISMS, specifically to establish ISMS policy, objectives, processes, and procedures relevant to managing risk and improving information security to deliver results in accordance with an organization's overall policies and objectives.
- The **Do** phase involves implementing and operating the ISMS, specifically to implement and operate the ISMS policy, controls, processes, and procedures.
- The **Check** phase involves monitoring and reviewing the ISMS, specifically to assess and, where applicable, measure process performance against ISMS policy, objectives, and practical experience and report the results to management for review.
- The **Act** phase involves maintaining and improving the ISMS, specifically to take corrective and preventive actions, based on the results of the internal

---

21. The PDCA (often called the Shewhart Cycle) is an iterative process used in business process improvement that was originally developed by Walter Shewhart and popularized by W. Edwards Deming.

ISMS audit and management review or other relevant information, to achieve continual improvement of the ISMS.

Of the ISO/IEC 27000-series standards, ISO/IEC 27001:2005—*Information technology—Security techniques—Information security management systems—Requirements*[22] is significant because it is the only ISMS standard that mandates behaviors (all the other ISMS standards offer guidance). ISO/IEC 27001 provides a detailed list of control objectives and controls that serve as the basis for certification as well as influencing the contents of many security checklists. These control objectives and controls are directly derived from and aligned with those listed in ISO/IEC 27002:2005 *Information technology—Security techniques—Code of practice for information security management.*[23]

COBIT

The Control Objectives for Information and Related Technologies version 4.1 or COBIT® 4.1[24] is an internationally accepted set of tools organized into a framework for IT governance, created by the Information Systems Audit and Control Association (ISACA®)[25] and the IT Governance Institute® (ITGI).[26] It provides a common language for executives and IT professionals to align IT with business objectives, deliver value, and manage associated risks. COBIT helps bridge the gaps between business requirements, control needs and technical issues as well as to communicate the level of control to stakeholders. It is a control model to meet the needs of IT governance and ensure the integrity of information and information systems.

The COBIT framework has been structured into 34 IT processes clustering interrelated life cycle activities or interrelated discrete tasks. These high-level IT processes cover 210 control objectives categorized into four domains:

- *Planning and Organization*—Provides direction to solution delivery and service delivery. It covers strategy and tactics, and concerns the identification of the way IT can best contribute to the achievement of the business objectives.
- *Acquisition and Implementation*—Provides the solutions and passes them to be turned into services. It is concerned with realizing the IT strategy through IT solutions that need to be identified, developed or acquired, as well as implemented and integrated into the business process; changes in and maintenance of existing systems are covered to make sure the solutions continue to meet business objectives.
- *Delivery and Support*—Receives the solutions and makes them usable for end users. It is concerned with the actual delivery of required services, which

---

22. Available from http://www.iso.org.

23. ISO/IEC 27002 was renumbered in July 2007 and was previously known as ISO/IEC 17799:2005 with the same title. Also available from http://www.iso.org.

24. At the time of this writing, COBIT 4.1 was the current version; however, COBIT Version 5 has recently been released in exposure draft. See http://www.itgi.org/cobit or http://www.isaca.org for additional information and downloads of COBIT.

25. See http://www.isaca.org for more information on ISACA.

26. See http://www.itgi.org for more information on the ITGI.

includes service delivery, management of security and continuity, service support for users, and management of data and operational facilities.

• *Monitoring and Evaluation*—Monitors all processes to ensure that the direction provided is followed. It is concerned with performance management, monitoring of internal control, regulatory compliance and governance.

IT control objectives are statements of managerial actions to achieve necessary outcomes or purposes to control risk and add value within a particular IT process. They are written as short, action-oriented management practices and expressed wherever possible in a life cycle sequence.

It should be noted that the Committee of Sponsoring Organizations of the Treadway Commission (COSO)[27] was used as source material for the business model, ISO 27002[28] was used for technical security guidance, and the Information Technology Infrastructure Library (ITIL®)[29] was used as service delivery guidance along with other standards, frameworks, and guidance to develop the control objectives. COBIT is not meant to replace any of these control models. It is intended to emphasize what control is required in the IT environment while working with and building on the strengths of these other control models.

National Identity Management Strategy

In recognizing the reality that online transactions on the Internet greatly increase the risk of potential losses associated with identity theft and fraud, the White House issued a National Strategy for Trusted Identities in Cyberspace: Creating Options for Enhanced Online Security and Privacy.[30] The strategy seeks to enable individuals and organizations to "utilize secure, efficient, easy-to-use, and interoperable identity solutions to access online services in a manner that promotes confidence, privacy, choice, and innovation."[31] The strategy envisions that the federal government will collaborate with the private sector, state, local, tribal and international governments to build and implement an interoperable identity infrastructure. While this proposed strategy is just one of a number of identity management models that have been developed over the past several years, and it may be viewed by some as akin to a national identity card. The issue of identity management is one overarching problem that must be addressed in order to develop secure computer networks that facilitate e-commerce and communication in the digital age.[32]

The goal of the strategy is to create an identity system that will ensure secure online transactions. Individuals would be able to use a multi-factor, interoperable credential to

---

27. See http://www.coso.org for more information on the COSO.

28. In actuality, the ISO/IEC 17799 standard was used in the original research, but ISO/IEC later renumbered the standard.

29. ITIL is a widely accepted approach to IT service management provides a cohesive set of best practice, drawn from the public and private sectors internationally. See http://www.itil-officialsite.com for additional information on ITIL.

30. National Strategy for Trusted Identities in Cyberspace, Creating Options for Enhanced Online Security and Privacy, Draft, June 25, 2010, *available at* http://www.nstic.ideascale.com.

31. *Id.* at 1.

32. *See generally* Lucy Thomson, *Critical Issues in Identity Management.* 47 JURIMETRICS J. 335–356 (2007).

authenticate themselves online for various transactions such as banking, accessing electronic health records, sending e-mail and making online purchases.[33]

THE SECURITY RESPONSE

In light of escalating cybercrime and the increasing number of data breaches, and as hackers become increasingly more sophisticated, information security experts are developing more focused approaches to securing digital information. In many cases hackers have penetrated the networks of organizations by exploiting vulnerabilities in the software or the implementation of system components. On the other hand, a large number of the cyber-intrusions and data breaches are the result of the failure to implement appropriate information security, such as transmitting unencrypted data in the clear, or to sloppy security practices resulting in lost or stolen laptops and other mobile devices containing unencrypted data. This chapter describes the important work of five organizations of security experts and policymakers who have recently begun to address the problem of data breaches by prioritizing and focusing security efforts where they will have the greatest impact. The high-level priorities of each organization are highlighted here to provide insight into the types of security initiatives and controls that are required to secure information systems from compromise by external hackers and malicious insiders, as well as from intentional or inadvertent disclosure by employees, contractors, clients, or others who may have authorized access to the system.

While the focus of each of the three organizations may be different, it is important to note that their recommendations are reasonably consistent, and thus, when considered along with the NIST guidance, they provide a core set of requirements that must be addressed to provide appropriate information security. As the next step, it is important to read the reports of these organizations carefully to understand the details behind their recommendations. Each organization must then conduct a risk assessment and develop a security plan in order to tailor the security controls to the unique requirements of the information system and the data and information to be protected.

Twenty Critical Controls for Effective Cyberdefense: Consensus Audit

In August 2009 a consortium of U.S. federal cybersecurity experts established a baseline standard of due care for cybersecurity—The Top Twenty Most Critical Controls—that defines the most critical security controls to protect federal and contractor information and information systems.[34] This approach is well suited to private sector organizations as well. This consensus document of 20 crucial controls is designed to begin the process of establishing a *prioritized baseline of information security measures and controls* that can be applied across federal enterprise environments. The 20 specific technical security controls are viewed as effective in blocking currently known high-priority attacks, as well as those attack types expected in the near future. Fifteen of these controls can be monitored, at least in part, automatically and continuously.

---

33. National Strategy for Trusted Identities in Cyberspace, Ibid.
34. SANS Inst., Twenty Critical Security Controls—Version 2.3 (Nov. 13, 2009), *available at* http://www.sans.org/cag/critical-security-controls/guidelines.php.

Critical controls subject to automated collection, measurement, and validation:

1. Inventory of authorized and unauthorized devices.
2. Inventory of authorized and unauthorized software.
3. Secure configurations for hardware and software on laptops, workstations, and servers.
4. Secure configurations for network devices such as firewalls, routers, and switches.
5. Boundary defense.
6. Maintenance, monitoring, and analysis of security audit logs.
7. Application software security.
8. Controlled use of administrative privileges.
9. Controlled access based on need to know.
10. Continuous vulnerability assessment and remediation.
11. Account monitoring and control.
12. Malware defenses.
13. Limitation and control of network ports, protocols, and services.
14. Wireless device control.
15. Data loss prevention.

Additional critical controls (not directly supported by automated measurement and validation):

16. Secure network engineering.
17. Penetration tests and red team exercises.
18. Incident response capability.
19. Data recovery capability.
20. Security skills assessment and appropriate training to fill gaps.

The consortium emphasized that securing our nation against cyberattacks has become one of the nation's highest priorities. To achieve this objective, networks, systems, and the operations teams that support them must vigorously defend against a variety of threats, both internal and external. Furthermore, for those attacks that are successful, defenses must be capable of detecting, thwarting, and responding to follow-on attacks on internal enterprise networks as attackers spread inside a compromised network.

Top 25 Most Dangerous Software Errors

The 2010 CWE/SANS Top 25 Most Dangerous Software Errors is a list of the most widespread and critical programming errors that can lead to serious software vulnerabilities.[35] These 25 flaws are the cause of almost every major cyber attack in recent history, with

---

35. The list is the result of collaboration between the SANS Institute, MITRE, and many top software security experts in the US and Europe. It leverages experiences in the development of the SANS Top 20 attack vectors (http://www.sans.org/top20/) and MITRE's Common Weakness Enumeration (CWE) (http://cwe.mitre.org/). MITRE maintains the CWE web site, with the support of the US Department of Homeland Security's National Cyber Security Division, presenting detailed descriptions of the top 25 programming errors along with authoritative guidance for mitigating and avoiding them. The CWE site contains data on more than 800 programming errors, design errors, and architecture errors that can lead to exploitable vulnerabilities; *available at* http://cwe.mitre.org/top25/.

cross-site scripting and SQL injection leading the list of security weaknesses—and the cause of many of the massive data breaches discussed throughout this book. They are often easy to find and easy to exploit. They are dangerous because they will frequently allow attackers to completely take over the software, steal data, or prevent the software from working at all.

The 2010 CWE/SANS website describes the purpose of the list:

> The Top 25 entries are *prioritized* using inputs from over 20 different organizations, who evaluated each weakness based on prevalence and importance. It is designed as a tool for education and awareness to help programmers to prevent the kinds of vulnerabilities that plague the software industry, by identifying and avoiding all-too-common mistakes that occur before software is even shipped. Software customers can use the same list to help them to ask for more secure software. Researchers in software security can use the Top 25 to focus on a narrow but important subset of all known security weaknesses. Finally, software managers and CIOs can use the Top 25 list as a measuring stick of progress in their efforts to secure their software.

A key weakness in the Top 25 Most Dangerous Software Errors addresses missing encryption of sensitive data (CWE 311), the cause of the massive data breaches discussed in chapter 5.[36]

Common Weakness Enumeration—Missing Encryption of Sensitive Data (CWE-311)

A key weakness is the finding that software does not encrypt sensitive or critical information before storage or transmission.

Whenever sensitive data is being stored or transmitted anywhere outside of your control, attackers may be looking for ways to get to it. Thieves could be anywhere—sniffing your packets, reading your databases, and sifting through your file systems. If your software sends sensitive information across a network, such as private data or authentication credentials, that information crosses many different nodes in transit to its final destination. Attackers can sniff this data right off the wire, and it doesn't require a lot of effort. All they need to do is control one node along the path to the final destination, control any node within the same networks of those transit nodes, or plug into an available interface. If your software stores sensitive information on a local file or database, there may be other ways for attackers to get at the file. They may benefit from lax permissions, exploitation of another vulnerability, or physical theft of the disk. You know those massive credit card thefts you keep hearing about? Many of them are due to unencrypted storage.

Insider Threats Must Be Countered

Defending an organization's perimeter from external attack does not protect against valuable information seeping out because of insider malfeasance, whether that behav-

---

36. *See also* CWE-312 Cleartext Storage of Sensitive Information and CWE-319 Cleartext Transmission of Sensitive Information.

ior is characterized as malicious, mischievous, or ignorant/accidental.[37] Carnegie Mellon University recommends a list of 16 best practices[38] to minimize the risk of insider threat:

1. Consider threats from insiders and business partners in enterprise-wide risk assessments.
2. Clearly document and consistently enforce policies and controls.
3. Institute periodic security awareness training for all employees.
4. Monitor and respond to suspicious or disruptive behavior, beginning with the hiring process.
5. Anticipate and manage negative workplace issues.
6. Track and secure the physical environment.
7. Implement strict password and account management policies and practices.
8. Enforce separation of duties and least privilege.
9. Consider insider threats in the software development lifecycle.
10. Use extra caution with system administrators and technical or privileged users.
11. Implement system change controls.
12. Log, monitor, and audit employee online actions.
13. Use layered defense against remote attacks.
14. Deactivate computer access following termination (employee).
15. Implement secure backup and recovery processes.
16. Develop an insider incident response plan.

These best practices also promote the protection of data from external threats.

Payment Card Industry Data Security Standard

The Payment Card Industry Data Security Standard (PCI DSS) is a worldwide security standard assembled by the Payment Card Industry Security Standards Council (PCI SSC).[39] The PCI security standards are technical and operational requirements that were created to help organizations that process card payments prevent credit card fraud, hacking, and various other security vulnerabilities and threats.

The PCI DSS consists of 12 requirements, such as installing a firewall and antivirus software and regularly updating virus definitions.[40] It also requires companies to encrypt data, to restrict data access to people who need it, and to assign a unique identifying number to people with access rights in order to monitor who views and downloads data.

Although the standard was developed by Visa and MasterCard, it is endorsed by other credit card companies. It applies to any merchant or service provider that processes, transmits, or stores credit card payments and places additional requirements on

---

37. *CSO*, 2006 eCrime Watch Survey (Sept. 6, 2006), *available at* http://www.cert.org/archive/pdf/ecrimesurvey06 .pdf. The survey was conducted by *CSO* magazine in cooperation with the U.S. Secret Service, Carnegie Mellon University Software Engineering Institute's CERT Coordination Center, and Microsoft Corp.

38. DAWN CAPELLI, ANDREW MOORE, TIMOTHY J. SHIMEALL & RANDALL TRZECIAK, COMMON SENSE GUIDE TO PREVENTION AND DETECTION OF INSIDER THREATS (July 2006), *available at* http://www.cert.org/insider_threat/.

39. PCI Sec. Standards Council, https://www.pcisecuritystandards.org.

40. *See* PCI SEC. STANDARDS COUNCIL, THE PRIORITIZED APPROACH TO PURSUE PCI DSS COMPLIANCE (2009), https://www.pcisecuritystandards.org/education/docs/Prioritized_Approach_PCI_DSS_1_2.pdf.

TABLE 16.1
Milestones for Prioritizing PCI DSS Compliance Efforts

Milestone	Goals
1	Remove sensitive authentication data and limit data retention. This milestone targets a key area of risk for entities that have been compromised. Remember—if sensitive authentication data and other cardholder data are not stored, the effects of a compromise will be greatly reduced. If you don't need it, don't store it.
2	Protect the perimeter, internal, and wireless networks. This milestone targets controls for points of access to most compromises— the network or a wireless access point.
3	Secure payment card applications. This milestone targets controls for applications, application processes, and application servers. Weaknesses in these areas offer easy prey for compromising systems and obtaining access to cardholder data.
4	Monitor and control access to your systems. Controls for this milestone allow you to detect the who, what, when, and how concerning who is accessing your network and cardholder data environment.
5	Protect stored cardholder data. For those organizations that have analyzed their business processes and determined that they must store primary account numbers, Milestone Five targets key protections mechanisms for that stored data.
6	Finalize remaining compliance efforts, and ensure all controls are in place. The intent of Milestone Six is to complete PCI DSS requirements and finalize all remaining related policies, procedures, and processes needed to protect the cardholder data environment.

Source: PCI Security Standards Council, The Prioritized Approach to Pursue PCI DSS Compliance.

card issuers, such as banks, to ensure that merchants and service providers comply with the requirements and report breaches in a timely manner.

Since 2001, any business wishing to process credit card transactions must sign a contract agreeing to the PCI standard and obtain a security audit from an approved assessor.

In April 2008 the PCI Standards group, leaders in the financial arena who have developed the Data Security Standard that governs credit card processing, issued a list of 10 priorities for financial organizations to follow to try to make their systems more secure.

The Prioritized Approach includes six milestones. Table 16.1 summarizes the high-level goals and intentions of each milestone. The rest of the Prioritized Approach maps the milestones to the 12 PCI DSS requirements and their subrequirements.

Cloud Security

For organizations using a cloud computing platform, the Cloud Security Alliance (CSA) Controls Matrix (CM) is designed to provide fundamental security principles to guide cloud vendors and to assist prospective cloud customers in assessing the overall security risk of a cloud provider.[41] The CSA CM provides a controls framework that provides a detailed understanding of security concepts and principles that are aligned to the Cloud Security Alliance guidance in 13 domains.

The CSA CM is intended to strengthen existing information security control environments by emphasizing business information security control requirements: to reduce and identify consistent security threats and vulnerabilities in the cloud, provide standardized security and operational risk management, and seek to normalize security expectations, cloud taxonomy and terminology, and security measures implemented in the cloud.

These are efforts to focus attention on the critical areas of information systems that must be secured to ensure that sensitive data and information are protected.

NOW IS THE TIME TO BECOME SERIOUS ABOUT INFORMATION SECURITY

Cyberattacks and massive data breaches are primarily the work of international cybercriminals. Global cybercrime and data breaches can and must be prevented. Information security solutions must address the threats and risks faced by every organization, and must be tailored to specific information practices and networks. Given the magnitude of the threats to the national security and economic viability of governments and private sector businesses and organizations around the world, business leaders and government executives must make cybersecurity the highest priority. Lax security practices that have led to data breaches of unencrypted personal information on lost or stolen mobile devices must also be addressed. Comprehensive security policies that address the threats and risks to sensitive personal data must be implemented, enforced, and continuously monitored.[42]

---

41. Cloud Security Alliance Controls Matrix (CSA CM) (April 27, 2010), *available at* http://www.cloudsecurity alliance.org/cm.html.

42. See chapter 2.

CHAPTER 17

Responding to Data Breaches

Ruth Hill Bro

Names, Social Security numbers, and various types of financial information are among the most common casualties in a growing number of data security breaches at leading organizations across the country. It seems that every week, a new data security breach involving the loss or disclosure of personally identifiable information (or "personal information") is reported in the media.

For most businesses, it is not a matter of *if*, but rather *when*, they will be subject to a data security breach. This is a phenomenon that does not discriminate: It touches all types of businesses, whether retailers, manufacturers, information brokers, financial institutions, healthcare companies, universities, law firms, or government entities.

Virtually all states now have, or are actively considering, statutes requiring that affected individuals be notified of the breach. At the same time, similar laws and regulations are emerging at the federal level and throughout the world. Taken as a group, these security breach notification laws generally require that any business possessing sensitive personal information about an individual must disclose a breach of the security of such information to the person affected. In some cases, others (e.g., government entities, credit reporting agencies) must be notified as well. Such notifications are designed to permit individuals to protect themselves against identity theft, described by some as the crime of the 21st century.

Consequences for noncompliance with these notification statutes can be significant; penalties vary from state to state, but can include substantial fines and private rights of action. Beyond the significant legal consequences, the public relations fallout associated with the data security breaches themselves can be considerable. As a result, it is important to identify *in advance* what incidents will trigger compliance obligations under these new statutes and what must be done to comply with such laws once a breach occurs.

Whether taking steps to prevent data security breaches or responding to the breaches themselves, it is vital for the organization to document what it did. When a data breach occurs (and it will), organizations will be in a much better position if they can point to evidence that they evaluated risks and took measures to address those risks before the breach. Equally important, when a breach occurs, businesses should keep records of their internal investigation and any determination that there is no real risk of harm to the data subjects, as well as other documentation supporting the organization's determination that data subjects did not need to be notified. Some state data security breach notification statutes require that such documentation be kept for as long as five years.

A data security breach can be a real wake-up call. In responding to such breaches, businesses need to be ready to RISE and SHINE:

Report immediately to a designated internal contact any discovered or suspected breach.
Investigate any reports promptly and thoroughly.
Stop the source of the breach and the associated harm.
Evaluate your legal obligations regarding the incident.

and

Strategize communications about the incident.
Help the data subjects.
Identify internal policies and procedures that should be immediately changed.
Notify the affected data subjects and other relevant entities where warranted.
Evolve practices and procedures on an ongoing basis.

Each of these actions is discussed in turn below. Organizations should review the following elements and develop a data breach protocol to supplement any existing incident response plans and security policies.

REPORT IMMEDIATELY TO A DESIGNATED INTERNAL CONTACT ANY DISCOVERED OR SUSPECTED BREACH

Businesses should start by establishing an initial point of contact internally (e.g., corporate security officer) to whom a discovered or suspected data breach can be reported. That person will turn to a broader cross-functional team to take follow-up steps. The response team may vary from business to business, but will likely include senior management, IT/security officers, and at least one person from the in-house legal department. As a backup, two others from the response team should be designated as alternate initial points of contact. The response team, with input from outside counsel as needed, must quickly decide whether the personal information at issue is covered by breach notification requirements in applicable laws, especially because some of these laws impose particularly short time frames for reporting such breaches. For a number of reasons, communications with others in the organization should be on a need-to-know basis (discussed below).

INVESTIGATE ANY REPORTS PROMPTLY AND THOROUGHLY

When it comes to responding to data security breaches, the devil is in the details. The facts discovered shortly after a data breach is first suspected or discovered can change from day to day, with one day's facts cutting in favor of notification to data subjects (and, in some cases, to a government authority), while new facts that come to light the next day might cut in favor of not notifying. At the same time, without having a proper grasp of the facts, it is difficult to take decisive action to prevent the incident from happening again. Thus, the first step in responding to a data breach is to promptly investigate to determine what went wrong and whether the breach was an isolated incident.

Investigations can vary widely, depending on the type of breach at issue. Many investigations have a significant technological component, given that a number of breaches involve laptops, Internet postings, network vulnerabilities, and the like. A substantial number of cases involve third parties, which adds another layer of complexity to the investigation.

A number of things, however, should be core to any investigation, including:

- Note dates and times throughout the investigation, including when the breach occurred, when it was discovered, and when each step thereafter was taken.
- Identify any representations made to the data subjects about how personal information they provided would be used, protected, and so on. Consider not only direct communications made to data subjects, but also representations posted on websites, on intranets, in employee handbooks, in corporate codes of conduct, and in places where more general promises about privacy and data security might have been made.
- Gather documentation regarding existing training programs, security measures, procedures, protocols, policies, audit trails, and so on. The company needs to be ready with facts and proof that processes were in place.

STOP THE SOURCE OF THE BREACH AND THE ASSOCIATED HARM

Stopping the source of the breach is one of the first things the organization should do, and this will typically occur long before the investigation is over. In some cases, it involves closing a security hole that allowed a hacker to get in. In others, it entails removing information inadvertently accessible to others via the Internet. In still other cases, it requires exhaustive tracking to locate a lost file box or laptop. Sometimes, where a bad actor is involved, it can entail contacting law enforcement authorities for assistance. In all cases, the organization must act swiftly and appropriately to stop the problem that caused the breach (or prompted the suspicion of breach).

EVALUATE YOUR LEGAL OBLIGATIONS REGARDING THE INCIDENT

While the factual investigation is occurring, it is critical to identify which laws apply to the breach in question. Consider federal, state, and local laws, whether in the United States or other countries. Applicable laws could include those in the state in which the breach occurred or the data is stored and in any state in which there are data subjects.

In evaluating the organization's legal obligations, it is important to keep in mind that this is an area that is rapidly changing, and many different (and new) laws could apply with each new incident. Some laws include very specific and short timeframes in which to provide necessary notifications—to affected data subjects, to government entities, to consumer reporting agencies, and so on. Ideally, organizations will have tracked most of these laws on an ongoing basis, with updating occurring at the time of an incident.

It is also important to keep in mind that the statutes in question were enacted only a short time ago (the earliest, from California, was in 2005) and thus are largely untested from a case law perspective, notwithstanding hundreds of reported data security breach incidents since that time. Likewise, data breach cases can have their own unusual facts that raise issues not squarely addressed by the black-letter language of the statutes.

Consider laws related to:

- data security breaches
- obligations to provide security
- the type of information at issue (e.g., Social Security numbers, credit card numbers, driver's license numbers, etc.)
- the means by which the breach occurred (e.g., e-mail, computer network, hard-copy mailing, website posting)
- the nature of the disclosure (e.g., directed to certain individuals, publicly posted)
- the means by which the information was first collected and representations made in connection with that collection
- industry-specific laws (e.g., company is in the financial or healthcare sector and subject to special regulations)
- other potentially applicable categories that could trigger legal requirements

These laws will, in turn, affect what must be done (the content of the notice and how it should be sent, obligations and time frames related to investigations and notices, corrective action that should be taken, and so on). In particular, consider:

- whether a *triggering event* has occurred—e.g., indications that the information is in the physical possession and control of an unauthorized person, has been downloaded or copied, or has been used by an unauthorized person (identity theft, opening accounts without authorization, etc.)
- whether *exceptions* might apply (e.g., was the data encrypted, was the breach unlikely to cause substantial harm, was good faith acquisition of data involved) and, if so, whether there are documentation or other obligations associated with such exceptions

The organization, consistent with corporate codes of ethics and commitment to retention of customers, employees, and good corporate standing, may wish to provide notice even if not legally required to do so—for example, where the incident was not a sufficient triggering event but the data in question was sensitive, or where some data subjects resided in states not requiring notice but the company believes it would not be right to notify some data subjects and not others. Taken as a whole, the laws and any related guidance issued by government authorities (e.g., the Federal Trade Commission; various states, including California; and various countries, including Canada) will help provide a sense of what might constitute good corporate practice in a given situation. Likewise, the extensive list of reported data security breaches maintained by the Privacy Rights Clearinghouse can shed light on what companies have previously considered to be reportable events.[1] Practically speaking, the organization may also want to notify

---

1. *See* Privacy Rights Clearinghouse, A Chronology of Data Breaches, *available at* www.privacyrights.org/data-breach (tracking of breach notifications from January 1, 2005, onward).

where many individuals internally know about the incident (which should only be communicated on a need-to-know basis), as loose lips can sink ships. The more people who know about the incident, the more likely that someone outside the organization will find out about it, including via an anonymous tip to the media from a disgruntled employee.

STRATEGIZE COMMUNICATIONS ABOUT THE INCIDENT

Plan how the company will respond if it receives a query from the press, a third party (including consumer watchdog groups), labor groups, or a government entity. This is particularly critical in the investigation phase and after any notice is provided. Ideally, the story that one would want to convey about the incident, if in fact there is a need to tell the story, is that the incident violated the organization's procedures and the organization immediately investigated and corrected the problem, promptly notified affected individuals, regrets that the incident occurred, and took responsibility for resolving it.

The organization should also consider early on the need for special communications—for example, with an employee or customer who first identified the problem. These individuals will require a more tailored response. Company policies (e.g., regarding an employee complaint or a customer complaint) may also need to be considered.

HELP THE DATA SUBJECTS

Beyond the mere act of notifying data subjects, the organization will want to consider other assistance it will provide. This other assistance is often included in the notification sent to the data subjects. In some cases, applicable law might dictate the minimum that must be provided; in other cases, it may be necessary to consider what should be provided based on emerging case law, media developments, government guidance, and other sources. For example, organizations might:

- arrange for a call center to answer questions and concerns from individuals regarding the incident and related matters. The notice to the data subjects should include a toll-free number and hours of operation (and how many months it will operate).
- indicate that they have informed the three major U.S. credit bureaus (Equifax, Experian, and TransUnion) about the incident and that, upon the data subject's request and at no expense to the data subject, the agencies will place a "fraud alert" on the individual's file to tell creditors to take additional steps to verify identity before granting credit in the individual's name. It should be explained that notifying one of the bureaus will result in notification to the remaining bureaus once the first confirms the fraud alert. The notice to data subjects should also warn that such a "fraud alert" can delay their own ability to obtain credit. The notice should include the name of each credit bureau, its toll-free phone number, and its website URL.
- arrange for credit monitoring at the option of the data subject. Such monitoring can provide notice to the data subject whenever there are key changes to their credit reports at any of the three credit bureaus or, if there are none, on a periodic (monthly) basis. Organizations vary in how they offer such

monitoring, whether it is free or on a copayment basis, whether it is for one year from the date of enrollment or more, and so on. While relatively inexpensive, the cost of credit monitoring can add significant costs where there are millions of data subjects at issue. On the other hand, litigation is emerging where data subjects have alleged that credit monitoring was provided for free only for a certain time period, but that the risk of harm extended beyond that time period. Instructions for sign-up should be included in the notice.

- notify data subjects of their right under applicable law (e.g., as in the United States) to one free credit report annually from each of the three major credit bureaus and how to order these reports (via www.annualcreditreport.com, or via toll-free number or mail).
- provide other information to data subjects about how to protect themselves against identity theft (e.g., the Federal Trade Commission's site at http://www .ftc.gov/bcp/edu/microsites/idtheft).

IDENTIFY INTERNAL POLICIES AND PROCEDURES THAT SHOULD BE IMMEDIATELY CHANGED

In the wake of any data security breach incident, a lot of introspection occurs (or should occur). For some organizations, the first data security breach incident can be the organization's call to action to take the steps it needs to avoid similar or worse incidents in the future. At the same time, taking corrective steps to prevent a similar incident from occurring can be key to managing the risks associated with the current incident. In making these assessments, organizations will often:

- *Identify and implement technological means of avoiding the problem*—e.g., a program to block all outbound e-mails with more than one address, a prompt that comes up when an out-of-the-ordinary field is selected for a mailing, or improved blocking of attempts at unauthorized access of computer systems.
- *Evaluate third-party relationships* that might have been involved in the incident and then act on that assessment by altering procedures and training, improving security measures, adding contractual safeguards, moving to a different vendor, and taking other appropriate steps. In particular, third parties should be contractually obligated to notify the organization immediately upon a breach or suspected breach.
- *Talk to affected employees* about the importance of privacy and data security. Consider the need for new training sessions (online training modules, inperson sessions, expanding detail in protocols, etc.) and ongoing means of training and awareness-raising.

NOTIFY THE AFFECTED DATA SUBJECTS AND OTHER RELEVANT ENTITIES WHERE WARRANTED

In the event of a security breach incident, the response team must determine not only whether affected data subjects must be notified (as discussed below) but also whether it is necessary or appropriate to notify law enforcement authorities (e.g., local law enforcement, the Federal Bureau of Investigation), consumer reporting agencies, or others. In some cases, this determination will be statute-driven, while in others it will be dictated by the need for assistance (e.g., in the case of a criminal ring), the desire to limit harm to the extent possible, and other concerns. Breaches involving significant numbers of data subjects will likely require coordination with the credit reporting agencies. In some cases, reporting the incident to law enforcement might result in a delay in notifying individuals, given that widespread notification could in certain cases compromise the investigation and tip off the bad actors in question.

In taking steps to promptly and appropriately notify affected individuals, a number of factors can come into play:

- *Legal requirements* (as discussed above) can vary from jurisdiction to jurisdiction and, in some instances, might even conflict; careful analysis of the requirements on an ongoing basis—with a refresher at the time of the incident—is critical. As mentioned above, if the incident involves criminal activity, the company may first need to notify law enforcement entities to coordinate notification and ensure that it does not impede the government's criminal investigation.
- The need for careful handling and prompt action increases with the *sensitivity* of the data or the breach in question.
- When it comes to the *mode of delivery*, individual notice is best. First-class mail is preferred. E-mail can be used if this is a standard means of communicating with the person, the person has provided consent to be contacted this way, and the notice otherwise complies with the federal E-SIGN law. Other more public means of notice (e.g., posting on a website, in major statewide media) might need to be used in certain situations, though these obviously have drawbacks. Mode of delivery will be affected by legal requirements, the incident in question, the type of data subject (e-mail can be more viable in employee scenarios), cost considerations, and so on.
- *Document* the basis for including data subjects to receive notification, and *double-check* before mailing or otherwise communicating with such individuals.
- In most cases, the following content at a minimum should be communicated (this will be influenced by legal requirements):
  - A general description of what occurred
  - The nature of the personal information at issue; the actual personal information at issue should not be included in the letter (e.g., refer to "Social Security number," but do not include the actual number in the letter)
  - What the company has done to protect the information from further disclosure
  - What the company is doing to assist individuals (e.g., providing a toll-free phone number, providing credit monitoring)
  - A reminder of the need to remain vigilant, as well as other information that might assist individuals—e.g., what action individuals should take regarding the incident in question, need to review account statements, how to contact credit reporting agencies

- *Readability* of the notice should also play a key role, not only from a communications perspective but also so that the letter will not be deemed to be insufficient because it is unlikely to draw the attention of the recipient or would not be readily understood when read. Drafting notices to data subjects (i.e., real human beings) can entail as much art as science (the latter being the legal requirements driving the content). The letter should strive to appropriately notify individuals regarding the required content, but without dramatizing the incident or using unnecessary language intensifiers. In particular:
    - Use clear, simple language, while avoiding jargon and technical language.
    - Use plenty of white space, headings (in a longer notice), and a large enough font size.
    - Include an "Re" line to focus attention on the issue; include attention-getting language (e.g., "Important notice regarding . . .").
    - Differentiate this mailing from others the organization has sent (avoid a standardized format that would promote complacency).
    - Do not combine the notice with other communications; make it a stand-alone communication, not part of a regular mailing.
    - Include the corporate message regarding the incident (see "Strategize Communications About the Incident" above) in the letter.

EVOLVE PRACTICES AND PROCEDURES ON AN ONGOING BASIS

Beyond the notification-related obligations, there is other potential fallout related to breaches. A breach may draw scrutiny to a business regarding its broader security practices and its compliance with statutes that impose an affirmative obligation to protect personal information; beyond these statutes, the FTC has indicated that every company must maintain an effective information security program if it is to avoid unfair and deceptive trade practice claims. At the same time, a well-publicized breach might reveal the vulnerability of the business to attack, not just with respect to personal information but also trade secrets and the like, thereby making the business an attractive target for a hacker or causing concern to clients who have entrusted confidential information to the business. The breach may also draw unwanted regulator and media scrutiny to other areas of legal compliance unrelated to personal information. Moreover, a data security breach can result in negative publicity, unflattering SEC disclosures, and other fallout. Businesses are increasingly recognizing that personal information is a valuable asset that—like trade secrets—needs to be protected. At the end of the day, failure to take appropriate steps could result in litigation, financial payouts, fines, damages, loss of business, loss of productivity, and higher insurance premiums.

It is therefore critical that businesses continually evolve their practices and procedures in this area. In particular, in addition to developing a written data security breach protocol, organizations should:

- *Conduct a data security assessment.* Businesses should identify the hardware, software, databases, and networks that require protection. Likewise, businesses should identify the material internal and external risks to the security, confidentiality, and integrity of the personal information that could result in the unauthorized disclosure, misuse, loss, alteration, destruction, or other compromise of such information, and assess the sufficiency of any safeguards in place to control these risks. Businesses should review and adjust safeguards as necessary on an ongoing basis.

- *Develop a written security program* to manage and control risk. This includes the design and implementation of reasonable administrative, technical, and physical safeguards to control the risks identified through the risk assessment. The security program should be consistent with applicable legal requirements and commonly known risks. For example, personal information shouldn't be stored for longer than company policies say (or the law allows) or in files with default user IDs or passwords. Likewise, companies should put appropriate authentication procedures in place, verify the IDs of those requesting access, be able to detect intrusions, and guard against commonly known attacks like SQL attacks. More and more, there is a trend toward encrypting personal information not only when it's transmitted, but also when it's stored, at least when it comes to sensitive personal data.
- *Identify applicable legal requirements and legislative trends*, and develop a compliance plan.
- *Identify existing data security promises* and make sure that they are accurate and consistent across the company (e.g., website privacy policies, online information collection forms, codes of conduct, employee policies).
- *Appoint persons responsible* for the company's privacy and data security program.
- *Implement an awareness, training, and education program* to make sure that all appropriate employees understand the privacy and security risks and their role in protecting against those risks. In particular, businesses should provide appropriate training for relevant personnel concerning the data security breach protocol. In any case, the consequences for failure to abide by the company's policies and breach protocol should be made clear.
- *Include appropriate security requirements in all contracts with third parties* that will have access to the company's personal information, and monitor compliance.

The wake-up call that is the data security breach can come at any time—often earlier than expected. Prudent organizations are taking steps to make sure they are ready to RISE and SHINE.

CHAPTER 18

Technology to Prevent Data Leaks

Jennifer Ann Kurtz

PROTECTION AT THE DATA LEVEL

Although no technical tool can protect an organization completely from the risk of losing confidential data and intellectual property that is contained in computing and communication devices, vendors are developing products to help prevent or detect the transmission of sensitive data from endpoints and laptops, whatever the network connection. Attorneys and business executives should be aware of the risk of data leakage (data seepage, information loss, information compromise) from inside the organization as well as outside, and what tools and practices can be implemented to mitigate its consequences.

Deloitte & Touche listed "data leakage" second in its list of Top 10 Security & Privacy Challenges in 2010. *Network World* identified data leakage prevention (DLP)[1] as the eighth "hottest" technology for 2008.[2] Considered as part of data protection, DPL grew in importance to third among the hot technologies for 2009.[3]

The *2010 Verizon Data Breach Investigations Report*, a study based on datasets obtained during investigations of data breach incidents performed by Verizon and the United States Secret Service, states that more than 143 million data records were compromised in 2009, the majority of breaches remained uncontained for weeks or months after detection, and that external discovery of compromise is still more likely than internal.[4]

The massive data breaches of Heartland, Hannaford, RBS WorldPay, TJX, and DSW discussed throughout this book illustrate how personal information about millions of

---

1. Also known as "data loss prevention."

2. Neal Weinberg, *Data Leakage Prevention: Hot Technology for 2008*, NETWORK WORLD, Jan. 14, 2008, *available at* http://www.networkworld.com/research/2008/011408-8-techs-data-leakage.html.

3. *Nine Hot Technologies for '09*, NETWORK WORLD, Jan. 2009, http://www.networkworld.com/supp/2009/outlook/hottech/.

4. *Verizon 2010 Data Breach Report*, in collaboration with U.S. Secret Service (July 2010), www.verizonbusiness.com/resources/reports/rp_2010-data-breach-report_en_xg.pdf, p. 47.

individuals can leak out. A culture of data stewardship is needed in organizations and continuity of care must be the underlying principle. Data stewardship encompasses an organization's responsibility for querying data quality, accuracy, and reliability. It cannot successfully be delegated to a single department or individual; it is a responsibility owned by all members of an organization. Continuity of care, as a medical principle, promotes understanding and treatment of an individual's health condition by reference to medical history. Applied to data, continuity of care informs the understanding about data provenance, its relationship to other data, its relevance to an organization's current business needs, its accessibility, and its volatility (e.g., if changed, how it was changed and by whom).

In several of the largest data breaches, the perpetrators gained access to the targets with stolen credentials, then used SQL code injections for a variety of purposes such as querying or modifying data in databases and delivering malware, often customized.[5] Over time, data flowed out of the organizations that had been compromised.[6] Although often not lost to the organization, in that the data is still available, possession is now shared. It is no longer under the exclusive control of the organization. Technology-based tools exist that can provide early detection assistance and assessments of an organization's data vulnerability.

Tools to mitigate data loss work by protecting

- networks and networked resources from rogue devices and software
- valued systems from inappropriate access
- data content from exposure, unwarranted alteration, or removal

One of the benefits of DLP products is early detection, acting as a kind of early warning system, or simply detection of any kind. DLP tools can scan outgoing e-mail, for example, and flag information such as credit card numbers, sensitive keywords, or other types of sensitive data.

The 2008 data breach at Heartland Payment Systems, Inc., for example, has heightened interest in DLP technology. According to company news releases, hackers planted malicious software on the Heartland processing system that was capable of sniffing payment card data as it moved across the company's network. The hackers then removed the data out of Heartland's system in encrypted data streams.[7] Apparently this malicious activity was not detected until Heartland was notified by Visa and MasterCard. Thus in this case a network server was sending data outside the network—even if the data was encrypted, a monitoring tool would have been able to see the traffic flows.

Early detection tip-offs there may have included: "1) abnormal increase in log data, 2) abnormal length of lines within files, 3) absence of (or abnormal decrease in) log

---

5. *Id.*, p. 47.

6. Figures 5.1 (Heartland), 5.2 (Hannaford), 5.3 (RBS WorldPay), 5.4 (TJX), and 5.5 (DSW) illustrate how hackers stole data from these companies and sent it to servers outside the United States.

7. Press Release, Heartland Payment Sys., http://www.2008breach.com/.

data."[8] According to the *Verizon 2010 Data Breach Report,* "a simple script to count log lines/length and send an alert if out of tolerance can be quite effective."[9]

Rogue Devices and Software

Rogue devices and software are most frequently introduced by end users and include seemingly innocuous tools to promote office or personal efficiency, such as PDAs, smart phones, digital cameras, flash drives, or other portable storage media. Users can connect them to system resources without alerting IT staff to their presence—or need for protection and monitoring. They are used both inside and outside an organization's physical or logical (i.e., network) boundaries and can transport large amounts of sensitive data: customer lists and pricing, contracts, images, and personally identifiable information.

Rogue devices are generally known to the end user, if not to the IT or security staff.

Rogue software, on the other hand, may or may not be introduced consciously to an organization's protected environment by a user. Recently discovered flaws in network browsers, for example, introduce the risk of exploitation by allowing malicious code to be loaded on devices connected to problem websites.[10] This exposes networked resources to botnet and other undesirable activity. Users may use Web proxies or anonymizers to circumvent Web filters installed by their organization.[11]

Access Control

Understanding who has access to system resources, what can be done with those resources, and under what circumstances (when, from what location, how) is addressed through a variety of technology tools that help an organization define business rules and manage key access control functions:

- *Authentication:* How a system challenges and validates user identification (you are who you say you are)
- *Authorization:* Privileges a user has on a system (what you can do, where you can do it from, how you can do it)
- *Administration:* Ongoing management of credentials and privileges by establishing procedures for keeping access control lists up-to-date, verifying documentation and/or requests for credentials, enforcing password policies, and monitoring audit trails and configuration changes

Data Protection

You have secured the network with the latest firewall software, conscientiously updated signatures for viruses, registered with do-not-call/do-not-send agencies, and even blocked voice access from certain troublesome area codes, and restricted e-mail access from, and Web surfing to, all but the most trusted URL domains. You've earned the

---

8. *Supra* note 4, p. 50.

9. *Supra* note 4, p. 57.

10. Robert McMillan, *New Web Attack Exploits Unpatched IE Flaw,* NETWORK WORLD, Dec. 9, 2008.

11. Kelly Jackson Higgins, *New Data Shows Businesses May Be Clueless About Proxy Abuse in Their Organizations,* DARK READING, Feb. 4, 2009.

right to feel snug and smug, knowing that your data is not vulnerable to cyberthreats, right? No—protections must be deployed at the data level. And encryption will not deliver organizations from data breach, leakage, or loss.

Encryption technology is discussed at length in other chapters of this book, so the following is just a brief caveat. Encryption can foil most of the technology used to screen outgoing e-mail messages or restrict copying sensitive material to portable storage media.[12] And that encryption does not need to be sophisticated or custom-designed. Simply connecting with an outbound SSL link to a website can create an encrypted pipe through which data that should not be leaving the network can be transmitted.

Defending an organization's perimeter from external attack does not protect against valuable information seeping out because of insider malfeasance, whether that behavior is characterized as malicious, mischievous, or ignorant/accidental.[13]

TOOLS FOR DLP RISK MITIGATION

Technology alone will not safeguard an organization from data leakage. Tools can, however, help monitor employee interactions with valuable information assets, identify patterns of use that can indicate ignorance—or abuse—of existing policies, and provide forensic evidence about how, when, and where sensitive information was transferred.

In brief, DLP tools are used to achieve different security objectives for different data states (see Table 18.1).

No single tool addresses all the DLP control mechanisms equally well.[14] Corporations should understand what their particular data and risk profile looks like before implementing a tool.[15] Products may focus on protecting endpoints (computers, servers, and portable devices like a BlackBerry), network gateways (switches and routers), or databases. Other products use semantic analysis or defined business rules to assess the content of outgoing e-mail messages, for example. A simple approach is to define certain data sets and restrict their transmission: a nine-digit pattern that could signal transmission of a Social Security number, for example, or a 16-digit pattern characteristic of a credit card number. In other words, an e-mail message containing such content would be diverted from leaving the corporation's network and put into a quarantine area for

---

12. Remarks at the 2008 Cerias Annual Research Symposium by Distinguished Professor Eugene Spafford, Executive Director, Center for Education and Research in Information Assurance and Security (CERIAS), a preeminent U.S. center of excellence, located at Purdue University.

13. CSO, 2007 eCrime Watch Survey (Sept. 11, 2007), *available at* http://www.cert.org/archive/pdf/ecrimesummary07 .pdf. The survey was conducted by *CSO* magazine in cooperation with the U.S. Secret Service, Carnegie Mellon University Software Engineering Institute's CERT Coordination Center, and Microsoft Corp.

14. Recognizing the need to offer their customers full-spectrum security solutions that include control mechanisms that work within the perimeters of an organization, a number of companies have added key DLP competencies, for example, Cisco (partner with EMC/RSA for access to the latter's Tablus), Symantec (Vontu), McAfee (Onigma and SafeBoot), WebSense (PortAuthority), Raytheon (Oakley), and Trend Micro (Provilla). CA announced its acquisition of Orchestria to combine the latter's DLP technology with CA's existing identity management and other infosec tools. Microsoft and RSA (The Security Division of EMC) announced in late December 2008 their intention to partner on data loss protection products, with the ultimate goal of building RSA technology into Microsoft platforms.

15. SANS INST., UNDERSTANDING AND SELECTING A DATA LOSS PREVENTION SOLUTION (June 2008), *available at* http://securosis.com/.

TABLE 18.1
Security Objects and Control Targets for Various Data States

Data State	Security Objective	Control Target
At rest	Content discovery	Network gateways Databases Servers Endpoints
In motion	Monitor, alert, protect session reconstruction Content analysis Hierarchical management	Data packets E-mail messages Instant messages
In use	Policy enforcement Leak prevention Content protection Semantic analysis	Data discovery Acceptable use monitoring

further attention. This kind of content awareness is particularly useful for acceptable use monitoring.

For data whose parameters are not so structured or easily defined, like intellectual property content (design descriptions, project references, and other patent or pricing information), semantic analysis can be used to identify what seems to be an inappropriate transmission of content. Another DLP tool captures all the content being transmitted from the corporate network, then automatically indexes and classifies that content, thus profiling network transactions. This provides information about how content is being used that can help corporations create new or revise existing data security policies.[16] It also captures metadata information that can be useful for litigation.

DLP tools can be modified to promote end-user awareness. One approach is to implement triggers that query a user before a suspect activity, asking for confirmation, for example, about the appropriateness of an e-mail message's content before transmitting it.

In addition to DLP products designed for data discovery and content awareness, analysis, and acceptable use monitoring, other products focus on protecting the end point and use data encryption for boot protection, compliance with regulated security mandates, elimination of costs associated with hard disk and data disposal, and information hardening. Whether in response to a specific data loss incident, the increasing globalization of information, or regulations like The Health Insurance Portability and Accountability Act (HIPAA), Gramm-Leach Bliley Act, and the Federal Trade Commission's privacy position, increased implementation of DLP tools is likely.

---

16. Matt Hines, *Data Leakage Prevention Becomes a Feature but Policy Management and Enforcement Pieces Are Key*, INFOWORLD, Nov. 2007.

DLP tools must be integrated into the existing security architecture. If the technology itself is poorly secured, it can actually become a great collection point for confidential or sensitive information that can seep through system cracks, rather than a prophylactic guard.

EFFECTIVE DATA SECURITY IS REQUIRED

It is important to remember that the information of your business or your client is subject to compromise, misuse, and loss from agents both outside and inside organizational boundaries. Increasing data security effectively requires a multidimensional effort to protect data from the inside out. Unlike perimeter protection measures that can be accomplished largely by IT staff or even outsourced, DLP initiatives require collaboration and commitment from the entire organization. A new culture of awareness must be created, with clear definitions about expectations for employee behavior, acceptable use of all corporate resources (physical, logical, and intellectual), procedures for monitoring compliance, and enforceable consequences for noncompliance. Business process owners must prioritize information under their purview according to its sensitivity and the business impact of its inappropriate use.

Technology-based tools can help set boundaries on the way information is handled by technical systems. For example, certain information could be restricted from being transmitted by e-mail or downloaded to a portable device. DLP tools can also reveal what prevailing organizational information transaction patterns look like so that more resilient business processes can be built to protect them. If an organization needs to deploy tools like these to protect sensitive information from inappropriate use by company insiders, other controls and policies may be deficient, misaligned, or inadequately enforced.

By making employee (and other trusted user) behavior more transparent, certain DLP tools also assist with the human engineering side of information protection. Companies are beginning to use these tools to analyze how to better align information policies and procedures with training and awareness programs. It is the combination of technology-based tools and well-designed management practices that will serve to reduce the risk of a data breach, whether the source is internal or external to the company, and help mitigate the consequences of a data incident.

CHAPTER **19**

Insurance Protection for Security Breaches

Lorelie S. Masters

News of security breaches today fills the pages of mainstream media,[1] and is the subject of debate not only in Congress but in bar association meetings commanding a national audience.[2] A business facing liability or loss from a security breach, as discussed in chapter 4, should assess the extent of its exposure and purchase appropriate insurance. Risk-management experts, insurance brokers specializing in insurance for loss from security breaches, and counsel experienced in advising companies regarding coverage for such exposures can help a business ensure that its insurance protection protects company assets from damage or liability that could arise from a security breach or failure of encryption. Once a loss or potential claim arises, the business should give notice to all potentially applicable sources of insurance protection and take steps to enforce the claim.

This chapter gives an overview of the kinds of insurance protection that may apply to protect a business facing liability or loss from a security breach or failure of data-security systems and discusses risk-management practices to help ensure that companies' insurance protection is available should a security breach or failure occur.

TYPES OF INSURANCE POTENTIALLY APPLICABLE TO LIABILITY OR LOSS FROM A SECURITY BREACH

Overview

Businesses seeking to protect their assets and operations from liability or loss from a security breach or failure of a company's data-security systems typically need both

---

1. *E.g.*, Saul Hansell, *A Lawsuit Tries to Get at Hackers Through the Banks They Attack*, N.Y. TIMES, Aug. 20, 2009, at B1.

2. ABA Section of Public Contract Law, New Realities for the Procurement Community in the Electronic Age and Emerging Issues in Global Anticorruption: Program Materials, Cybersecurity—Paradigm-Shifting Rules for Unparalleled Threats (Aug. 2, 2009).

"third-party" and "first-party" insurance.[3] First-party insurance protects the company's own property or operations, including both tangible or physical property like buildings, paper files, records, and equipment and intangible property like loss of income, expenses, and, in the case of certain coverages, money and financial instruments.[4] Third-party insurance covers the entity for defense costs and possible settlements or judgments that result from suits or claims brought by unrelated third-party claimants. The protection provided by third-party liability insurance is important even if the policyholder succeeds in defeating the underlying liability action because the cost of defense can be crippling.

With all insurance policies intended to cover a company's operations on the Internet, a policyholder should ensure that it applies on a worldwide basis. Many policy forms sold to smaller companies especially may limit the coverage territory for the policy to the United States.[5]

Commercial insurance policies, like those purchased by individuals, typically use standard-form contract language that is not negotiated by the policyholder. For that reason, generally accepted principles of insurance policy interpretation, including contra proferentem and the reasonable-expectations doctrine, should apply to protect the policyholder from application of ambiguous policy language to preclude coverage. In addition, because insurance is a state-law issue, the choice of law is often important and may be outcome-determinative.

First-Party Property Insurance

First-party property insurance, and related variations like inland marine insurance, protect a policyholder's property from damage due to security breaches. First-party property insurance may be written to cover only named perils or, as is typically the case today, on an "all-risk" basis. All-risk policies apply to cover loss from any risk except one that is explicitly excluded.[6] Policyholders should ensure that their property insurance applies on an all-risk basis. A first-party property policy typically pays to repair insured property that is damaged, and to pay the "actual cash value," "replacement value," or "agreed value" for insured property that is destroyed.[7]

Insurers may dispute coverage for business losses from security breaches and related system or security problems or from hackers breaking into the policyholder's computer systems or website on the ground that the cause of the damage was not a "covered peril" or did not constitute "direct physical loss."[8] Case law confirms that property and

---

3. For a discussion of first-party versus third-party insurance, see Tower Auto., Inc. v. Am. Prot. Ins. Co., 266 F. Supp. 2d 664, 670–71 (W.D. Mich. 2003).

4. *See, e.g.,* Parks Real Estate Purchasing Group v. St. Paul Fire & Marine Ins. Co., 472 F.3d 33, 41 (2d Cir. 2006) (applying New York law).

5. *See* CACI Int'l Inc. v. St. Paul Fire & Marine Ins. Co., 566 F.3d 150, 152, (4th Cir. 2009) (applying Virginia law) (rejecting coverage in part on the ground that "the underlying complaints cannot be read to allege events that happened in the coverage territory").

6. Sentinel Mgmt. Co. v. N.H. Ins. Co., 563 N.W.2d 296, 299 (Minn. Ct. App. 1997).

7. *E.g.,* Polytech, Inc. v. Affiliated FM Ins. Co., 21 F.3d 271, 273 (8th Cir. 1994) (applying Missouri law).

8. *E.g.,* Columbiaknit, Inc. v. Affiliated FM Ins. Co., No. Civ. 98-434-HU, 1999 WL 619100, at *3 (D. Or. Aug. 4, 1999).

business-interruption insurance applies unless an exclusion clearly applies to all aspects of the policyholder's loss.[9]

First-party property insurance often requires policyholders to provide a proof of loss, with appropriate backup, within a period of time specified in the conditions of the insurance policy, or after the insurer requests it.[10] First-party insurance policies also typically include suit-limitation clauses that act as contractual statutes of limitations, requiring a suit by the policyholder to enforce coverage to be filed within a certain period of time.[11] These contractual time periods can be extended by written agreement with the insurance company.

A company's first-party property insurance, either as a stand-alone coverage or provided as part of a package policy, should protect against damage caused by security breaches, but policyholders must carefully review the policy provisions and endorsements. According to one insurance industry professional, damages caused by computer viruses "are normally covered by any policy that covers programs and data."[12] Business personal property insurance policies may also cover damage to computer data and equipment.[13]

It is important with any of these first-party property coverages to review the policy form to be used carefully. Policyholders should specifically watch for addition of "Year 2000" endorsements, or their more recent descendents, given that insurers may use their extremely broad terms to try to preclude coverage for damage or loss unrelated to a "Y2K" or other programming issue.

Business-Interruption Insurance

Business-interruption insurance is a type of first-party property insurance and typically is purchased as part of a package of property insurance coverages. Business-interruption insurance protects a policyholder from (1) loss of income as a result of interrupted business operations; and (2) additional expenses incurred as a result of efforts to continue business operations.[14]

Some businesses, such as a website consulting business, may be able to resume operations relatively easily when business is interrupted from a security breach or other cause. In this situation, business-interruption insurance should cover the policyholder's additional expenses for relocation of employees, rental of temporary facilities, and procurement and installation of computers, telephones, and other necessary office equipment. Other businesses, such as computer or other manufacturing businesses, cannot relocate so easily. In that case, business-interruption insurance should protect the company against both a direct loss of income and the extra expenses incurred in paying fixed costs, retaining key employees, and replacing machinery.

---

9. Pillsbury Co. v. Underwriters at Lloyd's, London, 705 F. Supp. 1396, 1397–99 (D. Minn. 1989).

10. *E.g.*, Armco, Inc. v. Reliance Nat'l Ins. Co., 19 F. Supp. 2d 807, 810–11 (S.D. Ohio 1998).

11. *See, e.g.*, N.Y. Ins. Law § 3407(a) (insurer must request proof of loss from policyholder); Fid.-Phenix Fire Ins. Co. v. Benedict Coal Corp., 64 F.2d 347, 352 (4th Cir. 1933) (applying general principles; no state law applied).

12. James J. Markham, Property Loss Adjusting 2, 268 (2d ed.).

13. *Id.* at 267. Even boiler and machinery insurance policies may apply to a claim of damage to computer equipment and data. *Id.* at 269.

14. *See, e.g.*, Zurich Am. Ins. Co. v. ABM Indus., Inc., 265 F. Supp. 2d 302, 305–06 (S.D.N.Y. 2003) (business income) *aff'd in part, rev'd in part*, 397 F.3d 158 (2d Cir. 2005); Am. States Ins. Co. v. Creative Walking, Inc., 16 F. Supp. 2d 1062, 1063–64 (E.D. Mo. 1998) (extra expense).

Business-interruption insurance policies, like first-party property insurance generally, may require that the disruption of the business operation be caused by a "direct physical loss or damage." Insurers may argue that security breaches do not cause "physical loss," and often cite case law saying that the disruption must derive from a "fortuitous," or unexpected, event—a frequent source of dispute.[15]

Fidelity Insurance and Bonds

Standard package insurance policies purchased by many companies usually insure against loss because of fraud or theft. Such insurance may include "computer systems fraud" coverage, which protects against losses from fraudulent entry or alteration of data causing the unauthorized payment, transfer, or delivery of property or funds. Similarly, financial institution bonds protect against computer theft or fraud by bank employees. Some insurers offer banks supplemental insurance for losses or liability for crimes by nonemployees involving electronic equipment.

Similar to a financial institution bond, fidelity (or "crime") insurance typically provides insurance coverage for losses due to theft by employees or other agents of the policyholder. This kind of insurance, however, may not protect against theft or damage caused by nonemployees. Computer crime insurance policies typically insure against losses of, or sometimes damage to, electronic data.

Fidelity insurance may be available in the following kinds of insurance:

- Commercial crime insurance policies
- Dishonesty, disappearance, and destruction insurance policies
- "Blanket" bonds
- Financial institution bonds (banker's bonds, brokerage bonds, etc.)
- Endorsements to property insurance policies providing coverage for losses from theft
- Commercial general liability (CGL) insurance policies with credit card and depositors forgery endorsements
- Computer crime insurance policies

Fidelity bonds typically apply only to losses due to identified individuals or positions in the company. Fidelity bonds provide only a part of the insurance against theft that most companies need.

Fidelity coverages, like the property insurance policies, may require the policyholder to submit a proof of loss. They also typically require the policyholder to report the theft to authorities. Policyholders should examine policy conditions to determine time limitations that may apply to submissions of a proof of loss or to filing of suit against the insurer.

Electronic Funds Transfer Insurance

Electronic funds transfer (EFT) insurance is a cousin of fidelity insurance and bonds. EFT systems transfer hundreds of billions of dollars a day, and thefts from security breaches are an increasing concern.

---

15. *E.g.*, Pillsbury Co. v. Underwriters at Lloyd's, London, 705 F. Supp. 1396, 1399 (D. Minn. 1989).

This coverage applies whether the fraud or theft takes place over the Internet or in some other fashion, and computer crime insurance policies may cover EFT fraud. As an executive from one insurer has attested, "[T]here is no exclusion for Internet transactions that fits all other terms of the insuring clause [of the computer crime policy]."[16] These same insurance policies, however, often exclude insurance coverage for theft of confidential information. Some computer crime insurance riders provide insurance coverage for losses stemming from the "intentional, unauthorized, fraudulent creation of data."

Third-Party Liability Insurance

General Liability Insurance

The most common kind of liability insurance purchased by businesses to protect against claims by third parties is commercial general liability (CGL) insurance. References to "CGL insurance" typically encompass the primary, or "working," layer in a CGL insurance program, as well as the related umbrella and excess general liability insurance that companies may buy in layers for additional protection above the primary layer. CGL insurance may be written either on an occurrence basis, in which case the coverage in effect at the time of the injury, damage, or offense took place applies to the loss[17] or a claims-made basis, in which case the coverage in place at the time the claim is made against the policyholder applies.[18]

CGL insurance policies typically contain a variety of coverages, all of which should be reviewed carefully to determine whether they may apply to the claim in question. The CGL coverage part in a CGL insurance policy applies to protect the policyholder from liability for "bodily injury" or "property damage," as defined in the policy.[19] The advertising injury coverage part applies to protect the policyholder from liability for advertising injury or personal injury, which terms are defined to encompass liability from certain enumerated, intentional torts, including (among other things) "publication" of material that violates a person's right of privacy or that slanders or libels another or disparages another's goods, services, or products.[20] The contractual liability coverage part applies to protect the policyholder from liability arising out of an insured contract, as defined in the policy.[21] The insurance policy usually contains exclusions and terms that apply to all coverage parts in the policy. However, each coverage part typically will have exclusions and other terms that apply only to that coverage part. Policyholders should resist insurers' efforts to use exclusions or terms from one coverage part to deny coverage or reserve rights under another coverage part.

---

16. Ron Mund, senior claims attorney at St. Paul Fire & Marine Insurance Company, *quoted in* Janet Aschkenasy, *Wired for Fraud?* Treasury & Risk Mgmt. 34 (May/June 1996).

17. *E.g.*, EnergyNorth Nat. Gas, Inc. v. Underwriters at Lloyd's, London, 848 A.2d 715, 721–22 (N.H. 2004).

18. *See, e.g., In re* Ins. Antitrust Litig., 938 F.2d 919, 923 (9th Cir. 1991), *aff'd in part, rev'd and remanded in part sub nom.* Hartford Fire Ins. Co. v. California, 509 U.S. 764 (1993).

19. *See, e.g.*, ISO Form, *reprinted in* 1 Jack P. Gibson & Maureen McLendon, Commercial General Liability, at IV.T. 8, 16, 36, 43, 53–54 (2009). CGL and certain other kinds of insurance policies are drafted in insurance industry groups and thus contain standard-form language. The current insurance industry drafting group is the Insurance Services Office, Inc. (ISO). References herein to "CGL insurance" refer to CGL policies as a whole, not to a particular coverage part.

20. *See, e.g., id.* at IV.T.41, 152–53, 168.

21. *Id.* at IV.T. 23–28, 29–34.

CGL insurance defines "property damage" as "physical injury to tangible property, including loss of use therefrom; or loss of or property that is not physically injured."[22]

CGL insurers often refuse coverage for claims or suits arising from security breaches and damage to computer assets under the CGL coverage part, arguing, for example, that the damages sought do not qualify as "property damage." Courts are split on the issue of whether damage to computer data constitutes "property damage."[23] At a minimum, evidence that damage to the physical media and metal particles that preserve data on such media should satisfy that definition or at least constitute "loss of use to property that is not physically injured." Careful review of the policy language is required as definitions and policy terms, even in otherwise standard-form policies, may vary. The insurance industry has continued to revise the standard-form CGL policy language in an effort to diminish the likelihood that policyholders can prevail on this argument. For example, in *Eyeblaster, Inc. v. Federal Insurance Co.*,[24] the court accepted the insurer's argument, based on new standard-form policy language, that electronic data do not qualify as "tangible property." However, at a minimum, CGL insurance companies may be obligated to defend—in itself a costly proposition—as long as at least one claim against the policyholder is potentially covered.[25]

As defenses to coverage, including "expected or intended," CGL insurance policies also typically include exclusions that insurers may raise as "first publication," or "media" or "advertising" exclusions. Policyholders should remember that exclusions are strictly construed, and insurance companies have the burden to prove that all elements of the claim fall within the scope of an exclusion. In addition, an insurer should prevail only if its interpretation of the policy is the only reasonable interpretation.[26]

Insurers often use expected or intended exclusions to avoid their obligations under CGL insurance policies. These exclusions raise mixed questions of law and fact, and the fact issues, which typically require extensive written and oral discovery by the policyholder, can make the cost of a coverage dispute seem daunting. Although the legal standard may vary depending on the law applied, the exclusion, as most courts have found, is intended to preclude coverage only when the insurer proves that the policyholder intended the specific harm alleged in the underlying claim.[27]

Insurance companies may argue that a website or other content involved in a security breach was "published" before the policy period in question, thus asserting the "prior publication" exclusion to preclude coverage. This exclusion is found only in the adver-

---

22. *Id.* at IV.T.41, 43, 53, 55 150, 152, 166, and 167.

23. *Compare* Am. Guar. & Liab. Ins. Co. v. Ingram Micro, Inc., No. 99-185-TUC ACM, 2000 WL 726789 (D. Ariz. Apr. 18, 2000) (enforcing coverage), *and* Computer Corner, Inc. v. Fireman's Fund Ins. Co., 46 P.3d 1264 (N.M. Ct. App. 2002) (same), *with* Am. Online, Inc. v. St. Paul Mercury Ins. Co., 207 F. Supp. 2d 459 (E.D. Va. 2002), *aff'd*, 347 F.3d 89 (4th Cir. 2003) (rejecting coverage).

24. Civil No. 07-4379 ADM/JJK, 2008 U.S. Dist. Lexis 81912 (D. Minn. Oct. 7, 2008).

25. *See, e.g.*, Church Mut. Ins. Co. v. U.S. Liab. Ins. Co., 347 F. Supp. 2d 880, 884 (S.D. Cal. 2004). For a discussion of the principles applicable to an insurer's duty to defend, see EUGENE R. ANDERSON, JORDAN S. STANZLER, & LORELIE S. MASTERS, INSURANCE COVERAGE LITIGATION ch. 3 (Aspen Law & Business 2000 & Supp. 2009).

26. *E.g.*, Janart 55 W. 8th LLC v. Greenwich Ins. Co., 614 F. Supp. 2d 473 (S.D.N.Y. 2009).

27. *E.g.*, Stonewall Ins. Co. v. Asbestos Claims Mgmt. Corp., 73 F.3d 1178 (2d Cir. 1995), *modified on other grounds*, 85 F.3d 49 (2d Cir. 1996).

tising injury and personal injury coverage parts of a CGL insurance policy. Like the expected or intended exclusion, the prior-publication exclusion often raises fact issues that should preclude summary judgment in cases where genuine issues of material fact are in dispute. If the insurer cannot show when the publication in question actually took place, or that the injury involved the very same advertising or personal injury as involved in the claim, then the exclusion should not apply.[28] As one court explained, the exclusion "abrogates the insurer's duty to defend only where it can prove that the insured's prior publication of the same actionable, injurious material alleged in the underlying complaint occurred prior to the beginning of its policy."[29]

Insurers assert media or advertising exclusions to deny coverage for injuries allegedly arising out of a company's "media" activities (often undefined). These provisions should preclude coverage only for true media activities or advertising and should not be applied broadly to preclude coverage for any business with a website. These exclusions also should be read carefully to determine if exceptions apply to preserve coverage.

Media Liability Insurance

Media liability insurance traditionally was written for publishers, advertising agencies, and other companies involved in broadcasting or publishing for themselves or others. Its applicability to cyberrisks chiefly arises in connection with publishing-related liability exposures. Such policies may be written only for named "perils," meaning that the insurance will apply to cover liability only from events defined or enumerated in the policy.

Disputes may arise about whether the cause of the loss in question falls within one of the named perils identified in the insurance policy. Disputes also may arise about whether coverage extends only to the policyholder's own actions, and not for liability for actions of others (excluding professional liability, for example). Also, media insurance policies typically exclude coverage for liability for "property damage" and "bodily injury," which should be covered in a company's general liability insurance or "package" policies.

Directors and Officers and Fiduciary Liability Insurance

Directors and officers (D&O) insurance and fiduciary liability insurance both provide important protection for directors and officers and, depending on how "insured" is defined, other employees of a company and, in some circumstances, the company itself. D&O insurance protects insureds from liability for breaches of duty and "wrongful acts" as defined in the policy. Fiduciary liability insurance protects insureds, the company, and certain defined benefit plans from liability for alleged breaches of ERISA.[30] The provisions in such insurance policies, in many ways, are similar and thus the two types of coverage are discussed together in this section.

---

28. *E.g.*, Taco Bell Corp. v. Cont'l Cas. Co., 388 F.3d 1069, 1072–73 (7th Cir. 2004) (applying Illinois law).

29. Capitol Indem. Corp. v. Elston Self-Serv. Wholesale Groceries, Inc., 559 F.3d 616, 620 (7th Cir. 2009) (applying Illinois law).

30. Employee Retirement Income Security Act, 29 U.S.C. §§ 1001 *et seq.*

The insuring agreement, exclusions, and procedural requirements of such policies can vary widely from one insurance policy to the next, even within a single entity's D&O insurance program. Therefore, it is important to read each policy in an insurance program to determine the terms of coverage, and to ensure that notice is given in a timely and appropriate manner and the policy's other conditions are met.

D&O insurance policies typically include one or more of the following coverages:

- "Side A" coverage, to indemnify a director, officer, or other insured when the corporation or entity is not permitted to, or refuses to, indemnify the individual.
- "Side B" coverage, to reimburse the entity when it has indemnified individual directors and officers and other insureds for costs incurred in claims against the individuals.
- "Side C," or "Entity," coverage, to protect the entity for claims against the organization as a result of "wrongful acts" allegedly committed by directors, officers, or other insureds. This coverage typically applies to "securities claims," a defined term.

A D&O insurance policy also may include other coverages, often added by endorsement. Side A or B coverage is the coverage most likely to apply in the case of liability for security breaches. However, a company's failure to provide for adequate security to prevent breaches may, in the hands of creative plaintiff lawyers, provide the basis for claims that could fall within the coverage provided in Side C coverage.

D&O and fiduciary liability insurance policies typically pay defense costs "inside of" the limits of liability. Thus, the insurer's payment of defense costs erodes, or exhausts, the policy's limit of liability, and alone can exhaust the limits of a D&O or fiduciary liability insurance policy. In addition, unlike CGL policies, D&O and fiduciary liability insurance policies typically include a duty to pay defense costs, but not a duty to defend the insured.[31] This means that the insured has the responsibility to hire and pay defense counsel in the first instance and then to seek, or "demand,"[32] reimbursement of legal fees and expenses from the insurer.

D&O and fiduciary liability insurance policies usually are written on a claims-made basis and, thus, are activated, or triggered, by the timing of a claim against the policyholder. These policies typically also require that the claim be first made against the policyholder during the policy period in question. The issue of when a claim was first made frequently leads to disputes over whether coverage applies.[33]

D&O and fiduciary liability insurance policies contain a number of exclusions that seek to restrict coverage. These exclusions may be found not only in the exclusions

---

31. *See, e.g.,* ANDERSON, STANZLER, & MASTERS, INSURANCE COVERAGE LITIGATION, *supra* note 25, ch. 3, for a discussion of the difference between a duty to defend and a duty to pay defense costs.

32. In what policyholder lawyers consider an elevation of form over substance, some courts have held that an insured's "request" for reimbursement of defense costs does not adequately alert the insurance company to the fact that the policyholder expects reimbursement of defense costs. To avoid this absurd result, policyholders should "demand" that the insurer reimburse both defense and indemnity costs.

33. *E.g.,* H&R Block Inc. v. Am. Int'l Specialty Lines Ins. Co., No. 546 F.3d 937 (8th Cir. 2008) (applying Missouri law).

section of the policy but in the definition of "loss," or other definitions or provisions.[34] These exclusions may include an exception, however, preserving coverage for defense costs.[35] Although law on coverage for security breaches remains scant, it is worthwhile to address "conduct exclusions" in D&O and fiduciary liability policies. These exclusions seek to limit coverage for liability for dishonest, fraudulent, or illegal acts, or for acts resulting in personal profit or gain to which the insured was not entitled. Increasingly, these conduct exclusions are written to preclude coverage only if a "final adjudication" has established that the conduct in question occurred.[36] Exclusions that preclude coverage only if such conduct "in fact" occurred are less favorable to policyholders, allowing insurers to avoid payment until the facts are established.[37]

Errors and Omissions Insurance

Businesses that provide computer services should buy professional malpractice or errors and omissions (E&O) insurance to cover losses and liabilities stemming from their work. The scope of coverage, exclusions, and procedural requirements may differ from one insurance policy to the next. Like D&O and fiduciary liability policies, E&O insurance policies are written on a claims-made basis, as opposed to an occurrence basis.

Insurers sometimes argue that E&O coverage applies only to negligent acts or omissions. However, courts have rejected this argument, finding that E&O insurance also covers nonnegligent errors.[38] The term "professional services" in E&O insurance policies also gives rise to disputes, with insurers arguing that the activity in question does not constitute a professional service. Because most E&O insurance policies do not define the term, ambiguities should be construed in favor of coverage.[39]

Increasingly, disputes over coverage under E&O insurance policies focus on "prior knowledge" or "prior litigation" exclusions. Although these exclusions are found in other coverages, particularly D&O insurance, denials of coverage based on these exclusions often are the most hard-fought in cases involving E&O insurance. These exclusions seek to limit coverage for claims that are related or similar to claims or allegations made in prior policy periods,[40] or for claims related to earlier litigation.[41] These disputes can be fact-intensive, a situation that may help a policyholder avoid the insurer's effort

---

34. See, for example, the comparison of D&O policy forms in National Underwriter Co., FC&S—The Complete Property & Casualty Information Service, D&O Volume, at A.3-1 (2009).

35. For a discussion of case law on this oft-litigated exclusion, see JOHN MATHIAS, ET AL., DIRECTORS & OFFICERS LIABILITY: PREVENTION, INSURANCE, AND INDEMNIFICATION § 8.02 (Law J. Press 2008).

36. See, e.g., Atl. Permanent Fed. Sav. & Loan Ass'n v. Am. Cas. Co., 839 F.2d 212, 216–17 (4th Cir. 1988) (per curiam) (applying Virginia law).

37. See, e.g., Nat'l Union Fire Ins. Co. v. Cont'l Ill. Corp., 666 F. Supp. 1180, 1199 (N.D. Ill. 1987). Some insurance policies including "in fact" conduct exclusions allow the insurer to pursue an arbitration or other proceeding even when the investigation or lawsuit was resolved without any findings of fact by a court of law.

38. USM Corp. v. First State Ins. Co., 652 N.E.2d 613 (Mass. 1995).

39. See, e.g., Aetna Cas. & Sur. Co. v. Dannenfeldt, 778 F. Supp. 484, 495 (D. Ariz. 1991).

40. Compare Selko v. Home Ins. Co., 139 F.3d 146, 151–53 (3d Cir. 1998) (applying mixed subjective/objective standard under Pennsylvania law), with Westport Ins. Corp. v. Lilley, 292 F. Supp. 2d 165, 171–75 (D. Me. 2003) (rejecting objective, "foreseeability" standard).

41. Church Mut. Ins. Co. v. U.S. Liab. Ins. Co., 347 F. Supp. 2d 880, 889–90 (S.D. Cal. 2004); Home Ins. Co. v. Spectrum Info. Techs., Inc., 930 F. Supp. 825, 849–50 (E.D.N.Y. 1996).

to evade coverage under a motion for summary judgment. These exclusions further emphasize the importance of giving notice as soon as the policyholder has reason to believe that a claim or suit may arise.

CYBERRISK INSURANCE COVERAGE

The exposures and potential gaps in traditional insurance policies have created a market for new cyberrisk insurance policies. Cyberrisk insurance policies specifically seek to address concerns about traditional policies' coverage for "physical damage" to computer assets or from security breaches to or through computer systems or the Internet. These policy forms often are lengthy and complex, reflecting the unique nature of the risks they are intended to cover, and deserve careful review.

Types of Exposures Covered

Cyberrisk insurance policies available on the market today vary greatly in the nature and scope of coverage they offer. Some cover losses related to a policyholder's computer network in general while others focus on insuring risk relating to specific aspects of Internet commerce and security, or the operation and security of websites. Some cyberrisk insurance policies provide broad crime coverage. Others are hybrid, offering coverage for loss caused by fraudulent insider misuse of payment systems. Traditional policies covering financial institutions, for example, generally exclude theft by employees because coverage for such acts was available in the form of blanket bonds. Because corporations are now using EFT systems, they well may require separate coverage for such activities not provided by blanket bonds.

Most cyberrisk insurance policies contain multiple insuring agreements, relating to fraud and the use of electronic data, computer viruses, and business interruption, among other risks.

First-Party Versus Third-Party Coverage

One of the most significant factors distinguishing cyberrisk insurance policies is whether the coverage provided is first-party insurance, third-party, or both. Typical first-party losses covered include physical damage or damage to software or computer data caused by hackers or viruses; illicit computer transfer of money, securities, or tangible property; extortion; business interruption or denial of website service resulting from electronic vandalism or service (Internet service provider) outage; and loss-control costs. Loss-control costs are those reasonable expenses incurred by a policyholder to prevent further loss from a covered event. Cyberrisk first-party coverages may exclude coverage for loss caused by dishonest acts of insiders, failure to adhere to required system security practices or mismanagement of system, and remediation costs.

Third-party cyberrisk coverage insures against liability to third parties for loss due to exchange of data via e-mail or the Internet, denial of service, theft or destruction of data, unauthorized access, libel and slander, violation of privacy rights, misappropriation of ideas, and unfair competition. These coverages usually exclude coverage for failure to exercise reasonable care or due diligence; intentional or fraudulent acts; violation of laws such as antitrust, securities, or employment-related laws; legally protected rights, such as patent or copyright; and expenses incurred in the recall of products or services from the marketplace.

Role of Auditing and Loss Prevention

Cyberrisk insurance policies may require that an independent technical expert service, designated by the insurer for underwriting purposes, audit a prospective policyholder's operations. These policies also may require that the prospective policyholder undergo an ongoing loss-prevention program conducted by the same entity.

Cyberrisk policies providing first-party coverage often provide for the hiring of a crisis management consultant once a loss has occurred. The crisis management consultant may be preselected by the insurance company and will typically assess damages resulting from the covered loss and coordinate recovery efforts.

Cyberrisk policies continue to evolve. The magnitude of exposure is difficult to predict and underwrite, in particular because of the lack of strong actuarial backup and the complex nature of the risks involved.

RISK-MANAGEMENT TIPS

The following tips can help policyholders maximize the availability of their insurance should a claim for liability or loss arise.

Tips for Purchasing Insurance

Each insurance policy purchased should be reviewed both before purchase and once the policy itself is received to ensure that it matches what the company intended to purchase.

Prospective purchasers should consider the claims-handling practices and records of the insurers from whom they plan to purchase insurance. Policyholders also should consider the financial strength and stability of the insurer.

Policyholders should retain insurance policies and purchase documents indefinitely, particularly for occurrence-based coverages.

Many companies conduct an insurance policy audit at the time of purchase to ensure that their coverage is consistent through all layers of coverage. Insurance audits help to avoid common pitfalls that often arise at the point of claim.[42]

Tips for Making Claims

At the first indication that a data breach (or other loss) may arise, policyholders should identify all potentially applicable insurance policies and review them, or have them reviewed by someone in the risk-management or legal departments or by coverage counsel, to identify the sources of potential insurance protection. Policyholders also are well advised to follow the tips below.

---

42. For a checklist of points to consider in a D&O insurance audit, see Lorelie S. Masters, *Checklist for Renewing D&O Insurance Coverage*, JENNER & BLOCK'S INSURANCE COUNSELOR, Winter 2010, at 4, *available at* http://www.jenner.com/files/tbl_s20Publications/RelatedDocumentsPDFs1252/2760/Insurance%20Newsletter_10%20Winter.pdf.

All Claims

1. *Give notice promptly.* As with all kinds of insurance, the first rule is to give written notice as soon as possible, to all potentially affected insurers, at all potentially affected layers of coverage. Although most jurisdictions have abandoned the rule that an alleged delay in notice can defeat coverage regardless of prejudice to the insurer, establishing an early, cooperative relationship with the insurer can help ensure early payment and facilitate the claims process.[43]

2. *Cooperate with the insurance company.* Give the insurance company as much of the documentation requested as possible. Provide regular status reports and keep a written record of all of the information so provided. However, if the insurer has denied coverage or reserved its rights, production of privileged information to the insurer could effect a waiver of privilege.[44]

3. *Consider a standstill, or "nonwaiver," agreement.* Consider entering into a standstill agreement or tolling agreement so that you do not have to file litigation in the event of a dispute. A decision to enter a standstill agreement raises privilege and other concerns and should be the subject of careful consideration but may result in earlier payment of defense costs.

4. *Review policy conditions.* Particularly for claims made under first-party property coverages, carefully review the policy's conditions.

Claims Under Liability Insurance Policies

5. *Consider giving notice of circumstances.* Give notice as soon as you learn of facts, or, in insurance parlance, "circumstances," that you believe could lead to a claim. If the claim does arise or a suit is filed, send that claim or suit to the insurance company immediately.

6. *Give notice of potential settlements.* Give notice of potential settlements to the insurer before the settlement becomes final. An insurer's nominal right to "consent" to a settlement may be nullified, however, if the insurer denies coverage or reserves its rights.

7. *"Demand" coverage for defense costs.* Submit defense invoices to the insurers regularly for payment. Some courts have held that an insured's "request" for reimbursement of defense costs does not adequately alert the insurance company to the fact that the policyholder expects reimbursement of defense costs. To avoid this absurd result, policyholders should "demand" payment of defense and indemnity costs.

Claims Under First-Party Insurance Policies

First-party insurance policies typically include the following special requirements:

8. *Follow suit-limitation clauses.* Suit-limitation clauses state that the policyholder should file suit against the insurer within a certain period of time. These provisions act as contractual statutes of limitations in many states.

---

43. *See, e.g.,* N.Y. INS. LAW § 3420(a)(5) (adopted June 11, 2008). Even the state of New York, which for decades refused to adopt the modern rule on notice, has now adopted legislation to require insurers to prove prejudice before denying coverage on grounds that notice was "late."

44. *See, e.g.,* Hoechst Celanese Corp. v. Nat'l Union Fire Ins. Co., 623 A.2d 1118 (Del. Super. Ct. 1992).

9. *File proof of loss.* These provisions may require a policyholder to submit a proof of loss within a specified period of time or, in a provision more favorable to policyholders, may say that the policyholder should submit its proof of loss when "requested" by the insurer.

Both of these timing considerations may, as in New York, be affected or overridden by state statute. For that reason, it is important to check the relevant state statutes. Confirm all requests and agreements for extension of these time periods in writing.

Security Breach Notification Laws

SECURITY BREACH NOTIFICATION LAWS

Alaska	ALA. STAT. §§ 45.48.010 to .090
Arizona	ARIZ. REV. STAT. § 44-7501
Arkansas	ARK. CODE § 4-110-101 et seq.
California	CAL. CIV. CODE § 1798.82
Colorado	COL. REV. STAT. § 6-1-716
Connecticut	CONN. GEN STAT. 36A-701(b)
Delaware	DEL. CODE tit. 6, § 12B-101 et seq.
District of Columbia	D.C. CODE §§ 28-3851 et seq.
Florida	FLA. STAT. § 817.5681
Georgia	GA. CODE § 10-1-910 et seq.[1]
Hawaii	HAW. REV. STAT. § 487N-2
Idaho	IDAHO CODE §§ 28-51-104 to 28-51-107
Illinois	815 ILL. COMP. STAT. 530/1 et seq.
Indiana	IND. CODE § 24-4.9
Iowa	IOWA CODE § 715C.1–2, (2008 S.F. 2308)
Kansas	KAN. STAT. 50-7a01, 50-7a02
Louisiana	LA. REV. STAT. § 51:3071 et seq.
Maine	ME. REV. STAT. TIT. 10 §§ 1347 et seq.
Maryland	MD. CODE §§ 14-3501 thru 14-3508
Massachusetts	MASS. GEN. LAWS. ch. 93H
Michigan	MICH. COMP. LAWS 445.63, §§ 12, 12a, & 12b
Minnesota	MINN. STAT. § 325E.61, § 609.891
Mississippi	2010 MISS. H.B. 583
Missouri	MO. STAT. § 407.1500
Montana	MONT. CODE § 30-14-1701 et seq.
Nebraska	NEB. REV. STAT. 87-801 et. seq.
Nevada	NEV. REV. STAT. 603A.010 et seq.

1. Applies to information brokers only.

New Hampshire	N.H. Rev. Stat. 359-C:19 et seq.
New Jersey	N.J. Stat. 56:8-163
New York	N.Y. Bus. Law § 899-aa
North Carolina	N.C. Gen. Stat. § 75-65
North Dakota	N.D. Cent. Code § 51-30-01 et seq.
Ohio	Ohio Rev. Code §1349.19
Oklahoma	Okla. Stat. tit. 24, §§ 161 et seq.
Oregon	Or. Rev. Stat. § 646A
Pennsylvania	73 Pa. Cons. Stat. § 2303
Puerto Rico	2005 H.B. 1184
Rhode Island	R.I. Gen. Laws § 11-49.2-1 et seq.
South Carolina	S.C. Code § 39-1-90
Tennessee	Tenn. Code § 47-18-2107
Texas	Tex. Bus. & Com. Code § 35.58
Utah	Utah Code § 13-44-101 et seq.
Vermont	Vt. Stat. tit. 9 § 2430 et seq.
Virgin Islands (US)	14 V.I. Code § 2209
Virginia	Va. Code 18.2-186.6
Washington	Wash. Rev. Code § 19.255.010
West Virginia	W. Va. Code §§ 46A-2A-101 to -105
Wisconsin	Wis. Stat. § 895.507
Wyoming	Wyo. Stat. §§ 40-12-501, -502

For updates see: National Conference of State Legislatures—State Security Breach Notification Laws. http://www.ncsl.org/default.aspx?tabid=13489

Summary of Data Breach Notification and Encryption Laws

Stephen S. Wu

This Appendix summarizes selected encryption-related federal and state statutes, regulations, and regulatory guidance. Encryption is a crucial technology used to prevent security breaches. The encryption-related provisions covered here fall within three categories: (1) encryption to comply with legal requirements under federal law for information security in specific sectors of the economy, (2) state breach notification and general information security laws, and (3) laws intended to facilitate secure electronic commerce.*

---

*This summary is not intended to be an exhaustive list of encryption-related requirements. For example, the state breach notification and information security law table focuses only on selected states, even though almost all of the states have some form of breach notification law. Moreover, it does not include sector-specific state encryption laws, such as in the areas of medical records, genetic testing, or campaign finance laws. It does not include laws relating to liability for circumventing encryption protection of copyrighted material under the Digital Millennium Copyright Act or the protection of encrypted television signals. Moreover, this summary does not cover cybercrime involving the use of encryption. e.g., Nev. Rev. Stat. Ann. § 205.486. Finally, it does not cover laws that call for protections similar to those in the Payment Card Industry Data Security Standard, such as the disposal of PIN information after the completion of a payment transaction. e.g., Minn. Stat. § 325E.61. While encryption may help to prevent security breaches that are the subject of such laws, these laws do not require or mention encryption.

Encryption for Compliance with Federal Sectoral Information Security Requirements

Citation and Subject	Summary of the Requirement
1. Health Care: Health Insurance Portability and Accountability Act (HIPAA) and the HIPAA Security Rule supplemented by the Health Information Technology for Economic and Clinical Health (HITECH) Act within the American Recovery and Reinvestment Act of 2009, Pub.L. No. 1111-5.	
a. Protection of Protected Health Information	
42 U.S.C. § 1320d-2(d)(2) General statutory requirement of security of health information	A HIPAA-covered entity[1] that "maintains or transmits health information shall maintain reasonable and appropriate administrative, technical, and physical safeguards" to protect the health information.
45 C.F.R. § 164.304 Definition of encryption	"Encryption means the use of an algorithmic process to transform data into a form in which there is a low probability of assigning meaning without use of a confidential process or key."
45 C.F.R. § 164.312(a)(2)(iv) Technical safeguard: requirement of encryption to protect electronic protected health information	HIPAA-covered entities must (if reasonable and appropriate) encrypt electronic protected health information. Applies to data at rest and in transit during the communication process.
45 C.F.R. § 164.312(e)(2)(ii) Technical safeguard: requirement of encryption to protect electronic protected health information in transit	HIPAA-covered entities must (if reasonable and appropriate) encrypt electronic protected health information. Applies to data in transit during the communication process.
b. Breach Notification Requirements	
42 U.S.C. § 17932(a) HITECH Act's breach notification requirement for HIPAA covered entities. Notification of patients by covered entities.	"A covered entity that accesses, maintains, retains, modifies, records, stores, destroys, or otherwise holds, uses, or discloses unsecured protected health information (as defined in subsection (h)(1)) shall, in the case of a breach of such information that is discovered by the covered entity, notify each individual whose unsecured protected health information has been, or is reasonably believed by the covered entity to have been, accessed, acquired, or disclosed as a result of such breach."
42 U.S.C. § 17932(b) HITECH Act's breach notification requirement for HIPAA business associates. Notification of covered entities by business associates.	"A business associate of a covered entity that accesses, maintains, retains, modifies, records, stores, destroys, or otherwise holds, uses, or discloses unsecured protected health information shall, following the discovery of a breach of such information, notify the covered entity of such breach. Such notice shall include the identification of each individual whose unsecured protected health information has been, or is reasonably believed by the business associate to have been, accessed, acquired, or disclosed during such breach."

---

1. The HITECH Act makes the HIPAA security regulations apply to HIPAA business associates. 42 U.S.C. § 17931(a).

Citation and Subject	Summary of the Requirement
42 U.S.C. § 17932(h)(1) Definition of unsecured protected health information	"[T]he term 'unsecured protected health information' means protected health information that is not secured through the use of a technology or methodology specified by the Secretary in the guidance issued under paragraph (2)."
42 U.S.C. § 17932(h)(2) Specifying the guidance called for in 42 U.S.C. § 17932(h)(1)	"(2) Guidance. For purposes of paragraph (1) and section 13407(f)(3), not later than the date that is 60 days after the date of the enactment of this Act, the Secretary shall, after consultation with stakeholders, issue (and annually update) guidance specifying the technologies and methodologies that render protected health information unusable, unreadable, or indecipherable to unauthorized individuals, including the use of standards developed under section 3002(b)(2)(B)(vi) of the Public Health Service Act, as added by section 13101 of this Act."
45 C.F.R. § 164.402 Reference to Health and Human Services guidance on rendering protected health information unusable, unreadable, or indecipherable	"Unsecured protected health information means protected health information that is not rendered unusable, unreadable, or indecipherable to unauthorized individuals through the use of a technology or methodology specified by the Secretary in the guidance issued under section 13402(h)(2) of Public Law 111–5 on the HHS Web site."
74 Fed. Reg. 42740, 42742 Guidance specifying technologies and methodologies to render protected health information unusable, unreadable, or indecipherable, in an interim final rule document, which is posted on the HHS website: http://www.hhs.gov/ocr/privacy/hipaa/understanding/coveredentities/breachnotificationifr.html[2]	"Protected health information (PHI) is rendered unusable, unreadable, or indecipherable to unauthorized individuals if one or more of the following applies: (a) Electronic PHI has been encrypted as specified in the HIPAA Security Rule by "the use of an algorithmic process to transform data into a form in which there is a low probability of assigning meaning without use of a confidential process or key" and such confidential process or key that might enable decryption has not been breached. To avoid a breach of the confidential process or key, these decryption tools should be stored on a device or at a location separate from the data they are used to encrypt or decrypt. The encryption processes identified below have been tested by the National Institute of Standards and Technology (NIST) and judged to meet this standard. (i) Valid encryption processes for data at rest are consistent with NIST Special Publication 800–111, Guide to Storage Encryption Technologies for End User Devices. (ii) Valid encryption processes for data in motion are those which comply, as appropriate, with NIST Special Publications 800–52, Guidelines for the Selection and Use of Transport Layer Security (TLS) Implementations; 800–77, Guide to IPsec VPNs; or 800–113, Guide to SSL VPNs, or others which are Federal Information Processing Standards (FIPS) 140–2 validated." (footnotes omitted)

2. Breach Notification for Unsecured Protected Health Information Interim Final Rule, available at http://www.hhs.gov/ocr/privacy/hipaa/understanding/coverdentities/breachnotificationifr.html.

Citation and Subject	Summary of the Requirement
2. Financial Services: Gramm-Leach-Bliley Act (GLBA), Interagency Guidelines for Establishing Standards for Safeguarding Customer Information ("Interagency Guidelines"), and FFIEC Information Security Booklet (July 2006)[3]	
15 U.S.C. § 6801(b) General statutory requirement of security of customers' financial records and information	Regulatory agencies are to establish standards requiring financial institutions to ensure the security and confidentiality of customer records and information, protect against anticipated security threats, and protect against unauthorized access or use that "could result in substantial harm or inconvenience" to customers.
Regulations under GLBA: • For national banks: Office of the Comptroller of Currency (12 C.F.R. § 30.3(a)) • For foreign bank branches and bank holding companies: Federal Reserve Board (Federal Reserve Banks (12 C.F.R. §§ 208.3(d), 211.24(i)(i), 225.4(h)) • For commercial banks, state-insured foreign bank branches: Federal Deposit Insurance Corporation (12 C.F.R. § 308.302(a)) • For savings associations: Office of Thrift Supervision (12 C.F.R. § 568.5) • For federal credit unions: National Credit Union Administration (12 C.F.R. part 748 Appendix A) (Interagency Guidelines are not binding on federal credit unions)	Adoption of Interagency Guidelines for Establishing Standards for Safeguarding Customer Information as setting standards for security of customer information.
Interagency Guidelines, Section III.C.1.c Requirement of encryption for customer information	Financial institutions must adopt security measures if appropriate that include "[e]ncryption of electronic customer information, including while in transit or in storage on networks or systems to which unauthorized individuals may have access."
FFIEC Information Security Booklet at 56 Summary of encryption requirements for financial institutions to protect sensitive information	"Financial institutions should employ encryption to mitigate the risk of disclosure or alteration of sensitive information in storage and transit. Encryption implementations should include: • Encryption strength sufficient to protect the information from disclosure until such time as disclosure poses no material risk, • Effective key management practices, • Robust reliability, and • Appropriate protection of the encrypted communication's endpoints." Further detailed discussed in pp. 56–60.
3. Public Companies: Sarbanes-Oxley Act of 2002 (SOX) and IT Control Objectives for Sarbanes-Oxley (Sept. 2006)[4]	
15 U.S.C. § 7262(a)(1) Calls for rules to require public company reporting of efforts to maintain internal controls generally over financial reporting and supporting information	Section 404 of SOX calls for rules requiring public companies to report annually on the effectiveness of their internal controls in their annual reports. Internal control reports must acknowledge management's responsibility to establish and maintain "an adequate internal control structure and procedures for financial reporting."

3.   Fed. Fin. Insts. Examination Council (FFIEC), Information Security (July 2006), available at http://www.ffiec.gov/ffiecinfobase/booklets/information_security/information_security.pdf.

4.   IT Governance Inst., IT Control Objectives for Sarbanes-Oxley (2d ed., Sept. 2006), available at http://tinyurl.com/yanhe6n.

Citation and Subject	Summary of the Requirement
17 C.F.R. §§ 240.13a-15(c), 240.15d-15(c) Implementing a framework to assess the effectiveness of internal controls generally	Management must use a "suitable, recognized control framework" for assessing internal controls.
IT Control Objectives for Sarbanes-Oxley at 73 Example of control to prevent unauthorized use, disclosure, modification, damage, or loss of data: encryption for the confidentiality of financial information in transit	"When appropriate," public companies should "determine if encryption techniques are [to be] used to support the confidentiality of financial information sent from one system to another."
IT Control Objectives for Sarbanes-Oxley at 77	Public companies should define retention periods for data, including encryption keys and digital certificates used in connection with confidentiality encryption and authentication.
Example of control to ensure that data remains complete, accurate, and valid during storage	

Encryption Under State Breach Notification and General Information Security Laws

Citation and Subject	Summary of the Requirement
1. California	
Cal. Civil Code § 1798.29(a), (c) SB 1386, as amended: breach notification law covering state agencies	"Any agency that owns or licenses computerized data that includes personal information shall disclose any breach of the security of the system following discovery or notification of the breach in the security of the data to any resident of California whose unencrypted personal information was, or is reasonably believed to have been, acquired by an unauthorized person." Timing of the disclosure—"in the most expedient time possible and without unreasonable delay." Notification can be delayed due to "measures necessary to determine the scope of the breach and restore the reasonable integrity of the data system" or "if a law enforcement agency determines that the notification will impede a criminal investigation."
Cal. Civil Code § 1798.29(e) Definition of "personal information" applicable to state agency breach notification	"Personal information" under SB 1386, as amended, means "an individual's first name or first initial and last name in combination with any one or more of the following data elements, when either the name or the data elements are not encrypted: (1) Social security number. (2) Driver's license number or California Identification Card number. (3) Account number, credit or debit card number, in combination with any required security code, access code, or password that would permit access to an individual's financial account. (4) Medical information. (5) Health insurance information."

Citation and Subject	Summary of the Requirement
Cal. Civil Code § 1798.82(a), (c) SB 1386, as amended: breach notification law covering businesses that conduct business in California	"Any person or business that conducts business in California, and that owns or licenses computerized data that includes personal information, shall disclose any breach of the security of the system following discovery or notification of the breach in the security of the data to any resident of California whose unencrypted personal information was, or is reasonably believed to have been, acquired by an unauthorized person." Timing of the disclosure—"in the most expedient time possible and without unreasonable delay." Notification can be delayed due to "measures necessary to determine the scope of the breach and restore the reasonable integrity of the data system" or "if a law enforcement agency determines that the notification will impede a criminal investigation."
Cal. Civil Code § 1798.82(e) Definition of "personal information" applicable to business breach notification	Same definition as in Cal. Civil Code § 1798.29(e)
Cal. Civil Code § 1798.81.5(b) AB 1950 – general information security law. Sets a general standard for information security, without detail, unlike the approach taken in Massachusetts.	"A business that owns or licenses personal information about a California resident shall implement and maintain reasonable security procedures and practices appropriate to the nature of the information, to protect the personal information from unauthorized access, destruction, use, modification, or disclosure."
Cal. Civil Code § 1798.81.5(d)(1) Definition of "personal information" to be protected under AB 1950	"'Personal information' means an individual's first name or first initial and his or her last name in combination with any one or more of the following data elements, when either the name or the data elements are not encrypted or redacted: (A) Social security number. (B) Driver's license number or California identification card number. (C) Account number, credit or debit card number, in combination with any required security code, access code, or password that would permit access to an individual's financial account. (D) Medical information."
Cal. Civil Code § 1798.81 Information disposal requirement	"A business shall take all reasonable steps to dispose, or arrange for the disposal, of customer records within its custody or control containing personal information when the records are no longer to be retained by the business by (a) shredding, (b) erasing, or (c) otherwise modifying the personal information in those records to make it unreadable or undecipherable through any means."
Cal. Civil Code § 1798.84(f) Safe harbor for disposing of information securely, such as for landlords or storage companies	"(1) A cause of action shall not lie against a business for disposing of abandoned records containing personal information by shredding, erasing, or otherwise modifying the personal information in the records to make it unreadable or undecipherable through any means. (2) The Legislature finds and declares that when records containing personal information are abandoned by a business, they often end up in the possession of a storage company or commercial landlord. It is the intent of the Legislature in paragraph (1) to create a safe harbor for such a record custodian who properly disposes of the records in accordance with paragraph (1)."

Citation and Subject	Summary of the Requirement
Cal. Civil Code § 1798.85(a)(3) Protection of Social Security numbers	A person or entity may not "[r]equire an individual to transmit his or her social security number over the Internet, unless the connection is secure or the social security number is encrypted."
Cal. S.B. 30 (2007) (proposed Cal. Civil Code § 1798.10(a)(4)) Requirement of securing RFID used in connection with government-issued identification documents under the Identity Information Protection Act of 2007, which did not pass	"If personal information is transmitted remotely from the identification document, the identification document shall make the data unreadable and unusable by an unauthorized person through means such as encryption of the data during transmission, access controls, data association, encoding, obfuscation, or any other measures, or combination of measures, that are effective to ensure the confidentiality of the data transmitted between the identification document and authorized reader."
Cal. S.B. 30 (2007) (proposed Cal. Civil Code § 1798.135(i)) Definition of "encryption" under the Identity Information Protection Act of 2007, which did not pass	"'Encryption' means the protection of data in electronic form in storage or while being transmitted using an encryption algorithm implemented within a cryptographic module that has been adopted or approved by the National Institute of Standards and Technology, the Institute of Electrical and Electronics Engineers, Inc., the Internet Engineering Task Force, the International Organization for Standardization, the Organization for the Advancement of Structured Information Standards, or any other similar standards setting body, rendering that data indecipherable in the absence of associated cryptographic keys necessary to enable decryption of that data. That encryption shall include appropriate management and safeguards of those keys to protect the integrity of the encryption."
2. Illinois	
815 ILCS 530/5 Definitions of "data collector" entities and "personal information" covered by the breach notification law	"'Data Collector' may include, but is not limited to, government agencies, public and private universities, privately and publicly held corporations, financial institutions, retail operators, and any other entity that, for any purpose, handles, collects, disseminates, or otherwise deals with nonpublic personal information." "'Personal information' means an individual's first name or first initial and last name in combination with any one or more of the following data elements, when either the name or the data elements are not encrypted or redacted: (1) Social Security number. (2) Driver's license number or State identification card number. (3) Account number or credit or debit card number, or an account number or credit card number in combination with any required security code, access code, or password that would permit access to an individual's financial account."

Citation and Subject	Summary of the Requirement
815 ILCS 530/10 Breach notification covering "data collectors"	"Any data collector that owns or licenses personal information concerning an Illinois resident shall notify the resident at no charge that there has been a breach of the security of the system data following discovery or notification of the breach." Timing of the disclosure—"in the most expedient time possible and without unreasonable delay." Notification can be delayed due to "measures necessary to determine the scope of the breach and restore the reasonable integrity, security, and confidentiality of the data system" or "if an appropriate law enforcement agency determines that notification will interfere with a criminal investigation and provides the data collector with a written request for the delay."
815 ILCS 530/10(b) Breach notification by the data collector to the actual owner or licensee	"Any data collector that maintains computerized data that includes personal information that the data collector does not own or license shall notify the owner or licensee of the information of any breach of the security of the data immediately following discovery, if the personal information was, or is reasonably believed to have been, acquired by an unauthorized person"
815 ILCS 530/12 Breach notification covering state agencies	"Any State agency that collects personal information concerning an Illinois resident shall notify the resident at no charge that there has been a breach of the security of the system data or written material following discovery or notification of the breach." Timing of the disclosure—"in the most expedient time possible and without unreasonable delay, consistent with any measures necessary to determine the scope of the breach and restore the reasonable integrity, security, and confidentiality of the data system."
815 ILCS 505/2RR(a)(3) Protection of Social Security numbers	A person may not "[r]equire an individual to transmit his or her social security number over the Internet, unless the connection is secure or the social security number is encrypted."
3. Massachusetts	
Mass. Gen. L. ch. 93H, § 2(a) Legislation in Massachusetts calls for the Department of Consumer Affairs and Business Regulation to create regulations to safeguard the personal information of residents of Massachusetts. This is a general information security law. Massachusetts is a pioneer among states, in that the state regulations now call for businesses to implement a comprehensive written information security program to protect personal information of Massachusetts residents. The regulations specify details concerning the information security controls for the protection of personal information, unlike California's AB 1950.	"The department of consumer affairs and business regulation shall adopt regulations relative to any person that owns or licenses personal information about a resident of the commonwealth. Such regulations shall be designed to safeguard the personal information of residents of the commonwealth and shall be consistent with the safeguards for protection of personal information set forth in the federal regulations by which the person is regulated. The objectives of the regulations shall be to: insure the security and confidentiality of customer information in a manner fully consistent with industry standards; protect against anticipated threats or hazards to the security or integrity of such information; and protect against unauthorized access to or use of such information that may result in substantial harm or inconvenience to any consumer. The regulations shall take into account the person's size, scope and type of business, the amount of resources available to such person, the amount of stored data, and the need for security and confidentiality of both consumer and employee information."

Citation and Subject	*Summary of the Requirement*
201 CMR 17.02 Definitions within regulations adopted by Department of Consumer Affairs and Business Regulation	"Breach of security, the unauthorized acquisition or unauthorized use of unencrypted data or, encrypted electronic data and the confidential process or key that is capable of compromising the security, confidentiality, or integrity of personal information, maintained by a person or agency that creates a substantial risk of identity theft or fraud against a resident of the commonwealth. A good faith but unauthorized acquisition of personal information by a person or agency, or employee or agent thereof, for the lawful purposes of such person or agency, is not a breach of security unless the personal information is used in an unauthorized manner or subject to further unauthorized disclosure." "Encrypted, the transformation of data into a form in which meaning cannot be assigned without the use of a confidential process or key."
201 CMR 17.03 General requirement of a comprehensive written information security program for owners or licensees of personal information	"Every person that owns or licenses personal information about a resident of the Commonwealth shall develop, implement, and maintain a comprehensive information security program that is written in one or more readily accessible parts and contains administrative, technical, and physical safeguards that are appropriate to (a) the size, scope and type of business of the person obligated to safeguard the personal information under such comprehensive information security program; (b) the amount of resources available to such person; (c) the amount of stored data; and (d) the need for security and confidentiality of both consumer and employee information. The safeguards contained in such program must be consistent with the safeguards for protection of personal information and information of a similar character set forth in any state or federal regulations by which the person who owns or licenses such information may be regulated."
201 CMR 17.03(2)(j) Incident response requirement within the security program	A comprehensive information security program must include: "Documenting responsive actions taken in connection with any incident involving a breach of security, and mandatory post-incident review of events and actions taken, if any, to make changes in business practices relating to protection of personal information."
201 CMR 17.04 The written information security plan must include encryption of personal information in transit over public networks or transmitted wirelessly, and encryption of personal information stored on laptops or other portable devices (e.g., USB drives)	"Every person that owns or licenses personal information about a resident of the Commonwealth and electronically stores or transmits such information shall include in its written, comprehensive information security program the establishment and maintenance of a security system covering its computers, including any wireless system, that, at a minimum, and to the extent technically feasible, shall have the following elements: . . . (3) Encryption of all transmitted records and files containing personal information that will travel across public networks, and encryption of all data containing personal information to be transmitted wirelessly. . . . (5) Encryption of all personal information stored on laptops or other portable devices . . . ."

Citation and Subject	*Summary of the Requirement*
Mass. Gen. L. ch. 93H, § 3(a) Breach notification by a person or state agency to the actual owner or licensee	"A person or agency that maintains or stores, but does not own or license data that includes personal information about a resident of the commonwealth, shall provide notice, as soon as practicable and without unreasonable delay, when such person or agency (1) knows or has reason to know of a breach of security or (2) when the person or agency knows or has reason to know that the personal information of such resident was acquired or used by an unauthorized person or used for an unauthorized purpose, to the owner or licensor in accordance with this chapter. In addition to providing notice as provided herein, such person or agency shall cooperate with the owner or licensor of such information. . . ."
Mass. Gen. L. ch. 93H, § 3(b) Breach notification law covering businesses and state agencies	Similar definition as Mass. Gen. L. ch. 93H, § 3(a)
Mass. Gen. L. ch. 93H, § 4 Notification delay due to a criminal investigation	"Notwithstanding section 3, notice may be delayed if a law enforcement agency determines that provision of such notice may impede a criminal investigation and has notified the attorney general, in writing, thereof and informs the person or agency of such determination."
4. Nevada	
Nev. Rev. Stat. 603A.030 Definition of "data collector"	"'Data collector' means any governmental agency, institution of higher education, corporation, financial institution or retail operator or any other type of business entity or association that, for any purpose, whether by automated collection or otherwise, handles, collects, disseminates or otherwise deals with nonpublic personal information."
Nev. Rev. Stat. 603A.040 Definition of "personal information"	"'Personal information' means a natural person's first name or first initial and last name in combination with any one or more of the following data elements, when the name and data elements are not encrypted: 1. Social security number. 2. Driver's license number or identification card number. 3. Account number, credit card number or debit card number, in combination with any required security code, access code or password that would permit access to the person's financial account. The term does not include the last four digits of a social security number or publicly available information that is lawfully made available to the general public."

Citation and Subject	Summary of the Requirement
Nev. Rev. Stat. 603A.200 Information disposal requirement	"A business that maintains records which contain personal information concerning the customers of the business shall take reasonable measures to ensure the destruction of those records when the business decides that it will no longer maintain the records." "Reasonable measures to ensure the destruction" means any method that modifies the records containing the personal information in such a way as to render the personal information contained in the records unreadable or undecipherable, including, without limitation: (1)Shredding of the record containing the personal information; or (2) Erasing of the personal information from the records."
Nev. Rev. Stat. 603A.210(1) General information security law. Sets a general standard for information security, without detail, unlike the approach taken in Massachusetts.	"A data collector that maintains records which contain personal information of a resident of this State shall implement and maintain reasonable security measures to protect those records from unauthorized access, acquisition, destruction, use, modification or disclosure."
Nev. Rev. Stat. 603A.220(1) Breach notification covering "data collectors"	"Any data collector that owns or licenses computerized data which includes personal information shall disclose any breach of the security of the system data following discovery or notification of the breach to any resident of this State whose unencrypted personal information was, or is reasonably believed to have been, acquired by an unauthorized person. The disclosure must be made in the most expedient time possible and without unreasonable delay, consistent with the legitimate needs of law enforcement, as provided in subsection 3, or any measures necessary to determine the scope of the breach and restore the reasonable integrity of the system data."
Nev. Rev. Stat. 603A.220(2) Breach notification by the data collector to the actual owner or licensee	"Any data collector that maintains computerized data which includes personal information that the data collector does not own shall notify the owner or licensee of the information of any breach of the security of the system data immediately following discovery if the personal information was, or is reasonably believed to have been, acquired by an unauthorized person."
Nev. Rev. Stat. 603A.220(3) Notification delay due to a criminal investigation	"The notification required by this section may be delayed if a law enforcement agency determines that the notification will impede a criminal investigation. The notification required by this section must be made after the law enforcement agency determines that the notification will not compromise the investigation."

Citation and Subject	Summary of the Requirement
S.B. 227, 75th Leg. (2009) Law effective on 1/1/2010 requiring merchants to comply with the Payment Card Industry Data Security Standard, which requires the encryption of cardholder data, such as in Requirement 4 ("Encrypt transmission of cardholder data across open, public networks"). For a copy of the standard, see: https://www.pcisecuritystandards.org/security_standards/pci_dss_download.html[5]	"1. If a data collector doing business in this State accepts a payment card in connection with a sale of goods or services, the data collector shall comply with the current version of the Payment Card Industry (PCI) Data Security Standard, as adopted by the PCI Security Standards Council or its successor organization, with respect to those transactions, not later than the date for compliance set forth in the Payment Card Industry (PCI) Data Security Standard or by the PCI Security Standards Council or its successor organization." "2. A data collector doing business in this State to whom subsection 1 does not apply shall not: (a) Transfer any personal information through an electronic, nonvoice transmission other than a facsimile to a person outside of the secure system of the data collector unless the data collector uses encryption to ensure the security of electronic transmission; or (b) Move any data storage device containing personal information beyond the logical or physical controls of the data collector or its data storage contractor unless the data collector uses encryption to ensure the security of the information." 5(b). "'Encryption' means the protection of data in electronic or optical form, in storage or in transit, using: (1) An encryption technology that has been adopted by an established standards setting body, including, but not limited to, the Federal Information Processing Standards issued by the National Institute of Standards and Technology, which renders such data indecipherable in the absence of associated cryptographic keys necessary to enable decryption of such data; and (2) Appropriate management and safeguards of cryptographic keys to protect the integrity of the encryption using guidelines promulgated by an established standards setting body, including, but not limited to, the National Institute of Standards and Technology."
5. New York	
N.Y. State Technology Law § 208(2), (3) New York's Information Security Breach and Notification Act ("N.Y. Act") and its coverage of state agencies	"Any state entity that owns or licenses computerized data that includes private information shall disclose any breach of the security of the system following discovery or notification of the breach in the security of the system to any resident of New York state whose private information was, or is reasonably believed to have been, acquired by a person without valid authorization." Timing of breach notification for data owned or licensed by the state entity is the same as under California law. "Any state entity that maintains computerized data that includes private information which such agency does not own shall notify the owner or licensee of the information of any breach of the security of the system immediately following discovery, if the private information was, or is reasonably believed to have been, acquired by a person without valid authorization."

    5.   Payment Card Indus. Data Sec. Standard, Requirements and Security Assessment Procedures (Version 1.2.1, July 2009), https://www.pcisecuritystandards.org/security/pci_dss_download.html.

Citation and Subject	Summary of the Requirement
N.Y. State Technology Law § 208(1)(a) Definition of "private information" applicable to state agency breach notification	"'Private information' shall mean personal information in combination with any one or more of the following data elements, when either the personal information or the data element is not encrypted or encrypted with an encryption key that has also been acquired: (1) social security number; (2) driver's license number or non-driver identification card number; or (3) account number, credit or debit card number, in combination with any required security code, access code, or password which would permit access to an individual's financial account."
N.Y. Gen. Bus. Law § 899-aa(2), (3) N.Y. Act: breach notification law covering businesses that conduct business in New York	"Any person or business which conducts business in New York state, and which owns or licenses computerized data which includes private information shall disclose any breach of the security of the system following discovery or notification of the breach in the security of the system to any resident of New York state whose private information was, or is reasonably believed to have been, acquired by a person without valid authorization. The disclosure shall be made in the most expedient time possible and without unreasonable delay, consistent with the legitimate needs of law enforcement, as provided in subdivision four of this section, or any measures necessary to determine the scope of the breach and restore the reasonable integrity of the system." Timing of breach notification for data owned or licensed by the business is the same as under California law. "Any person or business which maintains computerized data which includes private information which such person or business does not own shall notify the owner or licensee of the information of any breach of the security of the system immediately following discovery, if the private information was, or is reasonably believed to have been, acquired by a person without valid authorization."
N.Y. Gen. Bus. Law § 899-aa(1) Definitions of "personal information" and "private information" applicable to business breach notification	"(a) 'Personal information' shall mean any information concerning a natural person which, because of name, number, personal mark, or other identifier, can be used to identify such natural person; (b) 'Private information' shall mean personal information consisting of any information in combination with any one or more of the following data elements, when either the personal information or the data element is not encrypted, or encrypted with an encryption key that has also been acquired: (1) social security number; (2) driver's license number or non-driver identification card number; or (3) account number, credit or debit card number, in combination with any required security code, access code, or password that would permit access to an individual's financial account. . . ."

Citation and Subject	Summary of the Requirement
N.Y. Gen. Bus. Law § 399-dd(2) Protection of Social Security numbers	"No person, firm, partnership, association or corporation, not including the state or its political subdivisions, shall do any of the following: . . . require an individual to transmit his or her social security account number over the internet, unless the connection is secure or the social security account number is encrypted."

Encryption (or Absence of Encryption) Under Laws Intended to Facilitate Secure Electronic Commerce

Citation and Subject	Summary of the Requirement
1. Federal Law	
15 U.S.C. § 7001(a) E-Sign Act—general federal law meant to facilitate the use of electronic signatures and records (which may have no cryptographic or other security whatsoever)	"Notwithstanding any statute, regulation, or other rule of law (other than this subchapter and subchapter II of this chapter), with respect to any transaction in or affecting interstate or foreign commerce— (1) a signature, contract, or other record relating to such transaction may not be denied legal effect, validity, or enforceability solely because it is in electronic form; and (2) a contract relating to such transaction may not be denied legal effect, validity, or enforceability solely because an electronic signature or electronic record was used in its formation."
2. California	
Cal. Civil Code § 1633.7 California's version of the Uniform Electronic Transactions Act (UETA)—a uniform state law meant to facilitate the use of electronic signatures and records (which may have no cryptographic or other security whatsoever)	"(a) A record or signature may not be denied legal effect or enforceability solely because it is in electronic form. (b) A contract may not be denied legal effect or enforceability solely because an electronic record was used in its formation. (c) If a law requires a record to be in writing, an electronic record satisfies the law. (d) If a law requires a signature, an electronic signature satisfies the law."

Citation and Subject	Summary of the Requirement
Cal. Gov't Code § 16.5(a) Facilitating the use of secure electronic signatures[6] for communications with the state government	"In any written communication with a public entity, as defined in Section 811.2, in which a signature is required or used, any party to the communication may affix a signature by use of a digital signature that complies with the requirements of this section. The use of a digital signature shall have the same force and effect as the use of a manual signature if and only if it embodies all of the following attributes:
	(1) It is unique to the person using it.
	(2) It is capable of verification.
	(3) It is under the sole control of the person using it.
	(4) It is linked to data in such a manner that if the data are changed, the digital signature is invalidated.
	(5) It conforms to regulations adopted by the Secretary of State. Initial regulations shall be adopted no later than January 1, 1997. In developing these regulations, the secretary shall seek the advice of public and private entities, including, but not limited to, the Department of Information Technology, the California Environmental Protection Agency, and the Department of General Services. Before the secretary adopts the regulations, he or she shall hold at least one public hearing to receive comments."

---

6. Although the statute speaks of a "digital signature," the statutory definition of "digital signature" does not correspond to, and is much broader than, the generally accepted technical definition of the term, which involves the use of asymmetric cryptosystems. The statute provides, "'Digital signature' means an electronic identifier, created by computer, intended by the party using it to have the same force and effect as the use of a manual signature." Cal. Gov't Code § 16.5(d). Thus, the legislature evidently was referring to what technologists would define as an "electronic signature," as opposed to a "digital signature."

Citation and Subject	Summary of the Requirement
Cal. Prob. Code § 4673(b) Support for digital signatures[7] for advance health care directives or health care powers of attorney	An electronic advance health care directive or power of attorney for health care is legally sufficient if it otherwise meets the requirements for these documents. Further, if a notary uses a digital signature for the notary's acknowledgement, the notary's digital signature must meet all of the following requirements: "(1) The digital signature either meets the requirements of Section 16.5 of the Government Code and Chapter 10 (commencing with Section 22000) of Division 7 of Title 2 of the California Code of Regulations or the digital signature uses an algorithm approved by the National Institute of Standards and Technology. (2) The digital signature is unique to the person using it. (3) The digital signature is capable of verification. (4) The digital signature is under the sole control of the person using it. (5) The digital signature is linked to data in such a manner that if the data are changed, the digital signature is invalidated. (6) The digital signature persists with the document and not by association in separate files. (7) The digital signature is bound to a digital certificate."
2. Illinois	
Ill. Comp. Stat., ch. 5, § 175/5-110 Support of electronic signature under Illinois' Electronic Commerce Security Act ("ECSA")	"Information, records, and signatures shall not be denied legal effect, validity, or enforceability solely on the grounds that they are in electronic form."

7. Under this section of the Probate Code, the legislature again seems to use the term "digital signature" in the more generic sense of "electronic signature," but sets forth validity criteria that require the use of asymmetric cryptography and therefore "digital signatures" in the technical sense, particularly the requirement of the use of a "digital certificate" in subsection (b)(7).

Citation and Subject	Summary of the Requirement
Ill. Comp. Stat., ch. 5, § 175/10-110 Meaning of "secure electronic signature"	"Secure electronic signature. (a) If, through the use of a qualified security procedure, it can be verified that an electronic signature is the signature of a specific person, then such electronic signature shall be considered to be a secure electronic signature at the time of verification, if the relying party establishes that the qualified security procedure was: (1) commercially reasonable under the circumstances; (2) applied by the relying party in a trustworthy manner; and (3) reasonably and in good faith relied upon by the relying party. (b) A qualified security procedure for purposes of this Section is a security procedure for identifying a person that is: (1) previously agreed to by the parties; or (2) certified by the Secretary of State in accordance with Section 10-135 as being capable of creating, in a trustworthy manner, an electronic signature that: (A) is unique to the signer within the context in which it is used; (B) can be used to objectively identify the person signing the electronic record; (C) was reliably created by such identified person, (e.g., because some aspect of the procedure involves the use of a signature device or other means or method that is under the sole control of such person), and that cannot be readily duplicated or compromised; and (D) is created, and is linked to the electronic record to which it relates, in a manner such that if the record or the signature is intentionally or unintentionally changed after signing the electronic signature is invalidated."

Citation and Subject	*Summary of the Requirement*
Ill. Comp. Stat., ch. 5, § 175/10-120 Presumptions resulting from the use of secure electronic signatures	"(b) In resolving a civil dispute involving a secure electronic signature, it shall be rebuttably presumed that the secure electronic signature is the signature of the person to whom it correlates. (c) The effect of presumptions provided in this Section is to place on the party challenging the integrity of a secure electronic record or challenging the genuineness of a secure electronic signature both the burden of going forward with evidence to rebut the presumption and the burden of persuading the trier of fact that the nonexistence of the presumed fact is more probable than its existence."
Ill. Comp. Stat., ch. 5, § 175/5-105 Definition of "digital signature"	"'Digital signature' means a type of electronic signature created by transforming an electronic record using a message digest function and encrypting the resulting transformation with an asymmetric cryptosystem using the signer's private key such that any person having the initial untransformed electronic record, the encrypted transformation, and the signer's corresponding public key can accurately determine whether the transformation was created using the private key that corresponds to the signer's public key and whether the initial electronic record has been altered since the transformation was made. A digital signature is a security procedure."
Ill. Comp. Stat., ch. 5, § 175/15-105 "Digital signature" technology is one form of qualified security procedure.	Secure electronic signature. A digital signature that is created using an asymmetric algorithm certified by the Secretary of State under item (2) of subsection (b) of Section 10-110 shall be considered to be a qualified security procedure for purposes of identifying a person under Section 10-110 if: (1) the digital signature was created during the operational period of a valid certificate, was used within the scope of any other restrictions specified or incorporated by reference in the certificate, if any, and can be verified by reference to the public key listed in the certificate; and (2) the certificate is considered trustworthy (i.e., an accurate binding of a public key to a person's identity) because the certificate was issued by a certification authority in accordance with standards, procedures, and other requirements specified by the Secretary of State, or the trier of fact independently finds that the certificate was issued in a trustworthy manner by a certification authority that properly authenticated the subscriber and the subscriber's public key, or otherwise finds that the material information set forth in the certificate is true.

Citation and Subject	Summary of the Requirement
3. Massachusetts	
Mass. Gen. L. ch. 110G, § 7 Massachusetts's version of the Uniform Electronic Transactions Act (UETA) – a uniform state law meant to facilitate the use of electronic signatures and records (which may have no cryptographic or other security whatsoever)	"(a) A record or signature may not be denied legal effect or enforceability solely because it is in electronic form. (b) A contract may not be denied legal effect or enforceability solely because an electronic record was used in its formation. (c) If a law requires a record to be in writing, an electronic record satisfies the law. (d) If a law requires a signature, an electronic signature satisfies the law."
4. Nevada	
Nev. Rev. Stat. 719.040 Nevada's version of the Uniform Electronic Transactions Act (again, which may have no cryptographic or other security whatsoever)	"1. A record or signature may not be denied legal effect or enforceability solely because it is in electronic form. 2. A contract may not be denied legal effect or enforceability solely because an electronic record was used in its formation. 3. If a law requires a record to be in writing, an electronic record satisfies the law. 4. If a law requires a signature, an electronic signature satisfies the law."
5. New York	
N.Y. State Technology Law § 304(2) Support of electronic signatures under New York's Electronic Signatures and Records Act ("ESRA") (which may have no cryptographic or other security whatsoever)[8]	"In accordance with this section unless specifically provided otherwise by law, an electronic signature may be used by a person in lieu of a signature affixed by hand. The use of an electronic signature shall have the same validity and effect as the use of a signature affixed by hand."
N.Y. State Technology Law § 305(3) Support of electronic records under ESRA	"An electronic record shall have the same force and effect as those records not produced by electronic means."

Updated through January 2010.

---

8. In 2002, New York law was changed to remove any security requirements relating to the definition of "electronic signature." S.B. 7289, 2002 N.Y. Laws 314.

APPENDIX C

Resources

DATA BREACH NOTIFICATION STATUTES

Health Information Technology for Economic and Clinical Health (HITECH), Title XIII of the American Recovery and Reinvestment Act of 2009 (ARRA), H.R. 1, Pub. L. No. 111-5, 123 Stat. 115 (2009); § 13402, Notification in the Case of a Breach, *available at* 42 U.S.C.A. § 17932; also see www.hipaasurvivalguide.com/hitech-act-text/html

Department of Veterans Affairs Information Security Enhancement Act of 2006, Pub. L. No. 109-461, http://www4.va.gov/ogc/docs/PL109-461.pdf

National Conference of State Legislatures, Breach of Information (overview), http://www.ncsl.org/programs/lis/cip/priv/breach.htm

National Conference of State Legislatures—State Security Breach Notification Laws, http://www.ncsl.org/Default.aspx?TabId=13489

National Conference of State Legislatures—Security Breach Legislation 2009, http://www.ncsl.org/default.aspx?tabid=18325

Commercial Law League of America, State Data Security/Breach Notification Laws (as of October 2010), http://www.clla.org/documents/breach.xls

Commonwealth of Massachusetts, Consumer Affairs & Business Regulation, Identity Theft, http://www.mass.gov/?pageID=ocatopic&L=3&L0=Home&L1=Business&L2=Identity+Theft&sid=Eoca

Compliance Checklist, 201 Mass. Code Regs. 17.00, http://www.mass.gov/Eoca/docs/idtheft/compliance_checklist.pdf

DATA BREACH NOTIFICATION REGULATIONS AND POLICIES

HHS Guidance Specifying the Technologies and Methodologies That Render Protected Health Information Unusable, Unreadable, or Indecipherable to Unauthorized Individuals for Purposes of the Breach Notification Requirements Under Section 13402 of Title XIII (Health Information Technology for Economic and Clinical Health Act) of the American Recovery and Reinvestment Act of 2009; HHS HITECH Act Breach Notification Guidance, 74 Fed. Reg. 19,006 (Apr. 27, 2009); 74 Fed. Reg. 42,767 (Aug. 20, 2009), http://www.hhs.gov/ocr/privacy/hipaa/administrative/breachnotificationrule/index.html, http://www.hhs.gov/ocr/privacy/hipaa/understanding/coveredentities/hitechrfi.pdf

Federal Trade Commission (FTC) Breach Notification Rule for Electronic Health Information, Apr. 16, 2009, 74 Fed. Reg. 17,914 (Apr. 27, 2009); 74 Fed. Reg. 42,962 (Final Rule) (Aug. 20, 2009), http://www.ftc.gov/opa/2009/04/healthbreach.shtm

Health Insurance Portability and Accountability Act of 1996 (HIPAA), 45 C.F.R. 160, 162, and 164

Department of Health and Human Services, Office for Civil Rights, HIPAA Privacy Rule, http://www.hhs.gov/ocr/privacy/hipaa/administrative/privacyrule/index .html

HIPAA Security Rule, http://www.hhs.gov/ocr/privacy/hipaa/administrative/securityrule/index.html

Securities and Exchange Commission, Final Rule: Privacy of Consumer Financial Information (Regulation S-P), 17 C.F.R. pt. 248 (amendments to the Gramm-Leach-Bliley Act and the Fair Credit Reporting Act), http://www.sec.gov/rules/final/34-42974.htm

Office of Management and Budget (OMB) Memorandum M-07-16, *Safeguarding Against and Responding to the Breach of Personally Identifiable Information* (May 22, 2007), http://www.whitehouse.gov/omb/memoranda/fy2007/m07-16.pdf

REPORTED DATA BREACHES AND TRENDS

Department of Health and Human Services, Health Information Privacy, Breaches Affecting 500 or More Individuals, http://www.hhs.gov/ocr/privacy/hipaa/administrative/breachnotificationrule/postedbreaches.html

Privacy Rights Clearinghouse, A Chronology of Data Breaches, http://www .privacyrights.org/ar/ChronDataBreaches.htm

Open Security Foundation, DataLoss DB, http://datalossdb.org

Office of Inadequate Security, http://www.databreaches.net

Identity Theft Resource Center (ITRC), *Data Breaches: The Insanity Continues* (Jan. 8, 2010), http://www.idtheftcenter.org/artman2/publish/lib_survey/Breaches_2009.shtml

ITRC Breach Report: 2009 Final, http://www.idtheftcenter.org/artman2/uploads/1/ITRC_Breach_Report_20100106.pdf

Breach, *The Web Hacking Incidents Database 2009, Biannual Report* (Aug. 2009), http://www.breach.com/resources/whitepapers/downloads/WP_TheWebHackingIncidents-2009.pdf

MAPS OF DATA BREACH STATUTES WITH LINKS TO UNDERLYING REGULATIONS AND STATUTES

CSO Disclosure Series, Data Breach Notification Laws, State by State, http://www .csoonline.com/article/221322/CSO_Disclosure_Series_Data_Breach_Notification_Laws_State_By_State

Privacy International, Data Protection Laws Around the World, http://www
.privacyinternational.org/survey/dpmap.jpg

COSTS OF RESPONDING TO DATA BREACHES

Ponemon Institute, PGP & Vontu, *2009 Annual Study: U.S. Cost of a Data Breach* (Nov.
2007), http://www.encryptionreports.com/costofdatabreach.html

Forrester Research, *Calculating the Cost of a Security Breach* (Apr. 2007), http://www
.forrester.com/rb/Research/calculating_cost_of_security_breach/q/id/42082/t/2

REPORTS AND BOOKS

American Medical Association (AMA), *HIPAA Security Rule: Frequently Asked Questions
Regarding Encryption of Personal Health Information* (Apr. 2010), http://www
.ama-assn.org/ama1/pub/upload/mm/368/hipaa-phi-encryption.pdf

U.S. Government Accountability Office (GAO), *Privacy: Lessons Learned about Data
Breach Notification*, GAO-07-657 (Apr. 2007), http://www.gao.gov/highlights/
d07657high.pdf

Gina Maria Stevens, *Federal Information Security and Data Breach Notification Laws*,
Congressional Research Services Report (updated Jan. 28, 2010), http://
opencrs.com/document/RL34120/2010-01-28/

Dawn Cappelli, Andrew Moore, Timothy J. Shimeall, & Randall Trzeciak, *Common
Sense Guide to Prevention and Detection of Insider Threats* (3d ed. v. 3.1, Jan. 2009),
http://www.cert.org/insider_threat/ (part of Carnegie Mellon University's
insider threat study with the U.S. Secret Service and others)

Cloud Security Alliance Controls Matrix (CSA CM) (April 27, 2010), http://www
.cloudsecurityalliana.org/cm.html

2010 CWE/SANS Top 25 Most Dangerous Software Errors, http://cwe.mitre.org/
top25/

CSO Magazine, *The Complete Guide to Security Breach Disclosure* (Feb. 29, 2008), six-part
series http://www.csoonline.com/article/217082; the series includes
- Interactive map of data breach notification laws in the United States
- Scott Berinato, *The Dos and Don'ts of Data Breach Notification Letters*, http://
www.csoonline.com/article/217018
- Kathleen Carr, *How to Respond to a Data Breach Notification Letter*, http://
www.csoonline.com/article/217049
- Katherine Walsh, *What California's New Medical Disclosure Law Means for the
Rest of Us*, http://www.csoonline.com/article/217010
- Scott Berinato, *What's Next with Disclosure Legislation?*, http://www.csoonline
.com/article/217027

Open Web Application Security Project (OWASP). "Top 10 2007—Insecure
Communications," http://www.owasp.org/index.php/Top_10_2007-A9

Symantec, *Managed Security in the Enterprise (U.S. Enterprise)* (Mar. 2009), http://www.symantec.com/content/en/us/about/media/managed_security_ent_US_12Mar09.pdf

2010 Verizon Breach Investigations Report (July 29, 2010), http://www.verizonbusiness.com/resources/reports/rp_2010-data-breach-report_en_xg.pdf

Verizon Business, *The Verizon Incident Sharing Framework* (beta version 1.1, Mar. 9, 2010), http://securityblog.verizonbusiness.com/wp-content/uploads/2010/03/Veris-Framework-Beta-1.pdf

Verizon Business Risk Team, *2009 Data Breach Investigations Report*, http://www.verizonbusiness.com/resources/security/reports/2009_databreach_rp.pdf; podcasts available at http://www.podtech.net/home/5218/verizon-business-2008-data-breach-investigations-report-part-i-2 (Part I) and http://www.podtech.net/home/5219/verizon-business-2008-data-breach-investigations-report-part-ii (Part II)

Verizon Business Risk Team, *2009 Data Breach Investigations Supplemental Report: Anatomy of a Data Breach*, http://www.verizonbusiness.com/resources/security/reports/rp_2009-data-breach-investigations-supplemental-report_en_xg.pdf

Interhack, *Using Science to Combat Data Loss: Analyzing Breaches by Type and Industry*, I/S: A Journal of Law and Policy for the Information Society, Volume 4, Issue 3 (Winter 2008-2009)

Utica College, Center for Identity Management and Information Protection, *Identity Fraud Trends and Patterns: Building a Data-Based Foundation for Proactive Enforcement* (Oct. 2007), http://www.cyber.st.dhs.gov/docs/Secret_Service_id_theft_study.pdf

SANS Institute, *Understanding and Selecting a Data Loss Prevention Solution*, http://sans.org/reading_room/dlp/87.pdf

Thomas Shaw, *Information Security and Privacy—A Practical Guide for Global Executives, Lawyers and Technologists* (American Bar Association 2011)

Harold F. Tipton & Micki Krause, *Information Security Management Handbook* (6th ed.), vol. 3

Seymour Bosworth, M. E. Kabay, & Eric Whyne, *Computer Security Handbook* (5th ed.)

Michael Gregg & David Kim, *Inside Network Security Assessment: Guarding Your IT Infrastructure*

ENFORCEMENT

U.S. Department of Justice, Computer Crime & Intellectual Property Section, http://www.justice.gov/criminal/cybercrime/

U.S. Department of Justice, Indictments, http://www.cybercrime.gov

Federal Bureau of Investigation, Cyber-Investigations, http://www.fbi.gov/cyberinvest/cyberhome.htm

Federal Trade Commission (FTC) Privacy Initiatives—Enforcement—Cases, http://www.ftc.gov/privacy/privacyinitiatives/promises_enf.html

IDENTITY THEFT

The President's Identity Theft Task Force, *Combating Identity Theft* (Apr. 2007), http://www.idtheft.gov/reports/StrategicPlan.pdf

U.S. Department of Justice, Identity Theft and Identity Fraud, http://www.justice.gov/criminal/fraud/websites/idtheft.html

Federal Trade Commission, Dealing with a Data Breach, Information Compromise and the Risk of Identity Theft: Guidance for Your Business, http://www.ftc.gov/bcp/edu/microsites/idtheft/business/data-breach.html

Federal Trade Commission, Peer-to-Peer File Sharing: A Guide for Business, www.ftc.gov/bcp/edu/pubs/business/idtheft/bus46.shtm. Tips for consumers about computer security and P2P can be found at OnGuard Online, http://www.onguardonline.gov/topics/p2p-security.aspx.

Federal Trade Commission, Guide for Assisting Identity Theft Victims (October 29, 2010), http://www.idtheft.gov/probono

Identity Theft Resource Center, http://www.idtheftcenter.org

Identity Theft Resource Center, *Identity Theft: The Aftermath 2007* (June 19, 2008), http://www.idtheftcenter.org/artman2/publish/m_press/Identity_Theft_The_Aftermath_2007.shtml

U.S. Department of Health and Human Services, Office of the National Coordinator for Health Information Technology, *Medical Identity Theft Final Report* (Jan. 2009), http://healthit.hhs.gov/portal/server.pt/gateway/PTARGS_0_10731_848096_0_0_18/MedIdTheftReport011509.pdf

World Privacy Forum, The Medical Identity Theft Information Page, http://www.worldprivacyforum.org/medicalidentitytheft.html

World Privacy Forum, *Medical Identity Theft: The Information Crime that Can Kill You* (Spring 2006), http://worldprivacyforum.org/pdf/wpf_Medicalidtheft2006.pdf

CRYPTOGRAPHY

RSA Laboratories, Cryptography Frequently Asked Questions, http://www.rsa.com/rsalabs/node.asp?id=2156

Schneier, Bruce, *Applied Cryptography* (Wiley, 1996)

Singh, Simon, *The Code Book, The Science of Secrecy from Ancient Egypt to Quantum Cryptography* (Anchor, 2000).

Wrixon, Fred. *Codes, Siphers, Secrets and Cryptic Communications.*

Information Systems Security Association (ISSA), www.issa.org

KEY MANAGEMENT

PCI Security Standards Council, *Payment Card Industry (PCI) Data Security Standard: Requirements and Security Assessment Procedures* (version 1.2.1, July 2009), https://www.pcisecuritystandards.org/security_standards/download.html?id=pci_dss_v1-2.pdf

National Institute of Standards and Technology (NIST) Key Management Project, http://csrc.nist.gov/groups/ST/toolkit/key_management.html

NIST SP 800-57, *Recommendation For Key Management—Part 1: General (Revised)* (Mar. 2007), http://csrc.nist.gov/groups/ST/toolkit/documents/SP800-57Part1_3-8-07.pdf

NIST SP 800-99, *Guidelines for Media Sanitation* (Sept. 2006), http://csrc.nist.gov/publications/nistpubs/800-88/NISTSP800-88_rev1.pdf

INFORMATION SECURITY AND PRIVACY GUIDELINES

Center for Strategic & International Studies, Consensus Audit Guidelines—*Twenty Important Controls for Effective Cyber Defense and FISMA Compliance*, (Aug. 10, 2009), http://csis.org/publication/twenty-important-controls-effective-cyber-defense-and-fisma-compliance

PCI Security Standards Council, *The Prioritized Approach to Pursue PCI DSS Compliance*, https://www.pcisecuritystandards.org/education/docs/Prioritized_Approach_PCI_DSS_1_2.pdf

Cloud Security Alliance, Cloud Controls Matrix V1 (April 27, 2010), http://www.cloudsecurityalliance.org/cm.html

National Institute of Standards and Technology (NIST), Computer Security Resource Center, http://csrc.nist.gov/publications/PubsDrafts.html. Publications available include

- *Information Security Handbook: A Guide for Managers*, NIST Spec Pub 800-100 (Oct. 2006)
- *Recommended Security Controls for Federal Information Systems*, NIST Spec Pub 800-53 Rev. 3 (Dec. 2009)
- *Guide for Assessing the Security Controls in Federal Information Systems*, NIST Spec Pub 800-53A (June 2008)
- *Guide for Applying the Risk Management Framework to Federal Information Systems: A Security Lifecycle Approach*, NIST Spec Pub 800-37 Rev 1 (public draft Nov. 2009)
- *An Introductory Resource Guide for Implementing the HIPAA Security Rule*, NIST Spec Pub 800-66-Rev 1
- *Guide to Storage Encryption Technologies for End User Devices*, NIST Spec Pub 800-111
- *Guidelines for the Selection and Use of Transport Layer Security (TLS) Implementations*, NIST Spec Pub 800-52

- *An Introductory Resource Guide for Implementing the Health Insurance Portability and Accountability Act (HIPAA) Security Rule,* NIST Spec. Pub. 800-66 Rev. 1 (Oct. 2008)
- *Guide to IPsec VPNs,* NIST Spec Pub 800-77
- *Guide to SSL VPNs,* NIST Spec Pub 800-113
- *Guidelines for Media Sanitization,* NIST Spec Pub 800-88
- *Guide to Protecting the Confidentiality of Personally Identifiable Information (PII),* NIST Spec Pub 800-122
- *Recommendation for the Transitioning of Cryptographic Algorithms and Key Sizes,* DRAFT NIST Spec Pub 800-133

Federal Financial Institutions Examination Council (FFIEC), *Information Security* (July 2006), http://www.ffiec.gov/ffiecinfobase/booklets/information_security/information_security.pdf

IT Governance Institute, *IT Control Objectives for Sarbanes-Oxley* (2d ed. Sept. 2006), http://www.isaca.org/Template.cfm?Section=Home&CONTENTID=32621&TEMPLATE=/ContentManagement/ContentDisplay.cfm

Internet Engineering Task Force (IETF), RFC 2898 PKCS #5: Password-Based Cryptography Specification Version 2.0

Information Systems Audit and Control Association (ISACA), *IS Standards, Guidelines, and Procedures for Auditing and Control Professionals* (Mar. 15, 2008), http://www.isaca.org/standards

ISO/IEC 10116:2006 Information technology—Security techniques—Modes of operation for an n-bit block cipher

ISO/IEC 11770-1:1996 Information technology—Security techniques—Key management—Part 1: Framework

ISO/IEC 11770-2:1996 Information technology—Security techniques—Key management—Part 2: Mechanisms using symmetric techniques

ISO/IEC 18033-1:2005 Information technology—Security techniques—Encryption algorithms—Part 1: General

ISO/IEC 18033-2:2006 Information technology—Security techniques—Encryption algorithms—Part 2: Asymmetric ciphers

ISO/IEC 18033-3:2005 Information technology—Security techniques—Encryption algorithms—Part 3: Block ciphers

ISO/IEC 18033-4:2005 Information technology—Security techniques—Encryption algorithms—Part 4: Stream ciphers

ISO/IEC 27001:2005 Information technology—Security techniques—Information security management systems—Requirements

ISO/IEC 27002:2005 Information technology—Security techniques—Information security management—Code of practice for information security management

NIST FIPS 197—Advanced Encryption Standard (AES)

NIST Special Publication 800-21, *Guideline for Implementing Cryptography in the Federal Government* (2d ed.)

NIST Special Publication 800-38A, *Recommendation for Block Cipher Modes of Operation—Methods and Techniques*

NIST Special Publication 800-38C, *Recommendation for Block Cipher Modes of Operation: the CCM Mode for Authentication and Confidentiality*

NIST Special Publication 800-38D, *Recommendation for Block Cipher Modes of Operation: Galois/Counter Mode (GCM) and GMAC*

NIST Special Publication 800-57 Part 1, *Recommendation on Key Management—Part 1: General (Revised)*

NIST Special Publication 800-57 Part 2, *Recommendation on Key Management—Part 2: Best Practices for Key Management Organization*

PCI Security Standards Council, *Payment Card Industry (PCI) Data Security Standard: Requirements and Security Assessment Procedures* (version 1.2.1, July 2009), https://www.pcisecuritystandards.org/security_standards/download.html?id=pci_dss_v1-2.pdf

Storage Networking Industry Association (SNIA), *Encryption of Data At-Rest—Step-by-Step Checklist* (rev. Sept. 2009), http://www.snia.org/forums/ssif/knowledge_center/white_papers

Storage Networking Industry Association (SNIA), Technical Proposal, *Storage Security Best Current Practices (BCPs) v2.1.0*, http://www.snia.org/forums/ssif/programs/best_practices/

Federal Trade Commission, Protecting Consumer Privacy in an Era of Rapid Change: A Proposed Framework for Businesses and Policymakers (December 1, 2010), http://www.ftc.gov/os/2010/101201privacyreport.pdf.

Important Cases Index

Index